The Bible Dilemma

Historical contradictions, misquoted statements, failed prophecies and oddities in the Bible

Imprisonment of the mind is the worst imprisonment of all.
It is without walls, without bars, without chains, without keys.
It is the most binding, the most self-imposing and self-inflicting.
It is blind, it is enslaving, and it has the most willing victim.

The Author

Table of Contents

Bibliography

I. Introduction

As the main religious text of Judaism, the Catholic Church, and all other Christian denominations, the Bible has been one of the strongest influences throughout history. It has instructed the formulation of laws and governments as well as the development of social norms and practices.

The exact interpretation of the Bible varies depending on denomination. The composition has also evolved over the centuries, based on decisions made by various religious councils, such as the hypothetical Jewish Council of Jamnia (AD 85-100), The First Council of Nicaea (AD 325), the Council of Trent (AD 1546), and the Hampton Court Conference (AD 1611) under the leadership of King James I of England.

In the past, church leaders declared canons and decrees limiting or prohibiting biblical reading. In November of 1229 AD, the Council of Toulouse created a special tribunal known as the Inquisition, issuing the following decree:

> Canon 14. We prohibit also that the laity should be permitted to have the books of the Old or the New Testament; unless anyone from motive of devotion should wish to have the Psalter or the Breviary for divine offices or the hours of the blessed Virgin; but we most strictly forbid their having any translation of these books.

On April 8, 1546, the Council of Trent also prevented laymen from accessing the Bible, stating that ordinary citizens must not rely on their own interpretations, but should refer to the ecclesiastical authorities for biblical guidance. On November 18, 1965, the Second Ecumenical Council of the Vatican, under the leadership of Pope John XXIII, issued a document called "Dogmatic Constitution on Divine Revelation" (Dei Verbum). This document declared God to be both the inspiration and author of the Old and New Testaments. The Council allowed the Catholic Bible to be read solely under a priest's guidance, and declared non-Catholic Bibles off-limits to Catholics.

Contradicting these determinations, in 1898, Pope Leo XIII decreed a three year indulgence of spiritual reading to anyone who read the Bible with great reverence for at least fifteen minutes a day. This decree was in line with the Handbook of Indulgences, which states that those who kiss the Gospel Book while reciting the following verses will be granted five hundred days of indulgences:

"May our sins be blotted out by virtue of the words of the Gospel,"
"May the reading of the Gospel be our salvation and protection,"
"May Christ teach us the words of the Holy Gospel."

Since its conception, the Bible has been highly regarded and widely read, serving as an essential guide and reference for human conduct. Since so many view its passages as the word of God, the Bible is considered beyond reproach. A closer look at biblical writings; however, reveal failed promises and prophecies, along with major contradictions.

This book is written to make a list of the major historical contradictions, misquotations, borrowed statements within the Bible and from non-biblical sources, failed promises and prophecies, scientific errors, and non-existing books mentioned in the Bible. It also makes a list of the different names of God, the gods in the Bible, the myths and legends similar to the biblical stories and the arguments against Jesus Christ being the Messiah.

The King James Bible [KJ] and the Douay Rheims Catholic Bible [DR] are the Bible versions used entirely in this book. Other Bible versions are occasionally used and mentioned for comparison and contrast.

II. Historical Contradictions and Absurdities

1. Old Testament

A. The story of creation

1. The chronological events of creation

> **Genesis 1:1-2:3** "In the beginning God created …"

Note: Genesis 1 and Genesis 2 have conflicting accounts of the chronology of creation.

a. Genesis 1:1-3 The first chronology of creation

i.	Day 1: Sky (heaven), Earth and light
ii.	Day 2: Heaven, water
iii.	Day 3: Plants
iv.	Day 4: Sun, Moon, stars
v.	Day 5: Animals
vi.	Day 6: Humans
vii.	Day 7: God rested

Note: How were days defined when days are defined in relation to the position of the earth and the sun? However, the sun was created only on the fourth day.

b. Genesis 2:4-25 The second chronology of creation

i.	Earth and heavens
ii.	Adam, the first man
iii.	Plants
iv.	Animals
v.	Eve, the first woman (from Adam's rib)

2. The creation of heaven and earth

On the first day
Genesis 1:1, 5 "God created the *heaven and the earth* … the first day."

On the second day
Genesis 1:6, 8 "God said, Let there be a firmament … God called the firmament Heaven … the second day."

Note: But heaven was already created on the first day.

On the third day
Genesis 1:9-10, 13 "[God said] let the dry land appear ... called the dry land Earth the third day."

Note: But earth was already created on the first day.

3. The waters had to be separated from the waters?

Genesis 1:6 "God said ... divide the *waters from the waters* ..."

4. When did God create the trees?

Trees were created before humans
Genesis 1:12, 27 "The earth brought forth ... the tree ... God created man in his own image ..."

Trees were created after humans
Genesis 2:7, 9 "The Lord God formed man ... out of the ground made ... to grow every tree ..."

5. The plants were all created for human consumption

Genesis 1:29 "God said, every herb [every tree] to you it shall be for meat."

Note: God said, the fruit of every tree is for man to eat, does this include the tree of life and the tree of knowledge of good and evil (Genesis 2:9)?

6. When did God create the animals?

God created animals before humans
Genesis 1:25, 27 "God [made] every thing that creepeth ... God created man"

God created animals after humans
Genesis 2:7, 19 "The Lord God formed man ... every beast ... every fowl ..."

7. Where did the birds come from?

All the birds came from the waters
Genesis 1:20 "God said, Let the waters bring forth ... fowl that may fly ..."

All the birds came from the ground
Genesis 2:19 "Out of the ground ... every fowl of the air ..."

8. Was man created in the image of God?

Yes, man was created in the image of God
Genesis 1:27 "God created man in his own image ... male and female"

No, man was not created in the image of God
[KJ] Genesis 2:7 "The Lord God formed man of the *dust of the ground* ..."
[DR] Genesis 2:7 "The Lord God formed man of the *slime of the earth* ..."
Genesis 3:22 "God said, Behold, the man [Adam] is become as one of us ..."

Note: Man was created from dust (or slime) and became like God after eating the fruit from the tree of knowledge of good and evil.

9. Were women and men created equal and at the same time?

Yes, man and woman were created equally together and at the same time
Genesis 1:27 "God created man ... male and female created he them."

No, man was created first, woman was created later to be his helpmate
Genesis 2:18, 23 "The Lord God said ... I will make him [Adam] a help meet ... she shall be called Woman, because she was taken out of Man."
I Timothy 2:13 "For Adam was first formed, then Eve."

10. Was man created to have dominion over the earth?

Yes
Genesis 1:28 "God [said] ... have dominion over ... the earth."

No
Genesis 2:8-15 "The Lord God took the man, and put him into the garden of Eden ... to keep it."

Note: It is commonly believed that the Garden of Eden was somewhere between the rivers Tigris and Euphrates in Mesopotamia, presently called Iraq (see Genesis 2:10-14).

11. All animals fear man

Genesis 9:2 "The fear ... [and] dread of you shall be ... upon all that moveth upon the earth ..."

Note: However, this statement is not true in the real world.

B. The story of Adam and Eve

1. God did not know Adam needed a woman

Genesis 2:18, 20 "The Lord God said, It is not good that the man should be alone (so) ... God formed every beast of the field ... *but for Adam there was not found an help meet for him.*"

Note: God made the animals and showed them to Adam to see if he would choose one of these animals to be his companion. After checking all the animals, Adam did not found his help meet. If God is all knowing, why did God not know that the animals were not a good help meet for Adam?

2. Who was deceived to eat the forbidden fruit?

Both Adam and Eve were deceived to eat the forbidden fruit
Genesis 3:6 "She took of the fruit ... gave [her husband] ... he did eat."
Genesis 3:13, 17 "God said unto Adam ... thou hast eaten of the tree ..."

Only Eve was deceived
I Timothy 2:14 "Adam was *not* deceived, but the woman being deceived was in the transgression."

3. Concerning the serpent

Genesis 3:14 "God said unto the serpent ... dust shalt thou eat ..."

Note: The serpent does not eat dust. How did the serpent move before tempting Eve? Did it walk with its legs? The argument about the serpent was one of the major contentions raised by Clarence Darrow in the Scopes Trial (1926).

4. Did everyone come from Adam and Eve?

Yes, everyone came from Adam and Eve
Genesis 3:20 "Adam called his wife's name Eve ... the mother of all living."

No
Hebrews 7:1, 3 "Melchisedec ... was without father, without mother, without descent, having neither beginning of days ..."
Genesis 4:16-17 "[Cain] dwelt in the land of Nod ... and Cain knew his wife"

Note: Because Cain left for Nod before having a wife, it is often assumed that his wife was a foreign woman and not a sibling.

5. Was Eve the mother of all living?

Eve was called the mother of all living when she was not yet a mother
Genesis 3:20 "Adam called his wife's name Eve ... the mother of all living."

Eve gave birth to Cain
Genesis 4:1 "Adam knew Eve his wife; and she conceived, and bare Cain ..."

Note: Why was Adam's wife called Eve (which means the mother of all living) when they were still in the garden of Eden, when she gave birth much later when they were already driven out of the garden?

6. God prepared some clothes for Adam and Eve

Genesis 3:21 "The Lord God make coats of skins, and clothed them."

Note: Did God kill some animals to make clothes for Adam and Eve?

7. Why was the Tree of Knowledge of Good and Evil unguarded?

Genesis 2:17, 3:22-24 "The tree of the knowledge of good and evil, thou shalt not eat of it … [God placed] Cherubims … to keep the way of the tree of life."

Note: If God placed the Eden Cherubims to guard the tree of life, why did God not place the Cherubims to guard both the tree of knowledge of good and evil and the tree of life at the very beginning?

8. Both the first male and female were called Adam

No, the woman was called Eve
Genesis 3:20 "Adam called his wife's name Eve."

Both the man and the woman were called Adam
Genesis 5:2 "Male and female created he them … called their name Adam"

Note: The suggestion that Adam was both male and female probably meant that Adam was a hermaphrodite. Or perhaps the name Adam referred to all humankind in the collective sense.

C. The sons of Adam and Eve

1. Abel was a herdsman and Cain was a farmer

[KJ] Genesis 4:2 "Abel was a keeper of sheep, [Cain] a tiller of the ground."
[DR] Genesis 4:2 "Abel was a shepherd, and Cain a husbandman."

Note: The first peoples of the earth were hunters and gatherers (Paleolithic Age) and not farmers nor herdsmen.

2. God favored Abel, thus Cain slew Abel

God favored Abel but not Cain
Genesis 4:4-5 "The Lord had respect unto Abel and to his offering: But unto Cain and to his offering he had not respect."

Note: If God is fair and just, why did God favor Abel but not Cain?

3. Did Cain become a fugitive and a vagabond?

God said Cain will become a fugitive and a vagabond
Genesis 4:9, 12 "The Lord said ... a fugitive and a vagabond shalt thou be"

Cain did not become a fugitive or a vagabond
Genesis 4:17 "Cain knew his wife ... bare Enoch ... builded a city ..."

Note: Cain had a family and built a city.

4. Cain was afraid another person will kill him after Abel's death

Genesis 4:14 "Every one that findeth me shall slay me."

Note: Why was Cain afraid when the only two people left were his parents?

5. Should death be repaid with death?

God protected Cain, a shedder of blood
Genesis 4:15 "The Lord set a mark upon Cain, lest any finding him should kill him."

A shedder of blood must die
Genesis 9:5-6 "Surely your blood of your lives will I require ... Who so sheddeth man's blood, by man shall his blood be shed."

Note: Why was there a need to mark Cain when there were only three persons left after the death of Abel?

6. Where did Cain's wife come from?

Cain got a wife who is not his sister
Genesis 4:16-17 "[Cain] dwelt in the land of Nod ... and Cain knew his wife"

Eve was the mother of all living
Genesis 3:20 "Adam called his wife's name Eve ... the mother of all living."

Note: In Genesis 4:16, Cain lived in the land of Nod (some Islamic writings indicate that Nod is the present day Yemen) where Cain got a wife.If Cain was able to get a wife who is not a descendant of Adam and Eve, Adam and Eve were not the only first couple that inhabited the earth. The Bible does not explain how Cain got a wife. However, in the Book of Jubilees, Cain took his sister Awan to be his wife and she gave birth to Enoch.

7. Cain and his wife built a whole new city in just two generations

Genesis 4:17 "Cain knew his wife ... bare Enoch: and he builded a city ..."

Note: How did Cain and his wife build a city in two generations? How many inhabitants were in that city?

8. Why should Lamech be avenged more?

Genesis 4:23-24 "Lamech [said] … I have slain a man to my wounding … If Cain shall be avenged sevenfold, truly Lamech seventy and sevenfold."

9. Is Enoch the sixth or the seventh generation from Adam?

Sixth, Adam, Seth, Enos, Cainan, Mahalaleel, Jared, Enoch
Genesis 5:3-18 "Adam … Seth … Enos … Cainan … Mahalaleel … Jared … Enoch."

Enoch is the seventh generation
Jude 1:14 "Enoch also, the seventh from Adam …"

D. Noah and the great deluge

1. Noah begat three sons in one year

Genesis 5:32 "Noah was five hundred years old … begat Shem, Ham and Japheth."

Note: Were Noah's sons triplets? Or did Noah's sons have different mothers?

2. The existence of Nephilim before and after the flood

There were Nephilim before and after the flood
Genesis 6:4 "There were Nephilim (giants) in the earth in those days …"
[KJ] Numbers 13:33 "We saw the giants, the sons of Anak …"
[DR] Numbers 13:33 "The people, that we beheld, are of a tall stature."

The flood annihilated all creatures other than Noah and his family
Genesis 7:21 "All flesh died that moved upon the earth …"

3. God killed everything when he was only displeased with men

Genesis 6:5-7 "God saw that *the wickedness of man* was great … the Lord said, I will destroy … both man, and beast … and the fowls of the air."

Note: Why did God destroy everything when he was only displeased with men? Why did God repent if God knows everything?

4. Because the human imagination is evil, what did God do?

God will destroy
Genesis 6:5, 7 "God saw ... every imagination of the thoughts of his [man] heart was only evil ... the Lord said, I will destroy man ..."

God will not destroy
Genesis 8:21 "The Lord said in his heart, I will *not* again curse the ground any more for man's sake; for the imagination of man's heart is evil ..."

Note: Why should the evil imagination of man be the reason for both his doom and salvation?

5. Was Noah perfect?

Yes, Noah was perfect
Genesis 6:9 "Noah was a just man and perfect ... Noah walked with God."
Genesis 7:1 "The Lord said... for thee have I seen righteous before me ..."

No, Noah was not perfect
Genesis 9:20-21 "He [Noah] ... was drunken ... was uncovered ..."

6. God killed so many creatures because of so much violence

[KJ] Genesis 6:13 "God said ... the earth is filled with violence ... I will destroy them ..."
[DR] Genesis 6:13 "God said ... the earth is filled with iniquity ... I will destroy them ..."

Note: Why kill all the living when only the humans were the ones at fault?

7. How many animals were in the ark?

Two of a kind
Genesis 6:19 "Of every living thing ... two of every sort ... into the ark."
Genesis 7:9, 15 "There went ... unto [the ark], two and two of all flesh ..."

Seven of a kind for every clean beast, and two for every unclean beast
Genesis 7:2, 3 "Every clean beast [take] *by sevens* ..."

8. Concerning animals that are clean and unclean

God ordered Noah to take seven of the clean and two of the unclean
Genesis 7:2 "Every clean beast [take sevens] beasts that are not clean [two]"

God declared what animals are clean and unclean
Leviticus 11:4-7 "Nevertheless these shall ye not eat of them that chew the cud ... To make a difference between the unclean and the clean ..."

Note: The law about clean and unclean animals was only declared in the Book of Leviticus, at a much later time than the time of Noah.

9. Noah and his family entered the ark twice?

Noah loaded the animals in seven days and entered the ark
Genesis 7:7-10 "Noah [and his family] went [into the ark] after seven days"

Noah loaded the animals in one day and entered the ark
Genesis 7:13-14 "In the selfsame day entered Noah [and his family] … into the ark."

Note: Noah and his wife Emzara, his sons Shem, Ham and Japheth and their wives entered the Ark.

10. Duration of Noah's Flood

A total of 40 days
Genesis 7:12 "The rain was upon the earth forty days and forty nights."

A total of 150 days
Genesis 7:24; 8:3 "The waters prevailed upon the earth an hundred and fifty days."

Note: A worldwide flood probably never happened and the story about Noah was most likely a local one.

11. When did the earth become dry?

Six hundredth and first year, in the first month, the first day of the month
Genesis 8:13 "In the six hundredth and first year, in the first month, the first day of the month, the waters were dried up … the ground was dry."

Second month, on the seven and twentieth day of the month
Genesis 8:14 "In the second month … seven and twentieth day of the month, was the earth dried."

Note: It is commonly believed that after the flood, Noah's ark rested upon the mountains of Ararat in Turkey (see Genesis 8:4).

12. Noah killed and offered some animals after saving the animals

Genesis 8:20 "Noah … took of every clean beast, and of every clean fowl, and offered burnt offerings on the altar."

Note: Noah killed one of every clean beast and every clean fowl after painstakingly trying to save seven of each clean animal.

E. The tower of Babel

1. How many languages were there before the tower of Babel?

Many languages
Genesis 10:5, 20, 31 "By these were the isles of the Gentiles divided in their lands; every one after his tongue ... after their families, after their tongues"

One language
Genesis 11:1 "The whole earth was of one language, and of one speech."

2. Who was the father of Shelah (Salah)?

Arphaxad was the father of Shelah
Genesis 11:12 "Arphaxad ... begat Salah."

Cainan the father of Shelah and Arphaxad was the grandfather of Shelah
Luke 3:35-36 "Salah, which was the son of Cainan ... the son of Arphaxad."

F. The time of Abraham and Isaac

1. How old was Terah when Abram was born?

Terah was seventy years old
Genesis 11:26 "Terah lived seventy years, and begat Abram ..."

Terah was 130 years old
Genesis 11:32 "Terah were two hundred and five years; and Terah died ..."
Genesis 12:4 "Abram was seventy and five years old ... (Terah was already dead)."

Note: Terah was 205 years old when she died. Abram was 75 years old when Terah died, therefore Terah was 130 years old when she begat Abram.

2. What was the age of Abram when he left Haran after Terah died?

Abram was one hundred thirty five
Genesis 11:26 "Terah lived seventy years, and begat Abram ..."
Genesis 11:32 "Terah were two hundred and five years; and Terah died in Haran"

Abram was seventy and five years old
Genesis 12:4 "Abram was seventy and five years old when he departed out of Haran."
Acts 7:4 "He [Abram] dwelt in Charran [Haran] when his father was dead"

Note: Terah's age when Abram was born (70), Terah's age when he died (205), thus Abram was 135 years old when Terah died. But the Bible says that Abram was 75 years old when he left Haran after Terah died.

3. The Chaldeans

The Ur of the Chaldeans
Genesis 11:31 "Terah took Abram … from Ur of the Chaldees …"
Genesis 15:7 "I … brought thee [Abram] out of Ur of the Chaldees …"

Note: But the Chaldeans did not come to the region of Ur until 1100 BCE, 700 years after Abraham's supposed migration from Ur.

4. Did Abraham know he was going to Canaan?

Yes, Abraham left to go to Canaan
Genesis 12:5 "Abram took Sarai … they went forth to go into the land of Canaan."

No, Abraham did not know where he was going
Hebrews 11:8 "By faith Abraham … went out, not knowing whither he went."

5. Abraham pimps his wife to the Pharaoh and to Abimelech

Abraham pimps his wife to the Pharaoh but God punished the Pharaoh instead
Genesis 12:14-17 "When Abram was come into Egypt the Egyptians beheld the woman [Sarai] that she was very fair ... and the woman was taken into Pharaoh's house … the Lord plagued Pharaoh and his house … because of Sarai Abram's wife."

Abraham pimps his wife to Abimelech but God did not punished Abimelech
Genesis 20:2-3, 14 "Abraham said of Sarah his wife, She is my sister: and Abimelech … took Sarah. But God [said] to Abimelech in a dream … the woman which thou hast taken; for she is a man's wife … and Abimelech … restored him Sarah his wife."

Note: Abraham pimp his wife to the Pharaoh to protect himself, and God plagued the Pharaoh's house for taking Abraham's wife. Why did God punish the Pharaoh instead of Abraham? Abraham also pimp Sarai to Abimelech but unlike the Pharaoh, God did not punish Abimelech. Sarai was approaching ninety years old and she was still desirable to the Pharaoh and Abimelech's eyes? And, because of Sarai's beauty the Pharaoh provided

Abraham with sheep, oxen, he asses, menservants, maidservants, she asses, and camels, and Abimelech gave Abraham sheep, oxen, men servants, and women servants.

When Abraham introduced his wife as his sister, Abraham was not lying, because his wife was actually his half-sister. Sarah was the daughter of Abraham's father, Terah.

6. Dan and Hebron

The place called Hebron
Genesis 13:18 "Abram [dwelt in] Mamre, which is in Hebron"
[KJ] Joshua 14:15 "The name of Hebron before was Kirjatharba"
[DR] Joshua 14:15 "The name of Hebron before was Cariath-Arbe"

The city of Dan
Genesis 14:14 "Abram ... pursued them unto Dan."
Judges 18:29 "The city Dan ... the name of the city was Laish"

Note: The place called Hebron was named Hebron at a much later date and the city of Dan was not named Dan until the time of Judges.

7. Who spoke with Hagar?

The angel
Genesis 16:7-11 "The angel of the Lord said ... Hagar ... Return to thy mistress ... the angel of the Lord said unto her [Hagar], Behold ..."

The Lord
Genesis 16:13 "She [Hagar] called the name of the Lord that spake unto her"

8. How many sons did Abraham have?

Two
Genesis 16:15; 21:2 "Hagar bare [a son Ishmael] ... Sarah ... bare [a son] ..."
Galatians 4:22 "Abraham had two sons ..."

One
Genesis 22:12 "He [God] said ... thy son [Isaac], thine only son ..."
Hebrews 11:17 "Abraham ... offered up Isaac ... his only begotten son."

Eight, since Abraham later bore six more children with Keturah
[KJ] Genesis 25:1-2 "Again Abraham took a wife [Keturah]. And she bare him Zimran, and Jokshan, and Medan, and Midian, and Ishbak, and Shuah."
[DR] Genesis 25:1-2 "Again Abraham took a wife [Keturah]. And she bare him Zamran, and Jecsan, and Madan, and Madian, and Jesboc, and Sue ..."

9. How old was Ishmael when he was abandoned?

More than thirteen years old
Genesis 16:16 "Abram was eighty-six years old when Hagar gave birth to ... Ishmael."
Genesis 17:25; 21:5 "Ishmael ... was thirteen years old ... Abraham was an hundred years old ..."

An infant
Genesis 21:14-15 "Abraham ... took bread ... and gave it unto Hagar, putting it on her shoulder, and the child, and sent her away: and she departed ... and cast the child under one of the shrubs."

Note: Ishmael was already 13 years old in Genesis 17, yet he was carried as an infant in Genesis 21.

10. God requires circumcision as a covenant between God and man

Genesis 17:9-14 "God said ... every man child among you shall be circumcised."

Summary: God requires every son who descended from Abraham and the son of his servants to be circumcised eight days after being born.

11. An uncircumcised child must be abandoned

Genesis 17:14 "The uncircumcised man child ... shall be cut off from his people; he hath broken my covenant."

12. Abraham scoffed the idea that he is going to have a child

Genesis 17:17 "Abraham [laughed and said] ... Shall a child be born unto him that is an hundred years old? And shall Sarah, that is ninety years old, bear?"

Note: Why should Abraham be concerned if he can still father a child at age 100 when his father Terah had him when he was 130 years old?

13. Abraham was circumcised when he was 99 years old

Genesis 17:24-27 "Abraham was ninety-nine years old when he was circumcised ... all the men of his house ... were circumcised with him."

Note: In Genesis 14:14, Abraham had a total of 318 servants. Abraham circumcised his entire household of 318 servants, his sons and himself when he was 99 years old.

14. Abraham fed God and God dined with Abraham

Genesis 18:1, 8 "The Lord appeared unto him … he [Abraham] took butter, and milk … and they did eat."

15. Did Sarah have faith that she would conceive?

Yes, Sarah had faith
Hebrews 11:11 "Through faith also Sara herself … conceive"

No, Sarah laughed at God
Genesis 18:10-15 "Sarah thy wife shall have a son … Sarah laughed within herself … the Lord said unto Abraham, Wherefore did Sarah laugh …"

16. Abraham scolded God

Genesis 18:23, 25 "Abraham … said [to God], Wilt thou also destroy the righteous with the wicked? … *Shall not the Judge of all the earth do right?*"

17. God helped in giving Abraham a son?

Abraham begat a son with the help of God
Genesis 21:2 "Sarah conceived … of which God had spoken to him."

Abraham begat six more children without the interference of God
Genesis 25:1-2 "Abraham took a wife … bare him (six children)."

Note: Why did God interfere in giving Abraham a son, when Abraham had six more children in the future?

18. Who named the place called Beersheba?

Abraham
[KJ] Genesis 21:31 "He [Abraham] called that place Beersheba …"
[DR] Genesis 21:31 "Therefore that place was called Bersabee …"

Isaac
[KJ] Genesis 26:33 "He [Isaac] called it Shebah … the city is [named] Beersheba unto this day."
[DR] Genesis 26:33 "He [Isaac] called it Abundance: and … the city was called Bersabee …"

Note: Bersabee is the Latin name of Beersheba.

19. The Land of the Philistines

Genesis 21:32-34 "The land of the Philistines …"

Note: But the Philistines did not come to the region of Canaan until 1200 BCE, 800 years after Abraham's supposed migration from Ur. The Philistines descended from Ham, son of Noah (see Genesis 10:6, 13, 14).

20. Did Abraham sacrifice Isaac to God?

God prevented Abraham from sacrificing Isaac
Genesis 22:12 "He [God] said, Lay not thine hand upon the lad ..."

Abraham went down from the mountains without mention of Isaac
Genesis 22:5, 16, 19 "Abraham said ... I and the lad will go yonder and worship, and come again to you ... Abraham returned unto his young men."

21. Was Abraham justified by faith?

By faith
Romans 4:2 "For if Abraham were justified by works, he hath whereof to glory."

By works
James 2:21 "Was not Abraham our father justified by works ..."

22. Who owns the sepulcher that Abraham purchased?

Ephron
Genesis 23:13-20 "He [Abraham] spake unto Ephron ... I will give [money for the field] ... I will bury my dead."

Hemor (Emmor)
Acts 7:15-16 "Jacob [died] ... and laid in the sepulchre that Abraham bought ... of the sons of Emmor the father of Sychem."

23. Who bought the sepulcher from Hemor (Emmor)?

Jacob
Joshua 24:32 "The bones of Joseph [buried] in Shechem ... which Jacob bought of the sons of Hamor ..."

Abraham
Acts 7:16 "The sepulchre that Abraham bought ... of the sons of Emmor ..."

24. How much was the sepulcher?

Four hundred shekels of silver
Genesis 23:16 "Abraham weighed to Ephron ... four hundred shekels of silver ..."

One hundred pieces of silver
[KJ] Joshua 24:32 "Jacob bought ... for an hundred pieces of silver ..."
[DR] Joshua 24:32 "Jacob bought ... for a hundred young ewes ..."

25. Abraham's servant swore with his hand under Abraham's thigh

Genesis 24:3, 9 "I will make thee swear by the Lord ... that thou shalt not take a wife unto my son of the daughters of the Canaanites ... And the servant put his hand under the thigh of Abraham ... and sware to him concerning that matter."

Note: Placing the hand under the thigh is a euphemism for holding the genitals (see Genesis 47:29). It is an ancient ritual of swearing called the Yarek Oath. Although Abraham's servant was unidentified, it is widely believed that he was Eliezer of Damascus (see Genesis 15:2).

26. Was Keturah Abraham's wife or concubine?

Abraham's wife
Genesis 25:1 "Abraham took a wife, and her name was Keturah."

Abraham's concubine
I Chronicles 1:32 "Keturah, Abraham's concubine ..."

Note: The Catholic Bible names the books I Chronicles and II Chronicles as the Ist Book of Paralipomenon and 2nd Book Of Paralipomenon.

27. Isaac visited the king of the Philistines

Genesis 26:1 "Isaac went unto Abimelech king of the Philistines unto Gerar."

Note: But the Philistines came to live in the region 800 years after Isaac.

28. Isaac pimps his wife to Abimelech

Isaac lies about his relationship with wife Rebekah and pimps her to Abimelech
Genesis 26:7 "The men of the place asked him [Isaac] of his wife; and he [Isaac] said, She is my sister: for he feared to say, She is my wife ..."

Note: Isaac pimped his wife Rebekah to the same king to whom his father Abraham also pimped his mother Sarai. (See Genesis 12:13).

G. Sodom and Gomorrah

1. Was Lot Abraham's brother or nephew?

Lot was Abraham's nephew
Genesis 11:27 "Terah begat Abram, Nahor, and Haran; and Haran begat Lot"
Genesis 12:5; 14:12 "Lot, Abram's brother's son ..."

Lot was Abraham's brother
Genesis 14:14, 16 "Abram heard that his brother [Lot] ..."

Note: Abram's name was changed to Abraham in Genesis 17:5:
Genesis 17:5 "Neither shall thy ... be called Abram, but ... Abraham."

2. Were Lot's daughters virgins?

Lot claims his daughters were virgins
Genesis 19:8 "I [Lot] have two daughters which have not known man ..."

Lot's daughters were married
Genesis 19:14 "Lot ... sons in law, which married his daughters ..."

Note: Lot's daughters named Pheine and Thamma were both married.

3. Was Lot a righteous man?

Yes, Lot was righteous
II Peter 2:7-8 "Just Lot, vexed with ... the wicked ..."

Lot pimps his daughters to the men of Sodom to protect his male visitors
Genesis 19:1-8 "There came two angels to Sodom (Lot received them in his house and the men of Sodom went to Lot's house to look for them and Lot replied) I have two daughters ... [let me] bring them out unto you ... only unto these men do nothing ..."

Summary: Lot pimps his daughters to protect his male visitors from the men in Sodom.
Note: Lot offered his daughters in exchange for the safety of his male visitors. A similar story is described in Judges 19. This gesture is a reflection of the hospitality norms and how women were valued less than men.

Lot lied about the virginity of his daughters
Genesis 19:8 "I have two daughters which have not known man."
Genesis 19:14 "Lot ... sons in law, which married his daughters"

Lot impregnated his daughters when he was drunk
Genesis 19:33-35 "They [Lot's daughters] made their father drink wine ... and lay with him ... both the daughters of Lot *with child by their father.*"

Note: The daughters of Lot thought their father was the only man on earth.

4. Who destroyed Sodom and Gomorrah?

The angels
Genesis 19:13 "The Lord hath sent us [angels] to destroy it."

God
Genesis 19:24 "The Lord rained upon Sodom and upon Gomorrah ..."

5. Was Sodom and Gomorrah the only destroyed cities?

Yes
Genesis 19:24 "The Lord rained upon Sodom [and] Gomorrah brimstone ..."

No, Sodom, Gomorrah, Admah and Zeboim
Deuteronomy 29:23 "The ... overthrow of Sodom, and Gomorrah, Admah, and Zeboim ..."

Note: Sodom, Gomorrah, Admah, Zeboim and Bela (Zoar) are collectively called the Cities of the Plain. Lot escaped to Zoar after fleeing from Sodom (Genesis 19:22). The destruction of these cities was most likely caused by a volcanic eruption. Today it is widely believed that the Dead Sea is where these cities were once located.

H. The time of Jacob and Esau

1. Esau sold his birthright to Jacob

Jacob and Esau were fighting each other inside the womb
Genesis 25:22 "The children struggled together within her."

Esau sold his birthright for a piece of bread and a bowl of lentil soup
Genesis 25:33-34 "He [Esau] sold his birthright (for) bread and pottage of lentils."

2. Jacob deceived Isaac

Jacob got his blessings from Isaac by pretending to be Esau
Genesis 27:19 "Jacob said unto his father, I am Esau thy first born; I have done according as thou badest me: arise, I pray thee, sit and eat of my venison, that thy soul may bless me."

Isaac blesses Jacob
Genesis 27:28-29 "Therefore God give thee of the dew of heaven, and the fatness of the earth ... and blessed be he that blesseth thee."

Note: Jacob pretended to be Esau in order to obtain blessings from his father Isaac. Isaac blessed Jacob in fulfillment of a prophecy (See Genesis 25:23).

Genesis 25:23 "The Lord [said] two nations are in thy womb ... one people shall be stronger than the other ... and the elder shall serve the younger."

3. Who were Esau's wives?

Judith, Basemath and Mahalath
Genesis 26:34; 28:9 "He [Esau] took as wives Judith, Basemath, Mahalath"

Adah, Aholibamah and Basemath
Genesis 36:2-3 "Esau took his wives Adah ... Aholibamah and Basemath"

4. Who was the daughter of Elon the Hittite, who was Esau's wife?

Basemath
Genesis 26:34 "He (took as wives) ... Basemath the daughter of Elon ..."

Adah
Genesis 36:2 "Esau took his wives ... Adah the daughter of Elon the Hittite"

5. Who was the father of Bashemath?

Elon the Hittite
Genesis 26:34 "Bashemath the daughter of Elon the Hittite."

Ishmael
Genesis 36:3 "Bashemath Ishmael's daughter ..."

6. Who was Laban's father?

Bethuel
Genesis 28:5 "Laban, son of Bethuel ..."

Nahor
Genesis 29:5 "Laban the son of Nahor (Nachor)"

7. Is Bethel and Luz the same place?

Yes
Genesis 28:19 "That place Bethel ... that city was called Luz (Luza) ..."
Genesis 35:6 "Jacob came to Luz (Luza) ... that is, Bethel ..."
Judges 1:23 "The house of Joseph ... descry Bethel. The city was formerly named Luz (Luza)."

No
Joshua 16:2 "From Bethel to Luz (Luza) ..."
Judges 1:26 "The man ... built a city, and called it Luz [Luza] ... the name thereof unto this day."

8. Jacob named a place called Bethel twice

Jacob names Bethel before meeting Rachel
Genesis 28:19 "Jacob] called … that place Bethel … was called Luz (Luza) …"

Jacob names Bethel before Rachel dies
Genesis 35:15 "Jacob called the name of the place … Bethel."

Jacob named a place Bethel that was already called Bethel
Genesis 12:8; 13:3 "East of Bethel … He went … to Bethel …"

9. Jacob did not know he was sleeping with the wrong woman

Genesis 29:21-25 "[Jacob said] Give me my wife … in the evening … [Laban] took Leah (Lia) … and brought her to him … [in the morning] he [Jacob] said … did not I serve … for Rachel?"

Note: Were Jacob's eyes closed all the time that he did not see he was sleeping with the wrong woman?

10. Rachel bartered Jacob to Leah in exchange for mandrakes

Genesis 30:15-16 "Rachel said, "Then he [Jacob] may lie with you tonight in exchange for … mandrakes" … Leah went to … [Jacob] and said, "You must come in to me, for I have hired you with my son's mandrakes." So he lay with her that night."

11. God wrestled with Jacob and Jacob won

Jacob prevailed against God so God dislocated Jacob's joint
Genesis 32:24-25, 28 "[Jacob] wrestled a man … the hollow of Jacob's thigh was out of joint, as he wrestled with him. And [Jacob] prevailed … he [God] said, Thy name shall be called no more Jacob, but Israel: for as a prince hast thou power with God and with men, and hast prevailed."

The Jews do not eat the sinew because of what happened to Jacob
Genesis 32:32 "The children of Israel eat not of the sinew … because he [God] touched the hollow of Jacob's thigh in the sinew that shrank."

12. What should Jacob be called?

God renames Jacob for the first time
Genesis 32:28 "He said, Thy name shall be called no more Jacob, but Israel."

God renames Jacob for the second time
Genesis 35:10 "God said … thy name shall not be called any more Jacob, but Israel …"

God calls Jacob, Jacob
Genesis 46:2 "God spake unto Israel … and said, Jacob, Jacob."

13. Dinah's brothers killed all the males in a city

Genesis 34:1-31 "[Shechem] saw her [Dinah] … [took her] and defiled her …
(Dinah's brothers deceivingly told Shechem to have him and all his people
circumcised) when they were sore… Dinah's brethren … slew all the males."

*Note: Shechem the son of Hamor the Hivite, prince of the country loved
Dinah dearly,   slept with her and asked her hand for marriage. But Dinah's
brothers disliked what Sechem did, so they convinced all the males (including
Shechem) in the city where Shechem lived, to be circumcised with the motive
of killing them all while they were still sore due to their circumcision.
Dinah's brothers killed all the males and plundered the city. The Bible did not
mention the name of the city where the killings took place but other writings
mentioned the name of the city is also Shechem.*

14. Reuben slept with his father's concubine

Genesis 35:22 "[Reuben] lay with Bilhah (Bala) his father's concubine."
Genesis 49:3-4 "Ruben, my firstborn … thou shalt not excel; because thou
wentest up to thy father's bed; then defiledst thou it."

*Note: Reuben angered his father Jacob for his actions that led Jacob to take
away from him his birthright. The right as firstborn was given to Joseph, the
right to rule the tribes was given to the sons of Judah and the right for
priesthood was given to the descendants of Levi. (See I Chronicles 5:1-2).*

15. How was Anah related to Zibeon?

Anah was the daughter of Zibeon (Sebeon)
Genesis 36:2, 14 "Anah the daughter of Zibeon (Sebeon) the Hivite …"

Anah was the brother of Zibeon
Genesis 36:20 "These are the sons of Seir … Zibeon (Sebeon), and Anah."
I Chronicles 1:38 "The sons of Seir: Zibeon, and Anah …"

Anah was the son of Zibeon
I Chronicles 1:40 "The sons of Zibeon (Sebeon); Aiah, and Anah.
Genesis 36:24 "The children of Zibeon; both Ajah, and Anah …"

16. Who were the sons of Eliphaz?

Teman, Omar, Zepho, Gatam, and Kenaz
Genesis 36:11 "The sons of Eliphaz … Teman, Omar, Zepho, Gatam, Kenaz."

Teman, Omar, Zepho, Kenaz, Korah, Gatam and Amalek
Genesis 36:15-16 "The sons of Eliphaz: Teman, Omar, Zepho, Kenaz, Korah, Gatam ... Amalek."

Teman, Omar, Zephi, Gatam, Kenaz, Timna, and Amalek
[KJ] I Chronicles 1:36 "The sons of Eliphaz: Teman, Omar, Zephi, Gatam, Kenaz, Timna and Amalek."

Theman, Omar, Sephi, Gathan, Cenaz, Thamna and Amalec
[DR] I Paralipomenon 1:36 "The sons of Eliphaz: Theman, Omar, Sephi, Gathan, Cenez, and by Thamna, Amalec."

17. Who was Korah's father?

Esau
Genesis 36:14 "Esau's wife: and she bare to Esau Jeush ... and Korah (Core)."

Eliphaz
Genesis 36:16 "Korah (Core) ... these are the dukes that came of Eliphaz ..."

Note: In Genesis 36:15-16, Esau was the grandfather of Korah.

18. To whom was Joseph sold by his brothers?

Ishmeelites
Genesis 37:28; 39:1 "[They] sold Joseph to the Ishmeelites ... bought of the Ishmeelites ..."

Midianites
[KJ] Genesis 37:36 "The Midianites sold him [Joseph] ... unto Potiphar ... an officer of Pharaoh's"
[DR] Genesis 37:36 "The Midianites sold him [Joseph] ... unto Potiphar ... an eunuch of Pharao"

Note: The Douay-Rheims Bible indicates that Potiphar was a eunuch of the Pharaoh. However, Potiphar was a married man and it was his wife who seduced Joseph in Egypt.

19. How did Joseph end up in Egypt?

The Ishmeelites brought Joseph into Egypt
Genesis 37:28 "They [Midianites] drew and lifted up Joseph ... sold Joseph to the Ishmeelites ... and they brought Joseph into Egypt."

The Midianites brought Joseph into Egypt
Genesis 37:36 "The Midianites sold him into Egypt ..."

Joseph's brothers sold him into Egypt
Genesis 45:4 "Joseph said ... I am Joseph your brother, whom ye sold into Egypt."

20. Er and Onan

Er, Judah's firstborn
Genesis 38:7 "[Er] was wicked in the sight of the Lord ... the Lord slew him."

Onan, spilled his 'seed' and the Lord also slew him
Genesis 38:8-10 "Judah said unto Onan, Go in unto thy brother's wife ... and raise up seed to thy brother. [But] Onan ... spilled it on the ground ... [it] displeased the Lord: [and] he slew him also."

Note: Onan had to marry Tamar, his brother's widow because of the Levirate Law defined in Deuteronomy 25:5-10. Judah asked Onan to impregnate Tamar; but Onan spilled his seed and God slew him. Because of the story of Onan many Christian groups ban the use of contraception and other non-procreational sexual acts (onanism).

21. Tamar dressed as a harlot and slept with her father-in-law

Genesis 38:13-18 "She [Tamar] ... covered her [self] with a vail ... sat in an open place ... Judah saw her, he thought her to be an harlot ... [and he] came in unto her, and she conceived by him."

Note: Tamar, the widow of Er and Onan, bore twins Pharez and Zarah from her union with her father-in-law whom she deceived by dressing up as a prostitute. Pharez, one of Tamar's sons, was an ancestor of Jesus.

22. Did seedtime and harvest stop for seven years?

Yes
Genesis 41:54-56 "The seven years of dearth began ... the famine waxed sore in ... Egypt."
Genesis 45:6 "For these two years hath the famine been in the land: and yet there are five years, in the which there shall neither be earing nor harvest."

No
Genesis 8:22 "Seedtime and harvest ... day and night shall *not* cease."

23. Where was Jacob buried?

Machpelah
[KJ] Genesis 50:13 "His [sons] ... buried him in the cave ... of Machpelah ..."

[DR] Genesis 50:13 "They buried him in the double cave which Abraham had bought ... of Ephron the Hethite over against Mambre."

Sychem (Shechem)
Acts 7:15-16 "Jacob [died] and was carried over into Sychem ..."

I. The tribes of Israel

1. How many relatives of Jacob went to Egypt?

Seventy
Genesis 46:27 "All ... [which came into Egypt] were *threescore and ten*."
Exodus 1:5 "All the souls ... *seventy* souls."

Seventy-five
Acts 7:14 "All his [Joseph] kindred, *threescore and fifteen* souls."

2. Who were the sons of Levi?

Gershon, Kohath, and Merari
Genesis 46:11 "The sons of Levi; Gershon, Kohath, and Merari."
I Chronicles 6:1, 16; 23:6 "The sons of Levi; Gershon, Kohath, and Merari."

Mahli (Moholi)
[KJ] Ezra 8:18 "Mahli, the son of Levi, the son of Israel."
[DR] I Esdras 8:18 "Moholi, the son of Levi, the son of Israel."

3. Who were the sons of Benjamin?

Belah, Becher, Ashbel, Gera, Naaman, Ehi, Rosh, Muppim, Huppim, Ard
[KJ] Genesis 46:21 "The sons of Benjamin were Belah, Becher, Ashbel, Gera, Naaman, Ehi, Rosh, Muppim, Huppim, and Ard."
[DR] Genesis 46:21 "The sons of Benjamin: Bela, Bechor, Asbel Gera Naaman, Echi, Ros, Mophim, Ophim and Ared."

Bela, Ashbel, Ahiram, Shupham, Hupham
Numbers 26:38-39 "The sons of Benjamin ... Bela, Ashbel, Ahiram, Shupham, Hupham ..."

Bela, Becher, Jediael
I Chronicles 7:6 "The sons of Benjamin; Bela, and Becher, and Jediael..."

Bela, Ashbel, Aharah, Nohah, Rapha
I Chronicles 8:1-2 "Benjamin begat Bela ... Ashbel, Aharah, Nohah, Rapha"

4. How was Naaman and Ard related to Benjamin?

They were sons of Benjamin
Genesis 46:21 "The sons of Benjamin were Belah ... Naaman ... and Ard."

They were grandsons of Benjamin
Numbers 26:38, 40 "The sons of Benjamin after their families: of Bela ... and the sons of Bela were Ard and Naaman."

5. How old was Benjamin when his family migrated to Egypt?

He was a child
Genesis 44:20, 22 "We have a father, an old man, and a child [Benjamin] of his old age, a little one ... the lad [Benjamin] cannot leave his father."

He was an adult with children
Genesis 46:8, 19, 21 "The children of Israel, which came into Egypt ... Benjamin ... and the sons of Benjamin were Belah, and ..."

6. Who were the fathers of the 12 tribes of Israel?

Reuben, Simeon, Levi, Judah, Zebulun, Issachar, Dan, Gad, Asher, Naphtali, Joseph, and Benjamin
Genesis 49:2-28 "Reuben ... All these are the twelve tribes of Israel."

Reuben, Simeon, Levi, Juda, Zabulon, Issachar, Manasses, Gad, Aser, Nepthalim, Joseph, and Benjamin
Revelation 7:4-8 "Of the tribe of Juda ... of the tribe of Benjamin ..."

Note: The book of Genesis excludes Manasses (Manasseh) but includes Dan. The book of Revelation includes Manasses (Manasseh) but excludes Dan.

7. Who was destined to rule Israel?

The tribe of Judah will reign
Genesis 49:10 "The sceptre shall not depart from Judah ..."

But King Saul was from the tribe of Benjamin
Acts 13:21 "Afterward they [Israelites] desired a king: and God gave unto them Saul... a man of the tribe of Benjamin ..."

J. Moses and the Exodus

1. Who wrote the Pentateuch?

Moses
Deuteronomy 1:1; 31:9 "These [Moses spake] ... Moses wrote this law"

There were other writers

Genesis 12:6 "The Canaanite *was* then in the land."
Genesis 13:7 "The Canaanite and the Perizzite dwelled then in the land."

Note: In Genesis 12:6 and Genesis 13:7, how did Moses know that the Canaanites will leave their land, when the Canaanites left Canaan after Moses passed away?

Numbers 12:3 "Now the man Moses was very meek ..."
Deuteronomy 34:5-6 "Moses ... died there in the land of Moab, according to the word of the Lord. And he buried him in a valley in the land of Moab, over against Bethpeor: but no man knoweth of his sepulchre unto this day."
Deuteronomy 34:10 "There arose not a prophet since in Israel like unto Moses, whom the Lord knew face to face."

Note: In the book of Numbers and Deuteronomy, Moses was being identified as a third person, which suggests there were other authors. In Deuteronomy, how did Moses write about his death and burial?

Moses predates the first king, King Saul
Genesis 36:31 "These are the kings that reigned in the land of Edom, *before there reigned any king over the children of Israel.*"

Note: How did Moses know in Genesis 36:31 that there will be kings in the future when Moses lived long before the first king, King Saul?

2. Moses said he has uncircumcised lips

Exodus 6:12 "Moses spake [saying] who am of uncircumcised lips?"

Note: According to legend Moses had a speech impediment. When Moses was a child he took the crown of the Pharaoh and placed it in his head. The court magicians were alarmed at the gesture and took it as a bad omen. So they tested him with a pan of burning coals and a pan of gold. Moses chose the pan of burning coals, took it in his mouth and damaged his mouth. If he had taken the pan of gold he would have been put to death.

3. When did the Exodus happen?

During the time of Thutmosis III (1448 BCE)
I Kings 6:1 "In the four hundred and eightieth year after the children of Israel were come out of the land of Egypt, in the fourth year of Solomon's reign over Israel ..."

Note: Solomon reigned from 971 to 931 BCE.

During the time of Rameses II (1279 - 1213 BCE)

[KJ] Exodus 1:11 "They built for Pharaoh treasure cities, Pithom and Raamses."
[DR] Exodus 1:11 "They built for Pharao cities *of tabernacles*, Phithom and Ramesses."

Note: It is widely believed that the cities Pithom and Raamses were built during the time of Rameses II.

During the time of Rameses III (1187 - 1156 BCE)
Exodus 13:17 "When Pharaoh had let the people go, that God led them not through the way of the land of the Philistines ..."

Note: The Philistines settled in Canaan towards the beginning of the 12th century BC during the time of Rameses III.

During the time of Ahmose I, (1600 BCE), coinciding with the volcanic eruption of Thera
Exodus 7:20-11:5 "Moses and Aaron ... lifted up the rod, and smote the waters and all the waters that were in the river were turned to blood ... (The ten plagues of Egypt)."
Exodus 14:21-22 "Moses stretched out his hand over the sea ... and the waters were divided."

Note: The eruption of the Aegean volcano of Thera (Santorini) is considered as one of the most plausible explanations for all the plagues and crossing of the Red Sea.

4. Did Moses fear the Pharaoh?

Yes
Exodus 2:14-15 "Moses feared ... when Pharaoh heard this thing, he sought to slay Moses. But Moses fled from the face of Pharaoh ..."

No
Hebrew 11:27 "By faith he [Moses] forsook Egypt, not fearing the wrath of the king."

5. Did God appear to Moses in the burning bush?

Yes
Exodus 3:4,6 "God called unto him out of the midst of the bush, and said, Moses, Moses ... Moses hid his face; for he was afraid to look upon God."

No, an angel
Exodus 3:2 "The angel of the Lord appeared unto him [Moses] in a flame of."

Acts 7:35 "This Moses ... God send [to be] a ruler and a deliverer by the hand of the angel which appeared to him in the bush."

6. Moses gave instructions to the Israelites to plunder the Egyptians

Exodus 3:22 "Ye shall spoil the Egyptians."
Exodus 12:35-36 "Israel did ... spoiled the Egyptians."

7. Who was the father-in-law of Moses?

Reuel
[KJ] Exodus 2:21 "He [Reuel] gave Moses Zipporah his daughter."

Raguel
[DR] Exodus 2:21 "He [Raguel] gave Moses Zipporah his daughter."
Numbers 10:29 "Hobab, the son of Raguel ... Moses' father in law."

Jethro
Exodus 3:1; 4:18; 18:1,5 "Jethro Moses' father in law ..."

Hobab
[KJ] Judges 4:11 "Hobab the father in law of Moses ..."
[DR] Judges 4:11 "Hobab the kinsman of Moses ..."

Note: Moses married two women, an Ethiopian woman (Numbers 12:1) and Zipporah. The Bible did not mention the Ethiopian woman's name, but Josephus (Antiquities of the Jews) identified the first wife of Moses as Tharbis, an Ethiopian princess whom Moses married for political reasons. The names mentioned above as father-in-law of Moses are assumed to be the father of Zipporah.

8. Who was Hobab?

The father-in-law of Moses
Judges 4:11 "Hobab the father in law of Moses ..."

The brother-in-law of Moses
[KJ] Numbers 10:29 "Hobab, the son of Raguel ... Moses' father in law"

A male relative
[DR] Numbers 10:29 "Moses said to Hobab ... his kinsman"

9. God wanted to kill Moses because his son was uncircumcised

Exodus 4:24-26 "[The Lord] sought to kill him [Moses]. Then Zipporah took a sharp stone, and cut off the foreskin of her son ... and said, A bloody husband thou art, because of the circumcision."

10. Who hardened the Pharaoh's heart?

God hardened the Pharaoh's heart many times
Exodus 4:21; 7:3, 13 "I [God] will harden Pharaoh's heart ..."
Exodus 9:12; 10:1, 20, 27; 11:10; 14:4, 8, 17 "[God] hardened Pharaoh's heart"

The Pharaoh hardened his own heart
Exodus 8:15 "He [Pharaoh] ... hardened his heart ..."
I Samuel 6:6 "As the Egyptians and Pharaoh hardened their hearts?"

Note: God was contradicting himself when He (God) hardened Pharaoh's heart and sent the plagues against the Egyptians so the Pharaoh will let the Israelites go. Ironically, the Egyptians do not have a recorded history of Moses and the Israelites and the name of the Egyptian Pharaoh was never mentioned in the Bible.

11. Who converted all the available water into blood?

Moses and Aaron
Exodus 7:20 "Moses and Aaron did so [all the waters] were turned to blood."

The magicians of Egypt
Exodus 7:22 "The magicians of Egypt did so [convert water into blood] ..."

Note: After Moses and Aaron converted all the water to blood, there will be no water left for the magicians of Egypt to convert.

12. Who were the magicians of Egypt?

Exodus 7:11, 22 "Then Pharaoh also called ... the magicians of Egypt ..."
II Timothy 3:8 "Now as Jannes and Jambres withstood Moses ..."

Note: The book of Exodus did not mention the names of the magicians but Paul identified the magicians of Egypt as Jannes and Jambres.

13. The cattle were killed twice and then all the firstborn cattle died

All the cattle and horses in Egypt died because of a very grievous murrain
Exodus 9:3, 6 "There shall be a very grievous murrain ... *all* the cattle [died]"

All the beasts (cattle and horses) in the field in Egypt died because of hail
Exodus 9:19 "For upon every man and beast which shall be found in the field ... the hail shall come down upon them, and they shall die."

All the firstborn cattle died
Exodus 12:29 "At midnight the Lord smote ... all the firstborn of cattle."

14. God will send plagues so people will know more about Him

Exodus 9:14 "[I will] send all my plagues ... that thou mayest know that there is none like me ..."

15. How long must the Israelites eat unleavened bread

Seven days
Exodus 12:15; 23:15 "Seven days shall ye eat unleavened bread."
Deuteronomy 16:3 "Seven days shall ye eat unleavened bread."

Six days
Deuteronomy 16:8 "Six days thou shalt eat unleavened bread ..."

Note: The Israelites celebrate the Passover as a commemoration of their freedom from slavery in Egypt. When God commanded the Israelites to leave Egypt, they left in great haste and did not have the time to make the bread dough rise. The Passover is celebrated by eating the unleavened bread.

16. All the houses in Egypt had at least one dead?

Exodus 12:29-30 "The Lord smote all the firstborn in the land of Egypt ... there was not a house where there was not one dead."

Note: Not all houses have children or firstborns. Therefore it is not correct to assume that every house in Egypt had at least one dead.

17. Concerning the Passover

Who can eat the Passover?
Exodus 12:44 "Every man's servant that is bought for money, when thou hast circumcised him, then shall he eat thereof."

Who cannot eat the Passover?
Exodus 12:43, 45, 48 "The Lord said ... There shall no stranger eat there of: A foreigner and an hired servant shall not eat thereof. And when a stranger shall sojourn with thee ... all his males be circumcised ... no uncircumcised person shall eat thereof."

How to eat the Passover?
Exodus 12:46 "In one house shall it be eaten; thou shalt not carry forth ought of the flesh abroad out of the house; neither shall ye break a bone thereof."

18. Why did the Israelites travel for forty years?

The Israelites might change their mind and return to Egypt

Exodus 13:17 "God led them not through the way of the land of the Philistines … the people [might] repent when they see war, and they return to Egypt."
All the generation that displeased the Lord must be consumed
Numbers 14:33; 32:13 "Your children shall wander in the wilderness forty years … until your carcases be wasted in the wilderness."

19. It took the Israelites forty years to travel from Egypt to Canaan

The shortest route from Egypt to Canaan is through the land of the Philistines
Exodus 13:17 "When Pharaoh had let the people go, that God led then not through … the land of the Philistines …"

Note: The shortest route from Egypt to Canaan is a ten-day trip through the land of the Philistines.
According to Jewish tradition, Bithiah, the Pharoah's daughter who found Moses as a baby in the Nile was banished from Egypt for taking Moses as her own child. She went with the Israelites during the Exodus and later married Mered, a Judahite and had children named Miriam, Shammai and Ishbah.

20. Did God lead the Israelites to the land of the Philistines?

No
Exodus 13:17 "God led them *not through* … the land of the Philistines …"

Yes
Judges 3:1-3 "Now these are the nations which the Lord left, to prove Israel by them … to teach them war … Namely, five lords of the Philistines, and all t he Canaanites … that dwelt in mount Lebanon, from mount Baalhermon unto the entering in of Hamath."

Note: The Philistines who descended from Casluchim (Genesis 10:14) migrated to Canaan at the beginning of 1200 B.C.E. as described in the book of Judges 3:3 about seven hundred years after it was called 'the land of the Philistines'.

The route taken by the Israelites took them forty years
Numbers 14:33; 32:13 "Your children shall wander … forty years …"
Exodus 16:35 "The children of Israel ate manna forty years … until they reached … Chanaan."

Note: The distance between Egypt and Canaan is a little over 200 miles and will take less than ten days to travel one way, but it took the Israelites 40 years to make such travel.

No	Numbers 33:1-49	Numbers	Exodus	Deuteronomy	Judges
1	Rameses (Goshen)		Rameses (12:37)		
2	Succoth		Succoth to (12:37)		
3	Etham		Etham to (13:20)		
4	Pi Hahiroth (near Migdol)		Pi Hahiroth (14:1,2,9)		
5	Marah				
6	Elim				
7	Red Sea (Sea of Reeds)		Red Sea (14:22)		Red Sea (Jud 11:16)
8	Desert of Sin		Shur (15:22)		Kadesh (Jud 11:16)
9	Dophkah		Marah (15:23)		Arnon (Jud 11:18)
10	Alush		Elim (15:27-16:1)		Sihon (Jud 11:21)
11	Kephidim		Sin (16:1,17:1)	Taberah (Deut. 9:22)	Heshon/Aroer (Jud 11:26)
12	Desert of Sinai		Rephidim (17:1)	Massah (Deut. 9:22)	
13	Kibroth Hattaavah	Kibroth Hattaavah (11:35)	Massah/Meribah (17:7)	Kibroth Hattaavah (Deut. 9:22)	
14	Hazeroth	Hazeroth (11:35)			
15	Rithmah	Paran (10:12,12:16)			
16	Kimmon Perez				
17	Libnah	Taberah (11:3)			
18	Rissah				
19	Kehelathah		Sinai (19:2)		
20	Mt. Shepher	Kadesh (13:26; 20:16,22)			
21	Haradah	Mt Hor (20:22)			
22	Makheloth				
23	Tahath				
24	Terah				
25	Mithcah				
26	Hashmonah				
27	Moseroth				
28	Bene Jaakan				
29	Hor Haggidgad			Gudgodah (Deut 10:7)	
30	Jotbathah			Jotbathah (Deut 10:7)	
31	Abronah	Oboth (21:11)			
32	Ezion Geber	Iye Abarim (21:11)		Horeb (Deut 1:2)	
33	Kadesh	Zered (21:12)		Kadesh-barnea (Deut 9:23)	
34	Mt. Hor	Arnon (21:13)			
35	Zalmonah	Beer (21:16)			
36	Punon	Mattanah (21:18)			
37	Oboth	Nahaliel (21:19)			
38	Iyim (Iye Abarim)	Bamoth (21:19)			
39	Dibon Gad	Moab (21:20)			
40	Almon Diblathaim	Heshon in Sihon (21:25)			
41	Abarim Mountains	Bashan (21:33)			
42	Moab Plains across Jericho	Moab (22:1)			

Exodus Route

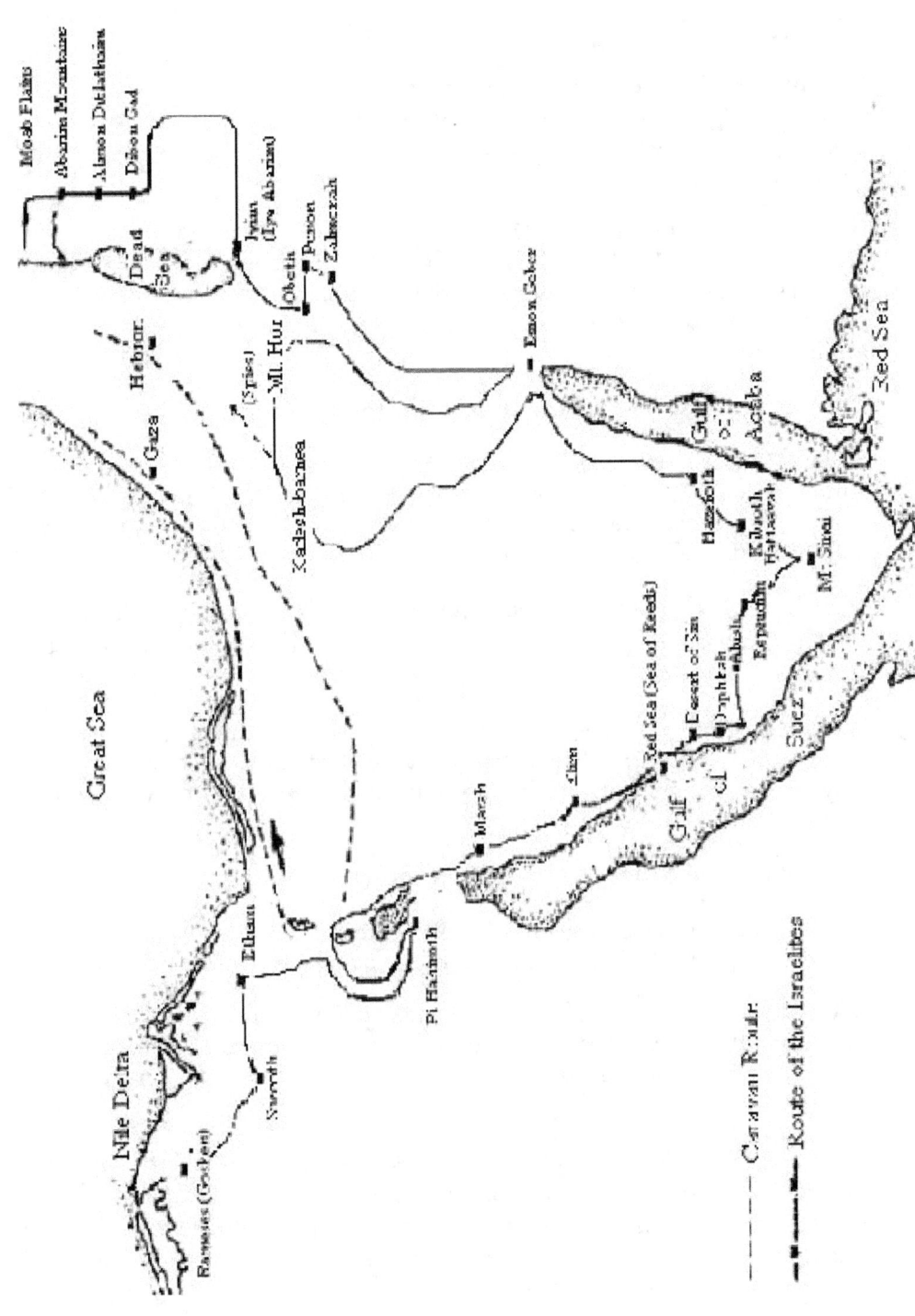

Moab Plains
Abarim Mountains
Almon Diblathaim
Dibon Gad
Dead Sea
Iyim (Ije Abarim)
Oboth
Punon
Zalmonah
Hebron
Gaza
(Spies)
Mt. Hor
Kadesh-barnea
Ezion Geber
Gulf of Aqaba
Red Sea
Hazeroth
Kibroth Hattaavah
Mt. Sinai
Rephidim
Alush
Dophkah
Desert of Sin
Red Sea (Sea of Reeds)
Elim
Marah
Great Sea
Nile Delta
Etham
Pi Hahiroth
Succoth
Rameses (Goshen)
Gulf of Suez

– – – – – Caravan Route
━━━━━ Route of the Israelites

45

21. Where did Moses get water from a rock?

In Rephidim from the wilderness of Sin
Exodus 17:1-7 "The congregation ... journeyed from the wilderness of Sin ... pitched in Rephidim ... the Lord said ... smite the rock, and there shall come water out of it ..."

In Kadesh from the desert of Zin
Numbers 20:1-8; 27:14 "Into the desert of Zin ... the people abode in Kadesh ... Moses ... smote the rock twice: and the water came out abundantly ..."
Deuteronomy 32:51 "Ye trespassed against me ... at the waters of MeribahKadesh."

22. Why was Moses forbidden to enter the Promise Land?

Because Moses struck the rock twice, instead of once
Numbers 20:7-12 "Moses ... smote the rock *twice* ... the Lord spake ... Because ye believed me not ... therefore ye shall not bring this congregation into the land which I have given them."

Note: The Lord spoke to both Aaron and Moses that they cannot enter the Promise Land because Moses struck the rock twice, was Aaron also punished for the misdeed of Moses?

Because the Lord considered the whole generation evil including Moses
Deuteronomy 1:34-37; 3:23-26 "I besought the Lord at that time, saying ... I pray thee, let me go over, and see the good land ... But the Lord was wroth with me for your sakes ..."

23. God denied Moses to enter the Promise Land

Moses pleaded with God to allow him to enter the Promise Land
Deuteronomy 3:25-26 "I pray thee, let me go over, and see the good land ..."

God only allowed Moses to see the Promise Land from afar
Deuteronomy 34:1-4 "Moses went up from the plains of Moab ... the Lord said ... I have caused thee to see it with thine eyes, but thou shalt not go over thither."

Note: Although Moses was God's faithful servant that led the Israelites to the Promise Land, God refused Moses entry to the Promise Land. Moses, after devoting his entire life to lead an entire nation to their destination, was so painfully close, only to be refused entry, and was allowed only to see it from afar.

24. Moses had to raise his hands so Israel will win the war

Exodus 17:11-12 "When Moses held up his hand, that Israel prevailed ... and his hands were steady until the going down of the sun."

Note: God required Moses to raise his hands in order for Israel to win the war.

25. Did God use an intermediary when He gave the law?

No, God gave the law directly to Moses
Exodus 20:1-17 "God spake [to Moses], saying, I am the Lord thy God ..."
Yes, the law was ordained by angels in the hand of a mediator
Galatians 3:19 "Wherefore then serveth the law? It was added because of transgressions ... and it was ordained by angels in the hand of a mediator."

26. God told the priests not to go to the altar and expose themselves

Exodus 20:26 "Neither shalt thou go up by steps unto mine altar, that thy nakedness be not discovered thereon."

27. What are the Ten Commandments? Are there just ten?

The commandments from Exodus 20
Exodus 20:1-17 "God spake all these words ...
1. Thou shalt have no other gods before me.
2. Thou shalt not make unto thee any graven image, or any likeness of any thing that is in heaven above, or that is in the earth beneath, or that is in the water under the earth.
3. Thou shalt not take the name of the Lord thy God in vain; for the Lord will not hold him guiltless that taketh his name in vain.
4. Remember the sabbath day, to keep it holy.
5. Honour thy father and thy mother: that thy days may be long upon the land which the Lord thy God giveth thee.
6. Thou shalt not kill.
7. Thou shalt not commit adultery.
8. Thou shalt not steal.
9. Thou shalt not bear false witness against thy neighbour.
10. Thou shalt not covet thy neighbour's house, Thou shalt not covet thy neighbour's wife, nor his manservant, nor his maidservant, nor his ox, nor his ass, nor any thing that is thy neighbour's."

The commandments from Exodus 34
Exodus 34:1, 14, 17-28 "The Lord said ... I will write upon these tables *the words that were in the first tables* ...
1. For thou shalt worship no other god.

2. Thou shalt make thee no molten gods.
3. The feast of unleavened bread shalt thou keep. Seven days thou shalt eat unleavened bread, as I commanded thee, in the time of the month Abib: for in the month Abib thou camest out from Egypt.
4. All that openeth the matrix is mine; and every firstling among thy cattle, whether ox or sheep, that is male. But the firstling of an ass thou shalt redeem with a lamb: and if thou redeem him not, then shalt thou break his neck. All the firstborn of thy sons thou shalt redeem. And none shall appear before me empty.
5. Six days thou shalt work, but on the seventh day thou shalt rest: in earing time and in harvest thou shalt rest.
6. And thou shalt observe the feast of weeks, of the firstfruits of wheat harvest, and the feast of ingathering at the year's end. The first of the firstfruits of thy land thou shalt bring unto the house of the Lord thy God.
7. Thrice in the year shall all your menchildren appear before the Lord God, the God of Israel.
8. For I will cast out the nations before thee, and enlarge thy borders: neither shall any man desire thy land, when thou shalt go up to appear before the Lord thy God thrice in the year.
9. Thou shalt not offer the blood of my sacrifice with leaven; neither shall the sacrifice of the feast of the passover be left unto the morning.
10. Thou shalt not seethe a kid in his mother's milk ... And he wrote upon the tables the words of the covenant, the ten commandments."

The commandments from Deuteronomy
Deuteronomy 5:6-21
1. "I am the Lord thy God, which brought thee out of the land of Egypt, from the house of bondage. Thou shalt have none other gods before me.
2. Thou shalt not make thee any graven image, or any likeness of any thing that is in heaven above ... Thou shalt not bow down thyself unto them, nor serve them:
3. Thou shalt not take the name of the Lord thy God in vain: for the Lord will not hold him guiltless that taketh his name in vain.
4. Keep the sabbath day to sanctify it.
5. Honour thy father and thy mother, as the Lord thy God hath commanded thee;
6. Thou shalt not kill.
7. Neither shalt thou commit adultery.
8. Neither shalt thou steal.
9. Neither shalt thou bear false witness against thy neighbour.
10. Neither shalt thou desire thy neighbour's wife, neither shalt thou covet thy neighbour's house, his field, or his manservant, or his maidservant, his ox, or his ass, or any thing that is thy neighbour's."

Note: The Ten Commandments in Exodus 20 came from the first tablets. However, Moses broke the original tablets. Moses came back to the mountain to get another set of tablets. But, the Ten Commandments in the second tablets listed in Exodus 34 are not the same as the first one.
The Protestant's Ten Commandments are slightly different from the Catholic's Ten Commandments. The Catholic's Ten Commandments does not include the prohibition of graven images and qualifies the Protestant's tenth commandment as two separate commandments namely: Thou shall not take thy neighbor's wife and Thou shall not take thy neighbor's goods.
The inclusion of the commandment 'Thou shalt not take thy neighbor's wife' and not vice versa is an indication that wives were regarded as mere properties.

28. Where did Moses receive the Ten Commandments?

Sinai
Exodus 31:18 "He [God] gave unto Moses ... upon mount Sinai, two tables"

Horeb
Deuteronomy 5:2 "The Lord our God made a covenant with us in Horeb."

Note: Horeb is said to be the other name of Mount Sinai. However, it is disputed as to whether this is true since Horeb is said to be the name of the mountain and Sinai is also the name of the desert and the peninsula. Mount Horeb or Mount Sinai is also referred to as Mount Musa, Jabal Musa and Gebel Musa.

29. Aaron must wear a bell when in the Holy Place or he will die

Exodus 28:34-35 "A golden bell ... upon the hem of the robe ... his sound shall be heard when he goeth in unto the holy place ... that he die not."

Note: The Holy Place is where the 'golden altar' in Exodus 40:26 is situated.

30. God gave instructions how to make and wear underwear

Exodus 28:42 "Thou shalt make them linen breeches to cover their nakedness; from the loins even unto the thighs they shall reach"

31. God appointed Aaron to become a high priest

Exodus 29:9 "Aaron and his sons ... and the priest's office shall be theirs for a perpetual statute: and thou shalt consecrate Aaron and his sons."

Note: Only the descendants of Aaron are worthy of priestly duties in perpetuity. Therefore the priests of today who are not blood descendants of Aaron are not worthy of their positions as priests.

32. God required the first census and taxation

Exodus 30:11-16 "The Lord [said] When thou takest the sum of the children of Israel ... then shall they give every man a ransom for his soul to the Lord ... they shall [give] half a shekel ... the offering to the Lord ..."

Note: Every person twenty plus years old must pay a ransom for his soul to the Lord.

33. Aaron and his sons must wash their hands and feet or die

Exodus 30:17-21 "For Aaron and his sons shall wash their hands and their feet thereat: When they go into the tabernacle ... that they die not ..."

34. Who created the molten calf?

Aaron created the molten calf
Exodus 32:2, 4 "[Aaron said] Break off the golden earrings ... [Aaron] made it a molten calf."

God accused the Israelites of making a molten calf
Exodus 32:8 "They [the Israelites] made them a molten calf ..."

Note: Aaron, the priest appointed by God made the molten calf himself not the Israelites.

35. Moses convinced God not to kill the Israelites

God wanted to kill the Israelites
Exodus 32:10 "My wrath may wax hot against them ... that I may consume them ..."

Moses convinced God not to pursue with His plans to kill the Israelites
Exodus 32:11-13 "Moses [said], Lord, why doth thy wrath wax hot against thy people ... Remember Abraham ... and saidst unto them, I will multiply your seed as the stars of heaven ..."

God repented for what He thought He will do
Exodus 32:14 "The Lord repented of the evil which he thought to do unto his people."

Note: Does God change his mind?

36. Moses required the Israelites to drink the grounded calf statue

Exodus 32:20 "[Moses] took the calf [ground it] made the children of Israel drink of it."

37. God made the people kill each other for dancing naked

[KJ] Exodus 32:25-28 "When Moses saw that the people were naked [for Aaron had made them naked] … [Moses said to the sons of Levi] Thus saith the Lord … slay every man his brother … his neighbour … and there fell … about *three thousand* men."
[DR] Exodus 32:28 "And the sons of Levi did according to the words of Moses, and there were slain that day about *three and twenty thousand* men."

Note: The people were punished for following the orders of Aaron, but Aaron (who was appointed by God) went unpunished for giving such orders.
The King James Bible shows three thousand men were killed, but the Douay Rheims Bible shows three and twenty thousand men were killed in the same verse.

38. God plagued the people after making them kill each other

Exodus 32:35 "The Lord plagued the people, because they made the calf, *which Aaron made."*

Note: God killed the Israelites for following the orders of His appointed high priest Aaron, but God did not kill Aaron the one who instigated everything.

39. Did Moses see God?

Yes
Exodus 33:11 "The Lord spake unto Moses face to face …"
Deuteronomy 34:10 "Moses, whom the Lord knew face to face."

Only His back
Exodus 33:20-23 "He [God] said, Thou canst not see my face: *for there shall no man see me, and live* … and thou shalt see my back parts."

40. Moses saw God but God mooned Moses

Exodus 33:23 "Then I will take away my hand, and you shall see my back, but my face shall not be seen."

41. Who wrote the words in the second set of tablets?

God will write the words

Exodus 34:1 "The Lord said ... I will write upon these tables the words that were in the first tables, which thou breakest."

Moses wrote the words
Exodus 34:27 "The Lord said unto Moses, Write thou these words ..."

Note: In Exodus 34:1. The Lord said he will write in the second set of tablets the same words that were written in the first set of tablets. However, Exodus 20:1-17 shows the commandments in the first set of tablets are different from the commandments in the second set of tablets as shown in Exodus 34:1, 14, 17-28.

42. Moses covered his face with a veil to avoid scaring the Israelites

[KJ] **Exodus 34:29-30** "Moses wist not that the skin of his face shone ... he put a vail on his face"
[DR] **Exodus 34:29-30** "When Moses came down ... he knew not that his face was horned ... Aaron and the children of Israel ... were afraid to come near.

43. Was the golden altar in the Holy Place or the Most Holy Place?

The tabernacle has 2 rooms, the Holy Place and the Most Holy Place
Hebrews 9:1-3 "For there was a tabernacle made; the first ... which is called the sanctuary. And *after the second veil*, the tabernacle which is called the Holiest of all"

The golden altar was placed in the Holy place
[KJ] **Exodus 40:26** "He put the golden altar in the tent ... *before* the vail."
[DR] **Exodus 40:26** "He put also the hanging in the entry of the tabernacle of the testimony."

The golden altar was placed in the Most Holy place
Hebrews 9:3-4 "*After the second veil*, the tabernacle which is called the Holiest of all; which had the *golden censer* ... and the tables of the covenant"

Note: The Most Holy Place also called the Holy of Holies is considered as a most sacred site and can only be entered by the High Priest once a year during Yom Kippur.

44. God killed the sons of Aaron because they offered 'strange fire'

Leviticus 10:1-3 "Nadab and Abihu, the sons of Aaron ... offered strange fire before the Lord, which he commanded them not ... Aaron held his peace."

Note: Aaron just watched his sons burned to death.

45. God gave a feast, changed his mind and gave a great plague

Numbers 11:31-33 "[The Lord] brought quails ... and let them fall by the camp ... the wrath of the Lord was kindled [and] smote the people with a very great plague."

46. Was Moses a meek man?

Moses was a very meek man
Numbers 12:3 "The man Moses was very meek ..."

Moses was a very cruel man
Numbers 31:15-17 "Moses said unto them ... kill every male among the little ones, and kill every woman that hath known man by lying with him."

47. Moses is the personification of the law

Romans 10:5 "For Moses describeth the righteousness which is of the law, that the man which doeth those things shall live by them."

48. The entire congregation must stone one person

Numbers 15:35-36 "The Lord said ... The man shall be surely put to death: all the congregation shall stone him ... with stones, and he died."

Note: The entire population of Israel must stone one person for violating the Sabbath.

49. Where did Aaron die?

Mount Hor
Numbers 20:27-28, 33:38 "Aaron died there in ... mount [Hor] ..."

Mosera
Deuteronomy 10:6 "Mosera: there Aaron died ..."

50. God ordered Moses to vex the Midianites but not the Moabites

The elders of Moab and Midian asked Balaam to curse the Israelites
Numbers 22:2, 5-7 "[Balak] saw all that Israel had done to the Amorites ... (Balak asked Balaam to put a curse on the Israelites. But Balaam refused, so Balak asked the elders of Moab and Midian to convince Balaam.) And the elders came unto Balaam and spake unto him the words of Balak."
Numbers 25:1-3 "Israel ... began to commit whoredom with the daughters of Moab ... and bowed down to their gods ..."
Numbers 25:6-15 "One of the children of Israel ... [brought] a Midianitish woman in the sight of Moses [and all congregation]"

Note: The Lord instructed the Israelites not to mingle with the Moabites and the Midianites because of their influence upon the Israelites to worship false gods. Phinehas killed Cosbi, the Midianitish woman; and Zimri, the son of Salu to avert the Lord's anger and punishment. Nonetheless, 24,000 died from the plague, the Lord's punishment.

Numbers 25:16-18 "The Lord spake ... vex the Midianites ... smite them ..."
Numbers 31:9-10, 15-18 "Israel took all the women of Midian captives, and their little ones ... and all their goods. And they burnt all their cities ..."

Note: Both the Moabite and the Midianite elders tried to persuade Balaam to put a curse on the Israelites upon the instigation of the Moab king. Both the Moabites and the Midianites were instrumental in leading the Israelites to worship other gods. But God ordered Moses to smite only the Midianites and not the Moabites. It seems the editors of the Bible steered clear from making statements that the Moabites were punished because King David, an ancestor of Jesus was the son of a Moabite woman.

51. Who hired Balaam to curse Israel?

The elders of Moab and the elders of Midian paid Balaam to curse Israel
Numbers 22:7 "The elders of Moab and ... Midian ... came unto Balaam, and spake unto him the words of Balak."

The Ammonites and the Moabites paid Balaam to curse Israel
Deuteronomy 23:2-3 "An Ammonite or Moabite shall not enter into the congregation of the Lord ... because they hired against thee Balaam ... to curse thee."
Nehemiah 13:1-3 "The Ammonite and the ... hired Balaam against them."

52. Ban those who hired Balaam forever

Deuteronomy 23:2-3 "An Ammonite or Moabite shall not enter into the congregation of the Lord ... because they hired against thee Balaam ... to curse thee."
Nehemiah 13:1-3 "The Ammonite and the Moabite should not come into the congregation of God for ever; Because they met not the children of Israel with bread and with water, but hired Balaam against them."

Note: But King David is the son of a Moabite woman. How about the Midianites? The elders of Midian also hired Balaam to curse Israel.

53. God got angry with Balaam for obeying His order to go

Numbers 22:20-22 "[God] said unto him [Balaam], If the men come to call thee, rise up, and go with them ... Balaam rose up in the morning [and] went with the princes of Moab. And God's anger was kindled because he went ..."

Note: God got angry with Balaam for doing exactly what God told him to do.

54. How many were killed for committing whoredom?

Twenty and four thousand (24,000)
Numbers 25:9 "Those that died ... were twenty and four thousand."

Three and twenty thousand (23,000)
I Corinthians 10:8 "And fell in one day three and twenty thousand."

55. What was the new moon sacrifice?

Two bullocks, 1 ram, and 7 lambs
Numbers 28:11 "In the beginnings of your months ye shall offer ... two young bullocks, and one ram, seven lambs ..."

One bullock, 1 ram, and 6 lambs
[KJ] Ezekiel 46:6 "In the day of the new moon it shall be a young bullock without blemish, and six lambs, and a ram."
[DR] Ezekiel 46:6 "And on the day of the new moon a calf of the herd without blemish: and the six lambs, and the rams shall be without blemish."

56. Did the Israelites kill all the males in Midian?

Yes
Numbers 31:7, 16-17 "They warred against the Midianites ... slew all [males]"

No
Judges 6:1-2 "The Lord delivered them into the hand of Midian seven years. And the hand of Midian prevailed against Israel."

Note: How did the Midianites thrive if all the males were killed?

57. God ordered the genocide of Midianites

Moses had all the Midianites killed except for the female virgins to be kept as sex slaves
Numbers 31:15-18 "Moses said ... kill every male, every woman that hath known man ...all the women children, that have not known a man ... keep alive for yourselves."

The plunder: 675,000 sheep, 72,000 cattle, 61,000 donkeys and 32,000 virgins

Numbers 31:32-35 "The plunder ... 675,000 sheep, 72,000 cattle, 61,000 donkeys and 32,000 women who had never slept with a man."

Note: God ordered the plunder and genocide of Midianites. The Israelites took all the women as captives and took all their possessions and presented them to Moses. Moses ordered all Midianites to be killed except the young virgins, which they will keep for themselves. Did they conduct some medical inspection to determine who were virgins?

58. Humans were offered to the Lord by Moses and Eleazar

Numbers 31:40 "The Lord's tribute was thirty and two persons."

59. Where did the Israelites go after Aaron's death?

Hor, Zalmonah and Punon
Numbers 33:39-42 "Aaron ... died in mount Hor ... they departed from mount Hor ... from Zalmonah, and pitched in Punon."

Mosera, Gudgodah and Jotbath
[KJ] **Deuteronomy 10:6-7** "Israel took their journey ... to Mosera: there Aaron died ... they journeyed unto Gudgodah ... to Jotbath ..."

Mosera, Gadgad and Jetebatha
[DR] **Deuteronomy 10:6-7** "Mosera ... they came to Gadgad ... Jetebatha"

60. Concerning the Moabites

Do not fight them and take their land
Deuteronomy 2:9 "The Lord [said] Distress not the Moabites, neither contend with them in battle: for I will not give thee of their land for a possession."

Kill them
Judges 3:28-30 "He [Joshua] said ... the Lord hath delivered your enemies the Moabites into your hand ... and they slew of Moab at that time ..."
Jeremiah 48:2 "Let us cut it [Moab] off from being a nation."

61. Did a Moabite enter the congregation of the Lord?

No
Deuteronomy 23:3 "An Ammonite or Moabite shall not enter into the congregation of the Lord"
Nehemiah 13:1 "The ... Moabite should not come into the congregation of God for ever."

Yes
Ruth 1:4, 4:13, 17 "They took them wives of the women of Moab ... Boaz took Ruth [as] his wife ... she bare a son named Obed ... the father of Jesse, the father of David."

62. What should be done with the Ammonites?

Do not fight them and do not take their land
Deuteronomy 2:19 "When thou comest nigh over against the children of Ammon, distress them not ... for I will not give thee of the land of the children of Ammon any possession ..."
Deuteronomy 2:37 "Only unto the land of the children of Ammon thou camest not... nor unto whatsoever the Lord our God forbad us."

Kill them
Judges 11:32 "Jephthah passed over unto the children of Ammon to fight against them; and the Lord delivered them into his hands."
Jeremiah 49:2 "I will cause an alarm of war to be heard in Rabbah of the Ammonites; and it shall be a desolate heap, and her daughters shall be burned with fire."

63. God ordered a genocide

Deuteronomy 7:1-2 "When the Lord thy God shall bring thee into the land whither thou goest to possess it, and hath cast out many nations before thee, the Hittites, and the Girgashites, and the Amorites, and the Canaanites, and the Perizzites, and the Hivites, and the Jebusites ... and utterly destroy them"

64. Concerning the Edomites

Be nice to them
Deuteronomy 23:7 "Thou shalt not abhor an Edomite; for he is thy brother."

Destroy them
Obadiah 1:1; 8:9 "Saith the Lord GOD concerning Edom ... rise up against her ... destroy the wise men out of Edom ..."
II Kings 14:7 "He slew of Edom in the valley of salt ten thousand ..."
Ezekiel 25:13 "I [God] will cut off man and beast from it [Edom]..."

65. Is Mount Nebo the same as Pisgah?

Pisgah
Deuteronomy 3:17, 27 "Get thee up into the top of Pisgah ..."
Deuteronomy 4:49 "All the plain on this side Jordan eastward ... under the springs of Pisgah."

Mount Nebo
Deuteronomy 32:49 "Get thee up ... unto mount Nebo"
Deuteronomy 34:1 "Moses went up ... unto the mountain of Nebo"

Note: A part of Mount Nebo is called Pisgah. The Bible used these names interchangeably.

66. Did the Israelites kill the trees in the places they invaded?

They saved the trees
Deuteronomy 20:19 "When thou shalt besiege a city ... thou shalt not destroy the trees ..."

They killed the trees
[KJ] II Kings 3:19 "Ye ... shall fell every good tree ..."
[DR] II Kings 3:19 "Ye shall ... cut down every fruitful tree..."

K. The conquest of Canaan

1. Was Canaan the land of plenty?

Yes
Exodus 3:8, 17 "A land flowing with milk and honey ..."
Ezekiel 20:6 "A land flowing with milk and honey ..."

No, the land devours its inhabitants
[KJ] Numbers 13:32 "The land ... eateth up the inhabitants thereof ..."
[DR] Numbers 13:33 "The land which we have viewed, devoureth its inhabitants"

2. Was Rahab saved by faith?

Yes, Rahab was saved by faith
Hebrews 11:31 "By faith the harlot Rahab perished not with them ..."

No, by works only Rahab the harlot shall live
Joshua 6:16-17 "When the priests blew with the trumpets ... And the city shall be accursed ... only Rahab the harlot shall live ... because she hid the messengers ..."

No, Rahab was justified by works
James 2:25 "Was not Rahab the harlot justified by works ..."

3. Who was the father of Achan?

Carmi
Joshua 7:1 "For Achan, the son of Carmi ..."

Zerah
[KJ] Joshua 7:24; 22:20 "Achan the son of Zerah ..."

Zare
[DR] Joshua 7:24; 22:20 "Achan the son of Zare ..."

4. Did Israel go to war against the people of Ai?

Joshua 8:3-29 "Joshua arose, and all the people of war, to go up against Ai"

Note: Historical records show that Ai was already an abandoned city during the time of the Israelites. The city where the battle may have taken place might be Et-Tell instead of Ai. But Et-Tell was unoccupied during the time the battle mentioned in Joshua 8 took place. There are speculations that the battle mentioned in Joshua 8 never really happened.

5. Was Ai inhabited after Joshua burned it?

No, Ai was totally destroyed by Joshua
Joshua 8:25-29 "All that fell that day ... all the men of Ai ... he [Joshua] had utterly destroyed all ... of Ai ... a great heap of stones, that remaineth unto this day."

Yes, Ai was inhabited
Nehemiah 7:32 "The men of Bethel and Ai, an hundred twenty and three."

6. Who captured Debir?

Joshua
Joshua 10:38-40 "Joshua returned ... to Debir; and fought against it ..."

Othniel
Judges 1:11-13 "Debir [was named] Kirjathsepher: And Caleb said, He that smiteth Kirjathsepher ... I give Achsah my daughter to wife. And Othniel ... took it [Debir]: and he gave him Achsah his daughter to wife."

7. Did Joshua and the Israelites capture Jerusalem?

Yes
Joshua 10:23, 40 "They ... brought forth those five kings unto him out of the cave, the king of Jerusalem ... So Joshua smote all the country ..."

No
Joshua 15:63 "As for the Jebusites the inhabitants of Jerusalem, the children of Judah could not drive them out; but the Jebusites dwell with the children of Judah at Jerusalem unto this day."

8. What was the former name of Debir?

Kirjathsepher
Joshua 15:15 "The name of Debir before was Kirjathsepher"
Judges 1:11 "The name of Debir before was Kirjathsepher"

Kirjathsannah
Joshua 15:49 "Kirjathsannah, which is Debir."

9. Was the city of Ai rebuilt after Joshua destroyed it?

No, it was never built again after Joshua destroyed it
Joshua 8:28 "Joshua burnt Ai … a desolation unto this day."

Yes, it existed at the time of the Babylonian captivity
Nehemiah 7:32 "The men of Bethel and Ai, an hundred twenty and three."

10. Which tribe received the cities of Exhtaol and Zoreah?

The tribe of Judah
Joshua 15:20, 33 "The inheritance … of Judah … Eshataol and Zoreah."

The tribe of Dan
Joshua 19:40-41 "Dan … their inheritance was Zorah, and Eshtaol."

11. Can God drive out the inhabitants with chariots of irons?

Yes, God can drive out the inhabitants with iron chariots
Joshua 17:18 "For thou shalt drive out the Canaanites, though they have iron chariots …"

No, God cannot drive out the inhabitants with iron chariots
[KJ] Judges 1:19 "The Lord was with Judah … but [they] could not drive out the inhabitants … because they had chariots of iron."
[DR] Judges 1:19 "[The Lord] was not able to destroy the inhabitants … because they had many chariots armed with scythes."

12. What was the tribe of Aijalon?

Dan
Joshua 21:23-24 "Out of the tribe of Dan … Aijalon with her suburbs …"

Ephraim
I Chronicles 6:66, 69 "The tribe of Ephraim … Aijalon with her suburbs"

L. The time of Judges

1. God sold the Israelites into slavery

Judges 3:5, 8 "He [Lord] sold them [Israelites] into the hand of Chushanrishathaim king of Mesopotamia ... Israel served Chushanrishathaim eight years."

2. God sent Ehud to disembowel Eglon

Judges 3:15, 17, 20-22 "The children of Israel cried unto the Lord, the Lord raised them up a deliverer, Ehud ... Ehud came unto him [Eglon] ... And said, I have a message from God ... [Ehud] took the dagger ... and thrust it into his belly ..."

3. Was Sisera asleep when he died?

Yes, he was asleep
Judges 4:21 "For he [Sisera] was fast asleep and weary. So he died."

No, he was standing
Judges 5:26-27 "At her feet he bowed, he fell, he lay down: at her feet he bowed, he fell: where he bowed, there he fell down dead."

4. God had to wet a fleece, make the ground dry and vice versa

Judges 6:36-40 "Gideon said unto God ... if the dew be on the fleece only, and it be dry upon all the earth beside, then shall I know that thou wilt save Israel by mine hand, as thou hast said. And it was so ... And Gideon said ... let it now be dry only upon the fleece, and upon all the ground let there be dew. And God did so that night."

Note: Gideon was not satisfied with God's answer, he told God to do the reverse if God really meant what He was saying.

5. God wanted only those men who drank like a dog to join Gideon

Judges 7:2-7 "The Lord said [every one that lappeth as a dog] him shalt thou set by himself ... and the number of them that lapped ... were three hundred men ... the Lord [said] By the three hundred men that lapped will I save you, and deliver the Midianites into thine hand ..."

Summary: The Lord told Gideon to ask for volunteers to join his army. However God wanted only a small group of people to join the war against the Midianites in order to prove that the war was miraculously won. After convincing those people who volunteered but were afraid to go to war to just return to their homes, God told Gideon to test the remaining volunteers to drink from a nearby body of water. Only those who drank like a dog will be allowed to fight in the war against the Midianites.

M. The Amalekites

1. How many times were the Amalekites totally destroyed?

First time
Genesis 14:7 "They ... smote all the country of the Amalekites ..."

Second time
I Samuel 15:7-8, 20 "Saul smote the Amalekites ... have utterly destroyed the Amalekites."

Third time
I Samuel 27:8-9 "David ... invaded ... the Amalekites ... left neither man nor woman alive ..."

Fourth time
I Samuel 30:17 "David smote them ... escaped not a man of them [Amalekites] ..."

Fifth time
I Chronicles 4:43 "They smote the rest of the Amalekites that were escaped"

Note: The Amalekites attacked the Israelites on their way to Egypt (Exodus 17:8) 400 years earlier. But in I Samuel 15:2-3, the Lord commanded Saul to destroy all the Amalekites. In I Samuel 15:2-3, 32-33 the Lord of hosts said, "I remember that which Amalek did to Israel... Now go and smite Amalek, and utterly destroy all that they have. . ." Then said Samuel, "Bring ye hither to me Agag the king of the Amalekites" Agag pleading for his life spoke to Samuel delicately. Agag said, "Surely the bitterness of death is past. Enough is enough." Don't you think Agag was right?

2. God ordered the total destruction of the Amalekites

Exodus 17:14 "The Lord said ... I will utterly put out the remembrance of Amalek from under heaven ..."
Deuteronomy 25:19 "You shall blot out the memory of Amalek ..."
I Samuel 15:1-3 "Now go and smite Amalek, and utterly destroy all that they have, and spare them not ..."

Note: God wanted the Amalekites to be destroyed because in verse Exodus 17:8, the Amalekites attacked the Israelites without provocation. After about 400 years, the succeeding generations of Amalekites had to pay the price for what their ancestors did. Was God being fair?

3. The Amalekites were destroyed before their ancestor was born

The Amalekites were destroyed
Genesis 14:7 "They returned … and smote all the country of the Amalekites"

Amalek is the ancestor of the Amalekites
Genesis 36:12 "Timna was concubine to Eliphaz ... and she bare … Amalek"
I Chronicles 1:36 "The sons of Eliphaz: Teman … and Amalek."

4. Who was Timna?

The concubine of Eliphaz, the mother of Amalek
Genesis 36:12 "Timna was concubine to Eliphaz ... she bare to Eliphaz Amalek"

The son of Eliphaz, the brother of Amalek
I Chronicles 1:36 "The sons of Eliphaz … Timna, and Amalek."

N. The Ark of the Covenant

1. Who made the Ark of the Covenant?

Bezaleel
Exodus 37:1 "Bezaleel made the ark of shittim wood ..."

Moses
Deuteronomy 10:3 "I [Moses] made an ark of shittim wood …"

2. What was the Ark of the Covenant made of?

Shittim wood
Deuteronomy 10:3 "I made an ark of shittim wood ..."

Shittim wood, gold
Exodus 25:10-18 "They shall make an ark of shittim wood [and] pure gold"

3. God punished the Philistines by giving them hemorrhoids

I Samuel 5:6, 8-9 "The Lord was heavy upon them [Philistines] … and smote them with emerods … and they had emerods in their secret parts."

Note: God gave the Philistines hemorrhoids in their private parts as punishment for getting and keeping the Ark of the Covenant.

4. The Philistines offered five golden tumors and five golden rats

I Samuel 6:1-5 "They [priests and diviners] said [to the Philistines] … return him [Lord] a trespass offering … Five golden emerods, and five golden mice

... Wherefore ye shall make images of your emerods, and images of your mice that mar the land ... give glory unto the God of Israel."

Note: For the glory of God, the Philistines offered five golden tumors, modeled after their hemorrhoids and five golden rats based on the images of the rats that ruin their land.

5. How long was the Ark kept in Abinadab's house?

20 years
I Samuel 7:1-2 "The men of Kirjathjearim ... fetched up the ark ... and brought it into the house of Abinadab ... the ark abode in Kirjathjearim ... for it was twenty years ..."
I Samuel 10:24 "Samuel said ... See ye him [Saul] whom the Lord hath chosen ... And all the people shouted, and said, God save the king."

More than 40 years
Acts 13:21 "God gave unto them Saul ... by the space of forty years."
II Samuel 6:2-3 "They ... brought it [ark] out of the house of Abinadab ..."

Note: Prior to the reign of Saul, the Philistines took the ark. But some of the Philistines were struck dead because they looked inside the ark. Those who survived, requested the inhabitants of Kiriath-jearim to take custody of the ark. In I Samuel 7:1-2, The inhabitants of Kiriath-jearim took the ark to the house of Abinadab and kept it there for 20 years. Shortly after the ark was transferred to the house of Abinadab, Saul was proclaimed king in I Samuel 10:24.In Acts 13:21, Saul reigned for 40 years until King David took over asking after the reign of Saul.In II Samuel 6:2-3, the ark was moved out of the house of Abinadab after King David took over Saul. Thus, the ark must have been kept in the house of Abinadab for at least 40 years.

6. What was in the Ark of the Covenant?

The two tables of stone of Moses
I Kings 8:9 "There was nothing in the ark save the two tables of stone ..."

The tables of Moses, a golden pot with manna, Aaron's rod that is budded
Hebrews 9:4 "The ark of the covenant ... wherein was the golden pot that had manna, and Aaron's rod that budded, and the tables of the covenant."

Note: According to legend, King Solomon gave the Ark of the Covenant to Menelik I, Solomon's son with the Queen of Sheba whose name is Makeda, and is supposedly kept in a chapel in Ethiopia to this day. Others claim that the Ark of the Covenant was hidden in some unknown cave by Jeremiah (Douay Rheims Bible: II Maccabees 2:4-7) and will later be revealed by God 'when God gathers His people again and shows mercy to them' as stated in II Maccabees 2:8.

7. When did David bring the Ark of the Covenant to Jerusalem?

After defeating the Philistines
II Samuel 5:19-20 "The Lord said unto David, Go up: for I will doubtless deliver the Philistines into thine hand. And ... David smote them ..."
II Samuel 6:10-11 "David carried it [ark] aside into the house of Obededom"

Before defeating the Philistines
I Chronicles 13:13 "David ... carried it aside into the house of Obed-edom"
I Chronicles 14:16 "David ... did as God commanded ... they smote ... the Philistines ..."

8. God struck Ussah dead when he tried to protect the ark

God declared the Kohathites the keepers of the ark
Numbers 3:27-32, 38 "The families of the sons of Kohath ... their charge shall be the ark ... and the stranger that cometh nigh shall be put to death."
Uzzah took care of the ark
II Samuel 6:6-8 "Uzzah put forth his hand to the ark of God, and took hold of it; for the oxen shook it ... and God smote him ..."

Note: The ox stumbled and Uzzah touched the ark to prevent it from falling. Uzzah devotedly took care of the ark for at least twenty years. But because Uzzah is not of Kohath origin, God struck Uzzah dead for touching the ark.

9. Where did God smite Uzzah?

At the threshingfloor of Nachon
II Samuel 6:6 "Nachon's threshingfloor ..."

At the threshingfloor of Childon
I Chronicles 13:9 "The threshingfloor of Childon ..."

10. Why did God bless Obededom the Gittite but not Ussah?

God declared the Kohathites the keepers of the ark
Numbers 3:27-32, 38 "The families of the sons of Kohath ... their charge shall be the ark ... and the stranger that cometh nigh shall be put to death."
God blessed Obededom the Gittite for taking care of the ark
II Samuel 6:11 "The ark of the Lord continued in the house of Obededom the Gittite ... and the Lord blessed Obededom ..."

God slayed Ussah for taking good care of the ark
II Samuel 6:6-8 "Uzzah put forth his hand to the ark … and God smote him"

Note: Obededom the Gittite is not a Kohatite, but God blessed him for keeping the ark.However, God slayed Ussah for protecting the ark.

O. The Kingdom of Israel (United Monarchy)

1. Was Samuel a Levite?

No, Samuel was an Ephraimite
I Samuel 1:1-2, 20 "Now there was a certain man of Ramathaimzophim, of mount Ephraim, and his name was Elkanah … Hannah had conceived … and called his name Samuel …"

Yes, Samuel was a Levite
I Chronicles 6:19, 28 "These are … the Levites … the sons of Samuel …"

Yes, Samuel offered sacrifices
I Samuel 7:9 "Samuel took a sucking lamb, and offered it for a burnt offering"

Note: In Leviticus 17:5 and Numbers 18:8, only Levites can offer sacrifices.

2. Who was Samuel's firstborn son?

Joel
I Samuel 8:2 "[Samuel's] firstborn son was Joel."

Vashni
I Chronicles 6:28 "The sons of Samuel; the firstborn Vashni."

3. About God choosing Saul to lead the Israelites

Yes, God chose Saul
I Samuel 9:17 "When Samuel saw Saul, the Lord said … Behold the man whom I spake to thee of! this same shall reign over my people."

God regretted choosing Saul
I Samuel 15:35 "The Lord repented that he had made Saul king over Israel."

4. Was Saul a prophet?

The spirit of God came upon Saul and Saul prophesied
I Samuel 10:10-12 "The Spirit of God came upon [Saul], and he prophesied"

The spirit of God was upon Saul and he prophesied while naked
I Samuel 19:23-24 "He [Saul] ... stripped off his clothes also, and prophesied before Samuel ..."

Note: Saul was both a prophet and a king?

5. How many sons did Jesse have?

Eight
I Samuel 16:10-11 "Jesse made seven of his sons to pass before Samuel ... he said, There remaineth yet the youngest, and, behold, he keepeth the sheep."
I Samuel 17:12 "Jesse ... he had eight sons."

Seven
I Chronicles 2:13-15 "Jesse [begat] Eliab ... Abinadab [second] Shimma [third], Nethaneel [fourth], Raddai [fifth], Ozem [sixth], David [seventh]."

6. Was David a brave warrior or an inexperienced lad?

A brave warrior, a man of war
I Samuel 16:18 "A son of Jesse ... a mighty valiant man, and a man of war ..."

An inexperienced lad
I Samuel 17:31-33 "Saul said to David ... thou art but a youth ..."

7. What was David's occupation?

A harp player to the king
I Samuel 16:17, 23 "Saul said ... Provide me now a man that can play well ... David took a harp, and played with his hand"

A warrior, a man of war
I Samuel 16:18 "A son of Jesse ... a mighty valiant man, and a man of war"

An armourbearer
I Samuel 16:21 "David became his [Saul's] armourbearer ..."

A shepherd
I Samuel 17:15 "David went ... to feed his father's sheep at Bethlehem."

A food delivery boy
I Samuel 17:18 "Carry these ten cheeses unto the captain of their thousand, and look how thy brethren fare, and take their pledge."

8. What was the character of David?

David obeyed God's commands and statutes

I Kings 3:14 "Walk in my ways, keep my statutes [as] thy father David did"
Acts 13:22 "David … which shall fulfill all my [Lord] will …"

David's heart was not perfect in the sight of the Lord
I Kings 15:3 "His heart was not perfect with the Lord …"

David's only sin was his sin concerning Uriah
I Kings 15:5 "David did that which was right in the eyes of the Lord … save only in the matter of Uriah the Hittite."

David always has the Spirit of God
I Samuel 16:13 "The Spirit of the Lord came upon David from that day forward."

David tortured and slayed thousands
I Samuel 18:6-7 "Saul hath slain his thousands, and David his ten thousands."
II Samuel 12:31 "He [David] brought forth the people … put them under saws … under axes of iron, and made them pass through the brick-kiln."

David fornicates with Bathsheba, Uriah's wife
II Samuel 11:2-4 "[David] saw a woman [the wife of Uriah] … [David] lay with her …"

Note: David murdered Uriah, Bathsheba's husband by giving instructions to his soldiers to retreat from him in battle. Uriah's wife was pregnant by King David through an adulterous affair.

David hates the blind and the lame, and rewards whoever kills them
II Samuel 5:8 "David said [Whosoever] smiteth the … lame and the blind that are hated of David's soul, he shall be chief and captain … the blind and the lame shall not come into the house."

David strips naked and dances in front of everybody
II Samuel 6:16, 20 "David leaping and dancing … uncovered himself [David] to day in the eyes of the handmaids of his servants, as one of the vain fellows shamelessly uncovereth himself!"

David and Jonathan 'loved' each other
I Samuel 20:30-31 "Saul… said unto him [Jonathan]… do not I know that thou hast chosen the son of Jesse [David] to thine own confusion, and unto the confusion of thy mother's nakedness?"
I Samuel 20:41 "They [David and Jonathan] kissed one another …"
II Samuel 1:26 "[David speaking] thy love to me… passing the love of women."

David wanted to fight for the Philistines against the Israelites
I Samuel 29:9 "Achish said [David] shall not go up with us to the battle."

Note: David wanted to fight for the Philistines against Saul and the Israelites, but Achish refused

David wanted a young virgin to keep him warm
I Kings 1:1-4 "David was old and stricken ... he got no heat ... So they sought for ... Abishag... the damsel ... cherished the king ... but the king knew her not."

David's dying wish to his son Solomon is to murder Joab
I Kings 2:9 "Now therefore hold him [Joab] not guiltless ... his hoar head bring thou down to the grave with blood."

Note: In I Kings 3:14 David was said to have followed the Lord. However, what the Bible shows about David raises some doubts if David was indeed right in the eyes of the Lord.

9. Did Saul know David?

Yes
I Samuel 16:19-21 "Saul [said] Send me David... [and David] became his armourbearer."

No
I Samuel 17:55-58 "Saul said to him [David], Whose son art thou ..."

Note: If David was the armourbearer of Saul, why was David unknown to Saul?

10. How many times did David kill Goliath?

First time, with a slingshot
I Samuel 17:50 "David... with a sling... smote the Philistine, and slew him"

Second time, with a sword
I Samuel 17:51 "David... took his sword... and slew him ..."

11. Who killed what giant?

Judah slew Ahiman, Sheshai and Talmai
Judges 1:10 "Judah... slew Sheshai, and Ahiman, and Talmai"
Judges 1:20 "He (Judah) expelled... Ahiman, Sheshai and Talmai."

David slew Goliath
I Samuel 17:50 "David [prevailed] with a sling and with a stone... slew him."

Elhanan slew Goliath, brother of Goliath and Lahmi
New International Version: II Samuel 21:19 "Elhanan... killed Goliath ..."
King James Version: II Samuel 21:19 "[Elhanan] slew the brother of Goliath"
I Chronicles 20:5 "Elhanan... slew Lahmi the brother of Goliath ..."

Note: The New American Standard Bible and the New International Version UK Bible shows that Goliath was killed by Elhanan.

Adeodatus slew Goliath
Douay Rheims Version: II Kings 21:19 "Adeodatus... slew Goliath ..."

Note: Goliath was killed either by David, Elhanan or Adeodatus, depending on the version of the Bible.

Abishai slew Ishbibenob (Ishbi-Benob)
II Samuel 21:17 "Abishai ... succoured him [Ishbibenob] ... and killed him."

Sibbechai slew Saph and Sippai
II Samuel 21:18 "Sibbechai ... slew Saph ... son of [a] giant."
I Chronicles 20:4 "Sibbechai ... slew Sippai ..."

Jonathan slew a huge man with six fingers on each hand and six toes on each foot
II Samuel 21:20-21 "A huge man with six fingers on each hand and six toes on each foot ... Jonathan ... killed him."

Benaiah slew two lionlike men and an Egyptian five cubits high
I Chronicles 11:22 "Benaiah ... slew two lionlike men of Moab ..."
I Chronicles 11:23 "Benaiah ... slew an Egyptian ... five cubits high."

12. The women celebrated when Saul and David slaughtered thousands

I Samuel 18:6-7 "The women came ... singing and dancing ... and said, Saul hath slain his thousands, and David his ten thousands."

13. Did David buy his wife with 200 foreskins?

Yes, 200 foreskins
I Samuel 18:25-27 "[David] slew of the Philistines *two hundred* men ... brought their foreskins ... to Saul ... and gave [David] his daughter to wife."

No, 100 foreskins
II Samuel 3:14 "Michal ...espoused to me [David] for *an hundred* foreskins of the Philistines."

14. Who was the father of Kish?

Abiel
I Samuel 19:1 "Kish, the son of Abiel."

Ner
I Chronicles 8:33 "Ner begat Kish."

15. Who was the high priest when David went to the house of God?

Ahimelech
I Samuel 21:1 "Then came David to Nob to Ahimelech the priest."

Abiathar
Mark 2:26 "[David] went into the house of God … Abiathar the high priest"

16. Was David by himself when he asked for the holy bread at Nob?

Yes, David was alone
I Samuel 21:1 "David [came] to Nob to Ahimelech … Ahimelech [said] … Why art thou *alone,* and *no man with thee*?"

No, David had company
Matthew 12:3-4 "He [Jesus] said … Have ye not read what David did, when he was an hungred, and *they that were with him* …"

17. David pretended to be insane for fear of Achish the king of Gath

I Samuel 21:11-15 "David … was sore afraid of Achish … he changed his behaviour … and feigned himself mad … [he] scrabbled on the doors of the gate, and let his spittle fall down upon his beard. Then said Achish … Lo, ye see the man is mad …"

18. Abiathar and Ahimelech, who was the father, who was the son?

Abiathar was the son of Ahimelech
I Samuel 22:20; 23:6 "Abiathar the son of Ahimelech …"

Ahimelech was the son of Abiathar
II Samuel 8:17 "Ahimelech the son of Abiathar …"
I Chronicles 18:16, 24:6 "Abimelech the son of Abiathar …"

19. Saul went to a necromancer after banning necromancy

Saul banned the use of necromancers
I Samuel 28:3 "Saul had put away those that had familiar spirits, and the wizards …"

Saul called the witch of EnDor, a necromancer to summon Samuel's ghost
I Samuel 28:3, 7, 8, 11, 15 "Samuel was dead ... Then said Saul ... seek me a woman that hath a familiar spirit ... Saul said, Bring me up Samuel ..."

Note: Saul forbade the use of necromancers. Saul wanted to talk to the dead Samuel and called Sedecla, a necromancer to summon Samuel for him.

20. Did Saul inquire about the Lord?

Yes
I Samuel 28:6 "When Saul enquired of the Lord, the Lord answered him not, neither by dreams, nor by Urim, nor by prophets."

No
I Chronicles 10:13-14 "Saul died for his transgression ... And enquired not of the Lord: therefore he slew him, and turned the kingdom unto David the son of Jesse."

21. David wanted to fight for the Philistines after killing Goliath

I Samuel 29:9-11 "Achish [said] He [David] shall not go up with us to the battle ... So David and his men rose up early to depart in the morning."

Note: David had a falling out with Saul and fled to Gath and became a subject of Achish, a Philistine king. After killing Goliath, a Philistine, David became a subject of a Philistine king and wanted to fight for the Philistines against the Israelite army. If David did kill Goliath and 200 Philistines to use their foreskins as dowry, why was David accepted by the Philistines and became a subject to their king?

22. Who killed Saul?

Saul killed himself
I Samuel 31:4 "Saul took a sword, and fell upon it ..."
I Chronicles 10:4 "Saul took a sword, and fell upon it."

An Amalekite killed Saul
II Samuel 1:8-10 "He [Saul] said unto me ... Stand, I pray thee, upon me, and slay me ... so I [Amalekite] stood upon him [Saul], and slew him ..."

The Philistines killed Saul
II Samuel 21:12 "The Philistines had slain Saul in Gilboa."

God killed Saul
I Chronicles 10:13-14 "Saul died for [the] he [Lord] slew him [Saul] ..."

23. Did Saul's family die with him?

No, Ishbosheth his son is alive
II Samuel 2:7-9 "Saul is dead ... Ishbosheth the son of Saul ..."

Yes
I Chronicles 10:6 "Saul died, and his three sons, and all his house died ..."

24. Who was the father of Heman?

Mahol
I Kings 4:31 "Heman, and Chalcol, and Darda, the sons of Mahol."

Zerah
I Chronicles 2:6 "The sons of Zerah; Zimri, and Ethan, and Heman ..."

Joel
 I Chronicles 6:33; 15:17 "Heman the son of Joel."

25. How many sons did Zerubbabel have?

Five
I Chronicles 3:19-20 "The sons of Zerubbabel; Meshullam, and Hananiah, and Shelomith their sister: And Hashubah, and Ohel, and Berechiah, and Hasadiah, Jushabhesed, five."

Note: However, the total count adds up to seven sons.

26. How many sons did Shemaiah have?

Six
I Chronicles 3:22 "The sons of Shemaiah; Hattush, Igeal, Bariah, Neariah, and Shaphat, six."

Note: However, the total count only adds up to five.

27. What is the lineage of Joram?

Joram, Ahaziah, Joash, Amaziah, Azariah, Jotham, Ahaz, Hezekiah, Manasseh...
I Chronicles 3:11-13 "Joram ... Ahaziah ... Joash ... Amaziah ... Azariah ... Jotham ... Ahaz ... Hezekiah ... Manasseh."

Joram, Ozias, Joatham, Achaz, Ezekias, Manasses, Amon...
Matthew 1:8-10 "Joram begat Ozias; Ozias begat Joatham; Joatham begat Achaz; Achaz begat Ezekias; Ezekias begat Manasses; Manasses begat Amon."

28. Who was the father of Jechoniah?

Jehoiakim
I Chronicles 3:15-16 "The sons of Josiah ... Jehoiakim ... the sons of Jehoiakim; Jeconiah ..."

Josias
Matthew 1:11 "Josias begat Jechonias ..."

Note: In I Chronicles 3:15-16, Josiah was the grandfather of Jeconiah.

29. Did Jeconiah sire any sons?

Jeconiah had many sons, and one of them was an ancestor of Jesus
I Chronicles 3:17-18 "The sons of Jeconiah; Assir, Malchiram [Nedabiah]."
Matthew 1:12 "Jeconiah begat Shealtiel."

No, The Lord cursed Jeconiah to be childless
Jeremiah 22:28-30 "Thus saith the Lord, write this man [Jeconiah] childless"

Note: Shealtiel was an ancestor of Jesus.

30. Who was the father of Zerubbabel?

Pedaiah
I Chronicles 3:19 "The sons of Pedaiah were, Zerubbabel ..."

Shealtiel (Salathiel)
Ezra 3:2 "Zerubbabel the son of Shealtiel, and his brethren ..."

31. Was Mahli the son of Levi?

Yes
Ezra 8:18 "Mahli, the son of Levi ..."

No, and the sons of Levi: Gershon, Kohath, and Merari
Genesis 46:11 "The sons of Levi; Gershon, Kohath, and Merari."
I Chronicles 6:1, 16; 23:6 "The sons of Levi; Gershon, Kohath, and Merari."

32. Who is the second son of David who was born in Hebron

Second son is Chileab
II Samuel 3:2-5 "Unto David were sons born in Hebron: Amnon ... his second, Chileab ..."

Second son is Daniel

I Chronicles 3:1-4 "The sons of David, [born in] Hebron; Amnon ... [then] Daniel ..."

33. Which sons of David were born in Jerusalem?

Shammuah, Shobab, Nathan, Solomon, Ibhar, Elishua, Nepheg, Japhia, Elishama, Eliada and Eliphalet
II Samuel 5:14-16 "The names of those that were born unto him in Jerusalem; Shammuah, and Shobab, and Nathan, and Solomon, Ibhar also, and Elishua, and Nepheg, and Japhia, And Elishama, and Eliada, and Eliphalet."

Shimea, Shobab, Nathan, Solomon, Ibhar, Elishama, Nogah, Nepheg, Japhia, Eliada and Eliphelet
I Chronicles 3:5-8 "These were born [in Jerusalem]; Shimea, Shobab, Nathan, and Solomon, four, of Bathshua the daughter of Ammiel: Ibhar, Elishama, Eliphelet, Nogah, Nepheg, Japhia, Elishama, Eliada, and Eliphelet, nine."

Shammua, Shobab, Nathan, Solomon, Ibhar, Elishua, Elpalet, Nogah, Nepheg, Japhia, Elishama, Beeliada, Eliphalet
I Chronicles 14:3-7 "David took more wives at Jerusalem ... his children which he had in Jerusalem; Shammua, Shobab, Nathan, Solomon, Ibhar, Elishua, Elpalet, Nogah, Nepheg, Japhia, Elishama, Beeliada, and Eliphalet."

34. Was Solomon the second son of David and Bathsheba?

Yes, the second son
II Samuel 12:15, 18, 24 "The Lord struck the [first] child ... and David ... lay with her: and she [Bathsheba] bare a son ... his name Solomon"

No, the fourth son
I Chronicles 3:5 "These were born unto him in Jerusalem; Shimea, Shobab, Nathan, and Solomon, four, of Bathshua the daughter of Ammiel."

35. Who was the father of Bathsheba (Bathsua)?

Eliam
II Samuel 11:3 "The man said, "Isn't this Bathsheba, the daughter of Eliam""

Ammiel
I Chronicles 3:5 "Bathshua the daughter of Ammiel."

36. When did Absalom rebel against David?

Less than forty years since David became king
II Samuel 5:4 "David was thirty years old when he began to reign, he [David] reigned forty years."

Note: Absalom rebelled against David when David was still king. David started to reign much earlier and David reigned for forty years. Therefore, Absalom rebelled against David less than forty years since David became king.

After forty years
II Samuel 15:7 "After *forty years*, that Absalom said unto the king, I pray thee, let me go and pay my vow, which I have vowed unto the Lord, in Hebron."

Note: Absalom cannot possibly rebel against David after forty years while David was still king since David only reigned for forty years. Newer versions of the Bible have a modified version of II Samuel 15:7, instead of forty years, the verse was changed to:
II Samuel 15:7 "After *four years* ..."

37. Did Michal have children?

No, Michal was childless
II Samuel 6:23 "Michal the daughter of Saul had no child ..."

Yes, Michal had five sons
II Samuel 21:8 "The five sons of Michal the daughter of Saul."

38. How many horsemen did David took after defeating Hadadezer?

Seven hundred
II Samuel 8:4 "David took ... seven hundred horsemen ..."

Seven thousand
I Chronicles 18:4 "David took ... seven thousand horsemen ..."

39. David told his men to return only when their beards have grown

II Samuel 10:2-5 "David [said], I will shew kindness unto Hanun (by sending my servants) ... Hanun took David's servants, and shaved off ... half of their beards, and cut off their garments in the middle ... and [David] said, Tarry at Jericho until your beards be grown, and then return."

Note: Hanun returned David's kindness by shaving off half of his servants' beards and cutting off their garments in the middle. And David told his servants to remain in Jericho until their beards have grown.

40. How many were killed by David when the Syrian fled before Israel?

The men of 700 chariots, 40,000 horsemen, and Shobach
II Samuel 10:18 "David killed … men of 700 chariots, 40,000 horsemen … Shobach"

The men of 7,000 chariots, 40,000 foot soldiers, and Shophach
I Chronicles 19:18 "David killed … men of 7,000 chariots and 40,000 foot soldiers, and put to death also Shophach …"

41. What was David's punishment for taking the wife of Uriah?

David's wives will be fornicating with his neighbors in public view
II Samuel 12:10-11 "Lord [said] I will take thy wives before thine eyes, and give them unto thy neighbour, and he shall lie with thy wives in the sight of this sun."

David's child with Bathsheba dies
II Samuel 12:13-15 "David said … I have sinned … Nathan said … because by this deed … the child … born unto thee shall surely die … the Lord struck the child …"

David's son Absalom fornicated with David's concubines
II Samuel 16:22 "Absalom went in unto his father's concubines …"

Note: Some Bible versions state that David's concubines will fornicate with someone close to him instead of his neighbors.

42. David wore a crown weighing a talent of gold (about 34 kgs)

II Samuel 12:30 "The weight [a talent of gold] … was set on David's head."
I Chronicles 20:2 "David took the crown … weigh a talent of gold"

Note: David wore a crown weighing a talent of gold which is about 34 kilograms.

43. Who was the daughter of Absalom?

Tamar
II Samuel 14:27 "Unto Absalom there were born … one daughter … Tamar"

Maachah
II Chronicles 11:20 "Maachah the daughter of Absalom …"

44. How many sons did Absalom have?

Absalom had three sons
II Samuel 14:27 "Unto Absalom there were born three sons."

None
II Samuel 18:18 "Absalom ... said, I have not son to keep my name ..."

45. Who was the father of Amasa?

Ishra an Israelite
[KJ] II Samuel 17:25 "Amasa was a man's son, whose name was Ishra an Israelite."

Jethra of Jezrael
[DR] II Samuel 17:25 "Amasa was the son of a man who was called Jethra of Jezrael."

Jether the Ishmaelite
I Chronicles 2:17 "The father of Amasa was Jether the Ishmaelite."

46. God cursed Israel because Saul slaughtered the Gibeonites

II Samuel 21:1, 6-9 "There was a [three year] famine ... and David enquired of the Lord. And the Lord answered, It is for Saul ... because he slew the Gibeonites. Let seven men of his sons be delivered unto us ... And he delivered them into the hands of the Gibeonites ... and they fell all seven together, and were put to death ..."

Note: Because Saul slaughtered the Gibeonites, God cursed Israel with three years of famine. To stop the famine, David had to atone for the sins of Saul by slaying seven grandsons of Saul. God ended the famine after seven grandsons of Saul were hanged and the bones of Saul, Jonathan and the sons of Saul were buried in the country of Benjamin.

47. Who was the father of Elhanan (Adeodatus)?

Jaareoregim the father of Elhanan
[KJ] II Samuel 21:19 "Elhanan the son of Jaareoregim ..."

Dodo
II Samuel 23:24 "Elhanan the son of Dodo of Bethlehem ..."
[KJ] I Chronicles 11:26 "Elhanan the son of Dodo of Bethlehem"
[DR] I Chronicles 11:26 "Elchanan the son of his uncle of Bethlehem"

Jair the father of Elhanan
[KJ] I Chronicles 20:5 "Elhanan the son of Jair ..."

Forrest the father of Adeodatus
[DR] II Samuel 21:19 "Adeodatus the son of the Forrest ..."

Saltus the father of Adeodatus
[DR] I Chronicles 20:5 "Adeodatus the son of Saltus a Bethlehemite ..."

Note: Elhanan and Adeodatus were used interchangeably in some versions of the Bible.

48. Who was David's mighty man?

Josheb-Basshebeth the Tachmonite
[KJ] II Samuel 23:8 "The Tachmonite ..."
[New King James Version] II Samuel 23:8 "Josheb-Basshebeth the Tachmonite ..."

Jashobeam, a Hachmonite
[New King James Version] I Chronicles 11:11 "Jashobeam the ... Hachmonite ..."

Jesbaham
[DR] II Samuel 23:8 "The names of the valiant men of David. Jesbaham ..."
[DR] I Chronicles 11:11 "Jesbaam the son of Hachamoni ..."

49. How many men did Jashobeam kill at one time?

Eight hundred
II Samuel 23:8 "He lifted up his spear against *eight* hundred ..."

Three hundred
I Chronicles 11:11 "He lifted up his spear against *three* hundred ..."

50. How many companions did David have?

Thirty
II Samuel 23:24-39 "Asahel the brother of Joab was one of the *thirty*."

Thirty seven
II Samuel 23:39 "Uriah the Hittite: thirty and seven in all."

Fifty one
I Chronicles 11:10-47 "The number of the mighty men whom David had ..."

51. Who were the mighty men of King David?

No.	II Samuel 23:8-39	I Chronicles 11:10-47
The Three		
1	Josheb-Basshebeth	Joshobeam the Hacmonite
2	Eleazar son of Dodai	Eleazar son of Dadai
3	Shammah son of Agee	

Not the Three		
1	Abishai son of Zeruiah	Abishai brother of Joab
2	Benaiah son of Jehoiada	Benaiah son of Jehoiada
The thirty (?)		
1	Asahel brother of Joab	Asahel the brother of Joab
2	Elhanan son of Dodo	Elhanan son of Dodo
3	Shammah the Harodite	Shammoth the Harorite
4	Elika the Harodite	
5	Helez the Paltite	Helez the Pelonite
6	Ira son of Ikkesh	Ira son of Ikkesh
7	Abiezer from Anathth	Abiezer from Anathoth
8	Mebunnai the Hushathite	Sibbecai the Hushathite
9	Zalmon the Ahohite	Ilai the Ahohite
10	Maharai the Netophathite	Maharai the Netophathite
11	Heled son of Baanah	Heled son of Baanah
12	Ithai son of Ribai	Ithai son of Ribai
13	Benaiah the Pirathonite	Benaiah the Pirathonite
14	Hiddai of Gaash	Hurai from Gaash
15	Abi-Albon the Arbathite	Abiel the Arbathite
16	Azmaveth the Barhumite	Azmaveth the Baharumite
17	Eliahba the Shaalbonite	Eliahba the Shaalbonite
18	Jonathan (of the sons of Jashen)	the sons of Hashem the Gizonite
19	Shammah the Hararite	Jonathan The son of Shagee
20	Ahiam son of Sharar	Ahiam of Sacar
21	Eliphelet son of Ahasbai	Eliphal son of Ur
22		Hepher the Mekerathite
23	Eliam son of Ahithophel	Ahijah the Pelonite
24	Hezrai the Carmelite	Hezro the Carmelite
25	Paarai the Arbite	Naarai son of Ezbai
26	Igal son of Nathan	Joel the brother of Nathan
27	Bani the Gadite	Mibhar son of Hagri
28	Zelek the Ammonite	Zelek the Ammonite
29	Nahari the Beerothite	Naharai the Berothite
30	Ira the Ithrite	Ira the Ithrite
31	Gareb the Ithrite	Gareb the Ithrite
32	Uriah the Hittite	Uriah the Hittite
33		Zabad son of Ahlai
34		Adina son of Shiza
35		Hanan son of Maacah
36		Joshaphat the Mithnite

37		Uzzia the Ashterathit
38		Shama and
39		Jeiel the sons of Hotham
40		Jediael son of Shimri
41		Joha the Tizite
42		Eliel the Mahavite
43		Jeribai and
44		Joshaviah (sons of Elnaam)
45		Ithmah the Moabite
46		Eliel
47		Obed and
48		Jaasiel the Mezobaite

52. Who told King David to take a census?

God
II Samuel 24:1 "He [Lord] moved David … Go, number Israel and Judah."

Satan
I Chronicles 21:1 "Satan … provoked David to number Israel."

53. God got angry with David for taking a census

God instructed Moses to conduct a census during the time of Moses
Exodus 30:11-12 "The Lord spake unto Moses, saying, When thou takest the sum of the children of Israel after their number … when thou numberest them; that there be no plague among them …"

God got angry when David conducted a census
I Chronicles 21:7-14 "God was displeased with this thing … So the Lord sent pestilence upon Israel: and there fell of Israel seventy thousand men."

Note: God got angry that David took a census and smote Israel and killed 70,000 men. Why did God get angry when David took a census? Who ordered David to take a census? In II Samuel 24, God ordered David to take the census. In Exodus 30:11, God ordered Moses to take a census, Moses did take a census and God did not get angry and promised not to plague Israel for doing so.

54. What was the total population of Israel?

The generations from Jacob to Moses: Jacob, Levi, Kohath, Amram and Moses
Genesis 49:2-28 "Sons of Jacob: … Levi …"

Exodus 6:16-20 "The son of Levi ... Kohath ... sons of Kohath ... Amram ... Moses."

There were 70 souls during the time of Jacob
Genesis 46:27 "All the souls of the house of Jacob ... *threescore and ten.*"
Exodus 1:5 "All the souls [from] the loins of Jacob were *seventy* souls."

There were 600,000 men during the time of Moses
Exodus 12:37 "Israel ... about six hundred thousand (men) on foot ... beside children."

There were 603,550 men (20 years old and over, excluding the tribe of Levi)
Exodus 38:25-26 "For every one that went to be numbered, from twenty years old and upward, for six hundred thousand and three thousand and five hundred and fifty men."
Numbers 1:45-46 "So ... from twenty years old and upward ... six hundred thousand and three thousand and five hundred and fifty. But the Levites ... were not numbered among them."

Jeroboam sent 800,000 Israelite men
II Chronicles 13:3 "Jeroboam also set the battle ... with eight hundred thousand ..."

Abijah slew 500,000 of Israel's chosen men
II Chronicles 13:17 "Abijah [slew] ... of Israel five hundred thousand ..."

Note: The population of Israel grew from seventy during the time of Jacob, to hundreds of thousands during the time of Moses. Moses was only four generations from Jacob.

55. The census numbers of Israel do not agree

Israel 800,000 and Judah 500,000
II Samuel 24:9 "Joab gave up the sum of the number of the people ... in Israel eight hundred thousand valiant men ... the men of Judah were five hundred thousand ..."

Israel 1,100,000 and Judah 470,000
I Chronicles 21:5 "Joab gave the sum of the number of the people ... they of Israel were a thousand thousand and a hundred thousand (one million one hundred thousand) men ... and Judah was four hundred threescore and ten thousand (four hundred seventy thousand) men ..."

56. Did David commit a sin when he took the census?

David committed a sin taking the census

II Samuel 24:10 "David's heart smote him after that he had numbered the people. And David said ... I have sinned greatly in that I have done."

David's only sin was his sin concerning Uriah
I Kings 15:5 "Because David did that which was right in the eyes of the Lord ... save only in the matter of Uriah the Hittite."

Note: Was David's only sin was his sin concerning Uriah? David murdered Uriah by having the soldiers abandon him in a battle so David can take Uriah's wife Bathsheba as his wife. What about the other killings made by David?

57. God asked David to choose his punishment for taking census

A famine of 7 years, 3 months of fleeing, 3 days of pestilence
II Samuel 24:13 "Gad [prophet of God] said ... seven years of famine ... or wilt thou flee three months before thine enemies ... or that there be three days' pestilence in thy land?"

A famine of 3 years, 3 months to be destroyed before thy foes, 3 days the sword of the Lord
I Chronicles 21:9-12 "Gad came to David, and said ... Choose thee either three years' famine; or three months to be destroyed before thy foes ... or else three days the sword of the Lord ..."

58. How much did David pay for the purchase of a threshingfloor?

Fifty shekels of silver
II Samuel 24:24 "David bought ... for fifty shekels of silver."

Six hundred shekels of gold
I Chronicles 21:25 "David gave ... six hundred shekels of gold by weight."

59. To whom did David pay for the purchase of a threshingfloor?

David paid Araunah (Areuna)
II Samuel 24:24 "[David] said unto Araunah ... bought the threshingfloor"

David paid Ornan
I Chronicles 21:22-25 "David said to Ornan, Grant me ... this threshingfloor"

60. Was Solomon the wisest?

Yes Solomon was the wisest
I Kings 3:12 "I have given thee [Solomon] a wise and an understanding heart; so that there was none like thee before thee, neither after thee shall any arise like unto thee."

No, his wives misled him into worshipping other gods
I Kings 11:4 "His [Solomon] wives turned away his heart after other gods."
I Kings 15:3 "He [Solomon] walked in all the sins of his father ... his heart
was not perfect with the Lord his God, as the heart of David his father."

61. How many stalls did Solomon have?

Forty thousand
I Kings 4:26 "Solomon had forty thousand stalls ..."
[DR] II Chronicles 9:25 "Solomon had forty thousand horses in the stables"

Four thousand
[KJ] II Chronicles 9:25 "Solomon had four thousand stalls ..."

62. What did Solomon give to Hiram the king of Tyre?

Wheat (20,000 measures), pure oil (20 measures)
I Kings 5:11 "Solomon gave Hiram twenty thousand measures of wheat ...
twenty measures of pure oil: thus gave Solomon to Hiram year by year."

Beaten wheat and barley (20,000 measures), wine and oil (20,000 baths)
II Chronicles 2:10 "Twenty thousand measures of beaten wheat, and ...
barley, and twenty thousand baths of wine, and ... oil."

63. When did Solomon reign?

After 476 years from the departure of Egypt
I Kings 6:1 "In the *four hundred and eightieth year* after the children of Israel
were come out of the land of Egypt in the *fourth year* of Solomon's reign"

Note: Four hundred eighty years minus four years is equal to 476.

After 570 years from the departure of Egypt
Acts 13:18, 20-21 "About the time of *forty years* suffered he [Lord] their
manners in the wilderness [after leaving Egypt] ... and after that he [Lord]
gave unto them judges about the space of *four hundred and fifty years* ... and
God gave unto them Saul ... by the space of *forty years* ..."
I Chronicles 29:27 "He [David] reigned over Israel was *forty years*."

*Note: The sum of 40 years (wandering in the wilderness), 450 years (time of
judges), 40 years (reign of Saul) and 40 years (reign of David) is 570 years.*

64. How many overseers were appointed for building the temple?

Three thousand and three hundred

I Kings 5:16 "Beside the chief of Solomon's officers ... three thousand and three hundred ..."

Three thousand and six hundred
II Chronicles 2:2 "Solomon told ... three thousand and six hundred to oversee ..."

65. How big was Solomon's temple?

It took 153,300 persons to build the temple
I Kings 5:15-16 "Solomon had threescore and ten thousand that bare burdens, and fourscore thousand hewers ... three thousand and three hundred ... ruled over ..."

Approximately twenty-seven meters by nine meters by fourteen meters
I Kings 6:2 "The house which king Solomon built ... the length thereof was threescore cubits ... breadth thereof twenty cubits ... height thereof thirty cubits."
II Chronicles 3:3 "The length by cubits after the first measure was threescore cubits, and the breadth twenty cubits."

It took seven years to build the temple
I Kings 6:38 "So was he seven years in building it."

It took 100,000 talents of gold and a million talents of silver for the temple
I Chronicles 22:14 "Hundred thousand talents of gold ... thousand thousand talents of silver ..."

Note: The size of the temple does not seem to match the time and resources used to make and run the temple.

66. What was the tribe of Hyram?

Naphtali
I Kings 7:13-14 "He [Hiram] was a widow's son of the tribe of Naphtali ..."

Dan
II Chronicles 2:13-14 "I have sent ... Huram ... The son of a woman of the daughters of Dan ..."

Note: Huram (Hiram or Hyram) Abiff, a master builder of King Solomon's temple is a main figure in Free Masonry. Masonic rituals for new members are reenactments of Hiram's murder and martyrdom for the Free Masonry cause.

67. How high were the two pillars built by Solomon?

Eighteen (18) cubits high
I Kings 7:15 "Two pillars of brass, of eighteen cubits high apiece "

Thirty-five (35) cubits high
II Chronicles 3:15 "Two pillars of thirty and five cubits high."

68. How many pomegranates for Solomon's mythical temple?

Two hundred
I Kings 7:20 "The pomegranates were two hundred ..."

One hundred
II Chronicles 3:16 "An hundred pomegranates ..."

69. What was the capacity of the molten sea in Solomon's temple?

Two thousand baths
I Kings 7:26 "It contained two thousand baths."

Three thousand baths
II Chronicles 4:5 "Held three thousand baths."

70. How many animals did Solomon sacrifice?

II Chronicles 7:5-9 "King Solomon offered a sacrifice of twenty and two thousand oxen, and an hundred and twenty thousand sheep ... kept the feast seven days ..."

Note: About 14+ animals were killed per minute for seven days.

71. How many chief officers were in charge of Solomon's temple?

Five hundred and fifty
I Kings 9:23 "The chief of the officers ... five hundred and fifty ..."

Two hundred and fifty
II Chronicles 8:10 "King Solomon's officers ... two hundred and fifty ..."

72. How many talents of gold came from Ophir?

Hiram brought 420
I Kings 9:26-28 "Hiram ... gold, four hundred and twenty talents ..."

Huram brought 450
II Chronicles 8:18 "Huram ... four hundred and fifty talents of gold ..."

P. The Kingdoms of Israel and Judah

1. Non-existing Pharaohs in the Bible

Shishak (Sesac)
I Kings 11:40 "Shishak (Sesac) king of Egypt."

So (Sua)
II Kings 17:4 "He had sent messengers to So (Sua) king of Egypt ..."

Hophra (Ephree)
Jeremiah 44:30 "Behold, I will give Pharaoh Hophra (Ephree) king of Egypt"

Note: Egyptologists therorized that Shishak (Sesac) was actually Pharaoh Shoshenq I and Hophra (Ephree) was actually Pharaoh Apries. However, Pharaoh So (Sua) remains unidentified by historians.

2. How were Abijam and Asa related?

Abijam was Asa's brother, they both had the same mother, Maachah
I Kings 15:1-2 "His [Abijam] mother's name was Maachah ..."
I Kings 15:9-10 "His [Asa] mother's name was Maachah."

Abijam was Asa's father
I Kings 15:8 "Abijam slept with his fathers ... Asa his son reigned ..."

3. What was the name of King Abijah's mother?

Maachah the daughter of Absalom
I Kings 15:1-2 "His [Abijam] mother ... Maachah"
II Chronicles 11:20 "Maachah ... bare him Abijah ..."

Michaiah the daughter of Uriel
II Chronicles 13:2 "His [Abijah] mother ... Michaiah the daughter of Uriel"

4. Did Asa remove the high places?

No
I Kings 15:14 "The high places were not removed"
II Chronicles 15:17 "The high places were not taken away out of Israel"

Yes
II Chronicles 14:3-5 "He [Asa] took away ... the high places ... he [Asa] took away... the high places and the images."

5. Did Asa reign peacefully?

No
I Kings 15:16 "There was war between Asa and Baasha king of Israel all their days."

Yes
II Chronicles 14:1, 5 "Asa … reigned in his stead. In his days the land was quiet ten years … and the kingdom was quiet before him."

6. In what year of King Asa's reign did Baasha die?

Baasha died during the twenty-sixth year reign of Asa
I Kings 16:6, 8 "Baasha slept with his fathers … in the twenty and sixth year of Asa …"

Baasha invaded Judah during the thirty-sixth year reign of Asa
[KJ] II Chronicles 16:1 "In the six and thirtieth year of the reign of Asa Baasha … came up against Judah … and Asa in the thirty and ninth year of his reign …"

Note: How can Baasha begin reigning during the 36ᵗʰ year of Asa's reign when he (Baasha) already passed away during the 26ᵗʰ year reign of Asa?

[DR] II Paralipomenon 16:1 "And in the *six and thirtieth year of his kingdom,* Baasa the king of Israel came up against Juda …"

Note: However, in the Douay Rheims Bible, the 36ᵗʰ year reign mentioned refers to the reign of Baasa.

7. How many years did Omri (Amri) reign over Israel?

Twelve years
I Kings 16:23 "Omri to reign over Israel, twelve years …"

Seven years
I Kings 16:23 ""In the thirty and first year of Asa king of Judah began Omri to reign over Israel, twelve years …"
I Kings 16:28-29 "Omri slept with his fathers … and in the thirty and eighth year of Asa… began Ahab the son of Omri to reign over Israel."

Note: Omri started to reign during the 31ˢᵗ year of Asa king of Judah. However, Omri passed away during the 38ᵗʰ year of Asa.

8. Who was the father of Jehoshaphat?

Asa
I Kings 15:24 "Asa slept with his fathers … Jehoshaphat his son …"

Nimshi
II Kings 9:2, 14 "Jehu the son of Jehoshaphat the son of Nimshi ..."

9. Was Jehu the son or grandson of Nimshi?

Jehu was the son of Nimshi
I Kings 19:16 "Jehu the son of Nimshi ..."
II Chronicles 22:7 "Jehu the son of Nimshi ..."

Jehu was the grandson of Nimshi
II Kings 9:2, 14 "Jehu the son of Jehoshaphat the son of Nimshi ..."

10. When did Elisha receive Elijah's mantle?

Before Elijah was taken up to heaven
I Kings 19:19 "Elijah ... cast his mantle upon him [Elisha]."

After Elijah was taken up to heaven
II Kings 2:11-13 "There appeared a chariot of fire ... Elijah went up by a whirlwind into heaven ... He [Elisha] took ... the mantle of Elijah ..."

Note: Elijah's mantle was used to part the river of Jordan (see II Kings 2:8).

11. A wall fell on 27,000 soldiers

I Kings 20:30 "A wall fell upon twenty and seven thousand of the men ..."

Note: A wall that fell on 27,000 soldiers must have been a very big wall indeed. The spectacle of a wall falling on thousands of soldiers seems quite incredulous and physically implausible.

12. Did Jehoshaphat remove the high places?

Jehoshaphat did not remove the high places
I Kings 22:42-43 "Jehoshaphat [began to reign] ... the high places were not taken away"

Jehoshaphat did remove the high places
II Chronicles 17:6 "He [Jehoshaphat] ... took away the high places ..."

13. Forty-two children were killed by bears for calling Elisha bald

II Kings 2:23-24 "He [Elisha] went up ... there came forth little children ... mocked him ... Go up, thou bald head ... he [Elisha] cursed them in the name of the Lord ... there came forth two she bears ... and tare forty and two children ..."

Note: If Elisha was indeed a man of God, why would he take the sneers from children personally and curse them to death?

14. When did Ahaziah (Ochozias) begin to reign?

In the twelfth year of Joram
II Kings 8:25 "In the twelfth year of Joram ... Ahaziah ... begin to reign."

In the eleventh year of Joram
II Kings 9:29 "In the eleventh year of Joram ... Ahaziah to reign over Judah."

15. How old was Ahaziah (Ochozias) when he began to reign?

Twenty-two years old
II Kings 8:26 "Two and twenty years old was Ahaziah when he began to reign ..."

Forty-two years old
II Chronicles 22:2 "Forty and two years old was Ahaziah when he began to reign ..."

16. How did Ahaziah (Ochozias) die?

He fled to Meggido and died
II Kings 9:27 "He fled to Megiddo, and died there."

He was brought to Jehu and slain
II Chronicles 22:9 "They [Jehu's men] ... brought him to Jehu ... they had slain him ..."

17. How did God react to Jehu for the killings at Jezreel?

God told Jehu to smite the house of Ahab and he and his descendants will be kings
II Kings 9:6-8 "[Elisha] said unto him [Jehu], Thus saith the Lord ... I have anointed thee king ... thou shalt smite the house of Ahab ..."
II Chronicles 22:7-8 "Jehu ... whom the Lord had anointed to cut off the house of Ahab ... he [Jehu] slew them [the house of Ahab]."

God condemned Jehu for doing the killings
Hosea 1:4 "The Lord said ... I [Lord] will avenge the blood of Jezreel upon the house of Jehu, and will cause to cease the kingdom of the house of Israel."

Jehu, Jehoahaz, Jehoash, Jeroboam II and Zechariah became kings
II Kings 10:30 "The Lord said unto Jehu, because thou hast done well in

executing that which is right in mine eyes ... thy children of the fourth generation shall sit on the throne of Israel."
II Kings 10:35 "Jehu slept with his fathers ... Jehoahaz his son reigned ..."
II Kings 13:9, 13 "Jehoahaz his son reigned ... Jeroboam sat upon his throne"
II Kings 14:29 "Zechariah his son succeeded him as king."
II Kings 15:12 "This was the word of the Lord which he spake unto Jehu, saying, Thy sons shall sit on the throne of Israel unto the fourth generation. And so it came to pass."

Note: Jehu killed Jehoram the son of Ahab and Jezebel in Jezreel thru the instructions of Elisha claiming it as a commandment from the Lord. However, in the book of Hosea, Jehu was avenged by the Lord for doing what he was told to do. Nonetheless, Jehu and the succeeding four generations reigned as kings of Israel fulfilling God's promise.

18. Was Joash buried in the sepulcher of the kings?

Yes, Joash was buried in the sepulchres of the kings
II Kings 12:20-21 "His [Joash] servants, smote him, and he died; and they buried him [Joash] with his fathers in the city of David."

No, Joash was not buried in the sepulchres of the kings
II Chronicles 24:24-25 "His Joash own servants ... slew him ... they buried him in the city of David, but they buried him [Joash] not in the sepulchres of the kings."

19. How long did Jotham reign?

At least 20 years
II Kings 15:30 "Hoshea ... made a conspiracy against Pekah ... and reigned in his stead, in the *twentieth year of Jotham* the son of Uzziah."

Sixteen years
II Kings 15:33 "Five and twenty years old was he [Jotham] when he began to reign, and he [Jotham] reigned *sixteen years* in Jerusalem ..."

20. How old was Ahaz when he became a father?

Based on the age of Hezekiah, Ahaz was a ten or eleven year old father
II Kings 16:2 "Twenty years old was Ahaz when he began to reign, and reigned sixteen years ..."
II Kings 16:20 "Ahaz slept with his fathers ... Hezekiah his son reigned ..."
II Kings 18:1-2 "Hezekiah ... began to reign. Twenty five years old was he"

Note: Ahaz started to reign when he was 20 years old, and he reigned for 16 years. Hezekiah succeeded his father when he was 25 years old. Thirty-six minus twenty-five is equal to eleven. Ahaz was about eleven years old when his son, Hezekiah was born.

21. Did the King of Syria conquer Ahaz?

The King of Syria and the son of the King of Israel did not conquer Ahaz
II Kings 16:5 "They [Rezin and Pekah] besieged Ahaz, but could *not* overcome him."

The King of Syria conquered Ahaz
II Chronicles 28:5 "The Lord … delivered him [Ahaz into] the king of Syria"

22. Was Ahaz buried in the sepulchre of the kings?

Yes
II Kings 16:20 "Ahaz… was buried with his fathers in the city of David."

No
II Chronicles 28:27 "Ahaz slept with his fathers … but they brought him not into the sepulchres of the kings of Israel."

23. Who is Adrammelech?

A god
II Kings 17:31 "The Sepharvites burnt their children in fire to Adrammelech and Anammelech, the gods of Sepharvaim."

son of Sennacherib king of Assyria
II Kings 19:36-37 "Adrammelech and Sharezer his [Sennacherib] sons …"

24. No other king like whom?

Hezekiah
II Kings 18:5 "After him [Hezekiah] was none like him among all the kings of Judah, nor any that were before him."

Josiah
II Kings 23:25 "Like unto him [Josiah] was there no king before him … neither after him arose there any like him."

25. Why was the sundial of Ahaz turned back by ten degrees?

A sign that Hezekiah will be healed
II King 20:8-11 "Hezekiah said … What shall be the sign that the Lord will heal me… let the shadow return backward ten degrees …"

A sign that Hezekiah will be healed and Jerusalem will be delivered from Assyria
Isaiah 38:5-8 "Thus saith the Lord ... I will add unto thy [Hezekiah] days fifteen years. And I will deliver ... this city [Jerusalem] out of the hand of the king of Assyria ... a sign unto thee ... I will bring... the sun dial of Ahaz, ten degrees backward."

26. The dead soldiers woke up and realized they were dead

[KJ] **II Kings 19:35** "The angel of the Lord [smote] ... an hundred fourscore and five thousand: and when they arose early in the morning, behold, they were all dead corpses."

27. Armenia or Urartu?

II Kings 19:37 "They escaped into the land of Armenia."

Note: Armenia was named Armenia around 190 BC. The place where they escaped must have been called Urartu.

28. Josiah was punished for the misdeeds of Manasseh

Josiah was punished because of his grandfather Manasseh
II Kings 23:25-27 "There [was] no king before him [Josiah], that turned to the Lord with all his heart ... [But the Lord's] ... anger was kindled against Judah, because of all the provocations that Manasseh had provoked him ..."

Manasseh asked for the Lord's forgiveness and was forgiven
II Chronicles 33:1-2, 12-13 "Manasseh ... was evil in the sight of the Lord ... [But] he [Manasseh] ... humbled himself greatly ... prayed unto him [God]: and he was intreated of him, and heard his supplication, and brought him again to Jerusalem into his kingdom."

Note: Manasseh, the grandfather of Josiah mended his ways and asked for the Lord's forgiveness and was forgiven by the Lord. Josiah was not yet born when Manasseh committed his evil deeds. Josiah was punished for the evil deeds of Manasseh when the Lord already forgave Manasseh himself.

29. How and where did Josiah die?

Josiah was slain by Pharaoh Neco and died in Megiddo and was brought to Jerusalem
II Kings 23:29-30 "He [Pharoah Neco] slew him [Josiah] at Megiddo ... and his servants carried him ... from Megiddo, and brought him to Jerusalem ..."

Josiah was shot by a group of archers and died in Jerusalem

II Chronicles 35:23-24 "The archers shot at King Josiah ... brought him to Jerusalem, and [died]"

30. Who succeeded Jehoiakim (Jehoiakin)?

His son Jehoiachin succeeded him as king
II Kings 24:6 "Jehoiakim slept with his fathers ... Jehoiachin his son reigned"

He had no one to succeed him
Jeremiah 36:30 "Saith the Lord, he [Jehoiakim] shall have none to sit upon the throne of David."

31. How old was Jehoiachin when he started to reign?

Eighteen years old
II Kings 24:8 "Jehoiachin was eighteen years old ..."

Eight years old
II Chronicles 36:9 "Jehoiachin was eight years old ..."

32. How long did Jehoiachim reign in Jerusalem?

Three months
II Kings 24:8 "[Jehoiachim] reigned in Jerusalem three months ..."

Three months and ten days
 II Chronicles 36:9 "[Jehoiachim] reigned three months and ten days ..."

33. Who was the successor of Josiah?

Jehoahaz
II Chronicles 36:1 "The people ... took Jehoahaz ... made him king ..."

Shallum
Jeremiah 22:11 "Shallum the son of Josiah ..."

34. What happened to Jehoiakim when he died?

He slept with his fathers
II Kings 24:6 "Jehoiakim slept with his fathers ..."

They bound him in fetters
II Chronicles 36:6 "And bound him in fetters, to carry him to Babylon."

He shall be buried with the burial of an ass
Jeremiah 22:18-19 "Therefore thus saith the Lord ... He shall be buried with the burial of an ass, drawn and cast forth beyond the gates of Jerusalem."

His dead body shall be cast out in the day to the heat and in the night to the frost
Jeremiah 36:30 "Therefore thus saith the Lord of Jehoiakim ... his dead body shall be cast out in the day to the heat, and in the night to the frost."

They put him in ward in chains and brought him into holds
Ezekiel 19:9 "They put him in ward in chains, and brought him to the king of Babylon: they brought him into holds, that his voice should no more be heard ..."

35. Where did Jehoiakim die?

Babylon
II Chronicles 36:6 "Against him [Jehoiakim] came up Nebuchadnezzar ... bound him in fetters, to carry him to Babylon."

Jerusalem
Jeremiah 22:18-19 "Thus saith the Lord ... he shall be buried with the burial of an ass, drawn and cast forth beyond the gates of Jerusalem."

36. What is the relationship of Zedekiah and Nebuchadnezzar?

Zedekiah was the uncle of Nebuchadnezzar
II Kings 24:17 "The king of Babylon made Mattariah his father's brother king in his stead, and changed his name to Zedekiah."

Zedekiah was the brother of Nebuchadnezzar
[KJ] II Chronicles 36:10 "King Nebuchadnezzar ... made Zedekiah his brother king ..."

Note: In the Douay Rheims Bible, Zedekiah was consistently identified as the uncle of Nebuchadnezzar.

37. Nebuchadnezzar or Nebuchadrezzar?

Nebuchadnezzar
[KJ] II Kings 24:1 "In his days Nebuchadnezzar king of Babylon ..."

Nebuchadrezzar
[KJ] Jeremiah 21:2 "Nebuchadrezzar king of Babylon ..."

Note: Nebuchadnezzar whose real name is Nabukudurriusur is sometimes called Nebuchadrezzar in the Book of Jeremiah and Ezekiel. However, in the Douay- Rheims Bible he is consistently called Nabuchodonosor.

38. When did the Israelites occupy Jerusalem?

During the time of Joshuah
Joshua 12:7-10 "Joshua gave unto the tribes of Israel [their lands] for a possession according to their divisions ... the Jebusites ... the king of Jerusalem ..."
Joshua 15:63 "The children of Judah could not drive them [Jebusites] out; but the Jebusites dwell with the children of Judah at Jerusalem unto this day."

After the death of Joshuah
Judges 1:8 "The children of Judah had fought against Jerusalem, and had taken it ..."
Judges 1:21 "The ... Jebusites dwell with the children of Benjamin in Jerusalem unto this day."
Judges 19:10-11 "When they were by Jebus (Jerusalem) ... the servant said ... Come, I pray thee, and let us turn in into this city of the Jebusites, and lodge in it. And his master said ... We will not turn aside hither into *the city of a stranger, that is not of the children of Israel;* we will pass over to Gibeah."

Note: In Joshua and Judges 1 it says, the Israelites lived in Jerusalem unto this day. However, in Judges 19 it says, there are no Israelites living in Jerusalem.

During the time of David
I Chronicles 11:4 "David and all Israel went to Jerusalem, which is Jebus."
II Samuel 5:6-7 "The king and his men went to Jerusalem unto the Jebusites ... David took the strong hold of Zion: the same is the city of David."

39. Did Zedekiah's eyes see the king of Babylon?

No, Zedekiah's eyes were removed before he reached Babylon
II Kings 25:7 "They ... put out the eyes of Zedekiah ... and carried him to Babylon."

Yes, Zedekiah saw the king of Babylon with his eyes
Jeremiah 34:3 "Thine (Zedakiah) eyes shall behold the eyes of the king ..."

40. On what day did Nebuzaradan burn the house of the Lord?

On the seventh day of the month
II Kings 25:8-9 "On the seventh day ... (Nebuzaradan) burnt the house of the Lord."

On the tenth day of the month
Jeremiah 52:12-13 "In the tenth day ... (Nebuzaradan) burned the house of the Lord."

41. What was the height of the chapiter?

3 cubits
II Kings 25:17 "The height of the chapiter was three cubits."

5 cubits
Jeremiah 52:22 "The height of one chapiter was five cubits."

42. How many men stood in the presence of the king of Babylon?

Five men
II Kings 25:19 "*Five* men ... were in the king's presence."

Seven men
Jeremiah 52:25 "*Seven* men ... were near the king's person ..."

43. What day was Jehoiachin released from prison?

On the 27th day of the month
II Kings 25:27 "On the *seven* and twentieth day of the month, that Evilmerodach ... lift up the head of Jehoiachin king of Judah out of prison."

On the 25th day of the month
Jeremiah 52:31 "In the *five* and twentieth day of the month, that Evilmerodach ... lifted up the head of Jehoiachin ... out of prison."

44. Was the heart of Asa perfect?

Yes
II Chronicles 15:17 "The heart of Asa was perfect all his days."

No
II Chronicles 16:7 "Hanani ... said unto him [Asa], Because thou hast relied on the king of Syria, and not relied on the Lord thy God ..."
II Chronicles 16:10 "Asa oppressed some of the people the same time."
II Chronicles 16:12 "Asa ... was diseased in his feet ... yet ... he sought not to the Lord, but to the physicians."

45. Ahaziah was two years older than his father Jehoram

II Chronicles 21:5, 20 "Jehoram was thirty two years old ... he reigned eight years in Jerusalem."
II Chronicles 22:1-2 "Forty-two years old was Ahaziah when he began to reign ..."

Note: Jehoram died at the age of forty and his son Ahaziah assumed the throne at age forty-two years old.

46. Who was the father of Zechariah (Zacharias)?

Jehoiada the priest
II Chronicles 24:20 "Zechariah the son of Jehoiada ..."

Jesus said Zacharias was the son of Barachias
Matthew 23:35 "Zacharias son of Barachias ..."

Note: The name Barachias or Barachiah is not in the Old Testament.

47. The capture and burning of Jerusalem

II Chronicles 36:11-12, 14, 15-17 "Zedekiah ... did that which was evil in the sight of the Lord ... Therefore ... the king of the Chaldees ... slew their young men ... and had no compassion upon young man or maiden ... or him that stooped for age."

Note: The inhabitants of Jerusalem together with the very old and the very young were punished for the sins of Zedekiah and his men..

Q. The Babylonian captivity

1. The total number of items is not equal to the sum total of items

Ezra 1:9-11 "This is the number of them: thirty chargers of gold, a thousand chargers of silver, nine and twenty knives, Thirty basons of gold, silver basons of a second sort four hundred and ten, and other vessels a thousand. All the vessels of gold and of silver *five thousand four hundred* ..."

Note: The total number of items is said to be 5400. But the total count is just 2499.

2. Who and how many came with Zerubbabel?

Ten
Ezra 2:2 "Which came with Zerubbabel: Jeshua, Nehemiah, Seraiah, Reelaiah, Mordecai, Bilshan, Mizpar, Bigvai, Rehum, Baanah."

Eleven
Nehemiah 7:7 "Who came with Zerubbabel, Jeshua, Nehemiah, Azariah, Raamiah, Nahamani, Mordecai, Bilshan, Mispereth, Bigvai, Nehum, Baanah."

3. How was Zechariah related to Iddo?

Zechariah was Iddo's son
Ezra 5:1, 6:14 "Zechariah the son of Iddo ..."

Zechariah was Iddo's grandson
Zechariah 1:1 "Zechariah, the son of Berechiah, the son of Iddo."

4. Medes and Babylon

Ezra 6:1-2 "Darius the king made a decree, and search was made in the house of the rolls, where the treasures were laid up in Babylon. And there was found at Achmetha, in the palace that is in the province of the Medes, a roll, and therein was a record thus written."

Note: Media is not part of Babylon. And Achmetha is the capital of Medes.

5. What was the total number of the whole assembly?

Forty and two thousand three hundred and threescore (42,360)
Ezra 2:64 "The whole congregation ... forty and two thousand three hundred and threescore."
Nehemiah 7:66 "The whole congregation ... forty and two thousand three hundred and threescore."

Family Of	Ezra	Nehemiah
Parosh	2172	2172
Shephatiah	372	372
Arah	**775**	**652**
Pahathmoab, Jeshua, Joab	**2812**	**2818**
Elam	1254	1254
Zattu	**945**	**845**
Zaccai	760	760
Bani (Binnui)	**642**	**648**
Bebai	**623**	**628**
Azgad	**1222**	**2322**
Adonikam	**666**	**667**
Bigvai	**2056**	**2067**
Adin	**454**	**655**
Ater	98	98
Bezai	**323**	**324**
Jorah (Hariph)	112	112
Hashum	**223**	**328**
Gibbar (Gibeon)	95	95
Bethlehem	**123**	**188**
Netophah	**56**	
Anathoth	128	128
Azmaveth (Bethazmaveth)	42	42

Kirjatharim, Chephirah, Beeroth	743	743
Ramah and Gaba	621	621
Michmas	122	122
Bethel and Ai	**223**	**123**
Nebo	52	52
Magbish	**156**	
Elam (other Elam)	1254	1254
Harim	320	320
Lod, Hadid, and Ono	**725**	**721**
Jericho	345	345
Senaah	3630	3930
Jedaiah	973	973
Immer	1052	1052
Pashur	1247	1247
Harim	1017	1017
The Levites: Jeshua and Kadmiel of the children of Hodaviah	74	74
The singers: the children of Asaph	**128**	**148**
The children of the porters:	**139**	**138**
The Nethinims and Solomon's servants:	392	392
Delaiah, Tobiah, Nekoda	**652**	**642**
Sub-Total (Numerical Count):	**29,818**	**31,089**
Servants	7337	7337
Singing men and women	**200**	**245**
Zerubbabel's companions	**10**	**11**
Total (Numerical Count):	**37,365**	**38,682**

6. The currency called Daric

American Standard Version: Nehemiah 7:70-72 "The governor gave to the treasury 1,000 darics of gold … And what the rest … gave was 20,000 darics of gold …"

Note: The Babylonian captivity happened in 586 BCE when the Kingdom of Judah fell to the Babylonian Empire. However the currency called Daric was introduced by King Darius at a much later date around 522-496 BC. Although the currency is nowhere to be found in the King James Bible, other Bible versions have included the Daric currency as early as in the book of Chronicles.

R. The Persian kings

1. Darius

Ezra 4:5 "Darius king of Persia …"

Note: The different books of the Bible have used the names Darius to refer to Darius I (Darius the Great - 522-486 B.C.), Darius II (Darius Nothus - 423-405 B.C.) and Darius III (Darius Codomannus - 335-330 B.C.). Darius II lived during the time of Nehemiah, so the Darius in the book of Nehemiah was most likely Darius II. However, historians have varying opinions about the identity of Darius mentioned in other books.

2. Ahasuerus or Cambysses?

Ezra 4:6 "In the reign of Ahasuerus …"
Ezra 4:7 "In the days of Artaxerxes [king of Persia] …"

Note: Some historians suspect that the Ahasuerus in Ezra 4:6 was actually Cambysses and the Artaxerxes in Ezra and Nehemiah was actually Pseudo Smerdis, a magician impostor who pretended to be the brother of Cambysses.

3. Who was Assuerus?

In the Book of Tobit, Assuerus is identified as an associate of Nebuchadnezzar
Douay-Rheims: Tobit 14:15 "Nabuchadnezzar and Assuerus …"

Note: Tobit is not part of the King James Bible. Catholic writers insist that the Assuerus in Tobit 14:15 was actually Cyaxares I.

4. Xerxes or Ahasuerus?

Ester 1:1 "Now it came to pass in the days of Ahasuerus, (this is Ahasuerus which reigned, from India even unto Ethiopia, over an hundred and seven and twenty provinces:)."

Note: Some historians suspect that Ahasuerus and Xerxes were one and the same in the book of Ester. However, others disagree.

5. Did the Persian Empire have 127 provinces?

Ester 1:1-2 "Ahasuerus (reigned) … over an hundred and seven and twenty provinces."

Note: Ahasuerus was said to have ruled over 127 provinces. However, there was no such division of the Persian Empire.

6. Did King Xerxes marry Ester after divorcing Vashti?

Ester 2:17 "The king loved Esther ... and made her queen instead of Vashti."

Note: In the King James Bible, it was King Ahasuerus who married Vashti and Ester. In other Bible versions, it was King Xerxes who married Vashti and Ester. There is no historical record indicating that King Xerxes had a wife named neither Esther nor Vashti. Some historians theorize that the real Ester is Amestris the wife of Xerxes I of Persia.

7. Ester had to enter a sex competition in order to become a queen

Ester 2:4-17 "Let the maiden which pleaseth the king be queen ... And the king loved Esther above all the women ... and made her queen instead of Vashti."

Note: The king decreed a sex competition and will choose the new queen among contenders to replace the queen. The king took another wife to become queen because queen Vashti refused the king's order to show herself to his friends.

8. Was Haman an Amalek or an Agagite?

No, the Amalekites were totally destroyed
I Samuel 15:7-8 "Saul smote the Amalekites ... destroyed all the people with the ... sword."

Yes, Haman was a descendant of Agag an Amalekite
Ester 3:1 "Haman the son of Hammedatha the Agagite ..."

9. King Xerxes allowed the Jews to attack his Persian subjects

Ester 8:11 "Wherein the king granted the Jews ... to stand for their life, to destroy, to slay and to cause to perish, all the power of the people and province that would assault them ... and to take the spoil of them for a prey."

Note: There is no record of this event. It is also highly improbable that a king would allow foreigners in his own country to attack his own people.

10. Ester wants to hang the dead sons of Haman

The ten sons of Haman were slain
Ester 9:10 "The ten sons of Haman ... slew they."

Ester wants to hang the already dead sons of Haman
Ester 9:13 "Then said Esther ... let Haman's ten sons be hanged upon the gallows."

Note: The Purim festival of the Jews celebrates Ester's victory over Haman.

11. Daniel's statement about the invasion of Judah

Daniel 1:1 "In the third year of the reign of Jehoiakim king of Judah came Nebuchadnezzar king of Babylon unto Jerusalem, and besieged it."

Note: Jehoiakim reigned as king of Judah from 609 to 598 BCE while Nebuchadnezzar reigned as king of Babylon from 605 to 562 BCE. During the third year of Jehoiakim's reign, Nebuchadnezzar was not yet the king of Babylon. However, when Nebuchadnezzar invaded Judah, Jehoiakim already passed away.

12. Was Belshazzar a king?

Daniel 5:1 "Belshazzar the king ..."

Note: Belshazzar was a co-regent but not king.

13. Who was the father of Belshazzar?

Daniel 5:2 "Belshazzar ... his father Nebuchadnezzar ..."

Note: Historical records show Nebonidus was the father of Belshazzar and not Nebuchadnezzar.

14. Did Darius the Median succeed Belshazzar?

Daniel 5:30-31 "In that night was Belshazzar the king of the Chaldeans slain. And Darius the Median took the kingdom ..."

Note: Historical records show that Cyrus succeeded Belshazzar and Darius the Median is a mere fictitious character that never existed. Darius the Median is not the same as Darius I. Darius I came in power in 521 BCE, 17 years after the fall of Babylon.

S. The men called Azariah

1. The Lord smote Azariah for not removing the high places

II Kings 3-5 "[Azariah] did that which was right in the sight of the Lord ... save that the high places were not removed [and] the Lord smote the king."

Note: Even if Azariah did what was right in the eyes of the Lord, the Lord smote Azariah with leprosy for not having removed the high places.

2. God turned Uzziah [Azariah] into a leper for burning incense

Uzziah [Azariah]
II Kings 15:5 "The Lord smote the king [Azariah], so that he was a leper ..."
II Chronicles 26:19-21 "Then Uzziah ... had a censer in his hand to burn incense ... the Lord had smitten him ... and Uzziah the king was a leper ..."

Azariah is a Levite
II Chronicles 29:12 "Then the Levites arose ... Azariah ..."

Note: Historians believe that Uzziah and Azariah was one and the same person. Uzziah was not a member of the Levite family and therefore did not have the privilege of performing priestly rites such as burning incense. If Uzziah and Azariah were one and the same, how come Azariah was a Levite and Uzziah was not? It seems that Azariah the Levite was not the same as Uzziah who became a leper for burning incense.

3. Who were the men named Azariah?

Azariah, king of Judah, son of Amaziah and Jecoliah
I Chronicles 3:12 "Amaziah his son, Azariah his son ..."

Azariah son of King Jehoshaphat of Judah, brother of Jehoram
II Chronicles 21:2 "He had brethren the sons of Jehoshaphat, Azariah, Jehiel, Zechariah, Azariah, Michael, Shephatiah: all these were the sons of Jehoshaphat ..."

Note: The name Azariah appears twice in the list of sons of Jehoshaphat.

Ahaziah king of Judah, son of Jehoram
II Kings 8:25 "Ahaziah the son of Jehoram king of Judah begin to reign."

Azariah son of Zadok, the priest, a prince of Solomon
I Kings 4:2 "These were the princes which he [Solomon] had; Azariah the son of Zadok the priest."

Azariah son of Nathan, in charge of the twelve officers of King Solomon
I Kings 4:5, 7 "Azariah the son of Nathan was over the officers. And Solomon had twelve officers over all Israel."

Azariah son of Ahimaaz, grandfather of Azariah
I Chronicles 6:9 "Ahimaaz begat Azariah, and Azariah begat Johanan."

Azariah son of Johanan, father of Amariah
I Chronicles 6:10-11 "Johanan begat Azariah, (he it is that executed the priest's office in the temple that Solomon built in Jerusalem:) And Azariah begat Amariah."

Azariah, the son of Hilkiah, the father of Seraiah
I Chronicles 6:13-14 "Hilkiah begat Azariah, and Azariah begat Seraiah."
Ezra 7:1 "Seraiah, the son of Azariah, the son of Hilkiah."

Azariah son of Hilkiah the grandson of Zadok
Nehemiah 11:11 "Seraiah... son of Hilkiah, son of Meshullam, son of Zadok"

Azariah son of Meraioth, father of Amariah
Ezra 7:3 "The son of Amariah, the son of Azariah, the son of Meraioth"

Azariah the chief priest during the time of King Hezekiah
II Chronicles 31:10, 13 "Azariah the chief priest of the house of Zadok... and Azariah the ruler of the house of God."

Note: May be the same as Azariah the son of Hilkiah the grandson of Zadok.

Azariah son of Ethan
I Chronicles 2:8 "The sons of Ethan; Azariah ..."

Azariah son of Jehu and father of Helez
I Chronicles 2:38-39 "Jehu begat Azariah, and Azariah begat Helez."

Azariah son of Zephaniah and father of Joel
I Chronicles 6:36 "Joel, the son of Azariah, the son of Zephaniah."

Azariah a prophet and the son of Oded who prophesied to Asa
II Chronicles 15:1 "The Spirit of God came upon Azariah the son of Oded."

Azariah son of Jeroham, one of those who overthrew Athaliah
II Chronicles 23:1 "Azariah the son of Jeroham."

Azariah son of Obed, one of those who overthrew Athaliah
II Chronicles 23:1 "Azariah the son of Obed."

Azariah the chief priest in the days of King Uzziah of Judah
II Chronicles 26:17, 20 "Azariah ... the chief priest ..."

Azariah son of Johanan and one of the Ephraimite chiefs
II Chronicles 28:12 "Azariah the son of Johanan ..."

Azariah a Kohathite Levite with a son named Joel, one of those who cleansed the Temple in the days of King Hezekiah

II Chronicles 29:12 "The Levites arose ... Joel the son of Azariah, of the sons of the Kohathites"

Azariah a Levite and a son of Jehalelel, one of the Merarites who cleansed the Temple at the time of King Hezekiah
II Chronicles 29:12 "The Levites arose ... Azariah the son of Jehalelel ..."

Azariah, son of Maaseiah, who repaired the wall of Jerusalem during Nehemiah's time
Nehemiah 3:23 "Azariah the son of Maaseiah ..."

Azariah, appointed to take part in the dedication of the wall of Jerusalem
Nehemiah 12:30-33 "The priests and the Levites purified themselves ... and after them went Hoshaiah ... and Azariah ..."

Azariah one of those who witnessed the sealing of the covenant
Nehemiah 10:2 "Now those that sealed were... Azariah ..."

Azariah, one of those who returned from exile with Zerubbabel
Nehemiah 7:7 "Who came with Zerubbabel ... Azariah."

Azariah, one of the Levites who helped the people understand the Law
Nehemiah 8:7 "Azariah ... caused the people to understand the law."

Azariah son of Hoshaiah, who ignored Jeremiah's advice and left for Egypt
Jeremiah 43:2 "Then spake Azariah the son of Hoshaiah ..."

Azariah, one of Daniel's companions
Daniel 1:6-7, 11, 19; 2:17 "Azariah ... [Daniel's] companions."

T. The man called Job

1. Did Satan visit God in heaven?

Job 1:6-7; 2:1 "Now there was a day when the sons of God came to present themselves before the Lord, and *Satan came also among them* ..."

Note: Satan came with the sons of God who visited God.Is Satan one of God's sons? Satan kept a casual conversation with God, could that mean that Satan and God are friends? If the story of Job is non-fiction who overheard and wrote the conversation between God and Satan?

2. Who brought evil upon Job?

Satan
Job 2:7 "Satan ... smote Job with sore boils from ... his foot unto his crown."

God
Job 42:11 "All the evil that the Lord had brought upon him [Job]."

U. The prophets Isaiah, Jeremiah and Ezekiel

1. God told Isaiah to walk naked and barefoot for three years

Isaiah 20:2-3 "At the same time spake the Lord ... Go and loose the sackcloth from off thy loins, and put off thy shoe from thy foot ... And the Lord said, Like as my servant Isaiah hath walked naked and barefoot three years for a sign and wonder upon Egypt and upon Ethiopia"

2. When did God kill the Leviathan and the sea dragon?

He will do it in the future
Isaiah 27:1 "In that day the Lord ... shall punish leviathan ... and he shall slay the dragon that is in the sea."

He already did it
Psalm 74:13-14 "Thou brakest the heads of the dragons in the waters. Thou brakest the heads of leviathan in pieces ..."

3. The people may eat their dung and drink their piss

Isaiah 36:12 "Rabshakeh said ... hath he not sent me to the men that sit upon the wall, that they may eat their own dung, and drink their own piss ..."

4. God compared the girdle to those who do not obey his orders

Jeremiah 13:1-11 "Thus saith the Lord ... Go and get thee a linen girdle... For as the girdle cleaveth to the loins of a man, so have I caused to cleave unto me the whole house of Israel ..."

Note: God told Jeremiah to wear a girdle, and not to wash the girdle but to hide it in a rock. Then God told Jeremiah to dig for the girdle in the rocks. The girdle was ruined, then God compared the girdle to those who do not obey His orders, they too will be ruined.

5. God told Ezekiel to eat a piece of scroll

[KJ] Ezekiel 3:1-3 "He [God] said ... eat this *roll* ... So I opened my mouth, and he caused me to eat that *roll*. And he said ... Son of man, cause thy belly to eat, and fill thy bowels with this *roll*"
[DR] Ezekiel 3:1-3 "He [God] said ... eat this *book* ... So I opened my mouth, and he caused me to eat that *book* ... Son of man, thy belly shall eat, and thy bowels shall be filled with this *book*"

6. God made Ezekiel stick his tongue to the roof of his mouth

Ezekiel 3:24-26 "Then the spirit entered into me ... and said ... I will make thy tongue cleave to the roof of thy mouth ..."

7. Ezekiel had to lie on his left side and then on his right side

Ezekiel had to lie on his left side for 390 days, on his right for 40 days
Ezekiel 4:4-8 "Lie thou also upon thy left side ... three hundred and ninety days ... lie again on thy right side ... forty days ..."

8. God ordered Ezekiel to make bread based on God's recipe

Ezekiel 4:9 "Take thou also unto thee wheat, and barley, and beans, and lentils, and millet, and fitches, and put them in one vessel, and make thee bread thereof ..."

9. God ordered Ezekiel to make and eat bread with human dung

Ezekiel 4:9 "Thou shalt eat it as barley cakes, and thou shalt bake it with dung that cometh out of man, in their sight."

10. Ezekiel had to hide his hair on his skirt

Ezekiel 5:1-4 "Take a razor [pass (it) upon thine head and beard] ... divide the hair ... burn with fire a third ... a third [smite with a knife]: a third scatter in the wind ... take ... a few... bind them in thy skirts ... cast them ... burn them in the fire; for thereof shall a fire come forth into all the house of Israel."

Note: God ordered Ezekiel to cut his hair, burn a third, smite a third, scatter a third and place some on his skirt.

V. The man called Jonah

1. Who threw Jonah to the sea?

The sailors
Jonah 1:15 "They look up Jonah, and cast him forth into the sea."

God
Jonah 2:3 "For thou [Lord] hadst cast me into the deep ..."

2. Fish or whale?

A fish swallowed Jonah
Jonah 1:17 "Now the Lord had prepared a great fish to swallow up Jonah."

Jonah lived inside a whale for three days
Matthew 12:40 "Jonah was three days and three nights in the whale's belly."

3. God spoke to a fish

Jonah 2:10 "The Lord spake unto the fish …"

4. God created a shade for Jonah and then God destroyed the shade

Jonah 4:6-7 "The Lord God prepared a gourd, and made it to come up over Jonah … God prepared a worm … and it smote the gourd that it withered."

5. Did God destroy Nineveh?

No, because they cannot tell their left from their right and too many cows
Jonah 4:11 "Should not I spare Nineveh … persons that cannot discern between their right hand and their left hand; and also much cattle?"

Yes Nineveh was destroyed
Nahum 3:7 "Nineveh is laid waste."

W. About the Old Testament

1. Regarding the book of Proverbs

Proverbs 25:1 "These are also proverbs of Solomon, which the men of Hezekiah king of Judah copied out."

Note: If Solomon wrote the book of Proverbs, why was Hezekiah mentioned in the said book? Solomon lived around 971-931 BCE while Hezekiah was said to have lived much later, sometime between 715-697 BCE.

2. Are the Old Testament laws still binding?

Yes, the Old Testament laws are binding forever
Exodus 12:14, 17, 24 "And ye shall observe this thing for an ordinance to thee and to thy sons for ever."
Leviticus 23:14, 21, 31 "It shall be a statute for ever …"
I Chronicles 16:15 "His [covenant] an everlasting covenant."
Luke 16:17 "It is easier for heaven and earth to pass, than one tittle of the law to fail."

No, Christians are not under the Old Testament law
Romans 6:14 "Ye are not under the law, but under grace."
Galatians 3:13 "Christ hath redeemed us from the curse of the law."
Colossians 2:14 "Blotting out the handwriting of ordinances … nailing it to his cross."

2. New Testament

A. The Genealogy of Jesus Christ

1. Which of the following genealogies of Jesus is correct?

King James	New Am. Standard	Douay Rheims	King James	New Am. Standard	Douay Rheims	King James	New Am. Standard	Douay Rheims
Matt 1:1-16	Matt 1:1-16	Matt 1:1-16	Luke 3:23-38	Luke 3:23-38	Luke 3:23-38	I Chron. 3:10-19	I Chron. 3:10-19	I Paralipomenon 3:1-19
			Adam	Adam	Adam			
			Seth	Seth	Seth			
			Enos	Enosh	Henos			
			Cainan	Cainan	Cainan			
			Maleleel	Mahalaleel	Malaleel			
			Jared	Jared	Jared			
			Enoch	Enoch	Henoch			
			Mathusala	Methuselah	Mathusale			
			Lamech	Lamech	Lamech			
			Noe	Noah	Noe			
			Sem	Shem	Sem			
			Arphaxad	Arphaxad	Arphaxad			
			Cainan	Cainan	Cainan			
			Sala	Shelah	Sale			
Abraham	Abraham	Abraham	Abraham	Abraham	Abraham			
Isaac	Isaac	Isaac	Isaac	Isaac	Isaac			
Jacob	Jacob	Jacob	Jacob	Jacob	Jacob			
Judas	Judah	Judas	Juda	Judah	Judas			
Phares	Perez	Phares	Phares	Perez	Phares			
Esrom	Hezron	Esron	Esrom	Hezron	Esron			
Aram	Ram	Aram	Aram	Ram	Aram			
				Admin				
Aminadab	Amminadab	Aminadab	Aminadab	Amminadab	Aminadab			
Naasson	Nahshon	Naasson	Naasson	Nahshon	Naasson			
Salmon	Salmon	Salmon	Salmon	Salmon	Salmon			
Booz	Boaz	Booz	Booz	Boaz	Booz			
Obed	Obed	Obed	Obed	Obed	Obed			
Jesse	Jesse	Jesse	Jesse	Jesse	Jesse			
King David	King David	King David	King David	King David	King David	King David	King David	King David
Solomon	Solomon	Solomon	Nathan	Nathan	Nathan	Solomon	Solomon	Solomon
Roboam	Rehoboam	Roboam	Mattatha	Mattatha	Mathatha	Rehoboam	Rehoboam	Roboam
Abia	Abijah	Abia	Menan	Menna	Menna	Abia	Abijah	Abia
Asa	Asa	Asa	Melea	Melea	Melea	Asa	Asa	Asa
Josaphat	Jehoshaphat	Josaphat	Eliakim	Eliakim	Eliakim	Jehoshaphat	Jehoshaphat	Josaphat
Joram	Jehoram	Joram	Jonan	Jonam	Jona	Joram	Joram	Joram
Ozias	Uzziah	Ozias	Joseph	Joseph	Joseph	Azariah	Ahaziah	Ochozias
Joatham	Jotham	Joatham	Juda	Judah	Judas	Joash	Joash	Joas
Achaz	Ahaz	Achaz	Simeon	Simeon	Simeon	Amaziah	Amaziah	Amasias
Ezekias	Hezekiah	Ezechias	Levi	Levi	Levi	Azariah	Azariah	Azarias
Manasses	Manasseh	Manasses	Matthat	Matthat	Mathat	Jotham	Jotham	Joatham
Amon	Amon	Amon	Jorim	Jorim	Jorim	Ahaz	Ahaz	Achaz
Josias	Josiah	Josias	Eliezer	Eliezer	Eliezer	Hezekiah	Hezekiah	Ezechias
Jeconias	Jeconiah	Jeconias	Jose	Joshua	Joshua	Manasseh	Manasses	Manasses

(Babylonian Captivity)	(Babylonian Captivity)	(Babylonian Captivity)						
Salathiel	Shealtiel	Salathiel	Er	Er	Her	Amon	Amen	Amen
Zorababel	Zerubbabel	Zorobabel	Elmodam	Elmadam	Helmadam	Josiah	Josias	Josiah
Abiud	Abiud	Abiud	Cosam	Cosam	Cosan	Jehoiakim	Joakim	Jehoiakim
Eliakim	Eliakim	Eliacim	Addi	Addi	Addi	Jeconiah	Jechonias	Jeconiah
Azor	Azor	Azor	Melchi	Melchi	Melchi			
Sadoc	Zadok	Sadoc	Neri	Neri	Neri			
Achim	Achim	Achim	(Babylonian Captivity)	(Babylonian Captivity)	(Babylonian Captivity)			
Eliud	Eliud	Eliud	Salathiel	Shealtiel	Salathiel			
Eleazar	Eleazar	Eleazar	Zorobabel	Zerubbabel	Zorobabel			
Matthan	Matthan	Mathan	Rhesa	Rhesa	Reza			
Jacob	Jacob	Jacob	Joanna	Joanan	Joanna			
Joseph	Joseph	Joseph	Juda	Joda	Juda			
Jesus	Jesus	Jesus	Joseph	Josech	Joseph			
			Semei	Semein	Semei			
			Matthathias	Matthathias	Mathathias			
			Maath	Maath	Mahath			
			Nagge	Naggai	Nagge			
			Esli	Hesli	Hesli			
			Naum	Nahum	Nahum			
			Amos	Amos	Amos			
			Matthathias	Matthathias	Mathathias			
			Joseph	Joseph	Joseph			
			Janna	Jannai	Janne			
			Melchi	Melchi	Melchi			
			Levi	Levi	Levi			
			Matthat	Matthat	Mathat			
			Heli	Eli (Heli)	Heli			
			Joseph	Joseph	Joseph			
			Jesus	Jesus	Jesus			

Note: *All the genealogies shown above are through the family of Joseph. However, Jesus is not the biological child of Joseph.*

2. How many generations from the Babylonian exile until Jesus Christ?

Thirteen
Matthew 1: 12-16 "After they were brought to Babylon, Jechonias begat Salathiel... Jacob begat Joseph the husband of Mary, of whom was born Jesus, who is called Christ."

Fourteen generations
Matthew 1:17 "And from the carrying away into Babylon unto Christ are fourteen generations."

Note: *However in Matthew 1:18, it is written that Jesus has no biological father.*

3. How many generations were there from Abraham to Jesus?

Forty-two generations
Matthew 1:17 "All the generations from Abraham to David are fourteen generations; and from David until the carrying away into Babylon are fourteen generations; and from the carrying away into Babylon unto Christ are fourteen generations."

Forty-one generations
Matthew 1:2-16 "Abraham begat Isaac; and ... Jacob begat Joseph the husband of Mary, of whom was born Jesus, who is called Christ."

4. How many generations were there from David to Jesus?

Twenty-eight generations
Matthew 1:17 "All the generations from Abraham to David are fourteen generations; and from David until the carrying away into Babylon are fourteen generations; and from the carrying away into Babylon unto Christ are fourteen generations."

Forty-three generations
Luke 3:23-31 "Jesus ... the son of Joseph, which was the son of Heli ... which was the son of Nathan, which was the son of David"

5. We should avoid genealogies

I Timothy 1:4 "Neither give heed to fables and endless genealogies ..."
Titus 3:9 "Avoid foolish disputes, genealogies ..."

Note: Matthew 1:1-17 and Luke 3:23-38 discusses about the genealogy of Jesus Christ.

B. The Nativity

1. Was Joseph the father of Jesus Christ?

Yes, Joseph was the father of Jesus Christ
II Timothy 2:8 "Remember that Jesus Christ of the seed of David ..."
Hebrews 2:16 "For verily he [Jesus] ... took on him the seed of Abraham."
Revelation 22:16 "I [Jesus] am the root and the offspring of David."

No, Joseph was not the father of Jesus Christ
Matthew 1:18 "Mary ... was found with child of the Holy Ghost."
Matthew 22:45 "If David then call him Lord, how is he his son?"

Note: According to the scriptures, the savior had to be a biological descendant of David. But Jesus was not a biological child of Joseph whose ancestor was David.

2. Did the angel visitation occur before Jesus was conceived?

No, after conception
Matthew 1:18-21 "Mary was espoused to Joseph … she was found with child … the angel of the Lord appeared unto him [Joseph] …"

Yes, before conception
Luke 1:26-31 "The angel came in unto her, and said, Hail, thou that art highly favoured, the Lord is with thee … behold, thou shalt conceive in thy womb"

Note: The book of Matthew is the only book that mentions about the angel visitation to Joseph, and the angel visitation to Mary can only be found in the book of Luke.

3. To whom did the angel spoke?

To Joseph
Matthew 1:20 "While he [Joseph] thought on these things, behold, the angel of the Lord appeared unto him in a dream …"

To Mary
Luke 1:28 "The angel came in unto her [Mary] …"

Note: The book of Matthew only mentions the angel visitation made to Joseph and the book of Luke only mentions the angel visitation to Mary.

4. Was Jesus born during the time of King Herod?

Yes, during the time of King Herod
Matthew 2:1 "Jesus was born … in the days of Herod the King …"

No, during the time of Quirinius (Cyrenius)
Luke 2:1-2 "Cyrenius (Quirinius) was governor of Syria … she [Mary] brought forth her … son"

Note: King Herod died ten years before Quirinius became the governor of Syria. If Jesus was born during the time of Quirinius, his nativity must be sometime during AD 6. If Jesus was born during the time of King Herod, his nativity must be sometime on or before 4 BC because Herod the Great died during 4 BC.

5. Where did Joseph and Mary reside prior to the birth of Jesus?

Bethlehem, traveled to Egypt and then moved to Nazareth

Matthew 2:1, 14, 21-23 "Jesus was born in Bethlehem ... he [Joseph] took the young child and his mother ... and departed into Egypt ... and dwelt in a city called Nazareth."

Nazareth, then traveled to Bethlehem
Luke 2:1-4 "Joseph also went ... unto the city of David, which is called Bethlehem; (because he was of the house and lineage of David)."

6. Was Jesus born in Bethlehem?

Joseph and Mary were already living in Bethlehem
Matthew 2:1 "Jesus was born in Bethlehem ..."

Joseph and Mary had to travel to Bethlehem
Luke 2:15-16 "Let us now go even unto Bethlehem ..."

Note: Did Joseph and Mary really have to travel to Bethlehem to take part in a census and taxation? People are taxed based on where they are and not on where they come from. The census ordered by Quirinius happened at a much later date and it only happened in Judea not in Galilee. It is highly unlikely that a very pregnant Mary could have traveled for 90 miles on a donkey without loosing her baby.

7. Who visited Jesus in his crib?

Astrologers, visited Jesus in a house
Matthew 2:1-2, 11 "There came wise men ... [saying] we have seen his star in the east, and are come to worship him ... they came into the *house* ..."

Shepherds visited Jesus in a manger
Luke 2:15-16 "They [shepherds] came ... and found ... the babe lying in a manger."

Note: The wise men visitation is mentioned only in the book of Matthew, and the shepherd visitation is mentioned only in the book of Luke. Jesus was visited by the wise men in a house indicating that the visitation happened at a much later time. The Bible did not give out the names of the three wise men. However, the three wise men are commonly known as Melchior, Caspar and Balthazar who gifted Jesus with gold, frankincense and myrrh.

8. Was the infant Christ taken to Egypt?

Yes, the family fled to Egypt
Matthew 2:14 "He ... took the young child and his mother ... into Egypt."

No, the family did no go anywhere and there was no slaughter of the infants
Luke 2:22, 39 "They brought him to Jerusalem ... [to] Galilee, to... Nazareth."

Note: John the Baptist must have been under two years old during the massacre of the infants but was spared of the infant killings. There is no historical account that the massacre of the infants ever took place other than the Bible.

9. Massacre of the innocents

Matthew 2:16 "Herod ... slew all the children [in Bethlehem] ... from two years old and under."

C. Mary the mother of Jesus Christ

1. Is Mary the mother of God?

Yes, Mary is the mother of God
Luke 1:43 "The mother of my Lord should come to me?"

Note: Mary was declared the mother of God with the Theotokos or the Mother of God dogma in the Ecumenical Council of Ephesus in 431 AD. A dogma based on Luke 1:43.

No, because Jesus Christ said he is not God
Matthew 19:17 "He [Jesus] said ... Why callest thou me good? there is none good but ... God."

2. Is Mary an ever virgin?

No
Matthew 1:25 "And [Joseph] knew her not till she had brought forth her firstborn son: and he called his name JESUS."
Matthew 13:55-56 "Is not this the carpenter's son? Is not his mother called Mary? And his brethren, James, and Joseph, and Simon, and Judas? And his sisters, are they not all with us?"

Note: The verse "And knew her not till ..." suggest that Mary was a virgin only up to the time of the birth of Jesus.

Yes
Ezekiel 44:2 "Then said the Lord unto me; This gate shall be shut, it shall not be opened, and no man shall enter in by it ... it shall be shut?"

Note: Mary's virginity was also written in the following verse from a non-

biblical book written about 150 AD,

The Proto-Gospel of James:
Proto-Gospel of James 19:3 "The midwife went out of the cave and Salome met her. And she said to her, "Salome, Salome, I can describe a new wonder to you. A virgin has given birth, contrary to her natural condition." Salome replied, "As the Lord of my God lives, if I do not insert my finger and examine her condition, I will not believe that the virgin has given birth."

The book History of Joseph the Carpenter says that the six children of Joseph were from a previous marriage and not with Mary. Joseph was about 90 years of age when he was asked to take the hand of Mary who was 12 years of age at that time. They lived together for two years until eventually he took her as his bride when she was 14 years of age. Joseph passed away at the age of one hundred and eleven years.

In the year 649 AD, the members of the Lateran Synod declared Mary as a forever virgin. The declaration of the perpetual virginity of Mary was based on Ezekiel 44:2.

3. Was Mary the Immaculate Conception?

Mary was declared the Immaculate Conception, born and conceived without original sin
Luke 1:28 "The angel … said, Hail, thou that art highly favoured, the Lord is with thee: blessed art thou among women."
Luke 1:48 "For he hath regarded the low estate of his handmaiden: for, behold, from henceforth all generations shall call me blessed."

Note: In 1476, Pope Sixtus IV declared Mary as the Immaculate Conception and declared December 8 to be the feast day of the Immaculate Conception. Pope Sixtus IV also declared that the Immaculate Conception is not a dogma and therefore the disbelief for such does not result to committing heresy. The Council of Trent (1545-1563) also confirmed the Immaculate Conception and declared it not a dogma. However, on December 8, 1854 Pope Pius IX officially declared the Immaculate Conception as a dogma in his constitution Ineffabilis Deus. The passages in Luke 1:28, 48 were used as the basis for declaring Mary as the Immaculate Conception.

But all have sinned and needs a savior
Luke 1:47 "My [Mary] spirit has rejoiced in God my Savior."
Romans 3:23 "For all have sinned and fall short of the glory of God"

Note: Why did Mary say she has a savior if she does not have the original sin and therefore does not need one?

4. Mary underwent purification for giving birth to the Son of God

Luke 2:22 "The days of her [Mary] purification ... were accomplished ..."

Note: Why should Mary undergo the purification rite for giving birth to the Son of God?

5. Did Mary go to heaven body and soul (Dogma of Assumption)?

No
I Corinthians 15:44, 50 "It is sown a natural body; it is raised a spiritual body ... flesh and blood cannot inherit the kingdom of God; neither doth corruption inherit incorruption."

Yes
John 14:3 "If I go and prepare a place for you, I will come again, and receive you unto myself; that where I am, there ye may be also."

Note: Pope Pius XII declared the dogma of the Assumption of the Blessed Virgin Mary also called Munificentissimus Deus on November 1, 1950. According to this dogma, Mary went to heaven body and soul. There is no biblical passage that supports the Assumption dogma. However, in 2004 Pope John Paul II quoted John 14:3 as the basis for the Dogma of Assumption.

6. Is Mary the mediator of mankind (The Mediatrix Dogma)?

No, only Jesus Christ is the mediator between God and men
I Timothy 2:5 "For there is ... one Mediator between God and men ..."

Note: However, in 1891, Leo XIII mentioned that no one can come to the Father except through the Son but also, no one can come to the Son except through the mother. In 1904, Pope Pius X described Mary as the connector between the Head of the Mystical Body and its Members. In the Second Vatican Council, in November 21, 1964, Pope Paul VI gave Mary the titles Advocate, Adjutrix, Auxiliatrix and Mediatrix, a mediator between man and God.

7. Is Mary the Mother of the Church?

The basis for the declaration of the Mediatrix Dogma
Genesis 3:15 "I will put enmity between thee and the woman ... between thy

seed and her seed ..."

Revelation 12:1-5 "There appeared a great wonder in heaven; a woman clothed with the sun... and she brought forth a man child, who was to rule all nations with a rod of iron: and her child was caught up unto God, and to his throne."

Note: On November 21, 1964, Pope Paul VI issued the Dogmatic Constitution called Lumen Gentium and declared Mary as the Mother of the Church.

8. Should Mary be declared as Co-Redemptrix?

Biblical verses used as reasons to declare Mary as co-redeemer of mankind
Luke 1:38 "Mary said, "Behold the maidservant of the Lord! Let it be to me according to your word.""
Luke 2:34-35 "Then Simeon blessed them, and said to Mary His mother, "Behold, this Child is destined for the fall and rising of many in Israel, and for a sign which will be spoken against (yes, a sword will pierce through your own soul also), that the thoughts of many hearts may be revealed."
John 1:14 "The Word became flesh and dwelt among us, and we beheld His glory, the glory as of the only begotten of the Father, full of grace and truth."
John 19:27 "Then He said to the disciple, "Behold your mother!" And from that hour that disciple took her to his own home"
Galatians 4:4 "But when the fullness of the time had come, God sent forth His Son, born of a woman, born under the law"

Note: Signatures were gathered to urge Pope John Paul II to declare Mary as coredeemer of mankind. In 1985, Pope John Paul II described Mary as co-redemptrix, a co-redeemer of mankind.

D. John the Baptist

1. Was John baptizing in Bethabara or Bethany?

John 1:28 "These things were done in Bethabara beyond Jordan ..."

Note: Some Bible versions renamed Bethabara as Bethany. If Bethabara is indeed Bethany, it is not beyond Jordan but in Jerusalem.

2. Was John imprisoned before Jesus called Peter and Andrew?

Yes, John was imprisoned before Peter and Andrew were called
Mark 1:14, 16-18 "Now *after that John was put in prison,* Jesus came into Galilee ... he saw Simon and Andrew ... And Jesus said ... Come ye after me, and I will make you to become fishers of men. And straightway they ... followed him."

No, Peter and Andrew were called before the imprisonment of John
John 1:40-42; 3:24 "Andrew, Simon Peter's brother. He first findeth his own brother Simon, and saith unto him, We have found the Messias ... And he brought him to Jesus ... *John was not yet cast into prison.*"

3. Was John the Baptist the reincarnation of Elijah?

Yes
Malachi 4:5 "Behold, I will send you Elijah the prophet ..."
Matthew 11:13-14 "For all the prophets and the law prophesied until John And if ye will receive it, this is Elias (Elijah) which was for to come."
Mark 6:14-15 "King Herod ... said, 'That John the Baptist was risen from the dead ... Others said 'That it is Elias (Elijah).'"

No
John 1:21 "They asked him [John the Baptist], What then? Art thou Elias? And he saith, I am not. Art thou that prophet? And he answered, No."

No, all men die once, then judgment follows
Hebrews 9:27 "As it is appointed unto men once to die, but after this the judgment."

4. Did John the Baptist baptize the Pharisees?

Yes
Matthew 3:7-8, 11 "He saw many of the Pharisees and Sadducees come to his baptism, he said unto them ... I indeed baptize you with water unto repentance."

No
Luke 7:29-30 "All the people that heard him ... justified God, being baptized [by] ... John. But the Pharisees and lawyers rejected the counsel of God against themselves, being not baptized of him."

5. Did Herod said that John the Baptist rose from the dead?

Yes
Mark 6:16 "He [Herod] said, It is John, whom I beheaded: he is risen from the dead."

No, Herod was perplexed of this belief
Luke 9:7 "Herod [was perplexed] ... that John was risen from the dead."

6. When did John found out Jesus was the Messiah?

John the Baptist knew Jesus right away

Matthew 3:11 "I indeed baptize you ... but he that cometh after me is mightier than I, whose shoes I am not worthy to bear ..."
John 1:29 "The next day John seeth Jesus ... saith, Behold the Lamb of God, which taketh away the sin of the world ..."

After baptism, while in prison John wanted to know if Jesus is the Messiah
Matthew 11:2-3 "John ... sent two of his disciples, And said unto him, Art thou he that should come, or do we look for another?"

7. Did Herod think that Jesus was John the Baptist?

Yes
Matthew 14:1-2 "Herod [said] ... This is John the Baptist ... risen from the dead ..."

No
Luke 9:9 "Herod said, John have I beheaded; but who is this ..."

8. Jesus mentioned that John the Baptist will restore all things

Matthew 17:11 "Jesus [said] ... Elias truly shall first come, and restore all things."

Note: What things did John the Baptist restore?

E. The baptism and temptation of Jesus Christ

1. Why did John the Baptist baptize Jesus Christ?

Matthew 3:11 "I indeed baptize you with water unto repentance."

Note: Why was Jesus Christ baptized unto repentance if he is God and had never committed a sin?

2. Did John the Baptist recognize Jesus before his baptism?

Yes
Matthew 3:13-14 "Then cometh Jesus ... unto John, to be baptized of him. But John forbad him, saying, I have need to be baptized of thee, and comest thou to me."

No
John 1:32, 33 "John [said] ... 'I saw the Spirit descending from heaven like a dove, and it abode upon him. And I knew him not ..."

3. Where was Jesus baptized?

River of Jordan
Matthew 3:13 "Then cometh Jesus ... to Jordan ... to be baptized of him"
Mark 1:9 "Jesus ... was baptized of John in Jordan."

In Bethabara, beyond Jordan
John 1:28-31 "These things were done in Bethabara beyond Jordan, where John was baptizing ... he [Jesus] should be made manifest to Israel, therefore am I come baptizing with water."

4. Where was Jesus the day after he was baptized?

He was in the wilderness for forty days
Mark 1:9, 12-13 "Jesus came from Nazareth of Galilee, and was baptized of John in Jordan ... and immediately the spirit driveth him into the wilderness"
Luke 4:1-8 "Jesus ... was led by the Spirit into the wilderness ..."

He recruited two disciples and attended a marriage in Cana
John 1:33, 35-37; 2:1 "But he that sent me to baptize with water ... and the two disciple ... followed Jesus ... there was a marriage in Cana of Galilee ..."

5. Who saw the Spirit descending?

Jesus
Matthew 3:16 "He [Jesus] saw the Spirit of God descending like a dove ..."

John
John 1:32 "John [said] I saw the Spirit descending from heaven like a dove"

6. What did the heavenly voice say?

This is...
Matthew 3:17 "A voice ... saying, 'This is my beloved Son, in whom I am well pleased.'"
Thou art ...
Mark 1:11 "A voice ... saying, 'Thou art my beloved Son, in whom I am well pleased.'"
Luke 3:22 "The Holy Ghost descended ... [a voice] said, 'Thou art my beloved Son; in thee I am well pleased.'"

7. In what order did Satan tempt Jesus?

Turn stones to bread, cast thy self down, worship me
Matthew 4:1-9 "Then was Jesus led up of the Spirit [he command]... these stones be made bread ... cast thyself down ... All these things will I give thee, if thou wilt fall down and worship me ..."

Turn stones to bread, worship me, cast thy self down
Luke 4:1-9 "The devil said … command this stone that it be made bread … If thou therefore wilt worship me, all shall be thine … cast thyself down from hence …"

8. Was Jesus tempted in the wilderness?

Yes, then Jesus was taken to a high mountain, and then he went to Galilee
Matthew 4:1, 8, 12 "Then was Jesus led up of the spirit into the wilderness to be tempted of the devil … the devil taketh him up into an exceeding high mountain … he departed into Galilee."

Yes, then Jesus went to Galilee
Mark 1:12-14 "The spirit driveth him [Jesus] into the wilderness … Jesus came into Galilee …"

No
John 2:1-2 "The third day there was a marriage in Cana of Galilee … And both Jesus was called, and his disciples, to the marriage."
James 1:13 "Let no man say when he is tempted, I am tempted of God: for God cannot be tempted with evil, neither tempteth he any man."

Note: If Jesus was tempted by the devil, Jesus is not God.

9. Did Jesus say we should be baptized?

Yes
Matthew 28:18-19 "Jesus [said] …Go ye therefore, and teach all nations, baptizing them in the name of the Father … of the Holy Ghost:"
Mark 16:16 "He that believeth and is baptized shall be saved; but he that believeth not shall be damned."

No
I Corinthians 1:17 "For Christ sent me not to baptize, but to preach the gospel …"

F. The nature and character of Jesus Christ

1. Who was Jesus?

God
John 1:1, 14 "In the beginning was the Word, and the Word was with God, and the Word was God … the Word was made flesh, and dwelt among us."
John 8:58 "Jesus said … I say unto you, Before Abraham was, I am."
John 10:30, 38-39, 14:9, 20:28 "I and my Father are one … The Father is in me, and I in him"

A Son of God
Acts 3:13, 26 "The God of Abraham ... hath glorified his Son Jesus ..."
Acts 4:27 "For of a truth against thy holy child Jesus ..."

A man
Matthew 19:17 "He [Jesus] said ... there is none good but one, that is, God."
Matthew 27:46 "Jesus [cried] My God, my God, why hast thou forsaken me?"
Mark 10:18 "Jesus said ... there is none good but one, that is, God."

A man, a servant of God
Isaiah 42:1 "Behold my servant, whom I uphold ..."
Matthew 12:18 "Behold my servant ..."

A man approved by God
Acts 2:22 "[Jesus] a man approved of God"

Note: Jesus said, "There is none good but one, that is God.", therefore he [Jesus] is saying that he is not good.

2. Was Jesus a ransom for all?

Yes
I Timothy 2:6 "Who gave himself a ransom for all ..."

No, for many
Matthew 20:28 "Even as the Son of man came ... a ransom for many."
Mark 10:45 "For even the Son of man came ... a ransom for many."

No, unless the Father chose to
John 6:44, 65 "No man can come to me, except the Father which hath sent me draw him."

3. God decides who can come to Jesus

Yes, the Father decides who can come to Jesus
John 6:44, 65 "No man can come to me, except the Father which hath sent me draw him."

No, man decides if they want to believe Jesus
John 5:38-43 "Ye have not his word abiding in you: for whom he hath sent, him ye believe not ... And ye will not come to me, that ye might have life ... ye have not the love of God in you. I am come in my Father's name, and ye receive me not."

4. Is Jesus equal to or lesser than the Father?

Yes, Jesus is equal to his father
John 1:1 "In the beginning was the Word ... and the Word was God."
John 10:30 "I and my Father are one."
Philippians 2:5-6, 11 "Who [Jesus], being in the form of God ... Jesus Christ is Lord ..."

No
Matthew 24:36 "But of that day and hour knoweth no man ... but my Father only."
John 14:28 "For my Father is greater than I."
I Corinthians 11:3 "The head of Christ is God."

5. Is Jesus and God the Father one and the same?

Yes
John 1:1, 14 "In the beginning was the Word ... And the Word was made flesh ..."
John 8:58 "Jesus said ... Before Abraham was, I am."
John 10:30-31, 38-39, 14:9, 20:28 "I and my Father are one ... The Father is in me, and I in him."

No
Matthew 24:36 "No one knows about that day or hour ... but only the Father."
John 14:28 "For the Father is greater than I."
I Corinthians 11:3 "The head of Christ is God."

6. Was Jesus the greatest of all?

Yes
Matthew 12:42 "Behold, a greater than Solomon is here."
Luke 11:31 "Behold, a greater than Solomon is here."
Colossians 2:2-3 "[Christ] are hid all the treasures of wisdom and knowledge."

No, Solomon
I Kings 3:12 "There was none like thee before thee, neither after thee shall any arise like unto thee."

No, John the Baptist
Matthew 11:11 "There hath not risen a greater than John the Baptist."

7. Who was the greatest of all the prophets?

Moses
Deuteronomy 34:10 "There arose not a prophet ... like unto Moses ..."

John the Baptist
Luke 7:28 "There is not a greater prophet than John the Baptist."

Jesus
Hebrews 3:1-3 "[Jesus] was counted worthy of more glory than Moses, inasmuch as he who hath builded the house hath more honour than the house."

8. Was Jesus the only one who raised the dead?

No, Elijah raised a woman's son
I Kings 17:17-22 "The son of the woman ... fell sick ... there was no breath left in him ... and he [Elijah] ... cried unto the Lord ... and the soul of the child came into him again, and he revived."

No, Elisha did before Jesus' time
II King 4:32-35 "When Elisha was come into the house, behold, the child was dead ... he went up ... and stretched himself upon the child nd the child opened his eyes."

9. Was Jesus the first to rise from the dead?

Yes, Jesus was the first to rise from the dead
Acts 26:23 "He [Christ] should be the first that should rise from the dead ..."
I Corinthians 15:20 "Christ risen from the dead, and become the firstfruits of them that slept."

No, a woman's son was raised by Elijah
I Kings 17:17-22 "The son of the woman ... fell sick ... there was no breath left in him ... And he [Elijah] ... cried unto the Lord ... and the soul of the child came into him again, and he revived."

No, a dead child was raised by Elisha
II King 4:32-35 "Elisha was come into the house, behold, the child was dead ... he went up ... and stretched himself upon the child ... and the child opened his eyes."

No, a dead man was raised from the dead who happened to touch Elisha's bones
II Kings 13:21 "As they were burying a man ... and when the man ... touched the bones of Elisha, he revived, and stood up on his feet."

Note: Elisha the son of Shaphat of Abel-Meholah, was an attendant and disciple of Elijah (I Kings 19:16-19).

No, Jesus raised Lazarus, a maiden, a widow's son and other people
Matthew 9:23-25 "He [Jesus] ... took her by the hand, and the maid arose."

Luke 7:12-15 "There was a dead man carried out ... And he [Jesus] said ... Arise. And he that was dead sat up, and began to speak."
John 11:43-44 "He [Jesus] cried with a loud voice ... he [Lazarus] that was dead came forth ..."

No, Jesus instructed his disciples to raise the dead
Matthew 10:8 "Heal the sick ... raise the dead ..."
Matthew 11:5 "The blind receive their sight ... the dead are raised up ..."

No, Moses and Elias rose from the dead (?)
Luke 9:29-30 "Behold, there talked with him ... Moses and Elias."

10. How powerful was Jesus?

Jesus did not have much power
Matthew 13:58 "He [Jesus] did not many mighty works ... because of their unbelief."
Matthew 20:23 "He saith ... to sit on my right hand, and on my left, is not mine to give ..."

Jesus had much power
Matthew 17:20 "Jesus said ... If ye have faith as a grain of mustard seed ... nothing shall be impossible unto you."
Mark 16:17-18 "In my name shall they cast out devils ... speak with new tongues ... and they shall recover."
Luke 17:6 "The Lord said, If ye had faith as a grain of mustard seed ..."
Jesus was all-powerful
Matthew 28:18 "Jesus [said] All power is given unto me in heaven and in earth."
John 3:35 "The Father ... hath given all things into his [Jesus] hand."

11. Was Jesus peaceable?

No
Matthew 10:21-22, 34-35 "The brother shall deliver up the brother to death ... ye shall be hated of all men for my name's sake ... I came not to send peace, but a sword ..."
John 15:6 "If a man abide not in me, he is cast forth as a branch, and is withered; and men gather them, and cast them into the fire, and they are burned."

Yes
Luke 2:13-14 "Suddenly ... [an] angel ... saying Glory to God in the highest, and on earth peace to men on whom his favor rests."
John 14:27 "Peace I leave with you, my peace I give unto you."

Note: The verse John 15:6 was used for centuries to justify the burning of people at stake for refusing to believe in Jesus Christ. It is the main basis and justification of the Roman Catholic tribunal called The Inquisition.

As Proverbs 6:16-19 says:
Proverbs 6:16-19 "These six things doth the Lord hate: yea, seven are an abomination unto him ... he that soweth discord among brethren."

If Jesus is sowing discord among families as stated in Matthew 10 and Luke 12, Jesus might be doing something that is considered an abomination to the Lord.

12. Unbelief of Jesus Christ is equated with evil

John 3:18-19 "He that believeth not is condemned already ... light is come into the world, and men loved darkness rather than light, because their deeds were evil."
Hebrews 3:12 "Take heed, brethren, lest there be in any of you an *evil heart of unbelief*, in departing from the living God."

13. Was Jesus meek and humble?

Yes
John 16:33 "These things I have spoken unto you, that in me ye might have peace ..."
Matthew 11:29 "Take my yoke upon you ... for I am meek and lowly in heart."

No
John 2:15 "He [Jesus] had made a scourge of small cords, he drove them all out of the temple ..."

14. Is Jesus the only way to God?

John: 14:6 "Jesus saith ... I am the way ... no man cometh unto the Father, but by me."

Note: The gospels Matthew, Mark and Luke did not mention this statement, which is quite an important one.

15. Are those who believe Jesus Christ for God?

Yes
I John 4:2 "Every spirit that confesseth that Jesus Christ is come in the flesh is of God."

I John 4:15, 5:1 "Whosoever shall confess that Jesus is the Son of God, God dwelleth in him, and he in God ... Whosoever believeth that Jesus is the Christ is born of God."

No
Matthew 8:29 "They [the devils] cried out, saying ... Jesus, thou Son of God?"
James 2:19 "Thou believest that there is one God ... the devils also believe, and tremble."

16. Is Jesus the same as Satan?

They are both the morning star
Isaiah 14:12 "How art thou fallen from heaven, O Lucifer, son of the morning"
Revelation 22:16 "I Jesus have sent mine angel to testify unto you these things in the churches. I am the root ... the bright and morning star."

Jesus is the Lion and the devil is like a lion
I Peter 5:8 "Be sober, be vigilant; because your adversary the devil, as a roaring lion, walketh about, seeking whom he may devour."
Revelation 5:5 "One of the elders saith unto me, Weep not: behold, the Lion of the tribe of Judah, the Root of David ..."

They both existed before the universe began
Job 38:4-7 "Where wast thou when I laid the foundations of the earth ... When the morning stars sang together, and all the sons of God shouted for joy?"
John 1:1 "In the beginning was the Word, and the Word was with God, and the Word was God."

They are both sons of God
Job 1:6, 2:1 "Now there was a day when the sons of God came to present themselves before the Lord, and Satan came also among them ..."
Mark 1:1 "The beginning of the gospel of Jesus Christ, the Son of God."

17. Who is a ransom for whom?

Jesus
Mark 10:45 "For even the Son of man came ... to give his life a ransom for many."
I Timothy 2:5-6 "Christ Jesus; Who gave himself a ransom for all, to be testified in due time."

The wicked and the transgressor

Proverbs 21:18 "The wicked shall be a ransom for the righteous, the transgressor for the upright"

18. Should Christ's followers keep all the provisions of the Jewish Laws?

Yes
Matthew 5:17-18 "Think not that I am come to destroy the law … Till heaven and earth pass, one jot or one tittle shall in no wise pass from the law, till all be fulfilled."

No
Romans 6:15 "What then? … we are not under the law, but under grace? God forbid."

19. Was Jesus trustworthy?

No
John 5:31 "If I bear witness of myself, my witness is not true."
John 7:10 "Went he [Jesus] also up unto the feast, not openly, but as it were in secret."

Yes
Matthew 5:37 "But let your communication be, Yea, yea; Nay, nay: for whatsoever is more than these cometh of evil."
John 8:14 "Though I bear record of myself, yet my record is true."
John 18:37 "Jesus answered … for this cause came I into the world, that I should bear witness unto the truth. Every one that is of the truth heareth my voice."

20. Did Christ receive testimony from man?

No
John 5:33-34 "Ye sent unto John, and he bare witness unto the truth. But I receive not testimony from man: but these things I say, that ye might be saved."

Yes
John 15:27 "Ye also shall bear witness, because ye have been with me from the beginning."

21. Did Jesus come to abolish the law?

No, the law is permanent
Matthew 5:17-19 "I am not come to destroy [the law], but to fulfill … Till

heaven and earth pass, one jot or one tittle shall in no wise pass from the law, till all be fulfilled."

Luke 16:17 "It is easier for heaven and earth to pass, than one tittle of the law to fail."

Yes

Ephesians 2:15 "Having abolished in his [Jesus] flesh the enmity, even the law of commandments contained in ordinances."

Hebrews 7:18-19 "For there is verily a disannulling of the commandment going before for the weakness and unprofitableness thereof. For the law made nothing perfect, but the bringing in of a better hope did."

22. Would Jesus inherit David's throne?

No

I Chronicles 3:16 "The sons of Jehoiakim: Jeconiah his son …"

Jeremiah 22:24 "As I live, saith the Lord, *through Coniah* … yet I pluck thee thence."

Jeremiah 22:30 "Thus saith the Lord, write ye this man (Coniah) childless … for *no man of his seed shall prosper, sitting upon the throne of David* …"

Jeremiah 36:30 "Therefore this saith the Lord of Jehoiakim king of Judah; *He shall have none to sit upon the throne of David.*"

Yes

Luke 1:32 "He [Jesus] shall be great, and shall be called the Son of the highest; and the Lord God shall give unto him the throne of his father David."

Note: Jeconiah (Coniah) and Jehoiakim were ancestors of Jesus Christ. Jeconiah and Jehoiakim were both cursed that they will have none of their descendants to sit at the throne of David.

23. Who can cast out the devils?

The followers of Jesus Christ

Mark 16:17 "In my name shall they cast out devils."

Even the non-followers can cast out devils

Matthew 7:22-23 "Many will say to me … in thy name have cast out devils? … And then will I profess unto them, I never knew you: depart from me …"

24. Was Jesus all-knowing?

Yes

John 16:30 "Now are we sure that thou knowest all things."

John 21:17 "Lord, thou knowest all things."

Colossians 2:3 "In whom [Jesus] are hid all the treasures of wisdom and knowledge."

No
Matthew 24:36 "But of that day and hour knoweth no man ... but my Father only."
Mark 13:32 "But of that day and that hour knoweth no man ... but the Father."
Luke 2:52 "Jesus increased in wisdom and stature, and in favour with God and man."
Luke 8:44-45 "[A woman] came ... touched ... his garment ... Jesus said, Who touched me?"

25. Jesus was not accepted by his own countrymen

Matthew 13:54-57 "When he was come into his own country ... they were astonished ... and offended in him. But Jesus said unto them, A prophet is not without honour, save in his own country, and in his own house."

G. The teachings of Jesus Christ

1. Comparison of the Beatitudes

[KJ] Matthew 5:3-11
"Blessed are the poor in spirit: for theirs is the kingdom of heaven.
Blessed are they that mourn: for they shall be comforted.
Blessed are the meek: for they shall inherit the earth.
Blessed are they which do hunger and thirst after righteousness:
	for they shall be filled.
Blessed are the merciful: for they shall obtain mercy.
Blessed are the pure in heart: for they shall see God.
Blessed are the peacemakers: for they shall be called the children of God.
Blessed are they which are persecuted for righteousness' sake:
	for theirs is the kingdom of heaven.
Blessed are ye, when men shall revile you, and persecute you,
	and shall say all manner of evil against you falsely, for my sake."

[DR] Matthew 5:3-11
"Blessed are the poor in spirit: for theirs is the kingdom of heaven.
Blessed are the meek: for they shall posses the land.
Blessed are they who mourn: for they shall be comforted.
Blessed are they that hunger and thirst after justice:
	for they shall have their fill.
Blessed are the merciful: for they shall obtain mercy.
Blessed are the clean of heart: for they shall see God.
Blessed are the peacemakers: for they shall be called the children of God

Blessed are they that suffer persecution for justice' sake:
    for theirs is the kingdom of heaven.
Blessed are ye when they shall revile you, and persecute you,
    and speak all that is evil against you, untruly, for my sake:"

Luke 6:20-22
    "Blessed be ye poor: for yours is the kingdom of God.
    Blessed are ye that hunger now: for ye shall be filled.
    Blessed are ye that weep now: for ye shall laugh.
    Blessed are ye, when men shall hate you,
        and when they shall separate you from their company,
        and shall reproach you, and cast out your name as evil,
        for the Son of man's sake."

2. Should we love our enemies?

Yes
Matthew 5:39 "Whosoever shall smite thee on thy right cheek, turn to him the other also."
Matthew 5:44 "Love your enemies, bless them that curse you, do good to them that hate you …"

Jesus hurled epithets at his opponents
Matthew 11:21-22 "Woe unto thee, Chorazin! woe unto thee, Bethsaida!… And thou, Capernaum … shalt be brought down to hell …"
Matthew 12:34, 16:3 "O generation of vipers … O ye hypocrites …"

God is likened to one who would destroy his enemies
Luke 19:27 "But those mine enemies … slay them before me."

Avoid anyone who does not hold the right doctrine
II John 1:9-11 "Whosoever transgresseth, and abideth not in the doctrine of Christ … receive him not … neither bid him God speed."

Jesus told the apostles not to go to the Gentiles and Samaritans
Matthew 10:5 "Jesus [said] … Go not into … the Gentiles … the Samaritans"

3. What did Jesus say about calling someone a fool?

We should not call someone a fool
Matthew 5:22 "[Jesus said] … whosoever shall say, Thou fool, shall be in danger of hell fire."

Jesus called someone a fool
Matthew 7:26 "Every one that heareth these sayings of mine, and doeth them not, shall be likened unto a foolish man …"

Matthew 25:1-12 "Then shall the kingdom of heaven be likened unto ten virgins, which took their lamps ... five were foolish."

4. Jesus said a man was born blind so God can show off his ability to heal

John 9:1-3 "Jesus [said about the blind man] ... Neither hath this man sinned, nor his parents: but that the works of God should be made manifest in him."

5. What did Jesus say about salvation?

Jesus said only few people will be saved
Matthew 7:14 "Because strait is the gate, and narrow ... few there be that find it."
Matthew 22:14 "For many are called, but few are chosen."

Jesus implied that all will be saved
John 12:32 "I, if I be lifted up from the earth, will draw *all men* unto me."

6. Should the gospel be preached to everyone?

No, the gospel should not be preached to the Gentiles and Samaritans
Matthew 10:5-6 "Jesus [said] Go not into ... the Gentiles ... But go rather to the lost sheep of the house of Israel."
Matthew 15:24 "I am not sent but unto the lost sheep of the house of Israel."
Acts 16:6 [Paul and his companions] ... were forbidden of the Holy Ghost to preach ... in Asia."

Yes, to everyone
Matthew 28:19 "Go ye therefore, and teach all nations, baptizing them ..."
Mark 16:15 "Go ... preach the gospel to every creature."

7. What did Jesus say about being killed?

Jesus taught his followers not to fear being killed
Matthew 10:28 "Fear not them which kill the body ..."
Luke 12:4 "I say ... Be not afraid of them that kill the body ..."

For fear of being killed, Jesus avoided the Jews
Matthew 12:14-16 "The Pharisees ... held a council [on] ... how they might destroy him ... He [Jesus] withdrew himself from thence ... [Jesus told the multitude] ... not [to] make him known."
John 7:1 "He [Jesus] would not walk in Jewry, because the Jews sought to kill him."

8. What did Jesus say concerning swords?

Jesus came not to send peace but a sword
Matthew 10:34 "I came not to send peace, but a sword."

Dispose of swords
Matthew 26:52 "Jesus unto him, Put up again thy sword into his place: for all they that take the sword shall perish with the sword."
John 18:11 "Then said Jesus unto Peter, Put up thy sword into the sheath: the cup which my Father hath given me, shall I not drink it?"

Note: John 18:11 was the basis for the formation of a group called Circumcellions (Agonistici). They would attack random travelers with clubs called 'Israelites' while shouting, "Praise God!" in Latin hoping to provoke retaliation and being killed in order to achieve martyrdom. They would also leap off from high walls or cliffs in order to die as martyrs.

Sell you garment to be able to buy a sword
Luke 22:36 "Then said Jesus ... he that hath no sword, let him sell his garment, and buy one."

9. Concerning the Christian yoke

The Christian yoke is easy
Matthew 11:30 "For my yoke is easy, and my burden is light."

The Christian yoke is not easy
John 16:33 "These things I have spoken ... In the world ye shall have tribulation."
II Timothy 3:12 "All that will live godly in Christ Jesus shall suffer persecution."
Hebrews 12:6-7 "For whom the Lord loveth he chasteneth ... If ye endure chastening, God dealeth with you as with sons ..."

10. Did Jesus say anything secretly?

Yes, Jesus said he spoke in parables, to keep his teachings secret to some
Matthew 13:10-11 "The disciples [asked Jesus] ... Why speakest ... in parables? He [Jesus] answered ... Because it is given unto you ... but to them it is not given."
Matthew 13:34 "All these things spake Jesus unto the multitude in parables."

No, Jesus said he did not taught things secretly but openly
John 18:20 "Jesus [said], I spake openly to the world ... and in secret have I said nothing."

Note: Unlike in other gospels, in the Gospel of John Jesus spoke in a more straightforward manner.

11. Jesus said beware of the leaven of whom?

The Pharisees and Sadducees
Matthew 16:6, 11 "Jesus said ... beware of the leaven of the Pharisees and of the Sadducees ... beware of the leaven of the Pharisees and of the Sadducees?"

The Pharisees and Herod
Mark 8:15 "Beware of the leaven of the Pharisees, and of the leaven of Herod."

12. Jesus criticized the Pharisees for not killing their disobedient children

Matthew 15:1-4 "Then came [the] ... Pharisees ... saying, Why ... wash not their hands when they eat bread. But he [Jesus] answered ... Why do ye also transgress the commandment of God ... Honour thy father and mother: and, He that curseth father or mother, let him die the death."

Note: The Pharisees criticized Jesus for not washing his hands. And Jesus criticized back at the Pharisees for not killing their disobedient children as required by the law (See Exodus 21:15, Leviticus 20:9, Deuteronomy 21:18-21).

13. Jesus compared moral character with personal hygiene

Matthew 15:16-20 "Jesus said ... whatsoever entereth in at the mouth goeth into the belly, and is cast out ... But ... to eat with unwashen hands defileth not a man."

14. Jesus told Peter to pay his taxes with a coin he will find in a fish

Matthew 17:27 "Take up the fish that first cometh up; and when thou hast opened his mouth, thou shalt find a piece of money: that take, and give unto them for me and thee."

15. Suffer the little children?

Matthew 19:14 "Jesus said, Suffer little children ... to come unto me ..."
Luke 18:16 "Jesus ... said, Suffer little children to come unto me ..."

Note: Both the King James and the Catholic Bible shows:
    "Suffer little children come to me ..."
This verse has been corrected in newer Bible translations as follows:
    "Allow the little children, and don't forbid them to come to me ..."

16. A camel or a rope?

It is easier for a camel to go through the eye of a needle
Matthew 19:24 "It is easier for a camel to go through the eye of a needle, than for a rich man to enter into the kingdom of God."

Note: The Greek word for rope is kamilos and for camel is kamelos. An error in translation of the original text of the Bible is perpetuated in every Bible that is written. What Jesus could have actually meant was, it is easier for a rope (instead of a camel) to enter the eye of a needle than for a rich man to enter the kingdom of heaven.

17. Jesus said call no man your father on earth

Yes
Matthew 23:9 "Call no man your father upon the earth: for one is your Father, which is in heaven."

No
Exodus 20:12 "Honour thy father and thy mother."
II Kings 2:12; 6:21 "Elisha ... cried, My father, my father ..."

18. What did Jesus say about his believers and followers?

Jesus said his followers will be killed
Matthew 24:9 "Then shall they deliver you up to be afflicted, and shall kill you."

Jesus said his followers will not be killed
John 8:51 "Verily, verily, I say unto you, If a man keep my saying, he shall never see death."

19. Jesus told his disciples to eat his body and drink his blood

Matthew 26:26-28 "Jesus [said], Take, eat; this is my body. And he took the cup ... saying, Drink ye all of it; For this is my blood ... which is shed for many for the remission of sins."

20. What did Jesus say about bearing his own witness?

My testimony is not true
John 5:31 "If I bear witness of myself, my testimony is not true."

My testimony is true
John 8:14 "Jesus answered ... 'Though I bear record of myself, yet my record is true ..."

John 8:18 "I am one that bear witness of myself, the Father that sent me beareth witness of me."

21. Did Jesus receive testimony from man?

Yes
John 5:33-34 "You have sent to John and he has testified to the truth. Not that I accept human testimony; but I mention it that you may be saved."

No
John 15:27 "You also must testify, for you have been with me from the beginning."

22. Did Jesus told his disciples all?

Yes
John 15:15 "For all things that I have heard of my Father I have made known unto you."

No
John 16:12 "I have yet many things to say unto you, but ye cannot bear them now."

23. Did Jesus come to this world to bear witness to the truth?

Yes, Jesus came to this world to bear witness to the truth
John 18:37 "Jesus answered … To this end was I born, and for this cause came I into the world, that I should bear witness unto the truth. Every one that is of the truth heareth my voice."

The truth has always been evident
Romans 1:18-20 "For the wrath of God is revealed from heaven against all ungodliness and unrighteousness of men, who hold the truth in unrighteousness; Because that which may be known of God is manifest in them; for God hath shewed it unto them. For the invisible things of him from the creation of the world are clearly seen, being understood by the things that are made, even his eternal power and Godhead; so that they are without excuse."

24. Does the Gospel of Luke include all the works of Jesus?

No
John 21:25 "There are also many other things which Jesus did, the which, if they should be written every one, I suppose that even the world itself could not contain the books that should be written."

Yes
Acts 1:1-2 "The former treatise have I made, O Theophilus, of all that Jesus began both to do and teach, Until the day in which he was taken up."

25. Luke admits his writing about Jesus is not a first hand account

Luke 1:1-4 "Forasmuch as many have taken in hand to set forth in order a declaration of those things which are most surely believed among us, *Even as they delivered them unto us, which from the beginning were eyewitnesses, and ministers of the word* ... wherein thou hast been instructed."

H. The public life of Jesus Christ

1. Was the crowd impressed with the miracle of loaves?

No
Mark 6:52 "For they considered not the miracle of the loaves: for their heart was hardened."

Yes
John 6:14 "Then those men, when they had seen the miracle that Jesus did, said, This is of a truth that prophet that should come into the world."

Note: The feeding of the multitude by Jesus Christ was very much similar to the feeding of the multitude by Elisha in II Kings 4:42-44.

2. Where did Jesus go after feeding the multitude?

Gennesaret
Mark 6:53 "They came into the land of Gennesaret ..."

Capernaum
John 6:17-25 "[They] ... went over the sea toward Capernaum ..."

3. The disciples asked how to feed a multitude after feeding a multitude

Jesus and his disciples fed a multitude through miraculous means
Matthew 14:16-21 "Jesus said ... give ye them [the multitude] to eat. And they [disciples] say unto him, We have ... five loaves, and two fishes ... And he [Jesus blessed] ... And they did all eat, and were filled ... about five thousand men, beside women and children."

The disciples asked how they can feed 4,000 after feeding about 5,000
Matthew 15:33 "His disciples say unto him, Whence should we have so much bread in the wilderness, as to fill so great a multitude?"

Note: The disciples wondered how they could feed a multitude of 4,000 when they just recently fed a multitude of 5,000 through some sort of miraculous means.

4. Where did the devil take Jesus?

The devil took Jesus to the pinnacle of the temple, and then to the mountaintop
Matthew 4:5-8 "Then the devil taketh him up into the holy city, and setteth him on a pinnacle of the temple ... Again, the devil taketh him up into an exceeding high mountain ..."

The devil took Jesus to the mountaintop, then to the pinnacle of the temple
Luke 4:5-9 "The devil, taking him up into a mountain. [And] set him on a pinnacle of the temple"

5. Did Jesus deliver his sermon on the mount?

Yes, Sermon on the mount
Matthew 5:1-3 "He [Jesus] went up into a mountain: and ... he opened his mouth ... saying, Blessed are the poor in spirit: for theirs is the kingdom of heaven ..."

No, Sermon on the plain
Luke 6:17-20 "He came down with them, and stood in the plain ... And he ... said, Blessed be ye poor: for yours is the kingdom of God ..."

6. Coming down from Jerusalem and Jericho

Luke 10:30 "Jesus ... said, A certain man went down from Jerusalem to Jericho ..."

Note: Although Jericho is way up north of Jerusalem; Jesus must be talking about the elevation of the place since Jerusalem is in a much higher elevation than Jericho.

7. To whom did Jesus recite the Lord's Prayer?

To the multitude
Matthew 5:1, 6:9-13, 7:28 "Seeing the multitudes, he [said] ... pray ye: Our Father which art in heaven, Hallowed be thy name ..."

To his disciples
Luke 11:1-4 "One of his disciples said ... Lord, teach us to pray ... And he [Jesus] said unto them, When ye pray, say, Our Father which art in heaven"

8. Did the Samaritans receive Jesus?

No, the Samaritans did not receive him
Luke 9:52-53 "They went [to] ... the Samaritans... they did not receive him."

Yes, the Samaritans received Jesus
John 4:39-40 "Many of the Samaritans of that city believed on him ... So when the Samaritans were come unto him, they besought him that he would tarry with them."

9. About the followers of Jesus

None will be lost
John 10:27-29 "I give unto them eternal life; and they shall never perish ... and no man is able to pluck them out of my Father's hand."

Some will depart from the faith
I Timothy 4:1 "Now the Spirit speaketh expressly, that in the latter times some shall depart from the faith ..."

10. Did Jesus loose the son of perdition?

Yes
John 17:12 "None of them is lost, but the son of perdition ..."
No
John 18:9 "That the saying might be fulfilled, which he spake, Of them which thou gavest me have I lost none."

11. Jesus said there is no sign for this generation

No sign for this generation
Matthew 12:39; 16:4 "But he answered ... an evil and adulterous generation ... there shall no sign be given to it but the sign of the prophet Jonas."

Jesus gave signs
Mark 16:20 "They ... preached every where, the Lord working with them, and confirming the word with signs following."
John 20:30 "Many other signs truly did Jesus in the presence of his disciples"
Acts 2:22 "Jesus ... a man approved of God among you by miracles and wonders and signs ..."

12. Did the centurion request Jesus personally to heal his slave?

Yes
Matthew 8:5-10 "When Jesus was entered into Capernaum, there came unto him a centurion, beseeching him, And saying, Lord, my servant lieth at home sick ..."

No, the centurion sent elders to ask Jesus
Luke 7:2-10 "A certain centurion's servant ... was sick ... he [centurion] sent unto him [Jesus] the elders of the Jews, beseeching him that he would come and heal his servant ..."

13. When did Jesus heal Simon's wife's mother?

After curing a centurion's servant
Matthew 8:13 "Jesus said ... Go thy way ... And his servant was healed ..."
Matthew 8:14-15 "When Jesus was come into Peter's house, he saw his wife's mother laid, and sick of a fever [Jesus] touched her ... the fever left her."

After curing a man with unclean spirit
Mark 1:23, 25-26 "There was in their synagogue a man with an unclean spirit ... And Jesus rebuked him ... he [unclean spirit] came out of him."
Mark 1:29-31 "But Simon's wife's mother lay sick of a fever ... and he came and took her by the hand ... and immediately the fever left her ..."

14. Did Jesus heal all the sick?

Yes, Jesus healed all the sick
Matthew 8:16 "He cast out the spirits ... and healed all that were sick."
Luke 4:40 "He laid his hands on every one of them, and healed them."
Jesus did not necessarily heal all the sick
Mark 1:34 "He [Jesus] healed many that were sick of divers diseases, and cast out many devils; and suffered not the devils to speak, because they knew him."

15. How many were possessed in the Gadarenes (Gergesenes) incident?

Two
Matthew 8:28 "When he was come to ... Gergesenes, there met him two possessed ..."

One
Mark 5:1-2 "They came [to] ... Gadarenes ... there met him ... a man with an unclean spirit ..."

Summary: One or two men was/were possessed by the devils and Jesus ordered the devils to possess the herd of swine instead and the herd drowned themselves.

Note: Jesus was concerned with the man (or men) possessed by the devils but was not concerned with the herd of swine that drowned and the fact that the herd of swine was someone else's property.

16. Where did Jesus meet the possessed man (or men)?

Gergesenes
Matthew 8:28 "When he was come to ... Gergesenes ..."

Gadarenes
Mark 5:1 "They came over [to] ... Gadarenes ..."
Luke 8:26 "They arrived at the country of the Gadarenes ..."

Note: Did the event concerning the possessed man/men and the herd of swine take place in Gadarenes or Gergesenes? Gadarenes is most likely Gadara and Gergesenes must be Gerasa. These are two different cities a few miles away from the Sea of Galilee.

17. Who was the man Jesus saw at the tax collector's office?

Matthew
Matthew 9:9 "He saw ... Matthew, sitting at the receipt of custom ..."

Levi
Mark 2:14 "He saw Levi the son of Alphaeus sitting at the receipt of custom"
Luke 5:27 "[He] saw ... Levi, sitting at the receipt of custom ..."

18. When Jesus met Jairus, was Jairus' daughter already dead?

Yes
Matthew 9:18 "While he spake ... a certain ruler [Jairus] saying, My daughter is even now dead."

No
Mark 5:23 "Besought him ... My little daughter lieth at the point of death."
Luke 8:41-42 "There came ... Jairus ... and he ... besought him [Jesus] ... and she lay a dying."

19. Where was the woman from, who asked help from Jesus?

Canaan
Matthew 15:22 "Behold, a woman of Canaan ..."

Greek
Mark 7:26 "The woman was a Greek ..."

Note: Jesus refused to heal the daughter of a non-Israelite. Was Jesus a racist?

20. Jesus called a woman a dog

Matthew 15:22, 25-26 "A woman [said] … Lord, help me. But he [Jesus] answered … It is not meet to take the children's bread, and to cast it to dogs."
Mark 7:26-27 "The woman … besought him … But Jesus said … it is not meet to take the children's bread, and to cast it unto the dogs."

21. Jesus healed a man by spittle

Mark 7:33 "He [Jesus] took him aside from the multitude, and put his fingers into his ears, and he spit, and touched his tongue."
John 9:6 "When he had thus spoken, he spat on the ground, and made clay of the spittle, and he anointed the eyes of the blind man with the clay."

Note: Jesus who claims to be all-powerful would heal by using spittle? This is an indication that Jesus Christ was probably an herbalist. The medical conditions described in the Bible such as deafness and blindness may actually be medical conditions of lesser gravity such as Otitis Media (instead of deafness) and Conjunctivitis (instead of blindness) which may be cured by herbal means.

22. When did Jesus and his friends went for the transfiguration?

After six days
Matthew 17:1-2 "After six days Jesus taketh Peter, James, and John … up into an high mountain apart … and was transfigured before them"

After eight days
Luke 9:28-29 "It came to pass about an eight days … he took Peter and John and James … And as he prayed, … his countenance was altered, and his raiment was white and glistering."

23. Who requested Jesus for a place in heaven?

The mother of James and John Zebedees asked Jesus a favor for her sons
Matthew 20:21 "She saith unto him, Grant that these my two sons may sit, the one on thy right hand, and the other on the left, in thy kingdom."

James and John Zebedees asked Jesus a favor for themselves
Mark 10:37 "They said unto him, Grant unto us that we may sit, one on thy right hand, and the other on thy left hand, in thy glory."

24. How many blind men asked the help of Jesus?

Two
Matthew 20:30 "Two blind men … cried out … Have mercy on us, O Lord"

One
Mark 10:46-52 "They came to Jericho ... blind Bartimaeus ..."
Luke 18:35 "A certain blind man sat by the way side begging."

25. When did Jesus heal the blind man/men?

After leaving for Jericho
Matthew 20:30 "As they departed from Jericho ... two blind men ..."
Mark 10:46 "As he went out of Jericho... blind Bartimaeus ..."

Before leaving for Jericho
Luke 18:35 "As he was come nigh unto Jericho, a certain blind man ..."

I. The twelve disciples

1. Where did Jesus first meet Simon Peter?

By the Sea of Galilee with his brother Andrew
Mark 1:16 "Now as he walked by the sea of Galilee, he saw Simon and Andrew his brother ..."

By the Lake of Gennesaret with James and John
Luke 5:1-11 "He stood by the lake of Gennesaret ... And so was also James, and John, the sons of Zebedee, which were partners with Simon. And Jesus said unto Simon ..."

By the banks of River Jordan with his brother Andrew
John 1:28, 40-42 "This all happened at Bethany on the other side of the Jordan ... One of the two ... was Andrew ... And he brought him [Simon] to Jesus"

2. Did Jesus baptize with his disciples?

Yes
John 3:22 "Jesus ... tarried with them, and baptized."

No
John 4:2 "Jesus himself baptized not, but his disciples."

3. Did Jesus give the disciples the power to heal?

Jesus gave his disciples the power to heal
Matthew 10:1 "He [Jesus] gave them power ... to heal all manner of sickness and ... disease."

The disciples cannot cure
Matthew 17:16 "I brought him to thy disciples, and they could not cure him."

4. Names of the 12(?) apostles

Apostle	Bible Verse	Comments
Andrew	Mt 10:2; Mk 3:18; Lk 6:14; Ac 1:13	Brother of Peter
Bartholomew	Mt 10:3; Mk 3:18; Lk 6:14; Jn 1:45, 21:2; Ac 1:13	Also Nathaniel
James	Mt 10:2; Mk 3:17; Lk 6:14; Ac 1:13	Son of Zebedee
James	Gal 1:19	Brother of Jesus
James	Mt 10:3; Mk 3:18; Lk 6:15; Ac 1:13	Son of Alphaeus
John	Mt 10:2; Mk 3:17; Lk 6:14; Ac 1:13	Brother of James; Boanerges
Judas	Mt 10:4; Mk 3:19; Lk 6:16	Iscariot
Judas	Lk 6:16; Ac 1:13	Brother of James
Jude	Mt 10:3; Mk 3:18	Also Lebbaeus; Thaddeus
Matthew	Mt 10:3; Mk 3:18; Lk 6:15; Ac 1:13	Tax collector/publican
Mathias	Ac 1:26	Replaced Judas Iscariot
Philip	Mt 10:3; Mk 3:18; Lk 6:14; Ac 1:13	From Bethsaida
Simon	Mt 10:4; Mk 3:18; Lk 6:15; Ac 1:13	Zelotes, the Canaanite
Simon Peter	Mt 10:2; Mk 3:16; Lk 6:14; Jn 1:42; Ac 1:13; I Cor 15:5	Son of Jona, Cephas*
Thomas	Mt 10:3; Mk 3:18; Lk 6:15; Ac 1:13	Called Didymus
Andronicus	Rm 16:7	A relative of Paul
Apollos	I Cor 3:5, 22	Also called Apolonius
Barnabas	Ac 14:14	Previous name was Joseph
Jesus	Heb 3:1	Paul called Jesus an apostle
Junia	Rm 16:7	Junia, a woman
Paul	Rm 1:1; 11:13; I Cor 1:1,3:22; Gal 2:8	Paul appointed himself
Silas	I Thess 1:1, 2:6	Also called Silvanus
Timothy	I Thess 1:1, 2:6	Also called Timotheus

Note: In John 1:42, Peter and Cephas are considered the same person. However, in I Corinthians 15:5, Cephas is not one of the twelve apostles. Therefore, Cephas and Peter might be two different persons.

5. Where did Peter and his brother Andrew come from?

Capernaum
Mark 1:21, 29 "They went into Capernaum ... they entered into the house of Simon and Andrew"

Bethsaida
John 1:44 "Now Philip was of Bethsaida, the city of Andrew and Peter."

6. Should Peter be an apostle to the Gentiles?

No
Matthew 10:5-6 "These twelve Jesus sent forth ... saying, Go not into the way of the Gentiles ..."

Yes
Acts 15:7 "Peter ... said ... that the Gentiles by my mouth should hear the word of the gospel ..."

7. What did Jesus said about keeping staff and shoes (sandals)?

Jesus said his apostles should not keep a staff or shoes for their journey
Matthew 10:9-10 "Provide [neither] scrip for your journey ... nor yet staves "

Jesus said his apostles should keep their staff and shoes on their journey
Mark 6:8-9 "[He] commanded them that they should take nothing for their journey, save a staff only ... But be shod with sandals."

8. When Jesus walked on water how did the disciples react?

They considered Jesus the Son of God
Matthew 14:33 "Then they that were in the ship came and worshipped him, saying, Of a truth thou art the Son of God."

They were just amazed and wondered
Mark 6:51 "They were sore amazed in themselves beyond measure, and wondered."

9. How did Peter found out that Jesus was the Christ?

He just knew
Matthew 16:15-16 "He [Jesus] saith unto them, But whom say ye that I am? And Simon Peter answered and said, Thou art Christ, the Son of the living God."

Thru his brother
John 1:41 "Simon, and saith unto him [Peter], we have found the Messias, which is, being interpreted the Christ."

10. Peter denied Jesus three times

Matthew 10:33 "But whosoever shall deny me before men, him will I also deny before my Father which is in heaven."

Note: Peter denied Jesus three times (Matthew 26:69-75, Mark 14:66-72, Luke 22:55-62, John.15:18-27), Jesus must have also denied Peter before God.

11. Who should feed the flock?

Peter
John 21:17 "Jesus saith unto him [Peter], Feed my sheep."

Peter was exhorting others to feed the Lord's flock
I Peter 5:2 "Feed the flock of God which is among you ..."

12. Was Peter the first head of the church of Christ?

Yes, Jesus considered Peter the head of his church
Matthew 16:18 "I say ... thou art Peter, and upon this rock I will build my church; and the gates of hell shall not prevail against it."

No, Jesus called Peter Satan
Matthew 16:23 "[Jesus] ... said unto Peter, Get thee behind me, Satan."
Mark 8:33 "But ... he rebuked Peter, saying, Get thee behind me, Satan."

No, James made the decisions in the Council of Jerusalem meeting
Acts 15:4-24 "When they were come to Jerusalem ... the apostles ... came together ... *James answered ... hearken unto me ... After this I will return, and will build again the tabernacle of David ... and I will set it up.*"

Note: According to some writers, the Council of Jerusalem was the first council and not the Council of Nicaea. The Book of Acts shows that James was the leader of the Council of Jerusalem and not Peter.

No, Paul mentioned James as the first pillar of the group
Galatians 2:9 "When James, Cephas, and John, who seemed to be pillars ..."

No, Paul mentioned about Peter's behavior when the group was in Antioch
Galatians 2:11-12 "When Peter was come to Antioch, I withstood him to the face, because he was to be blamed ... [Peter] *did eat with the Gentiles*: but when they [apostles] were come, *he withdrew and separated himself,* fearing them ..."

Note: Paul accused Peter of eating with the Gentiles and withdrawing and separating himself from the group.

No, Peter considered himself an elder like the rest and not their leader
I Peter 5:1 "The elders which are among you I exhort, who am also an elder"

J. The triumphal entry of Jesus Christ

1. How many animals were with Jesus?

Two
Matthew 21:2-7 "[Jesus said] ... ye shall find an ass tied, and a colt with her ... And the disciples went ... And brought the ass, and the colt ... and they set him thereon"

One
Mark 11:2-7 "[Jesus] saith …ye shall find a colt … and they brought the colt to Jesus … and he [Jesus] sat upon him."

Note: In Matthew 21:7, the verse says Jesus sat on both animals at the same time, but this is physically impossible.

2. Did Jesus found the animal/s himself?

No, he gave instructions to his disciples on how to find the animal/s
Matthew 21:2-6 "Saying unto them [disciples], Go into the village … ye shall find an ass tied, and a colt with her: loose them, and bring them unto me …"

Yes, Jesus found the animal himself
John 12:14 "Jesus … found a young ass, sat thereon."

3. What did Jesus ride into Jerusalem?

On an ass and a colt
Matthew 21:5-7 "Behold, thy King cometh unto thee, meek, and sitting upon an ass, and a colt the foal of an ass … And brought the ass, and the colt … and they set him [Jesus] thereon."

A colt
Mark 11:7 "They brought the colt to Jesus … and he sat upon him."
Luke 19:35 "They brought him to Jesus … and they set Jesus thereon."

An ass
John 12:14 "Jesus … found a young ass, sat thereon."

Note: Riding on an ass and a colt is not physically feasible.

K. The last days prior to the arrest of Jesus Christ

1. Did Jesus cleanse the temple the same day he went to Jerusalem?

Yes
Matthew 21:10-12 "When he came into Jerusalem … and Jesus went into the temple of God and cast out all them that sold and bought in the temple …"

No
Mark 11:11-15 "Jesus entered into Jerusalem … and now the eventide was come, he went out unto Bethany … And he came back to Jerusalem; and Jesus went into the temple, and began to cast out them that sold and bought in the temple …"

2. When did the cleansing of the temple happen?

The cleansing of the temple happened towards the end of the life of Jesus
Matthew 21:12-13 "Jesus went into the temple ... cast out all them that sold and bought ..."

The cleansing of the temple happened during the early part of Jesus' life
John 2:1, 13-15 "The third day there was a marriage in Cana ... and Jesus went up to Jerusalem. And found in the temple those that sold oxen and ... he drove them all out of the temple ..."

3. What was the temple compared to by Jesus during its cleansing?

A den of thieves
Matthew 21:13 "My house ... ye have made it a den of thieves."

A house of merchandise
John 2:16 "Make not my Father's house an house of merchandise."

4. Jesus with the moneychangers and Jesus' eventual arrest

Jesus cleansed the temple and a plan was made to arrest and kill him
Matthew 21:12-13, 23-25, 27; 26:3-4 "Jesus ... cast out all them that sold [in the temple] ... the chief priests and the elders came unto him and said, by what authority doest thou these things? Jesus [said] Neither tell I you by what authority I do these things. Then assembled together the chief priests, and the scribes ... consulted that they might take Jesus by subtilty, and kill him."
Mark 11:15, 27-30, 33; 14:1 "Jesus ... began to cast out them that sold [in the temple] ... there come to him the chief priests and the elders, And say unto him [Jesus], By what authority doest thou these things? ... Jesus [said] Neither do I tell you by what authority I do these things. The chief priests and the scribes sought how they might take him by craft, and put him to death."
Luke 19:45, 47, 20:1-8, 19-20 "He went into the temple, and began to cast out them that sold ... the chief priests and the scribes and the chief of the people sought to destroy him [Jesus] ... the chief priests ... came upon him saying, Tell us, by what authority doest thou these things? Jesus said ... Neither tell I you by what authority I do these things. And the chief priests ... sought to lay hands on him that so they might deliver him unto the power and authority of the governor."

Note: Jesus was most likely arrested and executed due to the events that took place in the temple between him and the moneychangers. The moneychangers were conducting their business with due approval from higher authorities and thus considered legitimate. Jesus was questioned by the chief priests, scribes and elders and was asked to give a reason for his actions and replied

'Neither I tell you by what authority I do these things'.

5. Did Jesus curse the fig tree to wither before purging the temple?

After
Matthew 21:12 "Jesus [cast out all] … that sold and bought in the temple …"
Matthew 21:19 "He saw a fig tree [and said] Let no fruit grow on thee … the fig tree withered away."

Before
Mark 11:12-14 "Seeing a fig tree … he came … he found nothing but leaves … And Jesus [said] No man eat fruit of thee hereafter for ever."
Mark 11:15 "Jesus went into the temple … cast out them that sold …"

6. When did the fig tree wither?

Immediately
Matthew 21:19 "When he saw a fig tree in the way, [Jesus] he came … and said unto it, Let no fruit grow on thee … And presently the fig tree withered away."

Not immediately but the following day
Mark 11:13-14 "Seeing a fig tree … [Jesus] said unto it, No man eat fruit of thee hereafter for ever. And his disciples heard it."
Mark 11:19-20 "When even was come … in the morning … they saw the fig tree dried up …"

Note: Jesus might be violating an Old Testament law that says you are not suppose to destroy trees classified as fruit bearing trees as stated in Deuteronomy 20:20:
Deuteronomy 20:20 "Only the trees which thou knowest that they be not trees for meat, thou shalt destroy and cut them down; and thou shalt build bulwarks against the city that maketh war with thee, until it be subdued."

7. Was the fig tree story an actual incident or a parable?

An actual incident
Matthew 21:19 "When he saw a fig tree … [Jesus] he came and said unto it, Let no fruit grow on thee … the fig tree withered away."
Mark 11:12-14 "[Jesus] said … No man eat fruit of thee hereafter forever."

A parable
Luke 21:29-30 "He spake to them a parable; Behold the fig tree … When they now shoot forth, ye see and know … summer is now nigh at hand."

Note: Why did Jesus curse the fig tree if the fig tree did not bear fruit, the fig

tree might have been just out of season. It would have been better if he used
his ability to perform miracles and blessed the fig tree to make it bear fruit.

8. How many days was Jesus in Bethany before he entered Nazareth?

Two
Matthew 26:2, 6 "Ye know that after two days is the feast of the Passover ...
Jesus was in Bethany, in the house of Simon the leper"
Mark 14:1, 3 "After two days was the feast of the Passover ... [Jesus was] ...
in Bethany in the house of Simon the leper ..."

Six
John 12:1 "Then Jesus six days before the passover came to Bethany ..."

9. Where was the anointing of Jesus?

In Bethany, in the house of Simon the leper
Matthew 26:6-7 "Now when Jesus was in Bethany, in the house of Simon ...
There came unto him a woman having an alabaster box of very precious
ointment, and poured it on his head ..."
Mark 14:3 "Being in Bethany in the house of Simon ... there came a woman
having an alabaster box of ointment of spikenard ... and poured it on his
head ..."

In a Pharisee's house
Luke 7:36-38 "And he went into the Pharisee's house ... a woman in the city
... brought an alabaster box of ointment ... and anointed [Jesus] ..."

In Bethany, where Lazarus was
John 12:1, 3 "Then Jesus ... came to Bethany, where Lazarus was ... Then
took Mary a pound of ointment of spikenard ... anointed the feet of Jesus ..."

10. Where was the oil poured when Jesus was anointed?

In Jesus' head
Matthew 26:7 "There came unto him a woman ... and poured it on his head"
Mark 14:3 "There came a woman ... and poured it on his head."

In Jesus' feet
Luke 7:38 "Stood at his feet ... and kissed his feet, and anointed them ..."
John 12:3 "Then took Mary ... and anointed the feet of Jesus ..."

11. Who did the anointment of Jesus?

An unknown woman
Matthew 26:7 "There came unto him a woman having an alabaster box ..."

Mark 14:3 "There came a woman having an alabaster box ..."

An unknown sinful woman
Luke 7:37 "Behold, a woman in the city, which was a sinner ..."

Mary, the sister of Lazarus
John 11:2; 12:3 "It was that Mary [whose brother Lazarus was sick] ... Then took Mary a pound of ointment ... and anointed [Jesus] ..."

Note: Traditionally, the Mary referred to who have anointed Jesus was Mary Magdalene. However, since the anointment took place in the house of Lazarus, Mary the sister of Lazarus seems to be the most logical Mary.

12. Who criticized the anointment made to Jesus?

The disciples
Matthew 26:8 "But when his disciples saw it, they had indignation, saying, To what purpose is this waste?"

Some people
Mark 14:4 "There were some that had indignation within themselves, and said, Why was this waste of the ointment made?"

Judas Iscariot
John 12:4-5 "Then saith ... Judas Iscariot ... Why was not this ointment sold for three hundred pence, and given to the poor?"

13. Did Jesus tell his disciples of his imminent death and resurrection?

Yes, Jesus did
Matthew 20:18-19 "The Son of man shall be betrayed ... they shall condemn him to death ... and to crucify him: and the third day he shall rise again."
Matthew 26:31-32 "Then saith Jesus ... for it is written, I will smite the shepherd, and the sheep ... shall be scattered abroad. But after I am risen again, I will go before you into Galilee."

No, Jesus did not
John 20:9 "For as yet they knew not the scripture, that he must rise again from the dead."

14. When did Satan enter Judas?

Satan entered Judas before the last supper
Luke 22:3, 14, 19 "Then entered Satan into Judas (Iscariot) ... And ... he sat down, and the twelve apostles with him. And he took bread, and gave thanks ... this do in remembrance of me."

Satan entered into Judas after the last supper
John 13:27 "Jesus answered, He it is, to whom I shall give a sop, when I have dipped it. And ... he gave it to Judas Iscariot ... And after the sop Satan entered into him. Then said Jesus unto him, That thou doest, do quickly."

15. When did Judas bargain with the chief priests?

Before the last supper
Matthew 26:14-15, 17 "Judas Iscariot, went unto the chief priests ... And they covenanted with him for thirty pieces of silver. And from that time he sought opportunity to betray him ... Now the first day of the feast of unleavened bread the disciples came to Jesus, saying unto him, Where wilt thou that we prepare for thee to eat the passover?"

After the last supper
John 13:2 "And supper being ended, the devil having now put into the heart of Judas Iscariot, Simon's son to betray him ..."

16. When did Jesus predict his betrayal?

Before communion
Matthew 26:20-21, 26-27 "Now ... he said, Verily I say unto you, that one of you shall betray me ... as they were eating, Jesus took bread, and blessed it ... And he took the cup ... gave it to them, saying, Drink ye all of it."
John 13:21, 26 "When Jesus ... said, Verily, verily, I say unto you, that one of you shall betray me ... Jesus answered, He it is, to whom I shall give a sop ... he gave it to Judas Iscariot ..."

After communion
Luke 22:17, 19, 21 "He took the cup ... and said, Take this, and divide it among yourselves: And he took bread ... gave unto them, saying, This is my body which is given for you ... the hand of him that betrayeth me is with me on the table."

17. What was the order of communion?

Bread, wine
Matthew 26:26, 27 "Jesus took bread ... and said, Take, eat; this is my body ... And he [Jesus] took the cup ... saying, Drink ye all of it.""

Wine, bread
Luke 22:17, 19 "He [Jesus] took the cup [and said] For I say unto you, I will not drink of the fruit of the vine, until the kingdom of God shall come ... he [Jesus] took bread ... gave unto them ..."

L. The arrest and trial of Jesus Christ

1. How many times did Jesus pray to avoid the cross?

Three
Matthew 26:36, 39 "Then cometh Jesus with them unto a place called Gethsemane ... And he ... prayed, saying, O my Father, if it be possible, let this cup pass from me: nevertheless not as I will, but as thou wilt."
Matthew 26:42 "He went away again the second time, and prayed, saying, O my Father, if this cup may not pass away from me, except I drink it, thy will be done."
Matthew 26:44 "He left them ... and prayed the third time ..."

One
Luke 22:39, 41-42 "He ... prayed, Saying, Father, if thou be willing, remove this cup from me: nevertheless not my will, but thine, be done."

None
John 12:27 "Now is my soul troubled; and what shall I say? Father, save me from this hour: but for this cause came I unto this hour."

2. How many times did the disciples fell asleep?

Three
Matthew 26:40, 43, 45 "He cometh unto the disciples, and findeth them asleep ... he came and found them asleep again ... he to his disciples, and saith ... Sleep on now, and take your rest."

One
Luke 22:45 "He rose up from prayer ... he found them sleeping for sorrow"

3. Did anybody ask Jesus where he was going?

Peter asked Jesus where he is going
John 13:36 "Simon Peter said unto him, Lord, whither goest thou?"

Thomas asked Jesus where he is going
John 14:5 "Thomas saith unto him, Lord ... how can we know the way?"

Jesus said nobody asked him where he is going
John 16:5 "But now I go my way to him that sent me; and none of you asketh me, Whither goest thou?"

4. Did Judas kiss Jesus?

Yes, for identification of Jesus
Matthew 26:48-49 "He that betrayed him gave them a sign ... he came to Jesus ... kissed him."

No, but Jesus expected the kiss
Luke 22:47-48 "He [Judas] ... drew near unto Jesus to kiss him. But Jesus said unto him, Judas, betrayest thou the Son of man with a kiss?"

No, Jesus introduced himself
John 18:3-5 "Judas [with a band of men and officers] ... cometh thither ... [Jesus] said unto them, 'Whom seek ye?' They answered him, 'Jesus of Nazareth.' Jesus said ... 'I am he.'"

5. Did Jesus heal the slave's severed ear?

No
John 18:10 "Simon Peter ... smote the high priest's servant, and cut off his right ear. The servant's name was Malchus."

Yes
Luke 22:50-51 "One of them smote the servant ... cut off his right ear ... he [Jesus] touched his ear, and healed him."

6. Was Jesus taken straight to Caiaphas when he was arrested?

Yes
Matthew 26:57 "They ... led him [Jesus] away to Caiaphas the high priest ..."
Mark 14:53 "They led Jesus away to the high priest."
Luke 22:54 "Then took they him ... and brought him into the high priest's house."

No, he was sent to Annas first
John 18:13, 24 "Led him ... to Annas first [and] sent him ... unto Caiaphas"

7. When was the initial hearing of Jesus?

During the night on Passover
Matthew 26:19-20 "They made ready the passover ... he sat down with the twelve."
Matthew 26:57 "They that had laid hold on Jesus led him away to Caiaphas"
Matthew 27:1-2 "When the morning was come, all ... took counsel against Jesus ..."

During the morning on Passover
Luke 22:13, 54, 66-67 "They made ready the Passover ... Then took they him ... into the high priest's house ... And as soon as it was day, the elders ... led him into their council ..."

During the day before Passover
John 18:28 "Then led they Jesus from Caiaphas unto the hall of judgment:"
John 19:14 "It was the preparation of the Passover ..."

8. Was Jesus silent during his trial?

Jesus was silent
Matthew 27:12-14 "When he was accused of the chief priests and elders, he answered nothing ... he answered him to never a word."

No, Jesus was not silent
Mark 14:61-62; 15:2 "The high priest asked him ... Art thou the Christ, the Son of the Blessed? And Jesus said, I am ... Pilate asked him, Art thou the King of the Jews? And he answering said unto them, Thou sayest it."
John 18:33-34 "[Pilate] said ... Art thou the King ... Jesus answered him ..."
I Timothy 6:13 "Christ Jesus, who before Pontius Pilate witnessed a good confession."

9. Did Jesus ask for the destruction of the temple?

Yes, Jesus asked for the destruction of the temple
John 2:19-21 "Jesus ... said unto them, Destroy this temple, and in three days I will raise it up"

No, the false witnesses were the ones who said that Jesus asked for the destruction
Matthew 26:60-61 "At the last *came two false witnesses*, And said, This fellow said, I am able to destroy the temple of God, and to build it in three days."
Mark 14:57-58 "There arose certain, and *bare false witness against him*, saying, We heard him say, I will destroy this temple ... and within three days I will build another ..."

10. Did Jesus appear before the Sanhedrin?

Yes, there was a trial
Matthew 26:59, 62 "Now the chief priests, and elders, and all the council, sought false witness against Jesus, to put him to death; And the high priest arose, and said unto him, Answerest thou nothing? what is it which these witness against thee?"

Yes, there were questions asked before the Sanhedrin
Luke 22:66-67 "The elders ... scribes ... led him into their council, saying, Art thou the Christ?"

No, there was no appearance before the Sanhedrin, only private hearings before Annas and Caiphas
John 18:13-24 "And led him away to Annas first ... Now Annas had sent him bound unto Caiaphas the high priest."

11. Were there false witnesses who testified against Jesus?

Yes, there were false witnesses
Matthew 26:59-61 "Now ... all the council, sought false witness against Jesus, to put him to death ... At the last came two false witnesses ..."

No, there were no false witnesses
Luke 22:70-71 "He [Jesus] said unto them, Ye say that I am. And they said, What need we any further witness? for we ourselves have heard of his own mouth."
John 18:19-20 "The high priest asked Jesus of his disciples ... his doctrine. Jesus answered him..."

12. Was Jesus asked if he is the Son of God?

Yes
Matthew 26:63 "The high priest [said] tell us whether thou ... the Son of God."

No, he was asked if he is the son of the blessed
Mark 14:61 "Again the high priest asked him ... Art thou the Christ, the Son of the Blessed?"

13. Did Jesus respond in a straightforward manner?

No
Matthew 26:64 "Jesus saith unto him, Thou hast said: nevertheless I say unto you, Hereafter shall ye see the Son of man sitting on the right hand of power, and coming in the clouds of heaven."
Luke 22:70 "Then said they all, Art thou then the Son of God? And he said ... Ye say that I am."

Yes
Mark 14:62 "Jesus said, I am: and ye shall see the Son of man sitting on the right hand of power, and coming in the clouds of heaven."

14. What did Jesus reply to the question "Are you the king of the Jews?"?

Thou sayest
Matthew 27:11 "Jesus said unto him, Thou sayest."

Thou sayest it
Mark 15:2 "He answering said unto them, , Thou sayest it."
Luke 23:3 "He answered him and said, Thou sayest it."

Sayest thou this thing of thyself, or did others tell it thee of me?
John 18:33-34 "Jesus [replied] Sayest thou this thing of thyself, or did others tell it thee of me?"

15. Did Jesus answer any of the charges at his hearing?

No, none at all
Matthew 27:14 "He answered him to never a word."

Yes all of them
John 18:33-37 "Then Pilate ... said ... Art thou the King of the Jews? Jesus answered him ..."

16. Did Herod question Jesus?

Yes
Luke 23:9 "Then he [Herod] questioned with him in many words; but he answered him nothing."

Note: The other gospels did not mention about Jesus being questioned by Herod.

17. What was Barabbas accused of?

Murder
Mark 15:7 "Barabbas ... who had committed murder in the insurrection."
Luke 23:18-19 "They cried out ... release unto us Barabbas: (Who for a certain sedition made in the city, and for murder, was cast into prison.)."
Acts 3:14 "But ye denied the Holy One ... and desired a murderer ..."

Robbery
John 18:40 "Barabbas. Now Barabbas was a robber."

18. Who persuaded the people to ask for the release of Barabbas?

The chief priests and elders
Matthew 27:20 "But the chief priests and elders persuaded the multitude that they should ask Barabbas, and destroy Jesus."

Only the chief priests
Mark 15:11 "But the chief priests moved the people (to) ... release Barabbas unto them."

The people decided for themselves
Luke 23:18, 21 "They cried out ... release ... Barabbas ... Crucify him [Jesus], crucify him."

M. The betrayal of Peter

1. How many times did Peter deny Jesus?

Three, denial made to a maid, another girl, and then to a group of people
Matthew 26:70 "But he denied before them all, saying, I know not what thou sayest."
Matthew 26:72 "And again he denied with an oath, I do not know the man."
Matthew 26:74 "Then began he to curse and to swear, saying, I know not the man."

Three, denial made to a maid, the same girl again, and then to a group of people
Mark 14:68 "He denied, saying, I know not, neither understand I what thou sayest."
Mark 14:69-70 "He denied it again."
Mark 14:71 "He began to curse ... saying, I know not this man of whom ye speak."

Three, denial made to a maid, a man, and then another man
Luke 22:57 "He denied him, saying, Woman, I know him not."
Luke 22:58 "Peter said, Man, I am not."
Luke 22:60 "Peter said, Man, I know not what thou sayest."

Two, a girl at the door, several people and one servant of the high priest
John 18:17 "He saith, I am not."
John 18:27 "Peter then denied again: and immediately the cock crew."

2. How many times did the cock crow?

One
Matthew 26:74 "Then began he to curse and to swear, saying, I know not the man. And immediately the cock crew."

Two
Mark 14:68, 72 "But he denied, saying, I know not, neither understand I what thou sayest ... and the cock crew... the second time the cock crew."

N. Concerning Judas Iscariot

1. What did Judas do with the blood money he received for the betrayal?

He threw the money
Matthew 27:5 "He [Judas] cast down the pieces of silver ... and departed ..."

He purchased a field
Acts 1: 18 "[Judas] purchased a field with the reward of iniquity ..."

2. How did Judas die?

By hanging himself
Matthew 27:5 "He [Judas] ... hanged himself."

By falling
Acts 1:18 "Falling headlong, he [Judas] burst asunder ... his bowels gushed out."

3. Who purchased the potter's field?

The chief priests
Matthew 27:6-8 "The chief priests ... bought ... the potter's field ..."

Judas
Acts 1:18 "Now this man [Judas] purchased a field with the reward of iniquity."

Note: The verse Matthew 27:8 that says 'Wherefore that field was called, the field of blood, unto this day' means that the gospels were written several years after and are not first hand accounts of the life of Jesus Christ.

O. The crucifixion and death of Jesus Christ

1. When was heaven prepared?

Before Ascension, from the foundation of the world
Matthew 25:34 "Then shall the King say unto them ... Come, ye blessed of my Father, inherit the kingdom prepared for you from the foundation of the world."

After Ascension
John 14:2-3 "In my Father's house ... I go to prepare a place for you. And if I go and prepare a place for you ..."

2. Was Jesus crucified during the Passover meal?

The day after Passover
Matthew 26:17 "Now the first day of the feast of unleavened bread the disciples came to Jesus, saying ... Where wilt thou that we prepare for thee to eat the passover?"
Matthew 27:1, 35 "When the morning was come, all the chief priests and elders of the people took counsel against Jesus to put him to death ... And they crucified him."

The day before Passover
John 19:14 "It was the preparation of the passover, and about the sixth hour: and he saith unto the Jews, Behold your King!"

John 19:16-18 "They took Jesus, and led him away ... into a place called the place of a skull, which is called in the Hebrew Golgotha: Where they crucified him."

3. Was it lawful for Jesus Christ to be put to death by the Jews?

No
John 18:31 "Pilate [said] unto them, Take ye him, and judge him according to your law. The Jews therefore said unto him, It is not lawful for us to put any man to death:"

Yes
John 19:7 "The Jews answered him, We have a law, and by our law he ought to die, because he made himself the Son of God."

4. Who dressed Jesus with a robe?

The soldiers of Pilate
Matthew 27:27-28 "The soldiers of the governor [Pilate] ... put on him a ... robe."

The soldiers of Herod
Luke 23:11 "Herod with his men of war ... arrayed him in a gorgeous robe"

5. What color was Jesus robe?

Scarlet
Matthew 27:28 "They stripped him and put on him a scarlet robe."

Purple
Mark 15:17 "They clothed him with purple ..."
John 19:2 "The soldiers ... put on him a purple robe."

6. Did Jesus bear his own cross?

No, Simon of Cyrene did
Matthew 27:32 "They found ... Simon ... they compelled to bear his cross."

Yes
John 19:17-18 "He [Jesus] bearing his cross went forth into a place ... [and] crucified him ..."

7. What did they give Jesus to drink in the cross?

Vinegar and gall
Matthew 27:34 "They gave him vinegar to drink mingled with gall."

Vinegar
Luke 23:36 "The soldiers ... offering him vinegar ..."

Vinegar and hyssop
John 19:29 "They filled a spunge with vinegar, and put it upon hyssop ..."

Wine with myrrh
Mark 15:23 "They gave him to drink wine mingled with myrrh."

8. Did Jesus drink what was given to him at the cross?

No
Mark 15:23 "They gave him to drink ... but he received it not."

Yes
John 19:29-30 "There was ... vinegar ... Jesus ... had received the vinegar ..."

9. What was written on the cross of Jesus?

This is Jesus, the king of the Jews
Matthew 27:37 "This is Jesus, the king of the Jews."
Mark 15:26 "The king of the Jews."

THIS IS THE KING OF THE JEWS
Luke 23:38 "A superscription ... in letters of Greek, and Latin, and Hebrew, THIS IS THE KING OF THE JEWS."

Jesus of Nazareth, the king of the Jews
John 19:19 "Jesus of Nazareth, the king of the Jews."

10. Were both thieves crucified with Jesus taunting him?

Yes
Matthew 27:44 "The thieves also ... crucified with him cast the same in his teeth."
Mark 15:32 "They that were crucified with him reviled him."

No, only one reviled Jesus
Luke 23:39-40 "One of the malefactors which were hanged railed on him, saying, If thou be Christ, save thyself and us. But the other answering rebuked him, saying, 'Dost not thou fear God, seeing thou art in the same condemnation?'"

Note: In the book Acts of Pilate the two thieves are identified as Dismas and Gestas. However, in the book The First Gospel of the Infancy of Jesus Christ, they were identified as Titus and Dumachus and were part of a gang who attacked Jesus, Mary and Joseph on their way to Egypt. Titus, the humane thief offered Dumachus 40 groats to leave the family unharmed. The infant Jesus told his mother that their paths will cross again after thirty years during his crucifixion and Titus shall go before him in paradise. This story was also mentioned in the poem The Golden Legend by Henry Wadsworth Longfellow.

11. What time of the day was Jesus crucified?

Sixth hour
Matthew 27:45-46 "Now from the sixth hour there was darkness ... unto the ninth hour ..."

Third hour
Mark 15:25 "It was the third hour, and they crucified him."

12. Who were present at the Crucifixion?

Mary of Magdala, James and Joseph's mother Mary, Zeebedees' mother, other women
Matthew 27:55-56 "Many women were there ... Among which was Mary Magdalene, and Mary the mother of James and Joses, and the mother of Zebedees children."

Mary of Magdala, James and Joseph's mother, Salome, other women
Mark 15:40 "There were also women ... among whom was Mary Magdalene, and Mary the mother of James the less and of Joses, and Salome."

His friends, and the women who had accompanied him from Galilee
Luke 23:27 "There followed him a great company of people, and of women"

His mother, her sister, Mary wife of Cleopas and Mary of Magdala
John 19:25-26 "Now there stood by the cross of Jesus his mother, and his mother's sister, Mary the wife of Cleophas, and Mary Magdalene."

13. Was Jesus in paradise the same day he died?

No
Matthew 12:40 "For as Jonah was three days and three nights in the whale's belly; so shall the Son of Man be three days and three nights in the heart of the earth."
Mark 10:34 "They shall mock him ... kill him: and the third day he shall rise again."
John 20:17 "Jesus saith ... I am not yet ascended to my Father."
Acts 1:3 "To whom also he shewed himself alive ... being seen of them forty days ..."

Yes
Luke 23:43 "Jesus said … Today shalt thou be with me in Paradise."

14. Where was Jesus at the sixth hour during the day of crucifixion?

On the cross
Matthew 27:45-46 "Now from the sixth hour there was darkness over all the land unto the ninth hour. And about the ninth hour Jesus cried with a loud voice, saying, Eli, Eli, lama sabachthani? that is to say, My God, my God, why hast thou forsaken me?"

In the judgment hall summoned by Pilate
John 19:9, 13-14 "[Pilate] went again into the judgment hall, and [Pilate] saith unto Jesus, Whence art thou? Jesus gave … no answer … and about the sixth hour: and he [Pilate] saith unto the Jews, Behold your King!"

15. In what language did Jesus say My God, my God?

Eli, Eli, lama sabachthani
Matthew 27:46 "Jesus cried … Eli, Eli, lama sabachthani?"

Eloi, Eloi, lama sabachthani
Mark 15:34 "Jesus cried … Eloi, Eloi, lama sabachthani?"

16. What were the last words of Jesus on the cross?

My God, my God, why hast thou forsaken me?
Matthew 27:46-50 "About the ninth hour Jesus cried … Eli, Eli, lama sabachthani? that is to say, My God, my God, why hast thou forsaken me? … Jesus … yielded up the ghost."

Father, into thy hands I commend my spirit
Luke 23:46 "Jesus [cried] … Father, into thy hands I commend my spirit … gave up the ghost."

It is finished
John 19:30 "[Jesus] said, It is finished … and gave up the ghost."

17. When did the curtain of the temple become torn?

After the death of Jesus
Matthew 27:50-51 "Jesus … yielded up the ghost … the veil of the temple was rent in twain from the top to the bottom."

Before the death of Jesus
Luke 23:45-46 "The veil of the temple was rent … he [Jesus] gave up the ghost."

18. Some zombie like creatures walked in the cities of Jerusalem

Matthew 27:50-53 "[Jesus] yielded up the ghost ... the graves were opened ... bodies ... came out of the graves ... went into the holy city, and appeared unto many."

Note: This story is not only bizarre, but is found nowhere in the other gospels.

19. What did the centurion say about Jesus during the crucifixion?

Jesus was the Son of God
Matthew 27:54 "The centurion [said] Truly this was the Son of God."
Mark 15:39 "The centurion [said] ... this man was the Son of God."

Jesus was a righteous man
Luke 23:47 "The centurion [said] Certainly this was a righteous man."

20. Where were the women during the crucifixion?

Afar off
Matthew 27:55 "Many women were there beholding afar off ..."
Mark 15:40 "There were also women looking on afar off ..."
Luke 23:49 "All his acquaintance, and the women ... stood afar off ..."

They stood near the cross
John 19:25 "There stood by the cross of Jesus his mother ... and Mary Magdalene."

21. Did Christ lay down his life for his friends?

Yes, Christ laid down his life for his friends
John 15:13 "Greater love hath no man than this, that a man lay down his life for his friends."
John 10:11 "I am the good shepherd: the good shepherd giveth his life for the sheep."

No, Christ laid down his life for his enemies
Romans 5:10 "For if, when we were enemies, we were reconciled to God by the death of his Son ... we shall be saved by his life."

22. Did Jesus Christ die to save the whole world?

No, every man shall be put to death for his own sin
Deuteronomy 24:16 "Every man shall be put to death for his own sin."

No, only those who believe in him
John 3:16 "God … gave his only begotten Son, that whosoever believeth in him should not perish, but have everlasting life."
John 10:27 "My sheep hear my voice, and I know them, and they follow me."
John 12:46 "I am come a light into the world, that whosoever believeth on me should not abide in darkness."
Romans 3:25 "Whom God hath set forth to be a propitiation through faith in his blood …"

No, only those who were chosen by God
John 6:44, 65 "No man can come to me, except the Father which hath sent me draw him: and I will raise him up at the last day … no man can come unto me, except it were given unto him of my Father."
Romans 8:30 "Moreover whom he did predestinate, them he also called: and whom he called, them he also justified: and whom he justified, them he also glorified."

Yes
John 1:29 "Behold the Lamb of God, which taketh away the sin of the world."
John 4:42 "Christ, the Saviour of the world."
I John 4:14 "The Father sent the Son to be the Saviour of the world."

23. Did Jesus Christ die to fulfill his role as a saviour?

No, Jesus was put to death for blasphemy, sedition and public disorder
Matthew 21:12-27, 26:3-4 "Jesus went into the temple of God, and cast out all them that sold and bought in the temple … And when he was come into the temple, the chief priests and the elders … came unto him [and said], By what authority doest thou these things? and who gave thee this authority? … And he [Jesus] said unto them, Neither tell I you by what authority I do these things … Then assembled together the chief priests, and the scribes … and consulted that they might take Jesus by subtilty, and kill him."
[Also in **Mark 11:15-33, 14:1; Luke 19:45-47, 20:1-8, 19-20**]
John 12:10-11, 47-48 "But the chief priests consulted that they might put Lazarus also to death; Because that by reason of him many of the Jews went away, and believed on Jesus …Then gathered the chief priests and the Pharisees a council, and said, What do we? for this man doeth many miracles. If we let him thus alone, all men will believe on him: and the Romans shall come and take away both our place and nation."

Note: The chief priests also considered putting Lazarus to death. Because of Lazarus, many Jews went to believe in Jesus.

Yes
John 1:29 "Behold the Lamb of God, which taketh away the sin of the world."
John 4:42 "Christ, the Saviour of the world."
I John 4:14 "The Father sent the Son to be the Saviour of the world."

Note: The Gospel of John and the writings of Paul indicated that Jesus died for the sins of the world. However, the gospels of Matthew, Luke and Mark shows that Jesus was arrested for public disorder and was crucified for blasphemy.

P. The burial and resurrection of Jesus Christ

1. Who buried Jesus Christ?

Joseph of Arimathaea
Matthew 27:57-60 "There came a rich man of Arimathaea, named Joseph ... Joseph had taken the body, he wrapped it in a clean linen cloth, And laid it in his own new tomb."

Joseph of Arimathaea and Nicodemus
John 19:38-42 "Joseph of Arimathaea ... took the body of Jesus. And there came also Nicodemus ... laid they [Joseph and Nicodemus] Jesus ..."

The Jews and their rulers
Acts 13:27-29 "For they that dwell at Jerusalem, and their rulers ... they took him down from the tree, and laid him in a sepulchre."

Note: According to legend, Joseph of Arimathea was the first keeper of the Holy Grail. The Holy Grail was the cup used by Jesus at the Last Supper and was the same cup used by Joseph of Arimathea to catch the blood of Jesus while he was being interred. The Holy Grail was later taken to Great Britain and became the conquest of several knights of King Arthur such as Sir Galahad, Sir Percival, Sir Lancelot and Sir Bors.

Some Christians believe that Joseph of Arimathea was the fulfillment of Isaiah 53:9.
Isaiah 53:9 "He made his grave with the wicked, and with the rich in his death; because he had done no violence, neither was any deceit in his mouth."
Isaiah 53 is also known as the 'Man of Sorrows'.

2. Was Jesus' body wrapped in spices before burial?

No
Matthew 27:59-60 "He [Joseph] wrapped it [Jesus] ... laid ... tomb ..."

Yes
John 19:39-40, 42 "There came also Nicodemus … brought a mixture of myrrh and aloes … Then took they the body of Jesus, and wound it in linen clothes with the spices, as the manner of the Jews is to bury. There laid they Jesus …"

3. Did Pilate order the guarding of the tomb of Jesus?

Yes
Matthew 27:62-63, 65 "Now the next day … the chief priests and Pharisees came together unto Pilate, Saying, Sir, we remember that that deceiver said, while he was yet alive, After three days I will rise again. Pilate said unto them, Ye have a watch: go your way, make it as sure as ye can."

No, nothing was mentioned about the guarding of Jesus' tomb
Mark 15:44-45 "Pilate marvelled if he were already dead: and calling unto him the centurion, he asked him whether he had been any while dead. And when he knew it of the centurion, he gave the body to Joseph."

Note: Since the women went to the tomb with their spices, probably there was no guard in the tomb.

4. How long was Jesus in the grave?

Three days and three nights
Matthew 12:40 "For as Jonas was three days and three nights in the whale's belly; so
shall the Son of man be …"
Matthew 17:23 "They shall kill him, and the third day he shall be raised again."

Two days and two nights
Mark 15:25, 42-46 "It was the third hour, and they crucified him … And now when the even was come … [Joseph] laid him in a sepulchre …"
Mark 16:9 "Now when Jesus was risen early the *first day* of the week …"

5. Did Jesus raise himself from the dead?

Yes
John 2:19-21 "Jesus answered … Destroy this temple, and in three days I will raise it up … he spake of the temple of his body."

No, God raised Jesus
Acts 2:32 "This Jesus hath God raised up …"

6. How many women came to the sepulcher?

One – Mary Magdalene
John 20:1 "The first day of the week cometh Mary Magdalene ..."

Two – Mary and Mary Magdalene
Matthew 28:1 "Mary Magdalene and the other Mary [came] to see the sepulchre."

Three – Mary, Mary Magdalene and Salome
Mark 16:1-2 "When the sabbath was past, Mary Magdalene, and Mary the mother of James, and Salome ... came unto the sepulchre ..."

Five (at least) - Mary Magdalene, Joanna, Mary and other women
Luke 24:10 "It was Mary Magdalene and Joanna, and Mary the mother of James, and other women that were with them ..."

7. When did the women buy the spices used for Jesus' body?

After the Sabbath was past
Mark 16:1 "When the sabbath was past, Mary Magdalene and Mary ... had bought sweet spices"

Before the Sabbath
Luke 23:55-56 "The women ... returned, and prepared spices and ointments; and rested the sabbath day according to the commandment."

8. What was the purpose of the women to go to the tomb?

To see the sepulchre
Matthew 28: 1 "Mary Magdalene and the other Mary [came] to see the sepulchre."

To anoint Jesus' body with spices
Mark 16:1 "Mary Magdalene, and Mary ... and Salome, had bought sweet spices, that they might come and anoint him."

The women did not enter the tomb, Jesus was already anointed with spices
John 19:39-40 "There came also Nicodemus ... and brought a mixture of myrrh and aloes ... Then took they the body of Jesus, and wound it in linen clothes with the spices ..."
John 20:11 "But Mary stood without at the sepulchre weeping: and as she wept, she stooped down, and looked into the sepulcher."

Note: If Nicodemus already brought spices and anointed Jesus why should the women do the same thing?

9. What time of the day did the women go to the tomb?

About dawn
Matthew 28:1 "As it began to dawn … came Mary Magdalene … to see the sepulchre."

After sunrise
Mark 16:2 "They came unto the sepulchre at the rising of the sun."

Early dawn
Luke 24:1 "Now … very early in the morning, they came unto the sepulcher"

It was still dark
John 20:1 "Cometh Mary Magdalene early, when it was yet dark …"

10. Where was the stone placed when the women arrived?

Closed, the angel rolled back the stone from the door
Matthew 28:2 "The angel of the Lord … rolled back the stone from the door"

Open, the stone was already rolled away
Mark 16:4 "When they looked … the stone was rolled away."
Luke 24:2 "They found the stone rolled away from the sepulchre."
John 20:1 "The first day of the week cometh Mary Magdalene … and seeth the stone taken away from the sepulchre."

11. Was there an earthquake when the women arrived in the tomb?

Yes, there was a great earthquake
Matthew 28:2 "Behold, there was a great earthquake."

No, there was no earthquake mentioned
Mark 16:5 "Entering into the sepulchre, they saw a young man sitting on the right side, clothed in a long white garment; and they were affrighted."

12. Did the women actually enter the tomb?

Yes
Mark 16:5 "Entering into the sepulchre, they saw a young man …"
Luke 24:3 "They entered in …"

No
John 20:1-2, 11 "The first day of the week cometh Mary Magdalene early … she runneth, and cometh to Simon Peter … Mary stood *without at the sepulchre* weeping: and as she wept, she stooped down, and looked into the sepulcher."

13. How many angels were within the sepulcher?

One angel, sitting down
Matthew 28:2 "The angel of the Lord ... rolled back the stone from the door"

A young man
Mark 16:5 "They saw a young man ..."

There were two men, standing up in dazzling garments
Luke 24:4 "Two men stood by them in shining garments:"

There were two angels sitting
John 20:11-12 "But Mary ... seeth two angels in white sitting ..."

14. Where the men (angels) inside the tomb?

Outside
Matthew 28:2 "The angel of the Lord descended from heaven, and came and rolled back the stone from the door, and sat upon it."

Inside
Mark 16:5 "Entering into the sepulchre, they saw a young man ..."
Luke 24:3-4 "They entered in ... behold, two men stood by them ..."
John 20:11-12 "But Mary ... and looked into the sepulchre, And seeth two angels ..."

15. Were the women told what happened to Jesus' body?

Yes
Matthew 28:5-6 "The angel answered ... He is not here: for he is risen ..."
Mark 16:5-6 "They saw a young man ... he saith unto them ... he is risen ..."
Luke 24:4-6 "Two men stood by them ... they said unto them ... He is not here, but is risen ..."

No
John 20:1-2 "The first day of the week cometh Mary Magdalene ... Then she runneth ... to Simon Peter ... and saith unto them, They have taken away the Lord out of the sepulchre, and we know not where they have laid him."

16. Did the women immediately inform the disciples about Jesus?

Yes, the women immediately informed the disciples
Matthew 28:8 "They departed quickly ... run to bring his disciples word."
Luke 24:8-9 "They remembered his words, And returned from the sepulchre, and told all these things unto the eleven, and to all the rest."

No, they told no one

Mark 16:8 "They went out quickly, and fled from the sepulcher ... neither said they any thing to any man; for they were afraid."

17. How did the women react knowing Jesus was not in the tomb?

They ran from the sepulchre with fear and great joy
Matthew 28:8 "They [the women] departed quickly from the sepulchre with fear and great joy."

Mary Magdalene told Peter and another disciple that the body was stolen
John 20:2 "Then she [Mary Magdalene] runneth, and cometh to Simon Peter ... and saith unto them, They have taken away the Lord ... and we know not where they have laid him."

18. What was the people's reaction about Jesus being resurrected?

With great belief
Matthew 28:9 "They went to tell his disciples, behold, Jesus met them, saying, All hail. And they came and held him by the feet, and worshipped him."

Disbelief, all doubted
Mark 16:11 "They, when they had heard that he was alive ... believed not."
Luke 24:11 "Their words seemed to them as idle tales, and they believed them not."

19. How did Mary Magdalene react when she saw Jesus?

She recognized Jesus and was filled with joy
Matthew 28:9 "As they [Mary Magdalene and the other Mary] went to tell his disciples, behold, Jesus met them, saying, All hail. And they came and held him by the feet, and worshipped him."

Jesus did not appear to Mary Magdalene
Luke 24:23 "When they found not his body, they came, saying, that they had also seen a vision of angels, which said that he was alive."

She did not recognize Jesus and was grieving
John 20:14 "[She] saw Jesus standing, and knew not that it was Jesus."

20. Who first saw Jesus after his resurrection?

Mary Magdalene and the other Mary
Matthew 28:9 "They [Mary Magdalene and the other Mary] went to tell his disciples, behold, Jesus met them ..."

Mary Magdalene

Mark 16:9 "Now when Jesus was risen ... he appeared first to Mary Magdalene ..."
John 20:14-16 "[She] saw Jesus standing, and ... Jesus saith unto her, Mary [Magdalene] ..."

Cleopas and another person
Luke 24:15-31 "Jesus himself drew near, and went with *them* ... And the one of them, whose name was Cleopas ... and their eyes were opened, and they knew him."

Cephas
I Corinthians 15:4-5 "He was seen of Cephas, then of the twelve:"

21. Where did Jesus first appear after his resurrection?

Near the tomb
Matthew 28:8-9 "They departed quickly from the sepulcher ... Jesus met them ..."

In Emmaus, about seven miles away from Jerusalem
Luke 24:13-15 "Behold, two of them went that same day to a village called Emmaus ... while they communed together ... Jesus himself drew near, and went with them."

At the tomb
John 20:14 "She turned herself back, and saw Jesus standing ..."

22. What was the order of appearances of Jesus after resurrection?

Mary Magdalene, the other Mary, the eleven disciples
Matthew 28:1, 9, 16-17 "Mary Magdalene and the other Mary [came] ... Jesus met them ... the eleven disciples ... saw him [Jesus] ..."

Mary Magdalene, Mary the mother of James and Salome, the eleven disciples
Mark 16:9, 12, 14 "Now when Jesus was risen ... he appeared first to Mary Magdalene. After that he appeared in another form unto two of them [Mary the mother of James and Salome] ... Afterward he appeared unto the eleven."

Cleophas and another person, then the eleven disciples
Luke 24:15, 33, 36 "They [Cleophas and another person] communed together and reasoned, Jesus himself drew near, and went with them ... Jesus himself stood in the midst of them [eleven disciples], and saith unto them, Peace be unto you."

Mary Magdalene, the disciples without Thomas, the eleven disciples with Thomas
John 20:14, 19, 26 "She turned herself back, and saw Jesus standing ... came Jesus and stood in the midst [of the disciples without Thomas], And after eight days again his disciples were within, and Thomas with them: then came Jesus ..."

Cephas, 12 apostles (but Judas was dead), 500+ people, James, all apostles, Paul
I Corinthians 15:5-8 "He was seen of Cephas, then of the twelve ... he was seen of above five hundred brethren ... After that, he was seen of James; then of all the apostles. And last of all he was seen of me [Paul] ..."

23. Were the disciples glad to see Jesus?

No, they were frightened
Luke 24:37 "But they were terrified and affrighted ..."

Yes, they were glad
John 20:20 "Then were the disciples glad, when they saw the Lord"

24. How many disciples saw Jesus after resurrection?

Eleven
Matthew 28:16 "The eleven disciples went away ... they saw him ..."

Ten (12 minus Thomas and Judas)
John 20:19-24 "Then ... the disciples were assembled ... came Jesus ... and saith unto them, Peace be unto you ... Thomas, one of the twelve, called Didymus, was not with them when Jesus came."

Twelve
I Corinthians 15:5 "He was seen of Cephas, then of the twelve."

Note: In verse I Corinthians 15:5, Jesus was seen by Cephas then the twelve, why twelve? Is Cephas [Peter] a different person from the twelve? Also, during this time Judas was already dead.

25. Did Jesus allow to be touched after resurrection?

Yes, his feet
Matthew 28:9 "Jesus met them ... they came and held him by the feet ..."

Yes, his hands and feet
Luke 24:39 "Behold my hands and my feet, that it is I myself: handle me."

No, he did not allow

John 20:17 "Jesus saith unto her, Touch me not."

Yes, after a week he allowed Thomas to touch him
John 20:27 "Then saith he to Thomas, Reach hither thy finger, and behold my hands; and reach hither thy hand, and thrust it into my side: and be not faithless, but believing."

26. What did the visitors do upon seeing Jesus back from the dead?

They ran to tell the disciples
Matthew 28:8 "They departed quickly ... run to bring his disciples word."

They said nothing to anyone
Mark 16:8 "They went out quickly ... neither said they any thing to any man."

They told the eleven and then the rest
Luke 24:9 "They remembered his words ... told all these things unto the eleven, and all the rest."

The disciples went home, Mary Magdalene stayed outside weeping
John 20:10-11 "Then the disciples went away again unto their own home. But Mary stood without at the sepulchre weeping."

27. Where should the disciples go after resurrection?

The disciples were instructed to go to Galilee right after the resurrection
Matthew 26:32 "But after I am risen again, I will go before you into Galilee."
Mark 16:7 "But go your way, tell his disciples and Peter that he goeth before you into Galilee: there shall ye see him ..."

The disciples were not suppose to leave Jerusalem
Luke 24:49 "But tarry ye in the city of Jerusalem ..."
Acts 1:4 "[Jesus] commanded them that they should not depart from Jerusalem ..."

Jesus did not say where his disciples should go
John 20:17 "But go to my brethren, and say unto them, I ascend unto my Father, and your Father; and to my God, and your God."

28. Where did Jesus first appear to his disciples after resurrection?

In a mountain in Galilee
Matthew 28:16-17 "Then the eleven disciples went away into Galilee, into a mountain where Jesus had appointed them. And ... they saw him ..."

In a room

Mark 16:14 "Afterward he appeared unto the eleven as they sat at meat ..."
John 20:19 "The doors were shut where the disciples were assembled ... came Jesus and stood in the midst, and saith unto them, Peace be unto you."

In a room in Jerusalem
Luke 24:33, 36 "They [Cleophas and another person] ... returned to Jerusalem ... the eleven gathered ... Jesus [stood] in the midst of them."
Acts 1:3-4 "To whom also he shewed himself alive ... being seen of them forty days ... being assembled together with them, commanded them that they should not depart from Jerusalem ..."

Q. The ascension of Jesus Christ

1. When was the ascension of Jesus Christ?

About a week
Luke 24:1-51 "Now upon the first day of the week, very early in the morning, they came unto the sepulcher ... he was parted from them, and carried up into heaven."
Mark 16:9-19 "Now when Jesus was risen early the first day of the week ... after the Lord had spoken unto them, he was received up into heaven, and sat on the right hand of God."

Several days after his resurrection
Acts 13:31 "He was seen many days of them which came up with him from Galilee to Jerusalem, who are his witnesses unto the people."

Forty days after his resurrection
Acts 1:2-3, 9 "Until the day in which he was taken up ... being seen of them forty days   ... while they beheld, he was taken up; and a cloud received him out of their sight."

2. Where did Jesus Christ ascend?

No mention was made about ascension, but Jesus' last moments was in Galilee
Matthew 28:16-20 "Then the eleven disciples went away into Galilee, into a mountain where Jesus had appointed them ... and, lo, I am with you always, even unto the end of the world."

Near Jerusalem, indoors
Mark 16:14-19 "Afterward he appeared unto the eleven as they sat at meat ... So then after the Lord had spoken unto them, he was received up into heaven, and sat on the right hand of God."

From Bethany, outdoors

Luke 24:50-51 "He led them out as far as to Bethany … while he blessed them, he was parted from them, and carried up into heaven."

From Mount Olivet, outdoors
Acts 1:9-12 "He was taken up; and a cloud received him out of their sight … Then returned they unto Jerusalem from the mount called Olivet …"

Note: Bethany is on the southeastern slope of the Mount of Olives.

3. How many people were present during the ascension of Jesus?

One hundred twenty
Acts 1:15 "The number … about an hundred and twenty."

Five hundred
I Corinthians 15:6 "He was seen of above five hundred brethren at once."

R. The return of Jesus Christ

1. When is the second coming of Jesus?

This generation shall not pass, till all these things shall be fulfilled
Matthew 16:28 "Verily I say unto you, There be some standing here, which shall not taste of death, till they see the Son of man coming in his kingdom."
Revelation 22:7, 12, 20 "Behold, I come quickly … I come quickly …"

Note: The prophecy about the second coming of Christ was written about 2,000 years ago. However, to this day the 'end of all things' has not yet happened and the second coming of Christ has not yet taken place.

2. What will happen during the second coming of Jesus Christ?

Jesus will descend from the clouds
Matthew 24:30 "They shall see the Son of man coming in the clouds of heaven …"
Acts 1:11 "Jesus, which is taken up from you into heaven, shall so come in like manner as ye have seen him go into heaven."
Revelation 1:7 "Behold, he cometh with clouds; and every eye shall see him."

Those who are alive will meet him in the air
I Thessalonians 4:16-17 "For the Lord himself shall descend from heaven with a shout, with the voice of the archangel, and with the trump of God: and the dead in Christ shall rise first: Then we which are alive and remain shall be caught up together with them in the clouds, to meet the Lord in the air."

Jesus will kill the unrepentant with his sharp two edged sword tongue

Revelation 1:5-7, 16; 2:16 "Behold, he cometh with clouds ... and out of his mouth went a sharp two edged sword ... Repent; or else I will come unto thee quickly, and will fight against them with the sword of my mouth."

S. The Holy Spirit

1. In whose name should one be baptized?

The Father, the Son and the Holy Ghost
Matthew 28:19 "Go ye therefore, and teach all nations, baptizing them in the name of the Father, and of the Son, and of the Holy Ghost."

Note: Holy Spirit and Holy Ghost are synonymous and are used interchangeably.

In Jesus name
Acts 8:16 "They were baptized in the name of the Lord Jesus."

2. Who sent the Holy Ghost?

Jesus
John 15:26 "But when the Comforter [Holy Ghost] is come, whom I will send unto you ..."

The Father
John 14:26 "But the Comforter, which is the Holy Ghost, whom the Father will send in my name"

3. When was the Holy Ghost given to the apostles?

The Holy Ghost was given before Pentecost
John 20:22 "He [Jesus] had said this ... Receive ye the Holy Ghost."

The Holy Ghost was given at Pentecost
Acts 1:8 "But ye shall receive power, after that the Holy Ghost is come upon you."
Acts 2:1-4 "When the day of Pentecost was ... come ... they were all filled with the Holy Ghost"

4. Was the Holy Ghost given after resurrection?

Yes
John 7:39 "The Holy Ghost was not yet given; because that Jesus was not yet glorified."
John 20:22 "He [Jesus] ... breathed on them, and saith ... Receive ye the Holy Ghost."

Acts 2:1-4 "When the day of Pentecost was fully come ... And they were all filled with the Holy Ghost, and began to speak with other tongues ..."

No, before resurrection
Mark 12:36 "For David himself said by the Holy Ghost, The Lord said to my Lord, Sit thou on my right hand, till I make thine enemies thy footstool."
Luke 1:15 "He [John the Baptist] shall be filled with the Holy Ghost ... from his mother's womb."
Luke 1:41 "Elisabeth was filled with the Holy Ghost."
Luke 1:67 "Zacharias was filled with the Holy Ghost."
Luke 2:25 "There was a man in Jerusalem, ... Simeon ... and the Holy Ghost was upon him."
Acts 1:16 "The Holy Ghost by the mouth of David spake ..."

5. The Holy Spirit cannot come to the world until after Jesus has departed

Yes
John 7:39 "But this spake he of the Spirit, which they that believe on him should receive: for the Holy Ghost was not yet given; because that Jesus was not yet glorified."
John 1:7 "The same came for a witness, to bear witness of the Light, that all men through him might believe."
Acts 1:2-5 "Until the day in which he was taken up, after that he through the Holy Ghost had given commandments unto the apostles whom he had chosen ... For John truly baptized with water; but ye shall be baptized with the Holy Ghost not many days hence."

No, David had it
I Samuel 16:13 "The Spirit of the Lord came upon David from that day forward."

No, John the Baptist had it
Luke 1:15 "For he shall be great in the sight of the Lord ... he shall be filled with the Holy Ghost, even from his mother's womb."

No, Elizabeth had it
Luke 1:41 "Elisabeth was filled with the Holy Ghost."

No, Zechariah had it
Luke 1:67 "His father Zacharias was filled with the Holy Ghost ..."

No Simeon had it
Luke 2:25 "Behold, there was a man in Jerusalem, whose name was Simeon ... and the Holy Ghost was upon him."

It can be obtained by prayer anytime
Luke 11:13 "If ye then, being evil, know how to give good gifts unto your children: how much more shall your heavenly Father give the Holy Spirit to them that ask him?"

T. After the ascension of Jesus Christ

1. Joshua or Jesus?

King James: Jesus
Acts 7:45 "Which also our fathers that came after brought in with *Jesus* into the possession of the Gentiles, whom God drave out before the face of our fathers, unto the days of David."

Revised Standard Version: Joshua
Acts 7:45 "Our fathers in turn brought it in with *Joshua* when they dispossessed the nations that God drove out before our fathers. So it was until the days of David"

2. When did King Herod intend to bring forth Peter to the people?

King James: After Easter
Acts 12:4 "When he [King Herod] had apprehended him [Peter], he put him in prison ... intending after *Easter* to bring him forth to the people."

Douay Rheims (Catholic): After Pasch
Acts 12:4 "When he [King Herod] had apprehended him [Peter], he put him in prison ... intending after the *pasch* to bring him forth to the people."

Revised Standard Version: After Passover
Acts 12:4 "When he had taken him, he put him in prison ... intending after the *Passover* to bring him forth to the people."

Note: Acts 12:4 either has Easter, Pasch or Passover depending on the Bible version. However, Easter was first established as a religious feast at the First Council of Nicaea (325 AD).

U. Concerning Paul

1. Did Paul ever meet Jesus?

No, Paul allegedly met Jesus in his visions
Acts 22:14 "He said, The God of our fathers hath chosen thee, that thou shouldest know his will, and see that Just One, and shouldest hear the voice of his mouth."

Acts 22:17-19 "When I was come again to Jerusalem, even while I prayed in the temple, I was in a trance; And saw him [Jesus] saying unto me, Make haste, and get thee quickly out of Jerusalem"

Paul said Jesus appeared to him
I Corinthians 15:7-8 "He [Jesus] was seen of James; then of all the apostles. And last of all he was seen of me also, as of one born out of due time."

Paul said he is not sure of his visions
II Corinthians 12:1-3 "It is not expedient for me doubtless to glory. I will come to visions and revelations of the Lord. I knew a man in Christ above fourteen years ago, (whether in the body, I cannot tell; or whether out of the body, I cannot tell: God knoweth;) such an one caught up to the third heaven. And I knew such a man, (whether in the body, or out of the body, I cannot tell: God knoweth;)."

Paul said he gets instructions from Jesus thru his visions
Galatians 1:11-12 "But I certify you, brethren, that the gospel which was preached of me is not after man … but by the revelation of Jesus Christ."

2. When Paul fell to the ground, did his companions also fell?

No
Acts 9:4, 7 "He [Paul] fell to the earth … the men which journeyed with him stood speechless …"

Yes
Acts 26:14 "When we were all fallen to the earth, I heard a voice …"

3. Did Paul's men hear a voice?

Yes, but saw no man
Acts 9:7 "The men which journeyed with him … hearing a voice, but seeing no man."

No, but saw a light
Acts 22:9 "They that were with me saw indeed the light, and were afraid; but they heard not the voice of him that spake to me."

4. Did Paul saw Jesus on the road to Damascus?

No, Paul did not see Jesus on the road to Damascus
Acts 9:8 "Saul arose from the earth; and when his eyes were opened, he saw no man."

Paul claims that Jesus showed himself to him
I Corinthians 15:8 "Last of all he [Jesus] was seen of me also …"

Note: Paul did not see Jesus on the road to Damascus. But Paul claims that Jesus showed himself to him.

5. Did the voice on the road to Damascus say what Paul's duties would be?

No
Acts 9:10 "I said, What shall I do, Lord? And the Lord said … go into Damascus; and there it shall be told thee of all things which are appointed for thee to do."

Yes
Acts 26:16-18 "Rise … I have appeared unto thee … to make thee a minister and a witness … they may receive forgiveness of sins …"

6. Did Paul say Christians should come together on Sundays?

Acts 20:7 "Upon *the first day of the week*, when the disciples came together to break bread, Paul preached unto them, ready to depart on the morrow; and continued his speech until midnight."
Colossians 2:14-17 "Blotting out the handwriting of ordinances that was against us, which was contrary to us, and took it out of the way, nailing it to his cross … Let no man therefore judge you in meat, or in drink, *or in respect of an holyday*, or of the new moon, *or of the sabbath days*: Which are a shadow of things to come; but the body is of Christ."

7. Paul became a ringleader of a sect of Nazarenes

Acts 24:5 "For we have found this man a pestilent fellow, and a mover of sedition among all the Jews throughout the world, and a ringleader of the sect of the Nazarenes."
Acts 28:22 "But we desire to hear of thee what thou thinkest: for as concerning this sect, we know that every where it is spoken against."

8. Paul was mistaken for a god

Acts 28:3-6 "Paul had gathered a bundle of sticks, and laid them on the fire … (a viper came out and Paul was not harmed), [the barbarians] said … he [Paul] was a god."

9. Did Paul went to Jerusalem immediately after his conversion

Yes
Acts 9:26 "When Saul was come to Jerusalem, he assayed to join himself to the disciples."

No, Paul went to Jerusalem three years after
Galatians 1:17-18 "Neither went I up to Jerusalem to them which were apostles before me ... Then after three years I went up to Jerusalem to see Peter, and abode with him fifteen days."

10. How many times did Paul go to Jerusalem?

Five times according to the Book of Acts

First visit to Jerusalem, right after his conversion in Damascus
Acts 9:26 "When Saul was come to Jerusalem, he assayed to join himself to the disciples ..."

Second visit to Jerusalem, to help for the relief of famine
Acts 11:29-30 "Then the disciples ... determined to send relief unto the brethren which dwelt in Judaea ... sent it to the elders by the hands of Barnabas and Saul."

Third visit, to attend Council of Jerusalem
Acts 15:2-4 "They determined that Paul and Barnabas ... should go up to Jerusalem ... And when they were come to Jerusalem, they were received of the church ..."

Fourth visit, to keep the feast
Acts 18:21-22 "But bade them farewell, saying, I [Paul] must by all means keep this feast that cometh in Jerusalem: but I will return again unto you, if God will. And he sailed from Ephesus ... and gone up, and saluted the church ..."

Fifth visit, Paul was arrested and killed
Acts 21:17, 30-31 "When we [Paul and company] were come to Jerusalem ... they took Paul ... they went about to kill him ... all Jerusalem was in an uproar."

Three times, according to other books

Paul did not visit Jerusalem immediately after his conversion
Galatians 1:17-18 "Neither went I up to Jerusalem to them ... Then after three years I went up to Jerusalem to see Peter, and abode with him fifteen days."

First visit to Jerusalem, met with Peter and James
Galatians 1:18 "Then after three years I went up to Jerusalem to see Peter, and abode with him fifteen days."

Second visit to Jerusalem, Paul met with Barnabas and Titus
Galatians 2:1 "Then fourteen years after I went up again to Jerusalem with Barnabas, and took Titus with me also ..."

Third visit to Jerusalem, Paul helped the poor
Romans 15:25 "But now I go unto Jerusalem to minister unto the saints."
I Corinthians 16:3 "When I come, whomsoever ye shall approve by your letters, them will I send to bring your liberality unto Jerusalem."

Note: Unlike in the Book of Acts, in the Book of Galatians, there was no visit to Jerusalem immediately after his conversion.

11. Whom did Paul meet in Jerusalem during his first visit?

Barnabas
Acts 9:26-27 "When Saul was come to Jerusalem ... Barnabas took him, and brought him to the apostles ..."

Peter and James
Galatians 1:18-19 "Then after three years I went up to Jerusalem to see Peter, and abode with him fifteen days. But other of the apostles saw I none, save James the Lord's brother."

12. A man was deliberately blinded by Paul

Acts 13:9-11 "Then Saul, (who also is called Paul,) filled with the Holy Ghost, set his eyes on him [Elymas]. And said ... behold, the hand of the Lord is upon thee, and thou shalt be blind, not seeing the sun for a season. And immediately there fell on him a mist and a darkness; and he went about seeking some to lead him by the hand."

Summary: Elymas, a sorcerer was deliberately blinded by Paul.

13. Paul was forbidden to teach in Asia by the Holy Ghost

Yes, Paul was forbidden
Acts 16:6 "[They] ... were forbidden of the Holy Ghost to preach the word in Asia."

But, Paul teaches in Asia anyway
Acts 19:9-10 "He [Paul] departed ... all they which dwelt in Asia heard the word of the Lord Jesus, both Jews and Greeks."

14. What is the fulfillment of the law?

Paul said, "Love your neighbor as yourself."
Romans 13:9-10 "Thou shalt love thy neighbour as thyself. Love worketh no ill to his neighbour: therefore love is the fulfilling of the law."

Jesus said, "Love God with all your heart and love your neighbor as yourself."

Matthew 22:37-40 "Jesus said, Thou shalt love the Lord thy God with all thy heart … with all thy soul … with all thy mind. This is the first and great commandment. And the second is Thou shalt love thy neighbour as thyself. *On these two commandments hang all the law and the prophets.*"

15. The gospel has already been preached all over the world

Romans 10:18 "But I say … Yes verily, their sound went into all the earth, and their words unto the ends of the world."

16. Paul was not sure if he baptized some people or not

I Corinthians 1:14-16 "I thank God that I baptized none of you, but Crispus and Gaius; Lest any should say that I had baptized in mine own name. And I baptized also the household of Stephanas: besides, I know not whether I baptized any other."

17. Paul was trying to create his own sect, cult or religion

I Corinthians 4:16; 11:1 "Wherefore I beseech you, be ye followers of me … Be ye followers of me, even as I also am of Christ."

18. Paul asked if members of Christ should be united with a harlot

I Corinthians 6:15-16 "Know ye not that your bodies are the members of Christ? shall I then take the members of Christ, and make them the members of an harlot? God forbid. What? know ye not that he which is joined to an harlot is one body? for two, saith he, shall be one flesh."

19. Those who are circumcised must not be uncircumcised

I Corinthians 7:18 "Is any man called being circumcised? let him not become uncircumcised. Is any called in uncircumcision? let him not be circumcised."

20. If you eat and drink unworthily you will get sick and die

I Corinthians 11:29-30 "For he that eateth and drinketh unworthily, eateth and drinketh damnation to himself, not discerning the Lord's body. For this cause many are weak and sickly among you, and many sleep."

21. Paul said that all prophecies will fail

I Corinthians 13:8 "Charity never faileth: but whether there be prophecies, they shall fail; whether there be tongues, they shall cease; whether there be knowledge, it shall vanish away."

Note: Paul made a prophecy that all prophecies will fail. If his prophecy is true, then all prophecies will fail even his own prophecy, thus making his own prophecy false.

22. Paul believed the story of Adam and Eve

II Corinthians 11:3 "But I fear ... as the serpent beguiled Eve ..."

23. Paul said he robs other churches

II Corinthians 11:8 "I robbed other churches, taking wages of them, to do you service."

24. Who attempted to seize Paul?

The governor under Aretas the king
II Corinthians 11:32-33 "In Damascus the governor under Aretas the king ... desirous to apprehend me."

The Jews
Acts 9:22-24 "But Saul ... confounded the Jews which dwelt at Damascus ... the Jews took counsel to kill him: But their laying await was known of Saul. And they watched the gates day and night to kill him."

25. Did Paul try to please men?

Paul said that if he pleased men, he should not be the servant of Christ
Galatians 1:10 "For if I yet pleased men, I should not be the servant of Christ."

Paul said he pleased men in all things
I Corinthians 10:33 "Even as I please all men in all things, not seeking mine own profit, but the profit of many, that they may be saved."

26. Anybody who is contrary to Paul's teachings will be accursed

Galatians 1:8-9 "But though we, or an angel from heaven, preach any other gospel unto you than that which we have preached unto you, let him be accursed. As we said before, so say I now again, if any man preach any other gospel unto you than that ye have received, let him be accursed."

27. Paul said, he was never taught by man but by Jesus Christ thru visions

Galatians 1:11-12 "But I certify you, brethren, that the gospel which was preached of me is not after man ... but by the revelation of Jesus Christ."

Note: However, Paul never met Jesus Christ.

28. Did Paul use trickery?

Yes
II Corinthians 12:16 "I did not burden you: nevertheless, being crafty, I caught you with guile."

No
I Thessalonians 2:3 "For our exhortation was not of deceit, nor of uncleanness, nor in guile."

29. Paul said, if you do everything he says, you will be at peace with God

Philippians 4:9 "Those things, which ye have both learned, and received, and heard, and seen in me, do: and the God of peace shall be with you."

30. Paul said Jesus Christ was insufficient and he will fill up what was lacking

Colossians 1:24 "Who now rejoice in my sufferings for you, and fill up that which is behind of the afflictions of Christ in my flesh for his body's sake, which is the church."

31. Paul said God's wrath would come upon the Jews

I Thessalonians 2:14-16 "For ye … have suffered like things of your own countrymen, even as they have of the Jews: Who both killed the Lord Jesus, and their own prophets, and have persecuted us … *for the wrath is come upon them to the uttermost.*"

32. What did Paul say about himself?

Paul claimed to be just, holy and blameless
I Thessalonians 2:10 "Ye are witnesses, and God also, how holily and justly and unblameably we behaved ourselves among you that believe."

Paul claimed he is the most sinful of all men
I Timothy 1:15 "Christ Jesus came into the world to save sinners; of whom I am chief."

33. Paul advised not to drink water but to drink wine

I Timothy 5:23 "Drink no longer water, but use a little wine for thy stomach's sake and thine often infirmities."

34. Paul gave a list of things that supposedly indicate the 'last days'

II Timothy 3:1-5 "This know also, that in the last days perilous times shall come. For men shall be lovers of their own selves ... lovers of pleasures more than lovers of God; Having a form of godliness, but denying the power thereof: from such turn away."

Note: What Paul indicated as a sign of the last days is just about the ugly side of human nature which is prevalent throughout history.

35. Did Paul violate a law in the book of Deuteronomy?

Paul returned Onesimus to his previous master
Philemon 1:10-16 "I beseech thee for my son Onesimus ... For perhaps he therefore departed for a season, that thou shouldest receive him for ever; Not now as a servant, but above a servant, a brother beloved ..."

Do not return a slave to his master
Deuteronomy 23:15-16 "Thou shalt not deliver unto his master the servant which is escaped from his master unto thee: He shall dwell with thee, even among you, in that place which he shall choose in one of thy gates, where it liketh him best: thou shalt not oppress him."

V. The kingdom of heaven

1. Who went to heaven?

Enoch
Genesis 5:24 "Enoch walked with God: and he was not; for God took him."
Hebrews 11:5 "By faith Enoch was translated that he should not see death; and was not found, because God had translated him."

Elijah went up to heaven
II Kings 2:11 "Elijah went up by a whirlwind into heaven."

Note: However, in verse II Kings 2:15, it says that Elijah was just carried away to a different place:
II Kings 2:15 "When the sons of the prophets ... said ... Elijah doth rest on Elisha ..."

In II Chronicles 21:12, Elijah sent a letter to King Jehoram:
II Chronicles 21:12 "There came a writing to him from Elijah the prophet, saying, Thus saith the Lord God of David thy father, Because thou hast not walked in the ways of Jehoshaphat thy father, nor in the ways of Asa king of Judah"

Moses (implied)
Matthew 17:1-8 "After six days Jesus taketh Peter, James, and John his brother, and bringeth them up into an high mountain ... behold, there appeared unto them Moses and Elias ..."

Only the Son of Man (Jesus) ascended to heaven
John 3:13 "No man hath ascended up to heaven, but he that came down from heaven, even the Son of man which is in heaven."

An unknown man
II Corinthians 12:1-4 "I knew a man ... one caught up to the third heaven. And I knew such a man ... he was caught up into paradise ..."

2. Did Jesus say that you could drink wine in heaven?

Matthew 26:29 "But I say unto you, I will not drink henceforth of this fruit of the vine, until that day when I drink it new with you in my Father's kingdom."

3. What Jesus said concerning heaven?

Luke 20:35 "But they which shall be accounted worthy to obtain that world, and the resurrection from the dead, neither marry, nor are given in marriage."

Note: Did Jesus say that only those who never got married would go to Heaven?

W. The end of the world

1. Will the earth be forever?

No
Psalm 102:25-26 "Of old hast thou laid the foundation of the earth ...They shall perish ... all of them shall wax old like a garment."
Isaiah 65:17 "For, behold, I create new heavens and a new earth: and the former shall not be remembered, nor come into mind."
Matthew 5:18 "Till heaven and earth pass ..."

Yes
Deuteronomy 4:40 "That thou mayest prolong thy days upon the earth, which the Lord thy God giveth thee for ever."
Psalm 37:29 "The righteous shall inherit the land, and dwell therein for ever."

2. Jesus gave a list of things that supposedly indicates the 'last days'

Matthew 24:4-12 "Jesus [said] ... Take heed that no man deceive you. For many shall come in my name, saying, I am Christ; and shall deceive many. And ye shall hear of wars ... And then shall many be offended, and shall betray one another, and shall hate one another ... the love of many shall wax cold."

Note: What Jesus was saying as signs of the last days have been happening all throughout history.

3. Is the day of the Lord close at hand?

Yes
I Thessalonians 4:15-17 "For this we say unto you by the word of the Lord, that we which are alive and remain unto the coming of the Lord shall not prevent them which are asleep ... Then we which are alive and remain shall be caught up together with them in the clouds, to meet the Lord in the air: and so shall we ever be with the Lord."
I Thessalonians 5:23 "Your whole spirit and soul and body be preserved blameless unto the coming of our Lord Jesus Christ."

No
II Thessalonians 2:3 "Let no man deceive you by any means: for that day shall not come, except there come a falling away first, and that man of sin be revealed, the son of perdition."

4. How will Jesus be revealed?

II Thessalonians 1:7 "Lord Jesus shall be revealed from heaven with his mighty angels."

5. Jesus will punish those who do not know God

II Thessalonians 1:7-9 "[Jesus] In flaming fire taking vengeance on them that know not God ... Who shall be punished with everlasting destruction from the presence of the Lord ..."

6. How will Jesus punish the wicked?

By consuming them with the spirit of his mouth and the brightness of his coming
II Thessalonians 2:8 "Then shall that Wicked be revealed, whom the Lord shall consume with the spirit of his mouth, and shall destroy with the brightness of his coming."

7. Is Satan all-powerful?

II Thessalonians 2:9 "Satan with all power and signs and lying wonders."

Note: If Satan is all-powerful, is Satan as powerful as God?

8. How will Jesus look like upon his return?

His hairs white as wool, eyes like fire, feet like brass and mouth with two sharp edged sword
Revelation 1:14-16 "His head and his hairs were white like wool, as white as snow; and his eyes were as a flame of fire; And his feet like unto fine brass ... in his right hand seven stars: and out of his mouth went a sharp two edged sword ..."

9. Are the false Jews but the synagogue of Satan?

Revelation 2:9; 3:9 "I know thy works, and tribulation, and poverty, (but thou art rich) and I know the blasphemy of them which say they are Jews, and are not, but are the synagogue of Satan ... Behold, I will make them of the synagogue of Satan, which say they are Jews, and are not, but do lie ..."

10. God has seven spirits, which have seven horns and seven eyes

Revelation 3:1; 5:6 "The seven Spirits of God, and the seven stars ... a Lamb as it had been slain, having seven horns and seven eyes, which are the seven Spirits of God ..."

11. The locusts and the burned grass

All the green grass will be burned
Revelation 8:7 "The first angel sounded, and there followed hail and fire ... and all green grass was burnt up."

The locust were told not to hurt the grass
Revelation 9:3-4 "There came out of the smoke locusts upon the earth ... And it was commanded them that they should not hurt the grass of the earth"

Note: The locust cannot hurt the grass, but all the grass were already burned.

12. Locusts with men's faces, women's hair, lion's teeth and scorpion's tails

Revelation 9:7-8, 10 "The shapes of the locusts were like unto horses ... their faces were as the faces of men ... the hair of women ... teeth were as the teeth of lions ... tails like unto scorpions"

13. Four angles with a 200 million army will kill one third of all the men

Revelation 9:15-16 "The four angels were loosed … to slay the third part of men. And the number of the army of the horsemen were two hundred thousand thousand."

14. An angel tells John to eat a book

Revelation 10:9-10 "I [John] went unto the angel, and said … Give me the little book. And he said unto me, Take it, and eat it up … I took the little book out of the angel's hand, and ate it up."

15. God will send an earthquake and 7,000 people will be killed

Revelation 11:13 "The same hour was there a great earthquake … slain of men seven thousand."

16. There will be a war between Michael, his angels and the dragon

Revelation 12:7 "There was war in heaven: Michael and his angels fought against the dragon; and the dragon fought and his angels."

17. Those with the mark of the beast will be tormented

Revelation 14:9-10 "If any man worship the beast and his image, and receive his mark in his forehead, or in his hand … shall drink of the wine of the wrath of God … [and] shall be tormented with fire and brimstone …"

18. Concerning the winepress of the wrath of God

Revelation 14:19-20 "The winepress [into the great winepress of the wrath of God] was trodden without the city, and blood came out of the winepress, even unto the horse bridles, by the space of a thousand and six hundred furlongs."

19. The seven vials of wrath

Revelation 16:1-21 "I heard a great voice out of the temple saying to the seven angels, Go your ways, and pour out the vials of the wrath of God upon the earth. And the first went, and poured out his vial upon the earth …"

Note: The seven vials of wrath: 1) a noisome and grievous sore upon the men which had the mark of the beast, and upon them which worshipped his image, 2) sea turned to blood, and every living soul died in the sea. 3) rivers and fountains of waters turned to blood, 4) people scorched with fire, 5) people gnawed their tongues in pain, 6) Euphrates dries up, 7) thunder, lightening, earthquake, and hail.

20. We must always wear clothes because Jesus will come like a thief

Revelation 16:15 "Behold, I come as a thief. Blessed is he that watcheth, and keepeth his garments, lest he walk naked, and they see his shame."

21. Jesus has a sharp sword sticking out of his mouth

Revelation 19:13, 15 "He was clothed with a vesture dipped in blood: and his name is called The Word of God. And out of his mouth goeth a sharp sword."

22. All the fowls will eat dead bodies, the supper of the great God

Revelation 19:17-18 "I saw an angel … saying to all the fowls that fly in the midst of heaven, Come and gather yourselves together unto the supper of the great God; That ye may eat the flesh of kings … and the flesh of all men, both free and bond, both small and great."

23. The beast and the false prophet are cast into a lake of fire

Revelation 19:20-21 "The beast was taken, and with him the false prophet … These both were cast alive into a lake of fire burning with brimstone. And the remnant were slain with the sword of him that sat upon the horse, which sword proceeded out of his mouth: and all the fowls were filled with their flesh."

Note: *The beast and the false prophet are cast into a lake of fire. The rest killed with the sword of Jesus and all the fowls filled with their flesh*

24. After a thousand years, God will send Satan to deceive us all

Revelation 20:7-8 "When the thousand years are expired, Satan shall be loosed out of his prison, And shall go out to deceive the nations which are in the four quarters of the earth."

Note: *The one thousand years are the years when Christ will reign before the final judgment. This belief is called Millennialism.*

25. God will send fire from heaven to devour people

Revelation 20:9 "Fire came down from God out of heaven, and devoured them."

26. Whoever isn't in the book of life will be cast into the lake of fire

Revelation 20:15 "Whosoever was not found ... in the book of life was cast into the lake of fire."

27. The fearful and unbelieving will be cast into a lake of fire

Revelation 21:8 "But the fearful, and unbelieving, and the abominable, and murderers, and whoremongers, and sorcerers, and idolaters, and all liars, shall have their part in the lake which burneth with fire and brimstone: which is the second death."

28. People were told not to change for the better

Revelation 22:11 "He that is unjust, let him be unjust still: and he which is filthy, let him be filthy still: and he that is righteous, let him be righteous still: and he that is holy, let him be holy still."

3. Unfulfilled promises and prophecies

A. Concerning prophets making mistakes

1. What does the Bible say if prophets make a mistake?

Prophets must be executed if they tell you to worship other gods
Deuteronomy 13:1-5 "If there arise among you a prophet ... saying, Let us go after other gods ... that prophet ... shall be put to death; because he hath spoken to turn you away from ... your God."

Prophets must be executed if they speak for God but God did not command them to
Deuteronomy 18:20 "But the prophet, which shall presume to speak a word in my name, which I have not commanded him to speak, or that shall speak in the name of other gods, even that prophet shall die."

Note: What is the basis of determining if a prophet was commanded by God or not?

2. Sometimes God makes his prophets lie

I Kings 22:22-23 "The Lord said ... I will be a lying spirit in the mouth of all his prophets ... the Lord hath put a lying spirit in the mouth of all these thy prophets ..."
II Chronicles 18:21-22 "He [a spirit] said, I will go out, and be a lying spirit in the mouth of all his prophets ... the Lord hath put a lying spirit in the mouth of these thy prophets ..."

3. The prophet's prophecies are lies

Jeremiah 5:31 "The prophets prophecy lies."

4. Those lying prophets will be killed

Jeremiah 14:14-15 "Then the Lord said to me, "The prophets are prophecying lies in my name. I have not sent them ... Those same prophets will perish by sword and famine."

5. Do not be afraid of false prophets

Deuteronomy 18:22 "When a prophet speaketh in the name of the Lord, if the thing follow not, nor come to pass, that is the thing which the Lord hath not spoken, but the prophet hath spoken it presumptuously: thou shalt not be afraid of him."

B. The early biblical prophecies

1. Did Adam die after eating the forbidden fruit?

God told Adam that he will die if he will eat from the forbidden fruit
Genesis 2:17 "But of the tree of the knowledge of good and evil, thou shalt not eat of it: for in the day that thou eatest thereof thou shalt surely die."

Adam did not die
Genesis 5:5 "Adam lived were nine hundred and thirty years: and he died."

Note: But then Adam and Eve ate the forbidden fruit from the tree in the middle of the garden. But did they die? Did God lie?

2. What will happen to Cain?

God said that Cain will become a fugitive and a vagabond
Genesis 4:9, 12 "The Lord said unto Cain ... a fugitive and a vagabond shalt thou be in the earth."

Cain did not become a fugitive or a vagabond, he had a family and built a city
Genesis 4:17 "Cain knew his wife; and she conceived, and bare Enoch: and he builded a city, and called the name of the city, after the name of his son, Enoch."

3. What was the covenant about the rainbow in the sky?

Genesis 9:9-11 "Behold, I establish my covenant with you ... neither shall all flesh be cut off any more by the waters of a flood; neither shall there any more be a flood to destroy the earth ..."

Note: After the Great Deluge during Noah's time, the rainbow was placed in the sky as a reminder of God's covenant – never will man be punished again by means of water. However, the existence of floods, tidal waves and tsunamis invalidates this statement. Does God break His promise? Does God forget?

4. God's promised to Abraham was unfulfilled

God promised Abraham the Land of Canaan
Genesis 12:7 "The Lord ... said, Unto thy seed will I give this land."

However, Abraham died without receiving God's promise
Genesis 25:8 "Abraham gave up the ghost, and died in a good old age ..."

God's promise to Abraham did not materialize
Acts 7:5 "He gave him none inheritance in it, no, not so much as to set his

foot on: yet he promised that he would give it to him for a possession, and to his seed after him, when as yet he had no child."

Hebrews 11:13 "These all died in faith, not having received the promises, but having seen them afar off, and were persuaded of them, and embraced them, and confessed that they were strangers and pilgrims on the earth."

5. God's promise to Jacob was also unfulfilled

Genesis 28:13 "Behold, the Lord stood above it, and said ... the land whereon thou liest, to thee will I give it, and to thy seed."

6. How long was the Egyptian captivity?

400 years
Genesis 15:13 "He [God] said ... thy seed shall be a stranger in a land that is not theirs ... they shall afflict them four hundred years"
Acts 7:6 "God spake ... his seed should sojourn in a strange land ... and entreat them evil four hundred years."

430 years
Exodus 12:40 "The children of Israel ... dwelt in Egypt ... four hundred and thirty years."
Galatians 3:17 "This I say, that the covenant, that was confirmed before of God in Christ, the law, which was four hundred and thirty years after ..."

7. When did Abraham's descendants return from Egyptian captivity?

Fourth generation
Genesis 15:16 "In the fourth generation they shall come hither again."

Seventh generation Abraham, Isaac, Jacob, Levi, Kohath, Amram, Moses
Genesis 21:3 "Abraham called the name of his son ... Isaac."
Genesis 25:19-26 "These are the generations of Isaac, Abraham's son: Abraham begat Isaac ... (and Isaac begat a son) ... and his name was called Jacob."
Genesis 35:22-23 "The sons of Jacob were ... Reuben ... Simeon ... *Levi* ..."
Exodus 6:16 "The sons of Levi... Gershon, and *Kohath* ..."
Exodus 6:18 "The sons of Kohath; Amram ..."
Exodus 6:20 "Amram took ... his father's sister to wife; and she bare him ... Moses."

Note: Moses was the seventh generation from Abraham and it was Moses who led the Israelites out of Egypt.

8. God promised Isaac his seed will be as many as the stars in heaven

Genesis 26:4 "I will make thy seed to multiply as the stars of heaven, and will give unto thy seed all these countries; and in thy seed shall all the nations of the earth be blessed."

Note: However, the Jews are still a minority to this day.

9. God promised to bring Jacob safely back to Israel from Egypt

God promised to bring Jacob back from Egypt
Genesis 46:4 "I [Lord] will go down with thee [Jacob] into Egypt; and I [Lord] will also surely bring thee [Jacob] up again."

But Jacob passed away in Egypt
Genesis 47:28-29 "Jacob lived in the land of Egypt … and the time drew nigh that Israel must die: and he called his son Joseph, and said … bury me not, I pray thee, in Egypt."

10. God will bring Joseph safely back to Israel from Egypt

God shall bring Joseph back to Israel
Genesis 48:21 "Israel said unto Joseph, Behold, I die: but God shall be with you, and bring you again unto the land of your fathers."

Joseph stayed and died in Egypt
Genesis 50:24 "Joseph said unto his brethren, I die: and God will surely visit you, and bring you out of this land unto the land which he sware to Abraham, to Isaac, and to Jacob."

11. The King of Israel will be from the tribe of Judah

The king will come from the tribe of Judah
Genesis 49:10 "The sceptre shall not depart from Judah, nor a lawgiver from between his feet, until Shiloh come; and unto him shall the gathering of the people be."

But King Saul is from the tribe of Benjamin
Acts 13:21 "Afterward they desired a king: and God gave unto them Saul the son of Cis, a man of the tribe of Benjamin."

12. Is this a prophecy about Jesus?

Genesis 49:11-12 "Binding his foal unto the vine, and his ass's colt unto the choice vine; he washed his garments in wine, and his clothes in the blood of grapes: His eyes shall be red with wine, and his teeth white with milk."

C. The Exodus promises

1. What did God promise Moses concerning other groups of people?

God promised to drive out the Canaanites, the Jebusites and other groups
Exodus 33:2 "I will send an angel before thee; and I will drive out the Canaanite, the Amorite, and the Hittite, and the Perizzite, the Hivite, and the Jebusite."
Deuteronomy 7:1 "When the Lord thy God shall bring thee into the land whither thou goest to possess it, and hath cast out many nations before thee, the Hittites, and the Girgashites, and the Amorites, and the Canaanites, and the Perizzites, and the Hivites, and the Jebusites, seven nations greater and mightier than thou …"
Joshua 3:10 "Hereby ye shall know that the living God is among you, and that he will *without fail* drive out from before you the Canaanites, and the Hittites, and the Hivites, and the Perizzites, and the Girgashites, and the Amorites, and the Jebusites."

God promised to destroy the Canaanites, the Jebusites and other groups
Deuteronomy 7:24 "He shall deliver their kings into thine hand, and thou shalt destroy their name from under heaven: there shall no man be able to stand before thee, until thou have destroyed them."
Deuteronomy 31:3 "The Lord thy God, he will go over before thee, and he will destroy these nations from before thee …"

But the promises were unfulfilled
Joshua 15:63 "As for the Jebusites the inhabitants of Jerusalem, the children of Judah could not drive them out; but the Jebusites dwell with the children of Judah at Jerusalem unto this day."
Judges 1:21, 27, 34-36 "The children of Benjamin did not drive out the Jebusites that inhabited Jerusalem; but the Jebusites dwell with the children of Benjamin in Jerusalem unto this day."
Judges 3:1-5 "Now these are the nations which the Lord left, to prove Israel by them, even as many of Israel as had not known all the wars of Canaan … And the children of Israel dwelt among the Canaanites, Hittites, and Amorites, and Perizzites, and Hivites, and Jebusites."

2. God promised the Israelites they would never be sick or barren

Deuteronomy 7:14-15 "Thou shalt be blessed above all people: there shall not be male or female barren among you, or among your cattle. And the Lord will take away from thee all sickness, and will put none of the evil diseases of Egypt, which thou knowest, upon thee; but will lay them upon all them that hate thee."

Note: God also promised He will inflict upon the enemies of the Israelites.

D. The time of Kings

1. How long was the drought during Elijah's time?

Three years
I Kings 17:1, 18:1 "Elijah … said unto Ahab, As the Lord God of Israel liveth, before whom I stand, there shall not be dew nor rain these years, but according to my word … [And] the Lord came to Elijah in the *third year*, saying, Go, shew thyself unto Ahab; and I will send rain upon the earth."

Three years and six months
Luke 4:25 "But I tell you … the heaven was shut up *three years and six months*, when great famine was throughout all the land"
James 5:17 "Elias … prayed earnestly that it might not rain: and it rained not on the earth by the space of *three years and six months*."

2. God promised Josiah a peaceful death

He will die a peaceful death
II Kings 22:20 "Behold therefore, I [God] will gather thee [Josiah] unto thy fathers, and thou shalt be gathered into thy grave in peace; and thine eyes shall not see all the evil which I will bring upon this place."

Josiah did not die a peaceful death, Pharaohnechoh slew Josiah in a battle
II Kings 23:29-30 "And he [Pharaohnechoh] slew him [Josiah] at Megiddo … his servants carried him in a chariot dead from Megiddo, and brought him to Jerusalem, and buried him …"

Josiah did not die a peaceful death, the archers shot at Josiah
II Chronicles 35:23-24 "The archers shot at King Josiah … and they [his servants] brought him to Jerusalem, and he died."

Note: Is this a failed prophecy of Huldah the prophetess, or a failed promise of God?

3. The prophecy of Jeremiah about Jehoiakim

Jeremiah prophesied that Jehoiakim will not have a successor
Jeremiah 36:30 "Therefore thus says the Lord concerning Jehoiakim king of Judah, he shall have none to sit on the throne of David."

The son of Jehoiakim succeeded him
II Kings 24:6 "So Jehoiakim slept with his fathers and Jehoiachin his son reigned in his stead."

4. Zedekiah was promised a peaceful death

God promised Zedekiah a peaceful death
Jeremiah 34:2, 4-5 "Thus saith the Lord ... to Zedekiah king of Judah ... Thou shalt not die by the sword: But thou shalt die in peace."

But Zedekiah did not die a peaceful death
Jeremiah 52:10-11 "The king of Babylon slew the sons of Zedekiah before his eyes ... Then he put out the eyes of Zedekiah; and the king of Babylon bound him in chains, and carried him to Babylon, and put him in prison till the day of his death."

5. God's promise concerning David and Solomon's kingdom

Solomon's kingdom will be the wealthiest ever
II Chronicles 1:12 "I will give thee riches, and wealth, and honour, such as none of the kings have had that have been before thee, neither shall there any after thee have the like."

David and Solomon's kingdom will be forever
II Samuel 7:13, 16 "*I will establish the throne of his kingdom for ever.* And thine house and thy kingdom shall be established for ever before thee: thy throne shall be established for ever."
Psalm 89:3-4, 34-37 "I have made a covenant with my chosen, I have sworn unto David my servant, Thy seed will I establish for ever ... His seed shall endure for ever, and his throne as the sun before me. *It shall be established for ever ...*"

Note: Solomon's kingdom no longer exists today, the last king was Zedekiah and it was totally destroyed 400 years after Solomon passed away. The kingdom fell in 586 BCE to the Babylonian Empire.

E. The prophets' prophecies

1. Prophecies about Judah

The Lord told Isaiah to tell Ahaz that Judah will not be invaded
Isaiah 7:3-7 "Then said the Lord unto Isaiah, Go forth now to meet Ahaz ... and say unto him ... [fear not for] Syria, Ephraim, and [Pekah] the son of Remaliah, have taken evil counsel against thee, saying, Let us go up against Judah ... saith the Lord GOD, *It shall not stand, neither shall it come to pass.*"

Judah was invaded by Rezin and Pekah
II Kings 16:5 "Then Rezin king of Syria and Pekah son of Remaliah king of Israel came up to Jerusalem to war: and they besieged Ahaz, but could not overcome him."

II Chronicles 28:5-6 "He [Ahaz] was also given into the hands of the king of Israel, who inflicted heavy casualties on him. In one day Pekah son of Remaliah killed a hundred and twenty thousand soldiers in Judah ..."

Judah will be desolate and a den of dragons
Jeremiah 10:22 "Behold, the noise of the bruit is come, and a great commotion out of the north country, to make the cities of Judah desolate, and a den of dragons."

Note: Judea (Judah) is presently occupied by agriculture and sheep farmers.

2. What will happen to Babylon?

The Jews will be exiled in Babylon and Babylon will be uninhabited
Jeremiah 25:8-9, 12 "Thus saith the Lord ... I will punish the king of Babylon, and that nation ... for their iniquity, and the land of the Chaldeans, and will make it perpetual desolations."

Babylon will never be inhabited
Isaiah 13:20 "It [Babylon] shall never be inhabited, neither shall it be dwelt in from generation to generation ..."
Jeremiah 51:37 "Babylon shall become heaps, a dwelling place for dragons, an astonishment, and an hissing, without an inhabitant."

Babylon will sink
Jeremiah 51:64 "Thou shalt say, Thus shall Babylon sink, and shall not rise from the evil that I will bring upon her."

Note: However, there are no dragons in Babylon. Babylon, presently called Iraq, was never desolate and is very much occupied.

3. The nation or kingdom that does not serve Israel will perish

Isaiah 60:12 "For the nation and kingdom that will not serve thee [Israel] shall perish; yea, those nations shall be utterly wasted."

4. Hazor will be a dwelling for dragons, and a desolation for ever

Jeremiah 49:33 "Hazor shall be a dwelling for dragons, and a desolation for ever: there shall no man abide there, nor any son of man dwell in it."

Note: Today Hazor is a large archeological excavation site. About 20,000 people once lived in Hazor during 200 BCE.

5. What did Isaiah say about the city of Damascus?

Damascus will cease to be a city

Isaiah 17:1 "Behold, Damascus is taken away from being a city, and it shall be a ruinous heap."

Note: Damascus is the capital of Syria and is still a city up to this day.

6. The prophecies about Tyre

Tyre will be laid waste for 70 years
Isaiah 23:1, 15 "The burden of Tyre ... for it is laid waste, so that there is no house, no entering in ... And it shall come to pass in that day, that Tyre shall be forgotten seventy years ... after the end of seventy years shall Tyre sing as an harlot."

Note: Tyre was never laid waste for 70 years.

Nebuchadnezzar will demolish Tyre
Ezekiel 26:7-21 "For thus saith the Lord God ... *I will bring upon Tyrus Nebuchadrezzar king of Babylon* ... thou shalt be built no more ... I shall make thee a desolate city ... thou shalt be no more: though thou be sought for, yet shalt thou never be found again ..."
Ezekiel 27:32 "What city is like Tyrus, like the destroyed in the midst of the sea?"
Ezekiel 27:36, 28:19 "The merchants among the people shall hiss at thee ... [Tyre] shalt be a terror, and never shalt thou be any more."

Note: Nebuchadnezzar tried to invade Tyre for 13 years without success. In 332 BC, 240 years later, Alexander the Great succeeded in invading Tyre. After a siege of seven months, Alexander the Great successfully invaded Tyre, which was situated in a well-fortified island, by using ship-mounted ballistae and by creating a causeway connecting it to the mainland of Lebanon.

Ezekiel admits his mistake and Nebuchadnezzar will demolish Egypt instead
Ezekiel 29:17-19 "The word of the Lord came unto me, saying, Son of man, Nebuchadrezzar king of Babylon caused his army to serve a great service against Tyrus ... *yet had he no wages, nor his army, for Tyrus, for the service that he had served against it:* Therefore thus saith the Lord GOD; Behold, I will give the land of Egypt unto Nebuchadrezzar king of Babylon; and he shall take her multitude, and take her spoil, and take her prey; and it shall be the wages for his army."

Jesus went to Tyre
Matthew 15:21 "Jesus withdrew to the region of Tyre ..."
Mark 7:24-31 "[Jesus] arose, and went into the borders of Tyre ..."

Luke 6:17 "He came down with them ... from the sea coast of Tyre ..."

Herod's kingdom had a relationship with Tyre
Acts 12:20 "Herod was highly displeased with them of Tyre and Sidon: but they came with one accord to him ..."

Paul and his companions went to Tyre
Acts 21:3, 7 "We... sailed into Syria, and landed at Tyre ... and when we had finished our course from Tyre, we came to Ptolemais ..."

Note: Tyre to this day is one of the largest cities of Lebanon.

7. The prophecies about Egypt

Egypt's River Nile will cease to be a river
Isaiah 19:5-6 "The waters shall fail from the sea, and the river shall be wasted and dried up. And they shall turn the rivers far away."

Note: However, the Nile is still a river, the longest river in the world and it never dried up to this day.

The land of Judah shall be a terror unto Egypt
Isaiah 19:17 "The land of Judah shall be a terror unto Egypt ..."

Note: Judah never invaded Egypt.

The Canaanite language will be spoken in Egypt
Isaiah 19:18 "In that day shall five cities in the land of Egypt speak the language of Canaan ..."

Note: The Canaanite language, which is now extinct, was never spoken in Egypt.

The Egyptians will bow down to the Lord of the Israelites
Isaiah 19:19 "The Lord shall be known to Egypt, and the Egyptians shall know the Lord in that day, and shall do sacrifice and oblation; yea, they shall vow a vow unto the Lord, and perform it."

Note: Judaism is not one of Egypt's religions. At present the Christians comprise about ten percent of the Egyptian population.

Egypt will have an alliance with Israel and Assyria
Isaiah 19:23-24 "In that day shall there be a highway out of Egypt to Assyria, and the Assyrian shall come into Egypt, and the Egyptian into Assyria, and the Egyptians shall serve with the Assyrians. In that day shall Israel be the third with Egypt and with Assyria, even a blessing in the midst of the land."

Note: The alliance between Egypt, Assyria and Israel never existed.

All those who will go to Egypt will die by the sword, famine and pestilence
Jeremiah 42:17 "So shall it be with all the men that set their faces to go into Egypt to sojourn there; they shall die by the sword, by the famine, and by the pestilence: and none of them shall remain or escape from the evil that I will bring upon them."

Note: Those who migrated to Egypt did not die from the sword, famine and pestilence.

Ezekiel predicted that Egypt will be a desolate and wasted land
Ezekiel 29:8-15 "Therefore thus saith the Lord GOD; Behold, I will bring a sword upon thee, and cut off man and beast out of thee. And the land of Egypt shall be desolate and waste ... I will make the land of Egypt utterly waste and desolate ..."

Note: Egypt has never been a desolate and wasted land.

Egypt will be uninhabited for forty years
Ezekiel 29:11 "No foot of man shall pass through it, nor foot of beast shall pass through it, neither shall it be inhabited forty years."

Note: Egypt has never been uninhabited and man and beast have always walked thru it.

Egypt will be desolate surrounded by more desolate countries
Ezekiel 29:12 "I will make the land of Egypt desolate in the midst of the countries that are desolate, and her cities among the cities that are laid waste shall be desolate forty years ..."

Note: Egypt has never been a desolate country surrounded by more desolate countries.

The Egyptians will be scattered among the nations
Ezekiel 29:12-14; 30:23, 26 "I will scatter the Egyptians among the nations, and will disperse them through the countries ... At the end of forty years will I gather the Egyptians from the people whither they were scattered: And I will bring again the captivity of Egypt, and will cause them to return into the land of Pathros, into the land of their habitation."

Note: Egypt never had a diaspora.

Egypt will be the basest of kingdoms

Ezekiel 29:14-15 "They shall be there a base kingdom. It shall be the basest of the kingdoms ... I will diminish them, that they shall no more rule over the nations."

Note: Egypt is not the basest of kingdoms.

Ezekiel predicted that Nebuchadrezzar of Babylon will conquer Egypt
Ezekiel 29:19-20, 30:10-11 "Thus saith the Lord GOD; Behold, I will give the land of Egypt unto Nebuchadrezzar ... I [Lord] have given him the land of Egypt for his labour ..."

Note: In 568 BCE, Nebuchadnezzar tried to conquer Egypt but failed and Egypt survived with no significant damage.

Ezekiel and Isaiah predicted that Egypt will be sold to an evil nation
Ezekiel 30:12 "I will make the rivers dry, and sell the land into the hand of the wicked: and I will make the land waste ... by the hand of strangers."
Isaiah 19:4 "I will hand the Egyptians over to the power of a cruel master, and a fierce king will rule over them, declares the Lord, the Lord Almighty."

Note: In 30 BC, Egypt was conquered by Rome and Christianity was introduced sometime in the mid-first century AD. Was God implying that the Roman Empire who introduced Christianity to Egypt, the wicked nation?

Ezekiel predicted that there will no longer be a prince in Egypt
Ezekiel 30:13 "Thus saith the Lord GOD ... there shall be no more a prince of the land of Egypt."

Note: The pharaohs ended their rule in Egypt sometime in 30 BC when the Roman Empire conquered it and became its province.

Ezekiel predicted that Egypt would be burned
Ezekiel 30:16 "I will set fire in Egypt ..."

Note: Egypt did not burn.

8. The prophecy about the Ammonites

Ezekiel 21:28-32 "Thus saith the Lord GOD concerning the Ammonites ... I will pour out mine indignation upon thee ... thou shalt be no more remembered: for I the Lord have spoken it."

Note: The Ammonites existed until the 2nd century AD.

9. The prophecy if Ephraim will return to Egypt

Yes, Ephraim will return to Egypt

Hosea 8:11-13 "Because Ephraim hath made many altars to sin, altars shall be unto him to sin … now will he remember their iniquity, and visit their sins: *they shall return to Egypt.*"

Hosea 9:3 "They shall not dwell in the Lord's land; but *Ephraim shall return to Egypt … "*

No, because Ephraim, does not want to return to Egypt

Hosea 11:5 "*He (Ephraim) shall not return into the land of Egypt,* and the Assyrian shall be his king, because they refused to return."

10. Amos' prophecy about Amaziah

Amos 7:17 "Therefore thus saith the Lord; Thy wife shall be an harlot in the city, and thy sons and thy daughters shall fall by the sword, and thy land shall be divided by line; and thou shalt die in a polluted land: and Israel shall surely go into captivity forth of his land."

Note: There is no evidence in the Bible that Amos' prophecy about Amaziah came true.

11. The prophecy about Nineveh

Jonah 3:4 "Jonah prophesies that in forty days Nineveh shall be overthrown. But it didn't happen because God repented."

Jonah 3:10 "God repented of the evil, that he had said that he would do unto them; and he did it not."

F. The prophecies and promises to Israel

1. Israel will dwell in their homeland safely and securely

II Samuel 7:10 "I will appoint a place for my people Israel, and will plant them, that they may dwell in a place of their own, and move no more."

Note: However to this day, the Israelites never had a peaceful relationship with their neighbors and their land ownership still falls into question.

2. God will kill all the people of Israel

Amos 8:2-3 "Then said the Lord unto me, *The end is come upon my people of Israel; I will not again pass by them any more* … there shall be many dead bodies in every place."

3. Predictions about Jerusalem

Isaiah's prediction about Jerusalem

Isaiah 52:1 "There shall no more come into thee [Jerusalem] the uncircumcised and the unclean."

Note: But many uncircumcised people have visited and occupied Jerusalem after this prophecy was made.

Jeremiah's prediction about Jerusalem

Jeremiah 3:17 "At that time they shall call Jerusalem the throne of the Lord; and all the nations shall be gathered unto it, to the name of the Lord, to Jerusalem ..."

Jeremiah 9:11 "I will make Jerusalem heaps, and a den of dragons; and I will make the cities of Judah desolate, without an inhabitant."

Note: Jeremiah prophesied that all nations would call Jerusalem the throne of the Lord. But this did not happen. Jeremiah also predicted that Jerusalem will be a ruinous heap and this also did not happen.

Micah predicted the destruction of Jerusalem

Micah 3:12 "Therefore shall Zion for your sake be plowed as a field, and Jerusalem shall become heaps, and the mountain of the house as the high places of the forest."

Note: Jeremiah said that the prediction of Micah did not come true because the Lord changed his mind.

Jeremiah 26:18-19 "Micah the Morasthite prophesied in the days of Hezekiah king of Judah, and spake to all the people of Judah, saying, Thus saith the Lord of hosts; Zion shall be plowed like a field, and Jerusalem shall become heaps ... and the Lord repented him of the evil which he had pronounced against them?"

Note: In 614 AD, Jerusalem was occupied by the Persians, and the looters took the True Cross where Jesus Christ was supposedly crucified. Jerusalem was invaded but not destroyed into ruinous heaps.

4. Jeremiah's prediction about the length of the Babylonian captivity

The Babylonian exile will last for 70 years

Jeremiah 25:11 "These nations shall serve the king of Babylon seventy years."

Jeremiah 29:4-5, 10 "Thus saith the Lord of hosts ... after seventy years be accomplished at Babylon I will visit you ..."

Note: The Babylonian captivity only lasted for about 49 years and not 70 years as Jeremiah predicted.

G. The prophecies concerning Jesus Christ

1. What should be the name of Jesus?

Emmanuel (or Immanuel)
Isaiah 7:14 "Therefore the Lord himself shall give you a sign; Behold, a virgin shall conceive, and bear a son, and shall call his name Immanuel."
Matthew 1:23 "Behold, a virgin shall be with child, and shall bring forth a son, and they shall call his name Emmanuel, which being interpreted is, God with us."

Jesus
Matthew 1:25 "And [Joseph] knew her not till she had brought forth her firstborn son: and he called his name JESUS."

2. Was Jesus' ride in Jerusalem a fulfillment of Zechariah's prophecy?

Zechariah 9:9-10 "Rejoice greatly, O daughter of Zion; shout, O daughter of Jerusalem: behold, thy King cometh unto thee: he is just, and having salvation; lowly, and riding upon an ass, and upon a colt the foal of an ass ... and his dominion shall be from sea even to sea, and from the river even to the ends of the earth."

Matthew 21:2, 4-5 "[Jesus said] unto them, Go into the village ... ye shall find an ass tied, and a colt with her ... bring them unto me. All this was done, that it might be fulfilled which was spoken by the prophet, saying, Tell ye the daughter of Sion, Behold, thy King cometh unto thee, meek, and sitting upon an ass, and a colt the foal of an ass."
John 12:14-15 "Jesus, when he had found a young ass, sat thereon; as it is written, Fear not, daughter of Sion: behold, thy King cometh, sitting on an ass's colt."

Note: The leader prophesied in the book of Zechariah was said to be warrior-like leader unlike Jesus.

3. Did the prophet Isaiah predict about the trial of Jesus?

According to Isaiah the Lord will not open his mouth before his accusers
Isaiah 53:6-7 "All we like sheep have gone astray; we have turned every one to his own way; and the Lord hath laid on him the iniquity of us all. He was oppressed, and he was afflicted, yet *he opened not his mouth:* he is brought as a lamb to the slaughter, and as a sheep before her shearers is dumb, so *he openeth not his mouth.*"

Yes, Jesus did not open his mouth before his accusers

Matthew 27:12-14 "When he was accused of the chief priests and elders, he answered nothing … he answered him [Pilate] to *never a word*; insomuch that the governor marveled greatly."

Jesus opened his mouth before his accusers
Mark 14:61-62, 15:2 "The high priest asked … Art thou the Christ, the Son of the Blessed? And *Jesus said*, I am … Pilate asked him, Art thou the King of the Jews? And he [answered] Thou sayest it."
Luke 23:34 "Then *said Jesus*, Father, forgive them …"
John 18:33-38 "Pilate… said unto him, Art thou the King of the Jews? *Jesus answered* him …"

4. The prophecy of angel Gabriel

Luke 1:31-33 "Behold, thou shalt conceive … and bring forth a son, and shalt call his name JESUS. He shall be great, and shall be called the Son of the Highest: and the Lord God shall give unto him the throne of his father David: And he shall reign over the house of Jacob for ever; and of his kingdom there shall be no end."

Note: Angel Gabriel appeared to Mary to foretell the birth of Jesus. He said that Jesus will be given King David's throne and he will reign over the house of Jacob forever, and his kingdom will never end. However, Jesus was crucified and did not rule as a king.

H. The promises and prophecies of Jesus Christ

1. Jesus said you will be immune to snakes and any deadly poison

Mark 16:16-18 "He that believeth and is baptized shall be saved … In my name shall they cast out devils … They shall take up serpents; and if they drink any deadly thing, it shall not hurt them; they shall lay hands on the sick, and they shall recover."
Luke 10:19 "Behold, I give unto you power to tread on serpents and scorpions, and over all the power of the enemy: and nothing shall by any means hurt you."

Note: Because of Mark 16:17-18 and Luke 10:19 some religious groups in the Appalachian Mountains and other parts of the United States i.e. Alabama, Georgia, Kentucky, West Virginia and Ohio practice snake handling. Church services often include not only the handling of venomous snakes but also handling fire and drinking water laced with poison such as strychnine and arsenic.

2. Jesus said that whoever believes in him will have eternal life

John 3:15 "Whosoever believeth in him should not perish, but have eternal life."

Note: However, in Genesis 5:22-29, Enoch who never learned about Jesus Christ went to heaven?

3. Jesus promised he will grant anything to those who pray to him

John 14:13-14 "Whatsoever ye shall ask in my name, that will I do … If ye shall ask any thing in my name, I will do it."

I. Prophecy of Jesus about the denial of Peter

1. What did Jesus say about Peter denying him?

Jesus said Peter will deny him thrice before the cock will crow once
Matthew 26:34 "Jesus said … before the cock crow, thou shalt deny me thrice."
Luke 22:34 "The cock shall not crow this day, before that thou shalt thrice deny …"
John 13: 38 "Jesus [said] The cock shall not crow, till thou hast denied me thrice.'"

Peter will deny Jesus thrice before the cock will crow twice
Mark 14:30 "Jesus saith … That this day, even in this night, before the cock crow twice, thou shalt deny me thrice."

2. How many times did the cock crow after Peter's denial of Jesus?

Peter denied Jesus thrice before the cock crowed once
Matthew 26:70 "But he denied before them all, saying, I know not what thou sayest."
Matthew 26:72 "Again he denied with an oath, I do not know the man."
Matthew 26:74 "Then began he … saying, I know not the man. And … the cock crew."
[Also in **Luke 22:57, 58, 60; John 18:17, 25, 27**]

The cock crowed twice, one after the first denial, the second after the third denial
Mark 14:68 "He denied, saying, I know not, neither understand I what thou sayest … and the cock crew."
Mark 14:70 "He denied it again."
Mark 14:71 "But he began to curse and to swear, saying, I know not this man of whom ye speak. And the second time the cock crew."

Note: The Gospel of Mark has a slightly different version about Peter's denial of Jesus.

J. Prophecies about the death, resurrection and return of Jesus

1. When will Jesus resurrect?

Jesus predicted he will rise from the dead after three days
Matthew 12:38-40 "He [Jesus] said unto them … For as Jonas was three days and three nights in the whale's belly; so shall the Son of man be three days and three nights in the heart of the earth."

Jesus rose from the dead after less than three days
Mark 15:37 "Jesus cried with a loud voice, and gave up the ghost …"
Mark 16:9 "Now when Jesus was risen early the first day of the week …"
Matthew 28:1, 5-6 "In the end of the Sabbath … toward the first day of the week … the angel [said] … He is not here: for he is risen, as he said."

2. Jesus will be buried with others

Yes, according to the prophecy
Isaiah 53:9 "He made his grave with the wicked, and with the rich in his death."

No
Matthew 27:59-60 "Joseph had taken the body … laid it in his own new tomb"
Mark 15:45-46 "[Pilate] gave the body to Joseph … [Joseph] laid him in a sepulcher … and rolled a stone unto the door …"
Luke 23:53 "He took it down … and laid it in a sepulcher …"
John 19:40-42 "Then took they the body of Jesus … wherein was never man yet laid. There laid they Jesus …"

3. When is the second coming of Jesus Christ?

Within the lifetime of Jesus
Matthew 16:28, 23:36, 24:34, 26:64 "There be some standing here, which shall not taste of death, till they see the Son of man coming in his kingdom … This generation shall not pass, till all these things be fulfilled … Hereafter shall ye see the Son of man sitting on the right hand of power, and coming in the clouds of heaven."
[Also in **Mark 9:1;13:30; 14:62; Luke 9:27; 21:32; 22:69; John 5:25; Romans 13:11**]

Before the gospel is preached to all the cities of Israel

Matthew 10:23 "Ye shall not have gone over the cities of Israel, till the Son of man be come."

After the gospel is preached all over the world
Matthew 24:14 "This gospel of the kingdom shall be preached in all the world … and then shall the end come."

Note: However, Paul said that the gospel was already preached to the entire world during his time:
Romans 10:18 "Yes verily … their words unto the ends of the world."
Colossians 1:23 "If ye continue in the faith … of the gospel, which ye have heard, and which was preached to every creature which is under heaven; whereof I Paul am made a minister"

According to Jesus he will return during John's time
John 21:22 "Jesus saith unto him, If I will that he tarry till I come, what is that to thee? follow thou me."

Paul expected Jesus to return within his lifetime
Romans 13:11-12 "The night is far spent, the day is at hand."
I Corinthians 1:7-8 "Waiting for the coming of our Lord Jesus Christ …"
Hebrews 10:37 "For yet a little while, and he that shall come will come …"

Paul said the rapture will happen in his lifetime
I Thessalonians 4:15-17 "For this we say unto you by the word of the Lord, that we which are alive and remain unto the coming of the Lord shall not prevent them which are asleep … we which are alive and remain shall be caught up together with them in the clouds, to meet the Lord in the air: and so shall we ever be with the Lord."

Note: The Rapture best described in I Thessalonians 4:16-17 is a belief by some Protestant denominations that the elect will rise up on the air to meet Jesus Christ in midair during his second coming.

Right after the Revelation was written
Revelation 1:1, 3; 22:10 "The Revelation of Jesus Christ … must shortly come to pass. For the time is at hand."
Revelation 3:11; 22:7, 12, 20 "Behold, I come quickly."

Note: John, the writer of Revelation, expected Jesus to return within his lifetime.

Paul changed his mind about the timing of Christ's return
II Thessalonians 2:2-6 "That ye be not soon shaken in mind … as that the day of Christ is at hand. Let no man deceive you by any means: for that day shall not come, except there come a falling away first, and that man of sin be

revealed, the son of perdition ... And now ye know what withholdeth that he might be revealed in his time."

Note: Paul said that Jesus Christ will return soon during his lifetime. However, upon realizing that Jesus will not return, Paul wrote some explanation why Jesus will not return as expected.

Jesus was not coming and an explanation was made
II Peter 3:3-8 "There shall come in the last days scoffers, walking after their own lusts, And saying, Where is the promise of his coming? ... But, beloved, be not ignorant of this one thing, that one day is with the Lord as a thousand years, and a thousand years as one day."

Note: The author of Peter II tried to explain that Jesus is not coming because what is one day with man is equivalent to one thousand years with the Lord.

K. Prophecies concerning the end of the world

1. The end will come soon

I Corinthians 7:29 "But this I say, brethren, the time is short: it remaineth ..."
I Peter 1:19-20 "But ... was manifest in these last times for you."
I Peter 4:7 "But the end of all things is at hand."
I John 2:18 "Little children, it is the last time: and as ye have heard that antichrist shall come, even now are there many antichrists; whereby we know that it is the last time."

2. The end of the world will be soon, there was no time for marriage

I Corinthians 7:29 "But this I say, brethren, the time is short: it remaineth, that both they that have wives be as though they had none"

3. The writer of Jude believed he was already living during the last times

Jude 1:17-18 "But, beloved, remember ye the words ... our Lord Jesus Christ; How that they told you there should be mockers in the last time ..."

Note: These passages were written 2000 years ago to warn about the immediate end of the world. But all that generation passed away without any of the prophecies being fulfilled thus making these passages contradictions.

4. The world will not end

Ecclesiastes 1:4 "One generation passeth away, and another generation cometh: but the earth abideth for ever."

5. Nobody knows except the Father

Matthew 24:36 "But of that day and hour knoweth no man … but my Father only."
Mark 13:32 "But of that day and that hour knoweth no man … but the Father."

L. Other prophecies

1. Is this prophecy about the alcohol prohibition in the United States?

Isaiah 24:5-11 "They have … changed the ordinance. There is a crying for wine in the streets; all joy is darkened, the mirth of the land is gone."

2. Is this prophecy about the whole Bible or just the Book of Revelation?

Revelation 22:18-19 "For I testify unto every man that heareth the words of the prophecy of this book, If any man shall add unto these things, God shall add unto him the plagues that are written in this book: And if any man shall take away from the words of the book of this prophecy, God shall take away his part out of the book of life, and out of the holy city, and from the things which are written in this book."

Note: The Bible has been modified and rewritten several times and in so doing, things have been added or deleted from it. Does the prophecy stated above refer to the whole Bible? The Book of Revelation was originally written without the intention of making it a part of the Bible, thus perhaps the prophecy was intended just for the book of Revelation.

In 1522, William Tyndale wrote an English translation of the Bible from the original Hebrew and Greek texts. Because of Tyndale's English translation of the Bible, he was arrested, jailed, convicted as a heretic, strangled to death and burned while at stake in 1536 in Vilvoorde, Belgium with copies of his Bible. However, the succeeding versions of the Bible including the Matthew Bible (1537) – the first authorized English version, the Protestant's King James Version (1611) and the Catholic's Douay-Rheims Bible (1582-1609) are primarily based on the Tyndale Bible.

III. Scientific Arguments, Errors and Oddities

1. The creation of the universe

A. The world was made in six days

Genesis 1:31 "God saw every thing that he had made ... the sixth day."
Exodus 20:11 "For in six days the Lord made the heavens and the earth ..."

Note: The book of Genesis clearly states that the universe was made literally in six days. However, scientific evidence shows the entire creation evolved thru billions of years and not in mere six days.

B. There were days and night before the sun was created

Genesis 1:1-2:3 "In the beginning God created ..."
   Day 1: Sky, earth, light
   Day 2: Heaven, water, both in ocean basins and above the sky
   Day 3: Plants
   Day 4: Sun, moon, stars (as calendrical and navigational aids)
   Day 5: Sea monsters (whales), fish, birds, land animals, creepy-crawlies (reptiles, insects, etc.)
   Day 6: Humans (apparently both sexes at the same time)
   Day 7: God rested

Note: There were days, evenings, and mornings before the sun was created on the fourth day.

C. Plants were created before the sun was created

Genesis 1:11 "God said, Let the earth bring forth grass, the herb yielding seed, and the fruit tree yielding fruit after his kind ... and it was so."
Genesis 1:14-19 "God said, Let there be lights in the firmament of the heaven to divide the day from the night ... And God made two great lights ..."

Note: How did the plants undergo photosynthesis without the sun?

D. Light was created before the sun and stars were created

Genesis 1:14-15 "God said, Let there be lights [to] give light upon the earth."
Genesis 1:16 "God made two great lights; the greater light to rule the day, and the lesser light to rule the night: he made the stars also."

Note: But light was created during the first day. How can there be light on the first day without the sun and the stars? How can there be day one when the sun was created on the fourth day.

E. Science is no explanation for God's work

Ecclesiastes 3:11 "No man can find out the work that God maketh from the beginning to the end."

F. There were prophets during the beginning of the world

Acts 3:21 "Whom the heaven must receive until the times of restitution of all things, which God hath spoken by the mouth of all his holy prophets since the world began."

2. Geometry

A. What is the value of Pi?

I Kings 7:23 "He made a molten sea, ten cubits from the one brim to the other: it was round all about … a line of *thirty cubits* did compass it round about."
II Chronicles 4:2 "He made a molten sea of ten cubits from brim to brim… and a line of *thirty cubits* did compass it round about."

Note: The value of pi is 3.1416 and not 3 (ten cubits x 3.1416 = 31.416 cubits).

3. Earth Science

A. Sodom and Gomorrah

Genesis 19:24 "[It] rained upon Sodom and Gomorrah brimstone and fire …"
Luke 17:29 "Sodom it rained fire and brimstone … and destroyed them all."

Note: Today the Dead Sea is commonly considered the place where Sodom and Gomorrah once stood. The cataclysmic event that happened in Sodom and Gomorrah was probably a volcanic eruption.
Lot's wife was turned into stone for disobeying the angel's instructions. A pillar of rock salt (halite) can be seen to this day near the Dead Sea. This rock formation is called Lot's Wife because it resembles a woman and is believed to be the remains of Lot's wife who was named Ado or Edith.

B. Continental drift

Genesis 10:25 "Unto Eber were born two sons: the name of one was Peleg; for in his days was the earth divided."

Note: Peleg means division. The earth was divided during Peleg's days. Is this division of the earth a description of the continental drift? When the earth's continents moved away from each other? Plant and animal fossils of similar nature were discovered at different continents around the world suggesting that the continents were once connected to each other as a single landmass called Gondwana.The continents slowly drifted apart from each other as they are now today.

C. Calamities are caused by God's anger

Isaiah 13:13 "Therefore I will shake the heavens, and the earth shall remove out of her place, in the wrath of the Lord of hosts, and in the day of his fierce anger."
Jeremiah 10:10 "At his [God] wrath the earth shall tremble ..."
Nahum 1:5 "The mountains quake at him, and the hills melt, and the earth is burned at his presence, yea, the world, and all that dwell therein."

D. What is the shape of the earth?

The earth is a circle
Isaiah 40:22 "It is he [God] that sitteth upon the circle of the earth ..."

The earth is flat
Job 11:9 "The measure thereof is longer than the earth ..."
Isaiah 24:1 "The Lord maketh the earth empty ... and *turneth it upside down*"
Revelation 1:7 "Behold, he cometh with clouds; and *every eye shall see him* ..."

The earth has ends, borders and corners
Deuteronomy 13:7 "One end of the earth even unto the other end of the earth"
Psalm 74:17 "Thou has set all the borders of the earth."
Isaiah 11:12 "The four corners of the earth."

E. What is holding the earth?

The earth is on top of pillars
I Samuel 2:8 "The pillars of the earth [Lord] hath set the world upon them"
Job 9:6 "Which shaketh the earth out of her place, and the pillars thereof tremble."
Psalm 75:3 "The earth ... dissolved: I bear up the pillars of it."

The earth is fixed on a foundation
II Samuel 22:16 "The foundations of the world were discovered"
I Chronicles 16:30 "All the earth: the world also shall be stable, that it be not moved."

The earth is upon nothing

Job 26:7 "[He] hangeth the earth upon nothing."

F. Does the earth travel around the sun?

No, the sun travels around the earth
Job 9:7 "Which commandeth the sun, and it riseth not."
Ecclesiastes 1:5 "The sun also ariseth, the sun goeth down, and hasteth to his place where he arose."

Note: The question whether the sun was commanded to rise or not implies a geocentric perspective.

The Bible, Copernicus and Galileo
Joshua 10:12-13 "Then ... he [Joshua] said in the sight of Israel, Sun, stand thou still upon Gibeon; and thou, Moon, in the valley of Ajalon. And the sun stood still, and the moon stayed ... So the sun stood still in the midst of heaven, and hasted not to go down about a whole day."
Psalm 19:1-5 "The ... firmament sheweth his [God] handywork ..."
Psalm 104:1-5 "Bless the Lord, O my soul. O Lord my God, thou art very great; thou art clothed with honour and majesty. Who coverest thyself with light as with a garment: who stretchest out the heavens like a curtain ..."
Isaiah 40:22 "It is he that sitteth upon the circle of the earth, and the inhabitants thereof are as grasshoppers; that stretcheth out the heavens as a curtain, and spreadeth them out as a tent to dwell in."
Acts 1:11 "Ye men of Galilee, why stand ye gazing up into heaven?"

Note: Because of Joshua 10:12-13, Martin Luther called Copernicus "a fool who went against Holy Writ" in response to the Copernican theory about the Solar System.
Tommaso Caccini, a Dominican priest cited Acts 1:11 as the basis for making statements against Galileo and his works. Galileo was tried and sentenced in 1633 for supporting the view that the earth revolves around the sun. Galileo's conviction was based on several passages in the Bible such as: Joshua 10:13, Psalm 19:1-5, Psalm 104:1-5 and Isaiah 40:22. In 1992, the Roman Catholic Church exonerated Galileo and admitted their mistake.

4. The heavens, the sky and the firmament

A. Heaven divides the higher waters from the lower waters

Genesis 1:6-8 "God said, Let there be a firmament in the midst of the waters, and let it *divide the waters from the waters* ... And God called the firmament Heaven."

B. The sun and the moon are attached to the firmament

Genesis 1:16-17 "God made two great lights ... and set them in the firmament of the heaven to give light upon the earth."

C. The sky is like a molten looking glass

Job 37:18 "The sky, which is strong, and as a molten looking glass?"

D. The sky is a solid dome

The sky is a solid dome where the sun, moon, and stars are attached
Ezekiel 1:22 "The likeness of the firmament upon the heads of the living creature was as the colour of the terrible crystal, stretched forth over their heads above."
Ezekiel 10:1 "Then I looked, and, behold, in the firmament that was above the head of the cherubims ..."
John 1:51 "Hereafter ye shall see heaven open, and the angels of God ascending and descending upon the Son of man."

E. The heavens were opened unto Jesus during his baptism

Matthew 3:16 "Jesus ... was baptized ... and, lo, the heavens were opened"

F. Heaven opened and a sheet came down to earth

Acts 10:11 "[I] saw heaven opened, and a certain vessel descending upon him, as it had been a great sheet knit at the four corners, and let down to the earth ..."

G. UFO?

II Kings 2:11 "There appeared a chariot of fire, and horses of fire, and parted them both asunder; and Elijah went up by a whirlwind into heaven."
II Kings 6:17 "Elisha prayed, and said, Lord, I pray thee, open his eyes... the Lord opened the eyes of the young man; and he saw ... the mountain was full of horses and chariots of fire round about Elisha."

Note: These passages led to the belief that extraterrestrials have visited humanity and is the basis for the so called 'UFO religions' such as Raelism and Scientology. However, the heaven mentioned in II Kings 2:11-13 may actually just refer to the clouds. Elijah was taken to the clouds and transported to a different place, similarly Phillip was transported to another place in Acts 8:39-40. In II Chronicles 21:12-13 Elijah sent a letter to King Jehoram, which indicates that Elijah was still earth bound.

5. The sun, the moon and the stars

A. The sun and the moon's cycle were altered

There was darkness in the land of Egypt for three days
Exodus 10:21-23 "Moses stretched forth his hand … and there was a thick darkness in all the land of Egypt three days …"

Sun, stand stood still upon Gibeon; and the Moon, in the valley of Ajalon
Joshua 10:12-13 "[Joshua] said … Sun, stand thou still upon Gibeon; and thou, Moon, in the valley of Ajalon. And the sun stood still, and the moon stayed …"
Habbakuk 3:11 "The sun and moon stood still in their habitation …"

The shadow returned backward ten degrees in the sundial of Ahaz
II Kings 20:11 "[Isaiah] brought the shadow ten degrees backward, by which it had gone down in the dial of Ahaz."
[Also in **Isaiah 38:8**]

The sun will set at noontime
Amos 8:9 "It shall come to pass in that day, saith the Lord GOD, that I will cause the sun to go down at noon, and I will darken the earth in the clear day."

During crucifixion
Matthew 27:45 "From the sixth hour there was darkness … unto the ninth hour."
[Also in **Mark 15:33; Luke 23:44-45**]

During the coming of the Lord
Joel 2:31 "The sun shall be turned into darkness, and the moon into blood, before the great and terrible day of the Lord come."
[Also in **Mark 13:24; Act 2:20**]

Note: Events such as 'the sun shall be darkened and the moon shall not give her light' were most likely solar and lunar eclipses. Solar and lunar eclipses are normal occurrences. However the Bible considers solar and lunar eclipses as signs of the second coming of the Lord.

B. The moon has its own light

Genesis 1:16 "God made two great lights; the greater light to rule the day, and the lesser light to rule the night."
Isaiah 13:10 "The moon shall not cause her light to shine."

C. Can the moon harm you?

Psalm 121:6 "The sun shall not smite thee by day, nor the moon by night."

Note: The moon does not have a light of its own. Its light is just a reflection from the sun.

D. The moon will be as bright as the sun

Isaiah 30:26 "Moreover the light of the moon shall be as the light of the sun"

E. Without the sun and moon there is still some light

Matthew 24:29-30 "Shall the sun be darkened, and the moon shall not give her light ..."

F. Stars fall to the ground and can be stamped upon

[KJ] **Daniel 8:10** "It cast down ... the stars to the ground, and stamped upon them."
[DR] **Daniel 8:10** "It threw down of the strength, and of the stars, and trod upon them."

G. Stars will fall from heaven unto the earth

Matthew 24:2, 29 "Jesus said ... the stars shall fall from heaven ..."
Mark 13:25 "The stars of heaven shall fall ..."

Note: Jesus thought that the stars are like small objects that will fall to earth.

H. What was the star of Bethlehem?

Matthew 2:2 "Saying, Where is he that is born King of the Jews? for we have seen his star in the east, and are come to worship him."

Note: According to Johannes Kepler, the star of Bethlehem was not a star but an alignment of the planets Jupiter, and Saturn. The alignment took place on three different occasions during 7 B.C., on May 7, September 15 and December 1st.

I. Jesus Christ will hold seven stars in his hand

Revelation 1:16 "He had in his right hand seven stars."

6. Wind and water

A. Whenever it rains the windows of heaven are open

Genesis 7:11-12, 8:2 "The windows of heaven were opened, and the rain was upon the earth ... the windows of heaven were stopped, and the rain from heaven was restrained."

Revelation 11:6 "These have the power to shut heaven, that it rain not in the days ..."

B. Water changes into blood

Exodus 7:20 "[Moses and Aaron] smote the waters that were in the river ... and all the waters ... turned to blood."

C. The sea parted with dry land in the middle

Exodus 14:21 "Moses stretched out his hand over the sea ... the waters were divided."

Note: The Red Sea where Moses and the Israelites crossed was most likely not the Red Sea but the Sea of Reeds. Some historians speculated that the parting of the Red Sea (or Sea of Reeds?) was caused by tidal waves due to the eruption of the Santorini volcano around 1600 BCE.

D. Water comes from a rock

Numbers 20:11 "[Moses] smote the rock ... the water came out abundantly"

E. Because of sin, heaven was shut and rains did not come

[KJ] I Kings 8:35 "When heaven is shut ... there is no rain, because they have sinned ..."

[DR] III Kings 8:35 "When heaven is shut ... there is no rain, because they have sinned ..."

[KJ] II Chronicles 6:26 "Heaven is shut ... there is no rain, because they have sinned ..."

[DR] II Paralipomenon 6:26 "Heaven is shut ... there is no rain, because they have sinned ..."

F. An iron ax floats

[KJ] II Kings 6:5-6 "The axe head fell into the water ... the iron did swim."

[DR] IV Kings 6:5-6 "The axe head fell into the water ... the iron did swim."

G. Snow and hail are stored for later use for battle and war

Job 38:22-23 "Hast thou entered into the treasures of the snow? or hast thou seen the treasures of the hail, which I have reserved against the time of trouble, against the day of battle and war?"

H. Elias prevented rain for three and a half years by praying

James 5:17 "[Elias] prayed earnestly that it might not rain: and it rained not on the earth by the space of three years and six months."

I. Jesus and Peter walks on water

Matthew 14:26-29 "The disciples saw him [Jesus] walking on the sea ... and when Peter was come down out of the ship, he walked on the water, to go to Jesus."

Note: Explanations were offered such as Jesus and Peter probably walked on a piece of ice, a sandbar or on top of rocks.

J. Jesus Christ said you cannot tell where the wind blows

John 3:8 "The wind bloweth ... but canst not tell whence it cometh, and whither it goeth."

Note: However with today's technology, it can be determined where the wind blows.

7. Biology and Ecology

A. Overpopulation

Genesis 1:26-28; 9:1 "God said ... Be fruitful, and multiply, and replenish the earth ..."

Note: Overpopulation is one of the main problems of mankind. Overpopulation leads to ecological imbalance causing the speedy extinction of

flora and fauna, shortage of food, scarcity of land, lack of potable water, over pollution, poverty and many others.

B. Jacob's odd Genetic Engineering

Genesis 30:37-39 "Jacob took him rods of green poplar, and of the hazel and chestnut tree; and pilled white strakes in them ... And the flocks conceived before the rods, and brought forth cattle ringstraked, speckled, and spotted."

Note: Jacob altered the genetic make-up of his cattle by making them stare at some streaked rods.

C. Mythical animals in the Bible

Cockatrices

[KJ] **Isaiah 11:8** "The ... the cockatrice' den."

[KJ] **Isaiah 59:5** "They [evil people] hatch cockatrice' eggs ..."

[KJ] **Jeremiah 8:17** "For, behold, I will send serpents, cockatrices ..."

Basilisks

[DR] **Psalm 90:13** "Thou shalt walk upon the asp and the basilisk."

[DR] **Proverbs 23:32** "It will ... spread abroad poison like a basilisk.

[DR] **Jeremiah 8:17** "For behold I will send among you serpents, basilisks ..."

Note: The King James and the Douay Rheims Bible have used Cockatrices and Basilisks interchangeably.

Satyrs

[KJ] **Isaiah 13:21** "Satyrs shall dance there ..."

[KJ] **Isaiah 34:14** "The satyr shall cry to his fellow ..."

Note: The Douay Rheims Bible used the description "the hairy ones" instead of satyrs.

Unicorns

Isaiah 34:7 "The unicorns shall come down with them ..."

Dragons

[KJ] **Isaiah 27:1** "He [Lord] shall slay the dragon that is in the sea ..."

Isaiah 43:20 "The beast of the field shall honor me, the dragons ..."

Fiery flying serpent

[KJ] **Isaiah 30:6** "The viper and fiery flying serpent."

[DR] **Isaiah 30:6** "The viper and the flying basilisk."

Mythical sea demon (Rahab)

[KJ] **Psalm 89:10** "Thou hast broken Rahab in pieces ..."

D. Unknown Beasts and Monsters

The Behemoth

Job 40:15 "Behold now behemoth ... he eateth grass as an ox."

Note: The behemoth is said to be a large animal that lives on land and it may be the hippopotamus, the dinosaur, the wildebeest, or the crocodile.

The Leviathan

Job 41:1-34 "Canst thou draw out leviathan with an hook ..."

Psalm 74:14 "Thou breakest the heads of leviathan in pieces ..."

Note: The Leviathan is a large sea creature and it may be a whale.In some chapters the King James and Douay Rheims have used dragons and Leviathans interchangeably.

E. Inaccurate facts about animals

The serpent talks with a woman
Genesis 3:1-4 "He [serpent] said unto the woman, Yea, hath God said ..."

The serpent eats dust
Genesis 3:14 "The Lord God said unto the serpent ... dust shalt thou eat ..."
Isaiah 65:25 "Dust shall be the serpent's meat ..."

Note: Serpents don't eat dust. How did the serpent move prior to the temptation of Adam and Eve, did it walk on some pair of legs? Or did it fly?

Rods turn to serpents
Exodus 7:10-12 "Aaron cast down his rod ... and it became a serpent ... every man his rod, and they became serpents."

Snails melt as they move
Psalm 58:8 "As a snail which melteth ..."

Worms will live forever
Isaiah 66:24 "For their worm shall not die ..."
Mark 9:44, 46, 48 "Where their worm dieth not ..."

Every beast will fear man
Genesis 9:2 "The fear ... and the dread of you shall be upon every beast ..."

Note: Not every beast fears man as stated in the Book of Proverbs 30:30.
Proverbs 30:30 "A lion which is strongest among beasts, and turneth not away for any ..."

An ass talks to Balaam
Numbers 22:28, 30 "The Lord opened the mouth of the ass, and she said unto Balaam, What have I done unto thee ..."

Horses fly like an eagle, swifter than leopards and fiercer than wolves
Habakkuk 1:8 "Their horses also are swifter than the leopards, and are more fierce than the evening wolves."

The wolf shall dwell with the lamb, the leopard with the kid, the calf with the lion and fatling
Isaiah 11:6 "The wolf also shall dwell with the lamb, and the leopard shall lie down with the kid; and the calf and the young lion and the fatling together."
Isaiah 65:25 "The wolf and the lamb shall feed together ..."

F. The birds and the bees

The bat is a bird
Leviticus 11:13, 19 "The fowls: ... and the bat."

Birds have four legs
Leviticus 11:20 "All fowls that creep, going upon all four."

Insects have four feet
Leviticus 11:21-23 "Every flying creeping thing that goeth upon all four ... all other flying creeping things, which have four feet ..."

Note: All insects either have six or eight legs.

Eagles carry their young on their wings
Deuteronomy 32:11 "As an eagle ... beareth them on her wings ..."

Note: Eagles do not carry their young on their wings.

The Lord commands ravens to feed Elijah
I Kings 17:4, 6 "I have commanded the ravens to feed thee there. And the ravens brought him [Elijah] bread and flesh ..."

Ostriches are cruel animals
Lamentations 4:3 "The daughter of my people is become cruel, like the ostriches ..."

Ostriches are stupid animals that abandon their eggs
Job 39:14-17 "Which leaveth her [ostrich] eggs in the earth ... God hath deprived her of wisdom, neither hath he imparted to her understanding."

Note: Ostriches do not abandon their eggs and are not stupid or cruel animals.

G. The hare and the coney

The coney chew their cud
Leviticus 11:5 "The coney, because he cheweth the cud ..."

The hare chew their cud
Leviticus 11:6 "The hare, because he cheweth the cud ..."

Note: Hares and rabbits both belong to the Leporidae family and are very similar in appearance. The main difference is in their young. A newborn rabbit is blind, hairless and helpless while a newborn hare has fur, can see clearly and can already fend for themselves quickly at birth.

H. The difference between a fish and a whale

Jonah lived inside a fish for three days
Jonah 1:17 "The Lord had prepared a great fish to swallow up Jonah."

Jonah lived inside a whale for three days
Matthew 12:40 "Jonah was three days and three nights in the whale's belly."

Note: Whales are classified as mammals while fish belongs to the Pisces classification. Whales are warm blooded while fish are cold blooded. Whales take oxygen from air, while fish takes oxygen from water. Whales use a blowhole on top of their head, while fish use their gills.

I. All animals

All animals are vegetarians
Genesis 1:30 "To every beast of the earth ... to every thing that creepeth upon the earth ... I have given every green herb for meat: and it was so."

All beasts, birds, serpents, and sea creatures had been tamed by humans
James 3:7 "For every kind of beasts, and of birds, and of serpents, and of things in the sea, is tamed, and hath been tamed of mankind."

8. Inaccurate facts about plants

A. All plants are food

Genesis 1:29 "God said ... I have given you every herb, every tree ... to you it shall be for meat."

Note: However, some plants are poisonous.

B. Eating the fruit of a tree will give knowledge of good and evil

Genesis 2:17, 3:5 "But of the tree of the knowledge of good and evil, thou shalt not eat of it: for in the day that thou eatest thereof thou shalt surely die ... For God doth know that in the day ye eat thereof, then your eyes shall be opened, and ye shall be as gods, knowing good and evil."

C. Eating the fruit of a tree will bestow immortality

Genesis 3:22 "Take also of the tree of life, and eat, and live for ever"

D. A voice comes from a burning bush

Exodus 3:4 "God called unto him out of the midst of the bush, and said, Moses ..."

E. The mustard seed

Matthew 13:32 "Which indeed is [mustard seed] the least of all seeds: but when it is grown, it is the greatest among herbs, and becometh a tree."
Mark 4:31 "It is like a grain of mustard seed, which ... is less than all the seeds that be in the earth."

Note: The mustard seed is not the smallest seed and the mustard plant is just a shrub.

F. Only dead seeds germinate

I Corinthians 15:36 "That which thou sowest is not quickened, except it die."

Note: A seed has to be alive to germinate.

9. The time of Adam and Eve

A. Adam names all the animals

Genesis 2:20 "Adam gave names to all cattle ... and to every beast of the field ..."

Note: Naming all the animals will take years for Adam to accomplish.

B. God created a woman out of Adam's rib

Genesis 2:21-22 "The Lord God ... took one of his [Adam] ribs ... and the rib, which the Lord God had taken from man, made he a woman ..."

Note: Both sexes have 12 pairs of ribs.

C. Did giants exist?

Genesis 6:4 "There were giants in the earth in those days."
Deuteronomy 2:20, 3:11 "Giants dwelt therein in old time ... nine cubits (13.5 feet)"
Amos 2:9 "The Amorite whose height was like the height of the cedars ..."
I Samuel 17:4 "Goliath, of Gath, whose height was six cubits and a span (9.5 feet)."

Note: There is no archeological evidence that giants ever existed. The giants referred to in the Bible may be humans with a pituitary disorder called acromegaly (pituitary gigantism). However humans with acromegaly could only be as tall as about eight feet. The giants mentioned were measured by cubits. The length of a cubit is derived from the elbow to the tip of the fingertip. This method of measurement makes the cubit different from one culture to another. But the standard cubit is 18 inch. There is a possibility that written accounts about how tall those giants were have been exaggerated. People suffering from acromegaly are said to be partially blind which possibly explains why the young David defeated Goliath.

D. Adam was created during the time the world began

Luke 3:23-38 "Jesus … the son of Joseph, which was the son of Heli … which was the son of Seth, which was the son of Adam, which was the son of God."

Note: If Adam was created on the sixth day during the time of the creation of the world, and Adam is only 76 generations away from Jesus Christ, it means that the world was created just a few thousand years ago. If the earth and the universe are more than 4 billion years old and Jesus Christ was born about two thousand years ago, the 76 generations from Adam to Jesus Christ does not add up.

E. Before Adam sinned nobody died

Romans 5:12 "Wherefore, as by one man sin entered into the world, and death by sin; and so death passed upon all men, for that all have sinned."
I Corinthians 15:22 "In Adam all die, even so in Christ shall all be made alive."

Note: Death is part of the cycle of life and has nothing to do with Adam and Eve. The Old Testament never mentioned that sin and death for mankind was caused by Adam's misdeed. It was Paul who wrote the concept of death and sin because of Adam's sin.

10. The time of Noah

A. Was Noah's ark feasible?

Genesis 6:15-16 "*The length of the ark shall be three hundred cubits, the breadth of it fifty cubits, and the height of it thirty cubits.* A window shalt thou make to the ark, and in a cubit shalt thou finish it above; and the door of the ark shalt thou set in the side thereof; with lower, second, and third stories shalt thou make it."

Note: Noah was told to make an ark that is 450 feet long. An ark this size will need an iron brace to counter warping. The ark must only have one window. How did the ark have proper ventilation with only one window? The ark must only have one door, how can all the animals load and unload in a short time with only one door? If all the 2,000,000 to 5,000,000 animal species were taken aboard, how did these animals fit inside the ark?

B. All the animals were loaded in the ark in one day

Genesis 6:16; 7:13-15 "A window shalt thou make to the ark ... and the door of the ark shalt thou set in the side thereof ... In the *selfsame day* entered Noah, and (his family) into the ark; They ... two and two of all flesh, wherein is the breath of life."

Note: With only one door how did a pair of all the animals in the world enter the ark in one day?

C. Noah had to save only a pair of each animal

Genesis 7:15-16 "They [animals] went in unto Noah into the ark, two and two of all flesh ... male and female of all flesh ..."

Note: Saving only a pair (male and a female) of each species would have lead to mass extinctions. The idea of having each specie or animal kind survive from only a pair is highly improbable due to a degraded gene pool and the destruction of the food chain and food web.

D. The flood covered the highest mountains

Genesis 7:20 "Fifteen cubits upward did the waters prevail; and the mountains were covered."

Note: Covering the highest mountains such as Mount Everest to a depth of 22 feet of water is highly improbable. No specific mountain was mention in this passage. In all likelihood it was referring to the hills that Noah could see.

E. It took only seven days to grow leaves

Genesis 8:8-11 "He [Noah] sent forth a dove ... to see if the waters were abated (the dove did not find a place to land, then after seven days ... the dove came ... in her mouth was an olive leaf ..."

F. The rainbow in the sky

Genesis 9:11, 13 "I will establish my covenant with you, neither shall all flesh be cut off any more by the waters of a flood ... I do set my bow in the cloud"

Note: After the Great Deluge during Noah's time, the rainbow was placed in the sky as a reminder of God's covenant – never will man be punished again by means of water. However, the existence of floods, tidal waves and tsunamis invalidates this statement. Does God break His promise? Does God forget?

G. Jesus believed Noah's flood was worldwide

Matthew 24:37 "But as the days of Noah ..."
II Peter 2:5 "And spared not the old world, but saved Noah the eighth person, a preacher of righteousness, bringing in the flood upon the world of the ungodly."
[Also in **Luke 17:26-27**]

Note: Noah's flood, if it ever really happened was most likely a local one.

11. Tower of Babel

A. God was violated by tall buildings?

Genesis 11:5-7 "The Lord came down to see the city and the tower ... And the Lord said ... nothing will be restrained from them, which they have imagined to do. Go to, let us go down, and there confound their language"

Note: To consider the desire to build a tall structure is wrong and a violation against God does not make sense considering the ancient Egyptian pyramids and the skyscrapers that are being built today.

B. One language

Genesis 11:1 "The whole earth was of one language, and of one speech."

Note: However, history and archeological evidence shows that different cultures have different languages.

C. How did language evolve?

Genesis 11:8-9 "The Lord scattered them ... Therefore is the name of it called Babel ... the Lord did there confound the language of all the earth."

Note: However, research shows that language evolved slowly thru time and not because of a single event.

12. The Israelites and the Exodus

A. Israel's population grew from 70 to millions in a few years

Israel's population grew from 70 to millions in a few hundred years
Exodus 1:5, 7 "All the souls [from] … the loins of Jacob were seventy …"
Exodus 2:37 "Children of Israel … six hundred thousand [men] …"
Exodus 38:26 "Every one that went to be numbered, from twenty years old

and upward, for six hundred thousand and three thousand and five
hundred and fifty men."

B. Moses and the burning bush

Exodus 3:2 "The angel of the Lord appeared unto him [Moses] in a flame of
fire out of the midst of a bush … and the bush was not consumed."

*Note: The burning bush in Exodus might be any of the following:
Dictamnus Gymnostylis Steven, Euonymus Alatus or Dictamnus Albus
(Fraxinella).*

C. The ten plagues of Egypt

First: The river turns to blood
Exodus 7:20-21 "All the waters that were in the river were turned to blood"

*Note: The waters turned into blood because the red tide algae produced
toxins.*

Second: The plague of frogs
Exodus 8:6 "The frogs came up, and covered the land of Egypt."

*Note: The toxins from the red tide resulted to a fish kill. The fish kill left the
frogs with no natural predators causing it to multiply in numbers.*

Third: The plague of lice
Exodus 8:17 "All the dust of the land became lice throughout all the land of
Egypt."

*Note: The fish kill also created an over polluted river which made the frogs
leave the rivers, and eventually the frogs died due to lack of moisture. When
the frogs died, the insects increased tremendously due to lack of predators for
the insects.*

Fourth: The plague of flies
Exodus 8:24 "There came a grievous swarm of flies into … all the land of
Egypt."

Note: The dead fish and frogs served as breeding grounds for flies.

Five: The plague of livestock death
Exodus 9:6 "All the cattle of Egypt died."

Note: The huge number of germ carrying insects resulted to livestock death.

Six: The plague of boils
Exodus 9:10 "A boil breaking forth with blains upon man, and upon beast."

Note: The large number of insects brought about livestock disease and boils.

Seven: The plague of hail
Exodus 9:23 "The Lord rained hail upon the land of Egypt."

Note: The hail may have been a natural weather event independent of all the other plagues.

Eight: The plague of locusts
Exodus 10:14 "Locust went up over all the land of Egypt."

Note: The large number of insects brought about the plague of gnats, flies and locusts.

Ninth: The plague of darkness
Exodus 10:22 "A thick darkness in all the land of Egypt three days."

Note: The plague of darkness could have been one of or a combination of volcanic activity, sand storms or large swarms of insects.

Tenth: The death of the firstborn
Exodus 11:5 "Every firstborn son in Egypt will die ..."

Note: The tenth plague may have been caused by food poisoning of whatever food is left. The firstborns were the most affected since traditionally firstborns had the highest pecking order when it comes to food rations and preferential treatment.

The ten plagues were said to be caused by the eruption of the Santorini volcano. The volcano eruption led to earthquakes, a rain of volcanic ash for days (causing the River Nile to turn red and three days of darkness) and limnic eruption. A limnic eruption is the release of large amounts of carbon dioxide from the ground causing people and animals close to the ground to die of carbon dioxide poisoning. Although the volcano is in Greece, the land of the Egypt was greatly affected because an earthquake fault line runs through Egypt, up to the Nile Delta.

D. Did manna come from heaven?

Exodus 16:14 "There lay a small round thing ... on the ground."
Psalm 78:24, 25 "And had rained down manna upon them to eat ..."
John 6:31 "Our fathers did eat manna in the desert."

Note: Is manna the lichen called Lecanora Esculenta? Is it the Coriander seed? Or is it the secretion of the tamarisk tree?

E. The exodus route took forty years

The route taken by the Israelites took them forty years
Exodus 16:35 "The children of Israel did eat manna forty years ..."
Deuteronomy 2:7; 8:2; 29:5 "Walking through this great wilderness: these forty years ..."
Act 7:36, 13:18 "In the wilderness forty years ..."

Note: The distance between Egypt and Canaan is a little over 200 miles and will take less than ten days of travel on foot.

F. Abstinence from food and drink

Moses survived 40 days and nights without food and water
Exodus 34:28 "He was there with the Lord forty days and forty nights; he [Moses] did neither eat bread, nor drink water."

Elijah survived 40 days and nights without food and water
I Kings 19:8 "He [Elijah] arose, and did eat and drink, and went in the strength of that meat forty days and forty nights unto Horeb ..."

Note: How did Moses and Elijah survive without eating and drinking for forty days and nights? In the case of Jesus Christ (see Luke 4:2, Matthew 4:2), he also fasted from food for 40 days; but the Bible does not say if he also fasted from water. A human being can survive forty days without food but not without water. Is it mere coincidence that Moses, Elijah and Jesus fasted for forty days and they were all participants in the so called Transfiguration of Jesus (see Matthew 7:1-9, Mark 9:2-8; Luke 9:28-36)?

G. Moses spoke to all Israel

Exodus 35:4 "Moses spake unto all ... the children of Israel ..."
Deuteronomy 1:1; 31:1 "These ... words which Moses spake unto all Israel"

Note: For Moses to be able to speak to at least 600,000 would be a physical impossibility during his time. Exodus 12:37 indicate that there were 600,000 men aside from children.

H. God gave the Israelites quails that filled the earth

Numbers 11:31 "There went forth a wind from the Lord, and brought quails from the sea ... two cubits high upon the face of the earth ..."

Note: Two cubits is approximately one meter high.

I. The walls of Jericho fell down

Joshua 6:5 "They make a long blast with the ram's horn ... wall of the city shall fall down ..."

Note: An earthquake was commonly given as an explanation for this particular event. However, the crumbling of the walls of Jericho may also mean a figurative one. Perhaps what the scripture meant was the inhabitants' loss of morale to fight and defend their ground against the Israelites.

13. Concerning Abijah

A. Abijah spoke to a million soldiers

II Chronicles 13:4 "Abijah said, Hear me all Israel (Abijah spoke to about 1.2 million soldiers)."

Note: For Abijah to be able to speak to about 1.2 million people would be a physical impossibility during his time.

14. The seat of conscience

A. Think with your heart

Esther 6:6 "Haman thought in his heart ..."
Isaiah 10:7 "Neither doth his heart think so"
Proverbs 23:7 "For as he thinketh in his heart ..."
Luke 2:19; 9:47 "Pondered them in her heart ... perceiving the thought of their heart"

B. Feel with your kidneys

Job 19:27 "My reins be consumed within me."
Psalm 16:7 "My reins also instruct me ..."
Proverbs 23:16 "Yea, my reins shall rejoice ..."

C. Your conscience is in your heart and kidneys

Psalm 7:9; 26:2; 73:21 "The righteous God trieth the hearts and reins [try] my reins and my heart … my heart was grieved, and I was pricked in my reins." Jeremiah 11:20; 17:10; 20:12 "Triest the reins and the heart … the LORD search the heart, I try the reins … seest the reins and the heart …"

15. Body parts

A. Joseph had horns like the horns of unicorns

Deuteronomy 33:17 "His horns are like the horns of unicorns."

B. Samson loses his strength if he loses his hair

Judges 16:17, 19 "I [Samson] have been a Nazarite unto God from my mother's womb: if I be shaven, then my strength will go from me … [Delilah] shave off the seven locks of his head … and his strength went from him."

Note: Samson, being a Nazirite, was not supposed to drink alcohol nor have any physical contact with a dead body and should never have a haircut.

C. Absalom's hair was as heavy as two hundred shekels

II Samuel 14:26 "He [Absalom] weighed the hair of his head at two hundred shekels after the king's weight."

Note: Absalom's hair weighed about 6 pounds (2.72 kilos).

D. Disembodied fingers wrote on a wall

Daniel 5:5 "In the same hour came forth fingers of a man's hand, and wrote over against the candlestick upon the plaister of the wall"

16. Concerning leprosy

A. Leprosy can be cured by bird and lamb blood

Leviticus 14:1-25 "The Lord spake this shall be the law of the leper in the day of his cleansing … he shall sprinkle [bird blood] upon him [seven times] the priest shall take some of the [lamb's] blood … put it upon the tip of the right ear … and upon the thumb of his right hand, and upon the great toe of his right foot …"

Note: God gave instructions on how to cure leprosy by using bird and lamb's blood.

B. A house infected with leprosy can be cleaned with bird blood

A house infected with leprosy can be cleaned by sprinkling bird blood
Leviticus 14:49-53 "For the cleansing of the house [infected with leprosy] he shall take two small birds ... cleanse the house with the blood of the bird ... So he shall make atonement for the house, and it shall be clean."

Note: God gave instructions on how to clean a house from leprosy with bird blood.

C. Dipping in the river Jordan seven times cured leprosy

II Kings 5:14 "Then went he down, and dipped himself seven times in Jordan ... and his flesh came again like unto the flesh of a little child."

17. Birth, life and death

A. Man came directly from dust

Genesis 2:7 "The Lord God formed man of the dust of the ground ..."

Note: Humans did not evolve directly from dust but from lower life forms.

B. Male and female

Mark 10:6 "From the beginning ... God made them male and female."

Note: However, single celled animals, where all life forms evolved do not have gender.

C. What is the maximum life span of humans?

One hundred and twenty years
Genesis 6:3 "The Lord said ... his days shall be an hundred and twenty years."

Life span of biblical characters:

Person	Age Died	Bible Verse
Adam	930	Genesis 5:5
Seth	912	Genesis 5:8
Enos	905	Genesis 5:11
Cainan	910	Genesis 5:14
Mahalaleel	895	Genesis 5:17
Jared	962	Genesis 5:20
Enoch*	365	Genesis 5:23
Methuselah	969	Genesis 5:27
Lamech	777	Genesis 5:31

Noah	950	Genesis 9:29
Shem	600	Genesis 11:10-11
Arphaxad	438	Genesis 11:12-13
Salah	433	Genesis 11:14-15
Eber	464	Genesis 11:16-17
Peleg	239	Genesis 11:18-19
Reu	239	Genesis 11:20-21
Serug	230	Genesis 11:22-23
Nahor	148	Genesis 11:24-25
Terah	205	Genesis 11:32
Abraham	175	Genesis 25:7
Ishmael	137	Genesis 25:17
Isaac	180	Genesis 35:28
Jacob	147	Genesis 47:28
Levi	137	Exodus 6:16
Kohath	133	Exodus 6:18
Amram	137	Exodus 6:20
Aaron	123	Numbers 33:39
Moses	120	Deuteronomy 34:7
Joshua	110	Joshua 24:29
Jehoida	130	II Chronicles 24:15
Job	140	Job 42:16

* Enoch did not die because God took him

D. Life comes from blood?

Leviticus 17:14 "For the life of every creature is its blood: its blood is its life."

E. Virgin birth

Matthew 1:20 "Mary ... is conceived in her is of the Holy Ghost."

F. Bringing back the dead to life

I Kings 17:21-22 "He [Elijah] stretched himself upon the child ... and the soul of the child came into him again, and he revived."
II Kings 4:32-35 "The child was dead [Elisha] prayed ... the child waxed warm ..."
II Kings 13:21 "When the [dead] man ... touched the bones of Elisha, he revived ..."
Acts 9:37-40 "She [died] Peter [said], Tabitha, arise ... she opened her eyes..."

Note: Until most recent times the permanent cessation of biological functions also called death was hard to determine. Deathlike symptoms described in the Bible may actually be just a profound state of unconsciousness.

G. Dried bones will come back to life

Ezekiel 37:4-10 "O ye dry bones, hear the word of the Lord. Thus saith the Lord GOD unto these bones; Behold, I will cause breath to enter into you, and ye shall live ... they lived, and stood up upon their feet, an exceeding great army."

H. Zombies rose from the dead during the crucifixion

Matthew 27:51, 52-53 "Jesus yielded up the ghost ... the graves were opened; and many bodies of the saints which slept arose ... and appeared unto many."

Note: The book of Matthew is the only book that mentions about the rising of zombies during the time of crucifixion. Scientifically, zombies do exist and is actually caused by a concoction of toad venom and poison from pupperfish (tetrodoxin). Such poisoning is so severe that the victim will appear to be dead for several hours. The poison leaves a permanent damage to the brain such that it impairs the victim's motor skills hence the so called zombie walk. Because the victim is usually buried after several hours of unconciousness, the brain is further damaged due to lack of oxygen.

I. Melchizedek had no beginning and no end

Hebrews 7:1-3 "For this Melchisedec ... Without father, without mother, without descent, having neither beginning of days, nor end of life."

J. Did Jesus Christ really die on a cross?

Matthew 27:45-50 "Now from the sixth hour there was darkness ... and about the ninth hour Jesus ... yielded up the ghost."
[Also in **Mark 15:33-37**]

Note: Jesus Christ was crucified only for several hours. Empirical evidence shows that it takes several days before a crucified person dies on the cross.

18. In health and in sickness

A. Who causes diseases?

God causes diseases
Exodus 4:11 "[The Lord said] who maketh the dumb, or deaf or the blind? have not I the Lord?"
Exodus 15:26 "If thou wilt diligently hearken to the voice of the Lord ... and keep all his statutes, I will put none of these diseases upon thee ..."
Numbers 11:33 "The Lord smote the people with a very great plague."

Demons causes diseases
Job 2:7 "So went Satan ... and smote Job with sore boils ..."
Matthew 9:33 "And when the devil was cast out, the dumb spake."
[Also in Matthew 12:22, 17:15-18; Mark 9:17, 25; Luke 9:39, 11:14, 13:11, 16]

According to Jesus, sin causes illness
John 5:14 "Jesus ... said ... Behold, thou art made whole: sin no more ..."
Acts 10:38 "Healing all that were oppressed of the devil."

B. What will prevent you from being sick?

If you follow God's commandments you will not be sick
Exodus 15:26 "And said, If thou wilt diligently hearken to the voice of the Lord thy God ... I will put none of these diseases upon thee ..."

C. Staring at a brass serpent will cure snakebite

Numbers 21:8-9 "The Lord said unto Moses, Make thee a fiery serpent, and set it upon a pole ... every one that is bitten, when he looketh upon it, shall live. And Moses made a serpent of brass, and put it upon a pole ..."

Note: This practice was probably derived from the symbol of the Greek god Asclepius. Today, instead of a single snake the symbol used for Medicine is a wand with two snakes also called Caduceus or wand of Hermes.

D. Belief in Jesus will make you immune to snakes and poison

Mark 16:16-18 "He that believeth and is baptized shall be saved ... They shall take up serpents; and if they drink any deadly thing, it shall not hurt them..."

E. Washing in the pool of Siloam cures blindness

John 9:7 "[Jesus] said unto him [blind man], Go, wash in the pool of Siloam ... He went ... and washed, and came seeing."

F. Prayer and faith alone can cure your illness

II Chronicles 16:12 "And Asa in the thirty and ninth year of his reign was diseased in his feet, until his disease was exceeding great: yet in his disease

he sought not to the LORD, but to the physicians.
Psalm 103:2-3 "The Lord ... healeth all thy diseases."
Matthew 9:22 "Jesus [said], Daughter ... thy faith hath made thee whole. And the woman was made whole from that hour."

Note: Rely on faith-based medicine for prayer and faith alone will cure you.

G. Belief in Jesus can make you heal the sick

Mark 16:17-18 "Them that believe; In my name shall they cast out devils ... speak with new tongues ... they shall lay hands on the sick, and they shall recover."

Note: Belief in Jesus can make you cast out devils, learn a new language and heal the sick.

H. Exorcism can cure mental and physical illness

Muteness
Matthew 9:33 "When the devil was cast out, the dumb spake ..."
Luke 11:14 "He was casting out a devil ... the devil was gone ... the dumb spake."

Blindness
Matthew 12:22 "He healed him ... the blind and dumb both spake and saw."

Epilepsy
Matthew 17:14-18 "Lord, have mercy on my son ... ofttimes he falleth ... Jesus rebuked the devil ... the child was cured ..."

Insanity
Matthew 4:23-24 "They brought unto him [Jesus] ... those ... which were lunatick, and those that had the palsy; and he healed them."
Mark 5:2-8 "There met him [Jesus] out of the tombs a man with an unclean spirit ... But when he saw Jesus afar off, he ran and worshipped him ... he said unto him, Come out of the man, thou unclean spirit."

Lameness
Luke 13:11, 13 "There was a woman which had a spirit of infirmity ... he [Jesus] laid his hands on her: and immediately she was made straight"
Acts 8:7 "Many taken [to Philip] ... that were lame, were healed."

I. Was it devil possession or food poisoning?

Matthew 17:15-18 "He [child] is lunatick ... Jesus rebuked the devil ... and the child was cured from that very hour."

Luke 9:39 "A spirit taketh him … it teareth him that he foameth again …"

Note: Symptoms attributed to witchcraft and devil possession may actually be ergot poisoning (ergotism). Ergot poisoning comes from the Claviceps purpurea fungus. Such contamination can occur by ingesting infected wheat, rye and other cereals. This fungus contains chemicals similar to the psychedelic drug called LSD. Symptoms of this poisoning include violent seizures, spasms, delusions, hallucinations, crawling sensations on the skin, headaches, nausea and vomiting.

J. Did Paul suffer from heatstroke?

Paul claims Jesus spoke to him in his trip to Damascus
Acts 9:8-9 "Saul arose from the earth; and when his eyes were opened, he saw no man … he was three days without sight, and neither did eat nor drink."

Note: After hours of traveling on foot under the sun on a hot midday Paul claimed to have met Jesus on the road to Damascus.Paul's symptoms - hallucinations, delusions, and temporary blindness points to a medical condition called heatstroke.

19. Angels and demons

A. Going to a pool stirred up by angels cured disease

John 5:4 "For an angel went down at a certain season into the pool, and troubled the water: whosoever … stepped in was made whole of whatsoever disease he had."

B. Angels open prison doors

Acts 5:19 "But the angel of the Lord by night opened the prison doors …"

C. Demons causes troubles and problems

Matthew 13:28 "An enemy hath done this."

IV. Borrowed statements and stories?

1. Misquoted and borrowed statements within the Bible

A. Misquoted and borrowed statements about the life of Jesus

1. Magnificat, the Song of Hannah and Psalm 113

The Magnificat
Luke 1:46-55 "Mary said, My soul doth magnify the Lord, And my spirit hath rejoiced in God my Saviour. For he hath regarded the low estate of his handmaiden: for, behold, from henceforth all generations shall call me blessed ..."

Psalm 113
Psalm 113 "Praise ye the Lord. Praise, O ye servants of the Lord, praise the name of the Lord. Blessed be the name of the Lord from this time forth and for evermore ..."

Song of Hannah
I Samuel 2:1-10 "Hannah prayed, and said, My heart rejoiceth in the Lord, mine horn is exalted in the Lord ... the Lord shall judge the ends of the earth ... and exalt the horne of his anointed."

Note: It is widely believed that The Magnificat (Luke 1:46-55) had been derived from the Song of Hannah (I Samuel 2:1-10). The Song of Hannah is also similar to Psalm 113.

2. Matthew misquoted Isaiah

Matthew 1:22-23 "Now all this was done, that it might be fulfilled which was spoken of the Lord by the prophet, saying, Behold, a virgin shall be with child, and shall bring forth a son, and they shall call his name Emmanuel, which being interpreted is, God with us."

Isaiah 7:14 "Therefore the Lord himself shall give you a sign; Behold, a virgin shall conceive, and bear a son, and shall call his name Immanuel ... For before the child shall know to refuse the evil, and choose the good, the land that thou abhorrest shall be forsaken of both her kings."

Note: Isaiah was referring to a child who will be born during his time and not a future event. Also the original text was referring to a young woman and not a virgin living at the time of the prophecy. Thus in effect prophesying that Judah will be saved from the threat of Rezin and Pekah as shown in the following verses:

Isaiah 7:16 "For before the child shall know to refuse the evil, and choose the good, the land that thou abhorrest shall be forsaken of both her kings (Rezin and Pekah)."

3. Matthew said Micah predicted that Jesus will become a ruler of Israel

Matthew 2:5-6 "They said unto him, In Bethlehem of Judaea: for thus it is written by the prophet, And thou Bethlehem, in the land of Juda, art not the least among the princes of Juda: for out of thee shall come a Governor, that shall rule my people Israel."

Micah 5:2, 6 "But thou, Bethlehem Ephratah, though thou be little among the thousands of Judah, yet out of thee shall he come forth unto me that is to be ruler in Israel; whose goings forth have been from of old, from everlasting …And they shall waste the land of Assyria with the sword, and the land of Nimrod in the entrances thereof: thus shall he deliver us from the Assyrian, when he cometh into our land, and when he treadeth within our borders."

I Chronicles 2:50-54 "These were the sons of Caleb the son of Hur, the firstborn of Ephratah; Shobal the father of Kirjathjearim. Salma the father of Bethlehem, Hareph the father of Bethgader. The sons of Salma; Bethlehem, and the Netophathites, Ataroth, the house of Joab, and half of the Manahethites, the Zorites."

Note: The Bethlehem mentioned in the book of Micah is about a clan mentioned in I Chronicles 2:50-54. While in the book of Matthew, the Bethlehem mentioned is a place. Micah also predicted that the future ruler would lead the Israelites against Assyria. But Jesus never led the Israelites against Assyria.

4. Out of Egypt have I called my son

Matthew 2:15 "And was there until the death of Herod: that it might be fulfilled which was spoken of the Lord by the prophet, saying, Out of Egypt have I called my son."

Hosea 11:1 "When Israel was a child, then I loved him, and called my son out of Egypt."

Note: Hosea the prophet said 'When Israel was a child, then I loved him, and called my son out of Egypt' this was a reference to the exodus of the Israelites from Egypt, a historical fact during Hosea's time. But Matthew mistranslated the statement as a prophecy of the future to refer to the flight of Jesus' family to Egypt.

5. Is the slaughter of the innocents a fulfillment of Jeremiah's prophecy?

Matthew 2:16-18 "Then Herod, when he saw that he was mocked of the wise men … slew all the children that were in Bethlehem … from two years old and under ... Then was fulfilled that which was spoken by Jeremiah the prophet, saying, In Rama was there a voice heard, lamentation, and weeping, and great mourning, Rachel weeping for her children, and would not be comforted, because they are not."

Jeremiah 31:15 "Thus saith the Lord; A voice was heard in Ramah, lamentation, and bitter weeping; Rachel weeping for her children refused to be comforted for her children, because they were not."

Note: In Jeremiah, Rachel wept for her children because they were carried away not slaughtered as in the book of Matthew. There is no historical or archeological evidence that shows that the massacre of the innocents by King Herod actually took place.

6. There is no reference to a prophecy that Jesus will be called a Nazarene

Matthew 2:23 "He came and dwelt in a city called Nazareth: that it might be fulfilled which was spoken by the prophets, He shall be called a Nazarene."

Note: No statement exists in the Old Testament. Jesus being a Nazarene implies that he is from Nazareth. However, there is no archeological evidence that supports the presence of Israelis during Jesus time in Nazareth.

7. The Devil quoted from the Book of Psalm

Matthew 4:6 "And saith unto him, If thou be the Son of God, cast thyself down: for it is written, He shall give his angels charge concerning thee: and in their hands they shall bear thee up, lest at any time thou dash thy foot against a stone."

Psalm 91:11-12 "For he shall give his angels charge over thee, to keep thee in all thy ways. They shall bear thee up in their hands, lest thou dash thy foot against a stone."

8. Was Jesus referring to a statement in Deuteronomy?

Matthew 4:10 "Then saith Jesus unto him, Get thee hence, Satan: for it is written, Thou shalt worship the Lord thy God, and him only shalt thou serve."

Luke 4:8 "Jesus … said unto him, Get thee behind me, Satan: for it is written, Thou shalt worship the Lord thy God, and him only shalt thou serve."
Deuteronomy 6:13 "Thou shalt fear the Lord thy God, and serve him, and shalt swear by his name."

Note: Jesus alluded from a passage in Deuteronomy in response to the Devil's statement, which was quoted from the book of Psalm.

B. Misquotations and alluded statements from Malachi

1. Was John the Baptist the reincarnation of Elijah?

John the Baptist was the reincarnation of Elijah
Matthew 11:10, 13-14 "For this is he … For all the prophets and the law prophesied until John. And if ye will receive it, this is Elias …"
Matthew 17:10-13 "Jesus [said] … Elias (Elijah) is come already … Then the disciples understood that he was spake unto them of John the Baptist."
Mark 6:14-16 "King Herod heard of him [and] said, 'That John the Baptist was risen from the dead … Others said 'That it is Elias (Elijah).'"
Luke 1:13-17 "But the angel said unto him … thy wife Elizabeth shall bear thee a son, and thou shalt call his name John … and he shall go before him in the spirit and power of Elias (Elijah) …"

John the Baptist refused to acknowledge being the reincarnation of Elijah
John 1:21 "They asked him, What then? Art thou Elias? And he saith, I am not. Art thou that prophet? And he answered, No."

Note: The Bible strongly suggests that reincarnation is a fact by saying that John the Baptist was a reincarnation of Elijah. However in John 1:21, John the Baptist said that he is not Elijah.

Malachi prophesied the return of Elijah
Malachi 3:1 "Behold, I will send my messenger, and he shall prepare the way before me: and the Lord, whom ye seek, shall suddenly come to his temple, even the messenger of the covenant, whom ye delight in: behold, he shall come, saith the Lord of hosts."
Malachi 4:5 "Behold, I will send you Elijah the prophet before the coming of the great and dreadful day of the Lord."

Note: However, Malachi prophesied the coming of the Lord as a great and dreadful day, which does not aptly describe the birth of Jesus Christ.

2. The Messiah will suddenly make an appearance at the temple

Mark 11:15-16 "They come to Jerusalem: and Jesus went into the temple, and began to cast out them that sold and bought in the temple …"

Malachi 3:1 "Behold, I will send my messenger, and he shall prepare the way before me: and the Lord, whom ye seek, shall suddenly come to his temple, even the messenger of the covenant, whom ye delight in: behold, he shall come, saith the Lord of hosts ..."

3. The Messiah will be the messenger of the covenant

Luke 4:43 "He said unto them, I must preach the kingdom of God to other cities also: for therefore am I sent."

Malachi 3:1 "Behold, I will send my messenger, and he shall prepare the way before me: and the Lord, whom ye seek, shall suddenly come to his temple, even the messenger of the covenant, whom ye delight in: behold, he shall come, saith the Lord of hosts ..."

4. The prophecy of Malachi about Elijah the prophet

Matthew, Mark and Luke were referring to John as Elijah, the fulfillment of the prophecy of Malachi
Matthew 11:13-14 "For all the prophets and the law prophesied until John And if ye will receive it, this is Elias (Elijah) which was for to come. Many will be lead to righteousness by the Messiah's forerunner."
Mark 1:3-5 "The voice of one crying in the wilderness, Prepare ye the way of the Lord, make his paths straight. John did baptize in the wilderness, and preach the baptism of repentance for the remission of sins. And there went out unto him all the land of Judaea, and they of Jerusalem, and were all baptized of him in the river of Jordan, confessing their sins."
Luke 1:16-17 "Many of the children of Israel shall he turn to the Lord their God. And he shall go before him in the spirit and power of Elias, to turn the hearts of the fathers to the children, and the disobedient to the wisdom of the just; to make ready a people prepared for the Lord."

Malachi 4:6 "He shall turn the heart of the fathers to the children, and the heart of the children to their fathers, lest I come and smite the earth with a curse."

C. Misquotations and alluded statements of Jesus

1. Jesus said the priests who profaned the Sabbath were blameless

Matthew 12:5 "Or have ye not read in the law, how that on the sabbath days the priests in the temple profane the sabbath, and are blameless?"

Note: No work must be performed on the Sabbath day. However priests were instructed to do certain things during Sabbath as stated in the following verses:

Leviticus 24:8 "Every sabbath he shall set it in order before the Lord continually, being taken from the children of Israel by an everlasting covenant."

Numbers 28:9 "On the sabbath day two lambs of the first year without spot … This is the burnt offering of every sabbath, beside the continual burnt offering, and his drink offering."

I Chronicles 9:32 "Other of their brethren, of the sons of the Kohathites, were over the shewbread, to prepare it every sabbath."

Ezekiel 46:4 "The burnt offering that the prince shall offer unto the Lord in the sabbath day shall be six lambs without blemish, and a ram without blemish"

Note: The statement made by Jesus refers to the priestly duties during Sabbath that are mentioned in the books of Leviticus, Numbers, I Chronicles and Ezekiel. These priestly duties contradict the law that says no work must be done on the Sabbath day.

2. Matthew 13:35 and Psalm 78?

Matthew 13:35 "That it might be fulfilled which was spoken by the prophet, saying, I will open my mouth in parables; I will utter things which have been kept secret from the foundation of the world."

Psalm 78:2-3 "I will open my mouth in a parable: I will utter dark sayings of old: Which we have heard and known, and our fathers have told us."

3. Jesus said his ride in Jerusalem was prophesied by Zechariah

Matthew 21:4-5 "All this was done, that it might be fulfilled which was spoken by the prophet, saying, Tell ye the daughter of Sion, Behold, thy King cometh unto thee, meek, and sitting upon an ass, and a colt the foal of an ass."

John 12:14-15 "Jesus, when he had found a young ass, sat thereon; as it is written, Fear not, daughter of Sion: behold, thy King cometh, sitting on an ass's colt."

Zechariah 9:9 "Rejoice greatly, O daughter of Zion; shout, O daughter of Jerusalem: behold, thy King cometh unto thee: he is just, and having salvation; lowly, and riding upon an ass, and upon a colt the foal of an ass"

Note: The leader prophesied in the book of Zechariah was said to be a warrior-like leader unlike Jesus.

Zechariah 9:10 "I will cut off the chariot from Ephraim, and the horse from Jerusalem, and the battle bow shall be cut off: and he shall speak peace unto the heathen: and his dominion shall be from sea even to sea, and from the river even to the ends of the earth."

4. Jesus said the Scriptures of the prophets be fulfilled

Matthew 26:52-56 "Then said Jesus unto him … Thinkest thou that I cannot now pray to my Father, and he shall presently give me more than twelve legions of angels? But how then shall the scriptures be fulfilled, that thus it must be? … But all this was done, that the scriptures of the prophets might be fulfilled. Then all the disciples forsook him, and fled."

Note: Jesus said the scriptures of the prophets should be fulfilled about his betrayal and arrest. However, there is no such prophecy in the Old Testament.

5. Did Jesus quote a statement from the Book of Isaiah and Malachi?

Mark 1:2 "As it is written in the prophets, Behold, I send my messenger before thy face, which shall prepare thy way before thee."

Note: No exact statement exists in the book of Old Testament. However, the following verses may be considered:

Isaiah 40:3 "The voice of him that crieth in the wilderness, Prepare ye the way of the Lord, make straight in the desert a highway for our God."

Malachi 3:1 "Behold, I will send my messenger, and he shall prepare the way before me: and the Lord, whom ye seek, shall suddenly come to his temple, even the messenger of the covenant, whom ye delight in: behold, he shall come, saith the Lord of hosts."

6. Jesus quotes a statement that is allegedly in the Old Testament

John 20:9 "For as yet they knew not the scripture, that he must rise again from the dead."

Note: No statement exists in the Old Testament.

7. Did Jesus misquote Isaiah?

Luke 4:16-19 "He came to Nazareth … he went into the synagogue on the sabbath day, and stood up for to read. And there was delivered unto him the book of the prophet Esaias. And when he had opened the book, he found the place where it was written, The Spirit of the Lord is upon me, because he hath anointed me to preach the gospel to the poor; he hath sent me to heal the brokenhearted, to preach deliverance to the captives, and recovering of sight to the blind, to set at liberty them that are bruised, To preach the acceptable year of the Lord."

Isaiah 61:1-2 "The Spirit of the Lord GOD is upon me; because the Lord hath anointed me to preach good tidings unto the meek; he hath sent me to bind up the brokenhearted, to proclaim liberty to the captives, and the opening of the prison to them that are bound; To proclaim the acceptable year of the Lord, and the day of vengeance of our God; to comfort all that mourn."

Note: Isaiah was talking about his present condition and not about a prophet or messiah in the future.

8. Did Jesus call himself the Son of Man based on Daniel?

Luke 17:22-24 "He [Jesus] said …The days will come, when ye shall desire to see one of the days of the Son of man, and ye shall not see it. And they shall say to you, See here; or, see there: go not after them, nor follow them. For as the lightning, that lighteneth out of the one part under heaven, shineth unto the other part under heaven; so shall also the Son of man be in his day."

Daniel 7:13-14 "I saw in the night visions, and, behold, one like the Son of man came with the clouds of heaven … And there was given him dominion … that all people … should serve him: his dominion … shall not pass away, and his kingdom that which shall not be."

9. Jesus claims that out of his belly shall flow rivers of living water

John 7:38 "He that believeth on me, as the scripture hath said, out of his belly shall flow rivers of living water."

Note: No direct statement exists in the Old Testament. Perhaps Jesus was referring to the following verses:
Isaiah 12:3 "Therefore with joy shall ye draw water out of the wells of salvation."
Isaiah 35:5-6 "Then the eyes of the blind shall be opened, and the ears of the deaf shall be unstopped. Then shall the lame man leap as an hart, and the tongue of the dumb sing: for in the wilderness shall waters break out, and streams in the desert."

10. Did Jesus quote a passage from the book of Psalm?

John 13:18 "I speak not of you all: I know whom I have chosen: but that the scripture may be fulfilled, He that eateth bread with me hath lifted up his heel against me."

Psalm 41:9 "Yea, mine own familiar friend, in whom I trusted, which did eat of my bread, hath lifted up his heel against me."

11. Jesus mentions a 'son of perdition' in the Old Testament

John 17:12 "While I was with them in the world, I kept them in thy name: those that thou gavest me I have kept, and none of them is lost, but the son of perdition; that the scripture might be fulfilled."

Note: No statement exists in the Old Testament.

12. What were the last words of Jesus during crucifixion?

The last words of Jesus according to the book of Mark and Matthew
Matthew 27:46 "About the ninth hour Jesus cried My God, my God, why hast thou forsaken me?"
Mark 15:34 "At the ninth hour Jesus cried ... My God, my God, why hast thou forsaken me?"
Psalm 22:1 "My God, my God, why hast thou forsaken me?"

The last words of Jesus according to the book of Luke
Luke 23:46 "When Jesus had cried ... Father, into thy hands I commend my spirit: and having said thus, he gave up the ghost."
Psalm 31:5 "Into thine hand I commit my spirit: thou hast redeemed me, O Lord God of truth."

D. Misquoted statements about the crucifixion of Jesus

1. John misquoted Exodus, Numbers and Psalm

John 19:32-36 "Then came the soldiers ... when they [soldiers] came to Jesus, and saw that he was dead already, they brake not his legs: But one of the soldiers with a spear pierced his side, and forthwith came there out blood and water. And he that saw it bare record, and his record is true: and he knoweth that he saith true, that ye might believe. For these things were done, that the scripture should be fulfilled, A bone of him shall not be broken."

Exodus 12:46 "In one house shall it [Passover lamb] be eaten; thou shalt not carry forth ought of the flesh abroad out of the house; neither shall ye break a bone thereof."
Numbers 9:12 "They shall leave none of it [Passover lamb] unto the morning, nor break any bone of it: according to all the ordinances of the passover they shall keep it."

Psalm 34:19-20 "Many are the afflictions of the righteous: but the Lord delivereth him out of them all. He keepeth all his [righteous people] bones: not one of them is broken."

Note: John 19:36 claims that the bones of Jesus Christ were not broken as a fulfillment of a prophecy. But there is no prophecy pertaining to this event. What is written in Exodus 12:46 and Numbers 9:12 were not prophecies but set of rules on how to handle the lamb for the Passover. The passage in Psalm 34:20 was not a prophecy but a statement about righteous people.

2. Who was pierced?

John 19:37 "Again another scripture saith, They shall look on him [Jesus] whom they pierced."

Zechariah 12:9-10 "On that day I will set out to destroy all the nations that attack Jerusalem. And I will pour upon the house of David, and upon the inhabitants of Jerusalem, the spirit of grace and of supplications: and they shall look upon me whom they have pierced, and they shall mourn for him, as one mourneth for his only son, and shall be in bitterness for him, as one that is in bitterness for his firstborn."

Note: Zechariah 12:10 points to a historical event during Zechariah's time and not a prophecy about a future event. The verse in Zechariah 12:9 does not seem to point to the crucifixion and death of Jesus Christ since no nation was destroyed during the crucifixion of Jesus Christ.

3. A statement that is allegedly in the Old Testament

John 20:9 "For as yet they knew not the scripture, that he must rise again ..."

Note: No statement exists in the Old Testament.

E. Misquoted statement about the potter's field

1. Did Jeremiah wrote about the potter's field?

Jeremy
Matthew 27:9-10 "Then was fulfilled that which was spoken by Jeremy the prophet, saying, And they took the thirty pieces of silver, the price of him that was valued, whom they of the children of Israel did value; And gave them for the potter's field, as the Lord appointed me."

Zechariah
Zechariah 11:12-13 "I said unto them, If ye think good, give me my price; and if not, forbear. So they weighed for my price thirty pieces of silver. And the

Lord said unto me, Cast it unto the potter: a goodly price that I was prised at of them. And I took the thirty pieces of silver, and cast them to the potter in the house of the Lord."

Note: Jeremiah did not write anything concerning the potter's field, but Zechariah did.

F. Misquotations of Jesus and Paul

1. Did Jesus and Paul misquote Hosea?

Luke 18:31-33 "Then he took unto him the twelve, and said unto them, Behold, we go up to Jerusalem, and all things that are written by the prophets concerning the Son of man shall be accomplished. For he shall be delivered unto the Gentiles, and shall be mocked, and spitefully entreated, and spitted on: And they shall scourge him, and put him to death: and the third day he shall rise again."

I Corinthians 15:3-4 "For I delivered unto you first of all that which I also received, how that Christ died for our sins according to the scriptures; And that he was buried, and that he rose again the third day according to the scriptures."

Hosea 6:2 "After two days will he [Lord] revive us [Israel]: in the third day he [Lord] will raise us [Israel] up, and we [Israel] shall live in his [Lord] sight."

Note: Hosea was referring to the Israelites living during his time and not about a future prophet.

2. Did Moses mention about Jesus?

Jesus said that Moses mentioned about him in his law
Luke 24:44-48 "He said unto them, These are the words which I spake unto you, while I was yet with you, that all things must be fulfilled, which were written in the law of Moses, and in the prophets, and in the psalms, concerning me. Then opened he their understanding, that they might understand the scriptures, And said unto them, Thus it is written, and thus it behooved Christ to suffer, and to rise from the dead the third day: And that repentance and remission of sins should be preached in his name among all nations, beginning at Jerusalem. And ye are witnesses of these things."
John 5:46 "For had ye believed Moses, ye would have believed me [Jesus]; for he wrote of me."

Paul said that Moses mentioned about Jesus
Acts 26:22-23 "Having therefore obtained help of God, I continue unto this

day, witnessing both to small and great, saying none other things than those which the prophets and Moses did say should come: That Christ should suffer, and that he should be the first that should rise from the dead, and should shew light unto the people, and to the Gentiles."

Note: There is no explicit statement stated by Moses about Jesus. The statement Jesus and Paul would be referring to might be Deuteronomy 18:15 which says:

Deuteronomy 18:15 "The Lord thy God will raise up unto thee a Prophet from the midst of thee, of thy brethren, like unto me [Moses]; unto him ye shall hearken."

G. Misquotations and alluded statements in the Book of Acts

1. Did Peter misquote the prophet Joel?

Acts 2:16-21 "But this is that which was spoken by the prophet Joel: And it shall come to pass in the last days, saith God, I will pour out of my Spirit upon all flesh: and your sons and your daughters shall prophesy, and your young men shall see visions, and your old men shall dream dreams: And on my servants and on my handmaidens I will pour out in those days of my Spirit; and they shall prophesy: And I will shew wonders in heaven above, and signs in the earth beneath; blood, and fire, and vapour of smoke: The sun shall be turned into darkness, and the moon into blood, before the great and notable day of the Lord come: And it shall come to pass, that whosoever shall call on the name of the Lord shall be saved."

Joel 2:28- 32 "And it shall come to pass afterward, that I will pour out my spirit upon all flesh; and your sons and your daughters shall prophesy, your old men shall dream dreams, your young men shall see visions: And also upon the servants and upon the handmaids in those days will I pour out my spirit. And I will shew wonders in the heavens and in the earth, blood, and fire, and pillars of smoke. The sun shall be turned into darkness, and the moon into blood, before the great and terrible day of the Lord come. And it shall come to pass, that whosoever shall call on the name of the Lord shall be delivered: for in mount Zion and in Jerusalem shall be deliverance, as the Lord hath said, and in the remnant whom the Lord shall call."

Note: Joel's prophecy is a failed prediction. Peter was wrong in quoting Joel's prophecy because it has nothing to do with the Pentecost and Jesus. Peter was wrong because Jesus did not come back as predicted and Peter was wrong about being in the last days. The descriptions made about the sun and the moon changing its' colors are eclipses which are today considered as natural occurrences with the scientific knowledge of Astronomy.

2. Was Acts 3:23 taken from Deuteronomy 18?

Acts 3:23 "And it shall come to pass, that every soul, which will not hear that prophet, shall be destroyed from among the people."

Deuteronomy 18:15,18-19 "I will raise them up a Prophet from among their brethren, like unto thee, and will put my words in his mouth; and he shall speak unto them all that I shall command him. And it shall come to pass, that whosoever will not hearken unto my words which he shall speak in my name, I will require it of him."

Note: In Acts 3:23, Peter said that whoever does not listen to the prophet will be destroyed. Was Peter quoting a verse in Deuteronomy? Was Peter referring to non-believers of Jesus Christ?

3. Was Acts 13:22 taken from I Samuel 13:14?

Acts 13:22 "And when he had removed him, he raised up unto them David to be their king; to whom also he gave their testimony, and said, I have found David the son of Jesse, a man after mine own heart, which shall fulfil all my will."

I Samuel 13:14 "But now thy kingdom shall not continue: the Lord hath sought him a man after his own heart, and the Lord hath commanded him to be captain over his people, because thou hast not kept that which the Lord commanded thee."

4. Was Acts 13:33 taken from Psalm 2:7?

Acts 13:33 "God hath fulfilled the same unto us their children, in that he hath raised up Jesus again; as it is also written in the second psalm, Thou art my Son, this day have I begotten thee."

Psalm 2:7 "I will declare the decree: the Lord hath said unto me, Thou art my Son; this day have I begotten thee."

5. Was Paul lying?

Acts 20:35 "I have shown you all things, how that so labouring ye ought to support the weak, and to remember the words of the Lord Jesus, how he said, 'It is more blessed to give than to receive.'"

Note: Jesus never made such biblical statement. Statements attributed to Jesus but were not included in the gospels are called Agrapha.

H. More misquotations and alluded statements by Paul

1. Paul wrote about Christ's superiority from angels

Paul said that Jesus Christ is superior from angels
Hebrews 1:4-5 "Being made so much better than the angels, as he hath by inheritance obtained a more excellent name than they. For unto which of the angels said he at any time, Thou art my Son, this day have I begotten thee? And again, I will be to him a Father, and he shall be to me a Son?"

Christ did not glorify himself to be made a high priest but as Son of God
Hebrews 5:5 "So also Christ glorified not himself to be made an high priest; but he that said unto him, Thou art my Son, to day have I begotten thee."

The passage in the book of Psalm
Psalm 2:7 "I will declare the decree: the Lord hath said unto me, Thou art my Son; this day have I begotten thee."

2. Was Romans 9:33 taken from Isaiah 28:16?

Romans 9:33 "As it is written, Behold, I lay in Sion a stumblingstone and rock of offence: and whosoever believeth on him shall not be ashamed."

Isaiah 28:16 "Therefore thus saith the Lord GOD, Behold, I lay in Zion for a foundation a stone, a tried stone, a precious corner stone, a sure foundation: he that believeth shall not make haste."

3. Was Romans 10:8 taken from Deuteronomy 30:14?

Romans 10:8 "But what saith it? The word is nigh thee, even in thy mouth, and in thy heart: that is, the word of faith, which we preach."

Deuteronomy 30:14 "But the word is very nigh unto thee, in thy mouth, and in thy heart, that thou mayest do it."

4. Did the scripture say this?

Romans 10:11 "For the scripture saith, Whosoever believeth on him shall not be ashamed."

Note: But there is no such statement in the Old Testament.

I Corinthians 9:10 "Or saith he it altogether for our sakes? For our sakes, no doubt, this is written: that he that ploweth should plow in hope; and that he that thresheth in hope should be partaker of his hope."

Note: But there is no such statement in the Old Testament.

5. Was Ephesians 4:8 taken from Psalm 68:18?

Ephesians 4:8 "Wherefore he saith, When he ascended up on high, he led captivity captive, and gave gifts unto men."

Psalm 68:18 "Thou hast ascended on high, thou hast led captivity captive: thou hast received gifts for men; yea, for the rebellious also, that the Lord God might dwell among them."

6. Was Hebrews 8:9 taken from Jeremiah 31:32?

Hebrews 8:9 "Not according to the covenant that I made with their fathers in the day when I took them by the hand to lead them out of the land of Egypt; because they continued not in my covenant, and I regarded them not, saith the Lord."

Jeremiah 31:32 "Not according to the covenant that I made with their fathers in the day that I took them by the hand to bring them out of the land of Egypt; which my covenant they brake, although I was an husband unto them, saith the Lord"

7. Was Hebrews 10:5-6 taken from Psalm 40:6?

Hebrews 10:5-6 "Wherefore when he cometh into the world, he saith, Sacrifice and offering thou wouldest not, but a body hast thou prepared me: In burnt offerings and sacrifices for sin thou hast had no pleasure."
Psalm 40:6 "Sacrifice and offering thou didst not desire; mine ears hast thou opened: burnt offering and sin offering hast thou not required."

I. A misquotation in the book of James

James 4:5 "Do ye think that the scripture saith in vain, The spirit that dwelleth in us lusteth to envy?"

Note: This passage is nowhere to be found in the Bible.

J. The Four Horsemen of the Apocalypse and Zechariah

Were the Four Horsemen of the Apocalypse derived from Zechariah?
Revelation 6:2-8 "[I saw] a white horse, [a] horse that was .red ... a black horse ... a pale horse"

Zechariah 6:1-3 "I looked, and, behold, there came four chariots ... In the first chariot were red horses; and in the second chariot black horses; And in the third chariot white horses; and in the fourth chariot grisled and bay horses."

K. Was the Book of Revelation based on the Book of Daniel?

Daniel 2:29 "As for thee, O king, thy thoughts came into thy mind upon thy bed, what should come to pass hereafter: and he that revealeth secrets maketh known to thee what shall come to pass."

Revelation 1:1 "The Revelation of Jesus Christ, which God gave unto him, to shew unto his servants things which must shortly come to pass."

Daniel 10:5 "Then I lifted up mine eyes, and looked, and behold a certain man clothed in linen, whose loins were girded with fine gold of Uphaz: His body also was like the beryl, and his face as the appearance of lightning, and his eyes as lamps of fire, and his arms and his feet like in colour to polished brass, and the voice of his --words like the voice of a multitude."

Revelation 1:13-14 "And in the midst of the seven candlesticks one like unto the Son of man, clothed with a garment down to the foot, and girt about the paps with a golden girdle. His head and his hairs were white like wool, as white as snow; and his eyes were as a flame of fire; And his feet like unto fine brass, as if they burned in a furnace; and his voice as the sound of many waters."

2. Borrowed and alluded statements outside the Bible

A. The Code of Hammurabi and the Covenant Code

Exodus 20:22-23:33 "The Lord said unto Moses, Thus thou shalt say unto the children of Israel, Ye have seen that I have talked with you from heaven ..."

Note: The Code of Hammurabi was written about 800 years earlier that the Book of Exodus. However, the two set of laws offers very similar sliding scale of punishment for crimes and offenses such as teft, adultery and murder.

B. The Ten Commandments and the Egyptian Book of the Dead?

The Ten Commandments
Exodus 20:7-16: "Thou shalt not take the name of the Lord thy God ..."

The Egyptian Book of the Dead: "I have done away sin for thee and not acted fraudulently or deceitfully. I have not belittled God. I have not inflicted pain or caused another to weep ..."

Note: Since the Ten Commandments were written after fleeing from Egypt, some historians believe that the Ten Commandments were derived from the Egyptian Book of the Dead.

C. The Lord's Prayer?

Matthew 6:9-13 "After this manner therefore pray ye: Our Father which art in heaven, Hallowed be thy name. Thy kingdom come, Thy will be done in earth, as it is in heaven. Give us this day our daily bread. And forgive us our debts, as we forgive our debtors. And lead us not into temptation, but deliver us from evil: For thine is the kingdom, and the power, and the glory for ever. Amen." [Also in **Luke 11:1-4**]

Note: The Lord's Prayer may have been copied from The First Book of Adam and Eve written 150 years prior to the birth of Jesus Christ.

The First Book of Adam and Eve: Chapter 23
Our Father, Who art in Heaven, be gracious unto us, O Lord our God, hallowed be Thy Name, and let the remembrance of Thee be glorified in Heaven above and upon earth here below. Let Thy kingdom reign over us now and forever. The Holy Men of old said remit and forgive unto all men whatsoever they have done unto me. And lead us not into temptation, but deliver us from the evil thing; for Thine is the kingdom and Thou shalt reign in glory forever and forevermore. AMEN.

D. Epimenides Cretica

Acts 17:28 "For in him we live, and move, and have our being ..."
Titus 1:12-13 "One of themselves, even a prophet of their own, said, the Cretians are always liars, evil beasts, slow bellies. This witness is true ..."

Epimenides' Cretica: Minos addresses Zeus
They fashioned a tomb for thee, O holy and high one
The Cretans, always liars, evil beasts, idle bellies!
But thou art not dead: thou livest and abidest forever,
For in thee we live and move and have our being.

Note: Epimenides, a Cretan poet quoted the following: Cretians are always liars. If he is a Cretan, is he lying? This is also known as the Epimenides paradox.

E. Phaenomena by Solensis Aratus

Acts 17:28 "As certain also of your own poets have said, For we are also his offspring."
Phaenomena (1-5) "Let us begin with Zeus, whom we mortals never leave unspoken. For every street, every market-place is full of Zeus. Even the sea and the harbour are full of this deity. Everywhere everyone is indebted to Zeus. *For we are indeed his offspring.*"

Note: Also used by Cleanthes in Hymn to Zeus.

F. Bacchae by Euripides

Acts 26:14 "And when we were all fallen to the earth, I heard a voice speaking unto me, and saying in the Hebrew tongue, Saul, Saul, why persecutest thou me? *it is hard for thee to kick against the pricks.*"

Bacchae: Line 936 "Better to yield him prayer and sacrifice Than kick against the pricks, Since Dionyse Is God, and thou but mortal."

G. Thais by Menander

I Corinthians 15:33 "Be not deceived: evil communications corrupt good manners."

Thais: Frg. 218 "Evil communications corrupt good manners"

H. Apocalypse of Ezra

Romans
Romans 5:12-21 "Wherefore, as by one man sin entered into the world, and

death by sin; and so death passed upon all men, for that all have sinned: For until the law sin was in the world: but sin is not imputed when there is no law …"

Apocalypse of Ezra 3:21 "For the first Adam clothers himself with the evil heart, and transgresses, and was overcome (and not only so) but also all who were begotten from him."

Apocalypse of Ezra 7:118 "Oh, what hast thou done, Adam! For though it was thou that didst sin, yet the evil was not thine alone, but ours also who are from thee!"

Revelation

Revelation 1:15 "And his feet like unto fine brass, as if they burned in a furnace; and his voice as the sound of many waters."

Revelation 14:2 "And I heard a voice from heaven, as the voice of many waters, and as the voice of a great thunder: and I heard the voice of harpers harping with their harps"

Apocalypse of Ezra 6:17 "And it came to pass that when I heard I stood upon my feet, and I heard, and lo ! a voice of one speaking, and his voice was as the voice of many waters."

I. Book of Enoch

Romans 8:38 and I Enoch 61:10

Romans 8:38 "For I am persuaded, that neither death, nor life, nor angels, nor principalities, nor powers, nor things present, nor things to come"

I Enoch 61:10 "And He will summon all the host of the heavens, and all the holy ones above, and the host of God, the Cherubic, Seraphin and Ophannin, and all the angels of power, and all the angels of principalities."

Romans 9:5 and I Enoch 77:1

Romans 9:5 "Whose are the fathers, and of whom as concerning the flesh Christ came, who is over all, God blessed for ever. Amen."

I Enoch 77:1 "And the first quarter is called the east, because it is the first: and the second, the south, because the Most High will descend there, yea, there in quite a special sense will He who is blessed for ever."

Deuteronomy 33:2, Jude 1:14-15 and I Enoch 1:9

Deuteronomy 33:2 "And he said, The Lord came from Sinai, and rose up from Seir unto them; he shined forth from mount Paran, and he came with ten thousands of saints: from his right hand went a fiery law for them."

Jude 1:14-15 "And Enoch also, the seventh from Adam, prophesied of these, saying, Behold, the Lord cometh with ten thousands of his saints, To execute judgment upon all, and to convince all that are ungodly among them of all their ungodly deeds which they have ungodly committed, and of all their hard speeches which ungodly sinners have spoken against him."

I Enoch 1:9 "And behold! He cometh with ten thousands of His holy ones To execute judgement upon all, And to destroy all the ungodly: And to convict all flesh Of all the works of their ungodliness which they have ungodly committed, And of all the hard things which ungodly sinners have spoken against Him."

J. Ecclesiasticus (Ben-Sirach)

Acts 17:30 "And the times of this ignorance God winked at; but now commandeth all men every where to repent"
Ecclesiasticus 28:7 "Remember the commandments, and do not bear your fellow ill-will, remember the covenant of the Most High, and ignore the offence."

Romans 12:15 "Rejoice with them that do rejoice, and weep with them that weep."
Ecclesiasticus 7:34 "Do not turn your back on those who weep, but share the grief of the grief-stricken."

K. Wisdom of Solomon

Romans 11:17-20 "And if some of the branches be broken off … The branches were broken off, that I might be grafted in … because of unbelief they were broken off …"
Wisdom of Solomon 4:5 "The imperfect branches shall be broken off, their fruit unprofitable, not ripe to eat, yea, meet for nothing [concerning the Gentiles and those in Israel who sinned]."

Romans 9:21-23 "Hath not the potter power over the clay, of the same lump to make one vessel unto honour, and another unto dishonour … And that he might make known the riches of his glory on the vessels of mercy, which he had afore prepared unto glory"
Wisdom of Solomon 15:7 "For the potter, tempering soft earth, fashioneth every vessel with much labour for our service: yea, of the same clay he maketh both the vessels that serve for clean uses, and likewise also all such as serve to the contrary: but what is the use of either sort, the potter himself is the judge"

Note: Ecclesiasticus and Wisdom of Solomon are Deutero-Canonical (Apocrypha) books and are not part of the Hebrew Bible. However these books are included in the Douay-Rheims Bible commonly called the Catholic Bible.

L. Aesop's Fables

1. The Logs and the Olive

Judges 9:7-15 "When they told it to Jotham, he went and stood in the top of mount Gerizim, and [said to the citizens of Shechem] … The trees went forth on a time to anoint a king over them; and they said unto the olive tree, Reign thou over us … And the bramble said unto the trees, If in truth ye anoint me king over you, then come and put your trust in my shadow: and if not, let fire come out of the bramble, and devour the cedars of Lebanon."

Aesop's Fable - The Logs and the Olive

Once the logs were consulting among themselves to elect a king. They asked the olive: 'Reign over us.' The olive tree replied:'What? Give up my oily liquor which is so highly prized by god and man to go reign over the logs?'And so the logs asked the fig:'Come and reign over us.' But the fig replied similarly:'What? Relinquish the sweetness of my delicious fruit to go and reign over the logs?'So the logs urged the thornbush:'Come and reign over us.'And the thorn replied: 'If you were really to anoint me king over you, you would have to take shelter beneath me. Otherwise the flames from my brushwood would escape and devour the cedars of Lebanon.'

Note: Judges 9:7-15 is also known as Jotham's parable.

2. The Fighting Cocks and the Eagle

Proverbs 16:18 "Pride goeth before destruction, and an haughty spirit before a fall."

Aesop's Fable - The Fighting Cocks and the Eagle

Two game cocks were fiercely fighting for the mastery of the farmyard. One at last put the other to flight. The vanquished cock skulked away and hid himself in a quiet corner, while the conqueror, flying up to a high wall, flapped his wings and crowed exultingly with all his might. An eagle sailing through the air pounced upon him and carried him off in his talons. The vanquished Cock immediately came out of his corner, and ruled henceforth with undisputed mastery. Pride goes before destruction.

3. The Mouse and the Bull

Ecclesiastes 9:11 "The race is not to the swift, nor the battle to the strong … but time and chance happeneth to them all."

Aesop's Fable - The Mouse and the Bull

A bull was bitten by a mouse, and, pained by the wound, tried to capture him. The mouse, however, reached his hole in safety. The bull dug into the walls with his horns until, wearied, he crouched down and slept by the hole. The mouse, peeping out, crept up his flank and, again biting him, retreated to his hole. The bull rising up, and not knowing what to do, was sadly perplexed. The mouse murmured, "The great do not always prevail." There are times when the small and lowly are the strongest to do mischief.

4. The Kingdom of the Lion

Isaiah 11:6-9 "The wolf also shall dwell with the lamb, and the leopard shall lie down with the kid ... And the cow and the bear shall feed; their young ones shall lie down together ... They shall not hurt nor destroy in all my holy mountain ..."

Aesop's Fable - The Kingdom of the Lion
The beasts of the field and forest had a lion as their king. He was neither wrathful, cruel, nor tyrannical, but he was just and gentle as a king could be. He made during his reign a royal proclamation for a general assembly of all the birds and beasts, and drew up conditions for a universal league, in which the wolf and the lamb, the panther and the kid, the tiger and the stag, the dog and the hare, should live together in perfect peace and amity. The hare said; "Oh, how I have longed to see this day, in which the weak shall take their place without fear by the side of the strong."

5. The Raven and the Swan

Jeremiah 13:23 "Can the Ethiopian change his skin, or the leopard his spots? then may ye also do good, that are accustomed to do evil."

Aesop's Fable - The Raven and the Swan
A raven envied a swan the whiteness of her plumage. Thinking that the swan's beauty was owing to the water in which she lived, the raven deserted the altars where he used to find his livelihood and took to the pools and streams. There he plumed and dressed himself and washed his coat, but all to no purpose, for his plumage remained as black as ever, and he himself soon perished for want of his usual food. Change of scene is not change of nature.

6. The Two Pots

Douay-Rheims: Ecclesiasticus 13:3 "What agreement shall the earthen pot have with the kettle? for if they knock one against the other, it shall be broken."

Aesop's Fable - The Two Pots
A river carried down in its stream two Pots, one made of earthenware and the other of brass. The Earthen Pot said to the Brass Pot, "Pray keep at a distance and do not come near me, for if you touch me ever so slightly, I shall be broken in pieces, and besides, I by no means wish to come near you." Equals make the best friends.

7. Wolf in Sheep's Clothing

Matthew 7:15 "Beware of false prophets, which come to you in sheep's clothing, but inwardly they are ravening wolves."

Aesop's Fable - The Wolf in Sheep's Clothing
A Wolf found great difficulty in getting at the sheep owing to the vigilance of the shepherd and his dogs. But one day it found the skin of a sheep that had been flayed and thrown aside, so it put it on over its own pelt and strolled down among the sheep. The Lamb that belonged to the sheep, whose skin the Wolf was wearing, began to follow the Wolf in the Sheep's clothing; so, leading the Lamb a little apart, he soon made a meal off her, and for some time he succeeded in deceiving the sheep, and enjoying hearty meals. Appearances are deceptive.

8. The Quack Frog

Luke 4:23 "He [Jesus] said unto them Ye will surely say unto me this proverb, Physician, heal thyself."

Aesop's Fable - The Quack Frog
A frog once upon a time came forth from his home in the marsh and proclaimed to all the beasts that he was a learned physician, skilled in the use of drugs and able to heal all diseases. A fox asked him, "How can you pretend to prescribe for others, when you are unable to heal your own lame gait and wrinkled skin?'

Note: Jesus was probably referring to an Aesop fable in Luke 4:23.

9. The Fisherman and His Pipe

Luke 7:31-32 "They are like unto children sitting in the marketplace, and calling one to another, and saying, We have piped unto you, and ye have not danced; we have mourned to you, and ye have not wept."

Aesop's Fable - The Fisherman and His Pipe
A fisherman skilled in music took his flute and his nets to the seashore. Standing on a projecting rock, he played several tunes in the hope that the fish, attracted by his melody, would of their own accord dance into his net, which he had placed below. At last, having long waited in vain, he laid aside his flute, and casting his net into the sea, made an excellent haul of fish. When he saw them leaping about in the net upon the rock he said: "O you most perverse creatures, when I piped you would not dance, but now that I have ceased you do so merrily."

10. The Ant and the Grasshopper

Proverbs 30:25 "The ants are a people not strong, yet they prepare their meat in the summer"

Aesop's Fable - The Ant and the Grasshopper
In a field one summer's day a Grasshopper was hopping about, chirping and singing to its heart's content. An Ant passed by, bearing along with great toil an ear of corn he was taking to the nest. "Why not come and chat with me," said the Grasshopper, "instead of toiling and moiling in that way?" "I am helping to lay up food for the winter," said the Ant, "and recommend you to do the same." "Why bother about winter?" said the Grasshopper; we have got plenty of food at present." But the Ant went on its way and continued its toil. When the winter came the Grasshopper had no food and found itself dying of hunger, while it saw the ants distributing every day corn and grain from the stores they had collected in the summer. Then the Grasshopper knew: It is best to prepare for the days of necessity.

11. The Ass in the Lion's Skin

Proverbs 13:3 "He that keepeth his mouth keepeth his life: but he that openeth wide his lips shall have destruction."

Aesop's Fable - The Ass in the Lion's Skin
An Ass once found a Lion's skin which the hunters had left out in the sun to dry. He put it on and went towards his native village. All fled at his approach, both men and animals, and he was a proud Ass that day. In his delight he lifted up his voice and brayed, but then every one knew him, and his owner came up and gave him a sound cudgelling for the fright he had caused. And shortly afterwards a Fox came up to him and said: "Ah, I knew you by your voice."

12. Aesop's Fable - The Belly and the Members

I Corinthians 12:14-23 "For the body is not one member, but many. If the foot shall say, Because I am not the hand, I am not of the body; is it therefore not of the body? And if the ear shall say ..."

Aesop's Fable - The Belly and the Members
One fine day it occurred to the Members of the Body that they were doing all the work and the Belly was having all the food. So they held a meeting, and after a long discussion, decided to strike work till the Belly consented to take its proper share of the work. So for a day or two, the Hands refused to take the food, the Mouth refused to receive it ... So thus they found that even the Belly in its dull quiet way was doing necessary work for the Body, and that all must work together or the Body will go to pieces.

13. Mercury and the Woodman

Kings II 6:4-6 "[Elisha] went with them. And when they came to Jordan, they cut down wood. But as one was felling a beam, the axe head fell into the water: and he cried, and said, Alas, master! for it was borrowed. And the man of God said, Where fell it? And he shewed him the place. And he cut down a stick, and cast it in thither; and the iron did swim."

Aesop's Fable – Mercury and the Woodman
A Woodman was cutting a tree by ther river bank when his axe fell into the water. As he stood by the water's edge lamenting his loss, Mercury appeared and upon learning what happened, dived into the river and, bringing up a golden axe, asked him if that was the one he had lost. The Woodman replied that it was not, and Mercury then dived a second time, and, bringing up a silver axe, asked if that was his. "No, that is not mine either," said the Woodman. Once more Mercury dived into the river, and brought up the missing axe. The Woodman was overjoyed at recovering his property, and thanked his benefactor warmly; and the latter was so pleased with his honesty that he made him a present of the other two axes."

M. The Satire of the Trades (The Instruction of Dua-Kheti)

[DR] Ecclesiasticus 38:24-39:11 "When the dead is at rest, let his remembrance rest ... The wisdom of a scribe cometh by his time of leisure ... With what wisdom shall he be furnished that holdeth the plough, and that glorieth in the goad ..."

Note: The Satire of the Trades also called The Instruction of Dua-Kheti is an ancient didactic Egyptian satire that describes the different manual professions in a very negative manner and extolling the advantages of being a professional scribe.

N. The Testaments of the Twelve Patriarchs

1. Matthew
Matthew 3:16-17 "Jesus, when he was baptized ... the Spirit of God descending like a dove, and lighting upon him: And lo a voice from heaven, saying, This is my beloved Son, in whom I am well pleased."
Testament of Levi 18:6-7 "The heavens shall be opened. And from the temple of glory shall come upon him sanctification, With the Father's voice as from Abraham to Isaac."

Matthew 5:28 "But I say unto you, That whosoever looketh on a woman to lust after her hath committed adultery with her already in his heart."

Testament of Benjamin 8:2 "He that hat a pure mind in love, looketh not after a woman with a view of fornication; for he hath no defilement in his heart bec the spirit of God resteth upon him."

Matthew 12:35 "A good man out of the good treasure of the heart bringeth forth good things: and an evil man out of the evil treasure bringeth forth evil things."

Testament of Asher 1:9 "For whenever it beginneth to do good, he forces the issue of the action into evil for him, seeing that the treasure of the inclination is filled with an evil spirit."

Matthew 12:45 "Then goeth he, and taketh with himself seven other spirits more wicked than himself, and they enter in and dwell there: and the last state of that man is worse than the first. Even so shall it be also unto this wicked generation."

Testament of Reuben 2:1 "And now hear me, my children, what things I saw concerning the seven spirits of deceit, when i repented."

Matthew 18:15, 35 "Moreover if thy brother shall trespass against thee, go and tell him his fault between thee and him alone: if he shall hear thee, thou hast gained thy brother.So likewise shall my heavenly Father do also unto you, if ye from your hearts forgive not every one his brother their trespasses."

Testament of Gad 6:3, 7 "Love ye one another from the heart; and if a man sin against thee, speak peaceably to him, and in thy soul hold not guile; and if he repent and confess, forgive him. But if he be shameless and persisteth in his wrong-doing, even so forgive him from the heart, and leave to God the avenging."

Matthew 19:29 "Every one that hath forsaken houses, or brethren, or sisters, or father, or mother, or wife, or children, or lands, for my name's sake, shall receive an hundredfold, and shall inherit everlasting life."

Testament of Zebulun 6:6 "Wherefore also the Lord satisfied me with aboundance of fish when catching fish; for he that shareth with his neighbor receiveth manifold more from the Lord."

Matthew 22:37-39 "Jesus said unto him, Thou shalt love the Lord thy God with all thy heart, and with all thy soul, and with all thy mind. This is the first and great commandment. And the second is like unto it, Thou shalt love thy neighbour as thyself."

Testament of Dan 5:3 "Love the Lord through all your life, And one another with a true heart."

Matthew 25:35-39 "For I was an hungred, and ye gave me meat: I was thirsty, and ye gave me drink: I was a stranger, and ye took me in: Naked, and ye clothed me: I was sick, and ye visited me: I was in prison, and ye came unto me. Then shall the righteous answer him, saying, Lord, when saw we thee an hungred, and fed thee? or thirsty, and gave thee drink? When saw we thee a stranger, and took thee in? or naked, and clothed thee? Or when saw we thee sick, or in prison, and came unto thee?"

Testament of Joseph 1:5-6 "I was sold into slavery, and the Lord of all made me free; I was taken into captivity, and His strong hand succoured me. I was beset with hunger, and the Lord Himself nourished me. I was alone, and God comforted me: I was sick, and the Lord visited me; I was in prison , and my God showed favour unto me; In bonds, and He released me"

Matthew 25:46 "These shall go away into everlasting punishment: but the righteous into life eternal."

Testament of Gad 7:5 "For if He taketh away (from a man) wealth gotten by evil means He forgiveth him if he repent, but the unrepentatn is reserved for eternal punishment."

Matthew 27:6 "The chief priests took the silver pieces, and said, It is not lawful for to put them into the treasury, because it is the price of blood."

Testament of Zebulun 3:2 "But Simeon and gad and six other of our bretheren took the price of Joseph, and bought sandals for themselves, and their wives and their children saying: We will not eat of it, for it is the price of our brother's blood ..."

2. Luke

Luke 1:17 "He shall go before him in the spirit and power of Elias, to turn the hearts of the fathers to the children, and the disobedient to the wisdom of the just; to make ready a people prepared for the Lord."

Testament of Dan 5:11 "And the captivity shall he take from Beliar [the souls of the saints], And turn disobedient hearts unto the Lord, And give to them that call upon him eternal peace."

Luke 10:19-20 "Behold, I give unto you power to tread on serpents and scorpions, and over all the power of the enemy: and nothing shall by any means hurt you. Notwithstanding in this rejoice not, that the spirits are subject unto you; but rather rejoice, because your names are written in heaven."

Testament of Simeon 6:6 "Then shall all the spirit of deceit be given to be trodden under foot, And men shall rule over wicked spirits."

Luke 17:3 "Take heed to yourselves: If thy brother trespass against thee, rebuke him; and if he repent, forgive him."

Testament of Gad 6:3 "Love ye one another from the heart; and if a man sin against thee, speak peaceably to him, and in thy soul hold not guile; and if he repent and confess, forgive him."

3. John
John 3:19 "This is the condemnation, that light is come into the world, and men loved darkness rather than light, because their deeds were evil."
Testament of Naphtali 2:10 "For if thous bid the eye to hear, it cannot; so neither while ye are in darkness can ye do the works of light."

John 4:14 "But whosoever drinketh of the water that I shall give him shall never thirst; but the water that I shall give him shall be in him a well of water springing up into everlasting life."
Testament of Judah 24:4 "This Branch of God Most High, And this Fountain giving life unto all."

4. Acts
Acts 8:23 "For I perceive that thou art in the gall of bitterness, and in the bond of iniquity."
Testament of Napthali 2:8 "For God made all things good in their order, the five senses in the head ... the gall for bitterness ..."

Acts 12:11 "When Peter was come to himself, he said, Now I know of a surety, that the Lord hath sent his angel, and hath delivered me out of the hand of Herod ..."
Testament of Simeon 2:8 "But his God and the God of his fathers sent forth His angel, and delivered him out of my hands."

5. Romans
Roman 1:21 "Because that, when they knew God, they glorified him not as God, neither were thankful; but became vain in their imaginations, and their foolish heart was darkened."
Testament of Reuben 3:8 "And so perisheth every young man, darkening his mind from the truth, and not understanding the law of God, nor obeying the admonitions of his fathers, as befell me also in my youth."

Romans 1:32 "Who knowing the judgment of God, that they which commit such things are worthy of death, not only do the same, but have pleasure in them that do them."
Testament of Asher 6:2 "For they that are double-faced are guilty of a twofold sin; for they both do the evil thing and they have pleasure in them that do it, following the example of the spirits of deceit, and striving against mankind."

Romans 2:15 "Which shew the work of the law written in their hearts, their conscience also bearing witness, and their thoughts the mean while accusing or else excusing one another;)"

Testament of Judah 20:5 "And the spirit of truth testifieth all things, and accuseth all; and the sinner is burnt up by his own heart and cannot raise his face to the judge."

Romans 9:21 "Hath not the potter power over the clay, of the same lump to make one vessel unto honour, and another unto dishonour?"

Testament of Naphtali 2:2 "For as the potter knoweth the vessel, how much it is to contain, and bringeth clay accordingly, so also doth the Lord make the body after the likeness of the spirit, and according to the capacity of the body doth He implant the spirit."

Romans 12:19 "Dearly beloved, avenge not yourselves, but rather give place unto wrath: for it is written, Vengeance is mine; I will repay, saith the Lord."

Testament of Gad 6:7 "But if he be shameless and persisteth in his wrong-doing, even so forgive him from the heart, and leave to God the avenging."

Romans 12:21 "Be not overcome of evil, but overcome evil with good."

Testament of Benjamin 4:3 "And though they devise with evil intent concerning him, by doing good he overcometh evil, being shielded by God."

6. II Corinthians

II Corinthians 6:14-15 "Be ye not unequally yoked together with unbelievers: for what fellowship hath righteousness with unrighteousness? and what communion hath light with darkness? And what concord hath Christ with Belial? or what part hath he that believeth with an infidel?"

Testament of Levi 19:1 "Choose therefore, for yourselves either the light or the darkness either the law of the Lord or the works of Beliar"

II Corinthians 7:10 "For godly sorrow worketh repentance to salvation not to be repented of: but the sorrow of the world worketh death."

Testament of Gad 5:7 "For true repentance after a godly sort [destroyeth ignorance, and] driveth away the darkness, and enlighteneth the eyes, and giveth knowledge to the soul, and leadeth the mind to salvation."

7. Ephesians

Ephesians 4:25 "Wherefore putting away lying, speak every man truth with his neighbour: for we are members one of another."

Testament of Dan 5:2 "Speak truth each one with his neighbor, So shall ye not fall into wrath and confusion; But ye shall be in peace, having the God of peace, So shall no war prevail over you."

Testament of Reuben 6:9 "I adjure you by the God of heaven to do truth each one unto his neighbor and to entertain love for each for his brother."

Ephesians 5:6 "Let no man deceive you with vain words: for because of these

things cometh the wrath of God upon the children of disobedience."
Testament of Naphtali 3:1 "Be ye, therefore, not eager to corrupt your doings through covetousness or with vain words to beguile your souls; because if ye keep silence in purity of heart, ye shall understand how to hold fast the will of God, and to cast away the will of Beliar."

Ephesians 5:18 "Be not drunk with wine, wherein is excess; but be filled with the Spirit"
Testament of Judah 14:1; 16:1 "And now, my children, I say unto you, be not drunk with wine ... Observe, therefore, my children, the right limit in wine..."

8. Philippians
Philippians 3:19 "Whose end is destruction, whose God is their belly, and whose glory is in their shame, who mind earthly things."
Testament of Judah 14:8 "But if he go beyond this limit the spirit of deceit attacketh his mind, and it maketh the drunkard to talk filthily, and to transgress and not be ashamed, but even to glory in his shame, and account himself honourable."

9. Colossians
Colossians 3:12 "Put on therefore, as the elect of God, holy and beloved, bowels of mercies, kindness, humbleness of mind, meekness, longsuffering"
Testament of Zebulun 7:3 "And if ye have not the wherewithal to give to him that needeth, have compassion for him in bowels of mercy."

10. I Thessalonians
I Thessalonians 2:16 "Forbidding us to speak to the Gentiles that they might be saved, to fill up their sins alway: for the wrath is come upon them to the uttermost."
Testament of Levi 6:11 "But the wrath of the Lord came upon them to the uttermost."

11. I Peter
I Peter 3:3-5 "Whose adorning let it not be that outward adorning ... But let it be the hidden man of the heart, in that which is not corruptible, even the ornament of a meek and quiet spirit, which is in the sight of God of great price ..."
Testament of Reuben 5:5 "Flee, therefore, fornication, my children, and command your wives and your daughters, that they adorn not their heads and faces to deceive the mind; because every woman who useth these wiles hath been reserved for eternal punishment."

12. Revelation
Revelation 3:12 "I will write upon him the name of my God, and the name of the city of my God, which is new Jerusalem, which cometh down out of

heaven from my God: and I will write upon him my new name."
Testament of Dan 5:12 "And the saints shall rest in Eden, And in the New Jerusalem will the righteous rejoice, And it shall be unto the glory of God for ever."

Revelation 5:8 "When he had taken the book, the four beasts and four and twenty elders fell down before the Lamb, having every one of them harps, and golden vials full of odours, which are the prayers of saints."
Testament of Levi 3:7 "And in the heaven below this are the angels who bear answers to the angels of the presence of the Lord."

Note: The Testaments of the Twelve Patriarchs predates Jesus Christ and Paul. Some of the teachings of Jesus Christ and Paul may have come from this book.

3. Similar Stories outside the Bible

	Biblical Story	Non-biblical Story
A	The Creation	Enuma Elish
B	Adam and Eve	The First Book of Adam and Eve The Second Book of Adam and Eve Adimo Heva Endiku Tala Vilasam
C	Noah's Flood	Epic of Gilgamesh Epic of Ziusudra Deucalion Satyavrata (King Manu) Pairachta Nuu
D	Tower of Babel	Enmerkar and the Lord of Aratta
E	Abraham and Sarah Abraham and Isaac	Brahma and Saraswati Agamemnon and Iphigenia
F	Moses	Sargon I of Akkad
G	Moses and The Ten Commandments	Zoroaster and Zend-Avesta Buddha and his ten commandments
H	Samson	Hercules
I	Jonah	Saktideva Hercules and a Dag
J	Jesus Christ	Buddha Mithra Krishna Jehoshua Ben Pandira Apollonous of Tyanna Vespasian
K	Jesus and Lazarus	Horus and Osiris (Egyptian Book of the Dead)

V. The God and gods of the Bible

1. Some of the names of God

A. Abba
Mark 14:36 "Abba, Father, all things are possible unto thee ..."
Romans 8:15 "We cry, Abba, Father."
Galatians 4:6 "God hath sent forth the Spirit of his Son ... crying, Abba, Father."

B. Jehovah
Psalm 83:18 "Thou, whose name alone is JEHOVAH"
[Also in **Exodus 6:3; Isaiah 12:2, 26:4**]

C. Jealous
Exodus 34:14 "For thou shalt worship no other god: for the Lord, whose name is Jealous ..."

D. Shem Ha Mephoresh, the 72 names of God
Exodus 14:19-21 "And the angel of God, which went before the camp of Israel, removed and went behind them; and the pillar of the cloud went from before their face, and stood behind them: And it came between the camp of the Egyptians and the camp of Israel; and it was a cloud and darkness to them, but it gave light by night to these: so that the one came not near the other all the night. And Moses stretched out his hand over the sea; and the Lord caused the sea to go [back] by a strong east wind all that night, and made the sea dry land, and the waters were divided."

Note: The 72 names of God were derived from Exodus 14:19-21. The method of derivaton used is called Boustrophedon. The term Shem Ha-Mephorash is substituted for the actual 72 names of God to avoid desecrating the actual names.The 72 fold name of God is an important aspect of Quabalistic studies and is used in amulets and magick rituals of some occult societies such as the Golden Dawn. The Seventy-two names are also called the Seventy-two leaves of the Tree of Life. According to legend the said 72 names of God were revealed to Moses in the burning bush and were instrumental in the parting of the Red Sea. Only the purest of the pure are suppose to utter the 72 names of God and each triad of the 72 names are used for praying for specific purposes such as health, love and finances.

Shem Ha Mephoresh: The 72-Names of God (also called the 216 Letter name of God)

כהת	אכא	ללה	מהש	עלם	סיט	ילי	והו
הקם	הרי	מבה	יזל	ההע	לאו	אלד	הזי
וזהו	מלה	ייי	נלך	פהל	לוו	כלי	לאו
ועֹר	לכב	אום	ריי	שֹאה	ירת	האא	נתה
ייז	רהע	ועם	אני	מנד	כוק	להֹו	ייזו
מיה	עולֹל	ערי	סאל	ילה	ולֹו	מיכ	ההה
פוי	מבה	נית	נלא	עמם	הוֹזע	דנֹי	והו
מוזי	ענֹו	יהה	ומב	מצֹר	הרוז	ייל	נמם
מום	היֹי	יבמ	ראה	וזבו	איע	מנֹק	דמב

I																	
K	L	H	H	M	I	H	L	A	H	K	A	L	M	O	S	I	V
L	A	Q	R	B	Z	H	A	L	Z	H	K	L	H	L	I	L	H
I	V	M	I	H	L	O	V	D	I	Th	A	H	Sh	M	T	I	V
18	17	16	15	14	13	12	11	10	9	8	7	6	5	4	3	2	1

H																	
M	K	L	I	V	L	A	R	Sh	I	H	N	Ch	M	I	N	P	L
N	V	H	Ch	Sh	K	V	I	A	R	A	Th	H	L	I	L	H	V
D	Q	Ch	V	R	B	M	I	H	Th	A	H	V	H	I	K	L	V
36	35	34	33	32	31	30	29	28	27	26	25	24	23	22	21	20	19

V																	
N	N	O	H	D	V	M	O	O	S	L	V	M	H	I	R	Ch	A
I	N	M	Ch	N	H	I	Sh	R	A	L	V	I	H	I	H	O	N
Th	A	M	Sh	I	V	H	L	I	L	H	L	K	H	Z	O	M	I
54	53	52	51	50	49	48	47	46	45	44	43	42	41	40	39	38	37

H																	
M	H	I	R	Ch	A	M	D	M	O	I	V	M	H	I	N	P	M
V	I	B	A	B	I	N	M	Ch	N	H	M	Tz	R	I	M	V	B
M	I	M	H	V	O	Q	B	I	V	H	B	R	Ch	L	M	I	H
72	71	70	69	68	67	66	65	64	63	62	61	60	59	58	57	56	55

I	H	V	H
1. Vehuiah	19. Leuviah	37. Aniel	55. Mebahiah
2. Jeliel	20. Pahaliah	38. Haamiah	56. Poiel
3. Sitael	21. Nelchael	39. Rehael	57. Nemamiah
4. Elemiah	22. Ieiaiel	40. Ieiazel	58. Ieialel
5. Mahasiah	23. Melahel	41. Hahahel	59. Harahel
6. Lelahel	24. Hahiuiah	42. Mikael	60. Mitzrael
7. Achaiah	25. Nith-haiah	43. Veualiah	61. Umabel
8. Cahethel	26. Haaiah	44. Ielahiah	62. Iahhel

9. Haziel	27. Ierathel	45. Sealiah	63. Anauel
10. Aladiah	28. Seheiah	46. Airiel	64. Mehiel
11. Lauviah	29 Reiiel	47. Asaliah	65. Damabiah
12. Hahaiah	30. Omael	48. Mihael	66. Manakel
13. Iezalel	31. Lecabel	49. Vehuel	67. Eiael
14. Mebahel	32. Vasiariah	50. Daniel	68. Habuhiah
15. Hariel	33. Iehuiah	51. Hahasiah	69. Rochel
16. Hakamiah	34. Lehahiah	52. Imamiah	70. Jabamiah
17. Lauviah	35. Chavakiah	53. Nanael	71. Haiaiel
18. Caliel	36. Menadel	54. Nithanael	72. Mumiah

However the following verse has a warning:
Exodus 20:7 "You shall not misuse the name of the Lord your God, for the Lord will not hold anyone guiltless who misuses his name."

2. Nature and Character of God

A. The number of Gods

1. How many Gods are there?

One
Deuteronomy 4:35, 39 "The Lord he is God; there is none else beside him … there is none else."
Deuteronomy 6:4 "Hear, O Israel: The Lord our God is *one* Lord."
Deuteronomy 32:39 "There is no god with me."
I Kings 18:39 "The Lord, he is the God; the Lord, he is *the* God."

More than One
Genesis 1:26 "And God said, let us make man in *our* image."
Genesis 3:22 "Behold, then man is become as one of *us* …"
Genesis 11:7 "[God speaking] Let *us* go down …"
Exodus 12:12 "And against all the *gods* of Egypt …"

2. Concerning the Holy Trinity

Matthew 3:16-17 "Jesus [was baptized] … the Spirit of God descending like a dove … upon him."
Matthew 28:19 "Baptizing them in the name of the Father, and of the Son, and of the Holy Ghost"
Luke 1:35 "And the angel [said], The Holy Ghost shall come upon thee …"
II Corinthians 13:14 "The grace of the Lord Jesus Christ, and the love of God, and the … Holy Ghost, be with you all. Amen."
Hebrews 9:14 "Christ, who through the *eternal Spirit* offered himself …"

I John 5:7-8 "For there are three that bear record in heaven, the Father, the Word, and the Holy Ghost: and these three are one. And there are three that bear witness in earth, the Spirit, and the water, and the blood: and these three agree in one."

Note: I John 5:7-8 also called Comma Johanneum, are the only verses in the Bible that explicitly refers to the Holy Trinity. These passages were not included in the original Greek manuscripts prior to the 16th century. Some Bible translations have excluded these verses entirely since it was only a recent 'insertion' to the Latin Vulgate edition of the Bible. However Jesus himself contradicted these verses when he said he is not God (see Matthew 19:16-17, Mark 10:17-18, Luke 18:18-19).

3. How many sons does God have?

One, Jesus is the only Son of God
John 3:16, 18 "God ... gave his *only* begotten Son ..."
I John 4:9 "God sent his *only* begotten son into the world."

More than one, Adam was also God's son
Luke 3:38 "Adam, which was the son of God."

More than one, some of God's sons mated with women and produced a race of giants
Genesis 6:2 "That the *sons* of God saw the daughters of men ..."

More than one, Satan and his companions were sons of God
Job 1:6, 2:1 "The sons of God came to present themselves before the Lord, and Satan came also among them."

More than one, God's sons were present when the universe was created
Job 38:6-7 "Whereupon are the foundations thereof fastened ... and all the *sons* of God shouted for joy?"

More than one, Christians are God's sons
John 1:12 "But as many as received him ... to become the *sons* of God."

B. How powerful is God?

1. Is God all-powerful?

Yes, God is all powerful
Genesis 18:14 "Is any thing too hard for the Lord?"
Job 42:1-2 "Then Job ... said, I know that thou canst do every thing ..."
Jeremiah 32:17 "Lord God ... there is nothing too hard for thee ..."

Yes, God had the strength of a unicorn?
Numbers 23:22 "God ... hath as it were the strength of an unicorn."

Yes, God can break the heads of dragons and leviathans
Psalm 74:13-14 "Thou brakest the heads of the dragons in the waters. Thou brakest the heads of leviathan in pieces ..."

No, God was no match to the chariots of iron
Judges 1:19 "The Lord was with Judah ... but could not drive out the inhabitants of the valley, because they had chariots of iron."

No, God cannot lie
Hebrews 6:18 "It was impossible for God to lie."

2. Can God lie?

Yes, God placed a 'lying spirit' in the mouth of his prophets
I Kings 22:22-23 "The Lord said unto him, Wherewith? And he [a spirit] said, I will go forth, and I will be a lying spirit in the mouth of all his prophets ..."

No, God cannot lie
Hebrews 6:18 "It was impossible for God to lie."

3. Can God stop the iron chariots?

Yes
Joshua 17:18 "Thou shalt drive out the Canaanites, though they have iron chariots ..."
Judges 4:13-15 "The Lord discomfited Sisera, and all his chariots ..."

No
Judges 1:19 "But [the Lord] could not drive out the inhabitants of the valley, because they had chariots of iron."

4. Can God alone do great wonders?

Yes, God alone can do great wonders
Psalm 136:4 "To him who alone doeth great wonders."

No, Satan can do too
II Thessalonians 2:9 "Even him, whose coming is after the working of Satan, whith all power and signs and lying wonders."

C. Is God omnipresent?

1. Is God everywhere?

Yes
Job 42:2 "No thought can be withholden from thee."
Proverbs 15:3 "The eyes of the Lord are in every place, beholding the evil and the good."
Psalm 44:21 "For he knoweth the secrets of the heart."

No, God was asking Adam where he is
Genesis 3:8-9 "Adam and his wife hid themselves ... And [God] said ... Where art thou?"

No, God was asking Cain for Abel's whereabouts
Genesis 4:9 "The Lord said unto Cain, Where is Abel thy brother?"

No, Cain hid from God
Genesis 4:14, 16 "Behold, thou hast driven me out this day from the face of the earth; and from thy face shall I be hid. And Cain went out from the presence of the Lord ..."

No, God had to come down to see the city and the tower
Genesis 11:5 "The Lord came down to see the city and the tower ..."

No, God asked Abraham the whereabouts of Sarah
Genesis 18:9 "They said unto him, Where is Sarah thy wife?"

No, God had to go down to see what is happening
Genesis 18:20-21 "The Lord said ... I will go down now, and see whether they have done altogether according to the cry of it [and if not], I *will* know."

No, God needs the Israelites to put blood in their doors so God can identify them
Exodus 12:13 "The blood shall be to you for a token upon the houses where ye are: and *when I see the blood, I will pass over you ...*"

No, God asked Balaam who his companions were
Numbers 22:9-10 "God ... said, *What men are these with thee?*"

No, God asked Satan where he went
Job 1:7 "The Lord said unto Satan, Whence comest thou?"

No, Jonah fled from the presence of the Lord
Jonah 1:3,10 "But Jonah rose up to flee unto Tarshish from the presence of the Lord ... For the men knew that *he fled from the presence of the Lord,* because he had told them."

No, God is not everywhere God is in heaven
Matthew 5:45 "Your Father which is in heaven ..."
Matthew 7:21 "My Father which is in heaven."

2. Where does God live?

God lives in the heavens, but heaven was created only on the second day
Genesis 1:6-8 "God said, Let there be a firmament … and God called the firmament Heaven. And the evening and the morning were the second day."

Note: If God created Heaven on the second day, where did God live prior to that day?

Solomon built a temple for God's dwelling
I Kings 8:13 "I have surely built thee a house to dwell in … for thee to abide in for ever."
Acts 7:47 "Solomon built him [God] an house."

God dwells in temples
II Chronicles 7:12 "The Lord appeared to Solomon by night, and said unto him, I have heard thy prayer, and have chosen this place to myself for an house of sacrifice."
II Chronicles 7:16 "For now have I chosen and sanctified this house, that my name may be there for ever: and mine eyes and mine heart shall be there perpetually."

God lives in Zion
Psalm 9:11 "The Lord, which dwelleth in Zion."
Psalm 76:2 "His dwelling place is in Zion."
Joel 3:17, 21 "I am the Lord your God dwelling in Zion … the Lord dwelleth in Zion."

God lives in the heavens
Psalm 123:1 "O thou that dwellest in the heavens."
Ecclesiastes 5:2 "For God is in heaven, and thou upon earth."

God lives in heaven and hell
Psalm 139:8 "If I ascend up into heaven, thou art there: if I make my bed in hell thou art there."

3. Does God live in the light?

Yes
Daniel 2:22 "He [God] knoweth what is in the darkness, and the light dwelleth with him."

No
II Samuel 22:12 "He made darkness pavilions round about him, dark waters, and thick clouds of the skies."

4. Does God dwell in temples?

Yes, Solomon built a temple for God's dwelling
I Kings 8:13 "I have surely built thee an house to dwell in, a settled place for thee to abide in for ever."
Acts 7:47 "But Solomon built him (God) an house."

Yes, God dwells in temples that he chose
II Chronicles 7:12 "And the Lord appeared to Solomon by night, and said unto him, I have heard thy prayer, and have chosen this place to myself for an house of sacrifice."

No, God does not dwell in temples
Acts 7:48 "Howbeit the most High dwelleth not in temples ..."

5. Does God rule heaven?

Yes
Matthew 6:10 "Thy will be done in earth, as it is in heaven."

No
Revelation 12:7 "There was war in heaven."

6. Does God rule the earth?

Yes, God is the ruler of the earth
Joshua 3:13 "The Lord, the Lord of all the earth ..."
I Chronicles 16:14, 31 "He is ... our God; his judgments are in all the earth"

No, Satan
Matthew 4:8-9 "Again, the devil ... sheweth him [Jesus] all the kingdoms of the world ... And saith unto him, All these things will I give thee ..."
Luke 4:5-6 "The devil ... shewed unto him [Jesus] all the kingdoms of the world ... and said ... All this power will I give thee ..."
John 12:31 "Now is the judgment of this world: now shall the prince of this world be cast out."

7. How long is a day as far as God is concerned?

An evening and a morning
Genesis 1:13 "The evening and the morning were the third day"

A thousand years
II Peter 3:8 "But, beloved, be not ignorant of this one thing, that one day is with the Lord as a thousand years, and a thousand years as one day."

D. Is God all-knowing?

1. Does God know everything?

Yes
I John 3:20 "For if our heart condemn us, God is greater than our heart, and knoweth all things."

No, God did not know that Adam needed a mate
Genesis 2:18-20 "The Lord God said, It is not good that the man should be alone; I will make him an help meet for him ... the Lord God formed every beast of the field, and every fowl of the air ... but for Adam there was not found an help meet for him."

No, God had to test Abraham if he would withheld his son
Genesis 22:12 "For now I [God] know that thou fearest God, seeing thou hast not withheld thy son ... from me."

No, God asked Jacob for his name
Genesis 32:27 "He [God] said unto him [Jacob], What is thy name?"

No, God did not know what was in the hearts of the Israelites
Deuteronomy 8:2, 13:3 "God led thee these forty years in the wilderness ... to know what was in thine heart. The Lord your God proveth you, to know whether ye love the Lord your God."

No, Samuel had to inform God about what he heard from others
I Samuel 8:21 "Samuel heard all the words of the people, and he rehearsed them in the ears of the Lord."

No, God did not know what was in Hezekiah's heart
II Chronicles 32:31 "God left him, to try him, that he might know all that was in his heart."

No, Israel made princes and he knew it not
Hosea 8:4 "They have set up kings ... made princes, and I knew it not."

No, we have to make our request made known to God
Philippians 4:6 "Be careful for nothing; but in every thing by prayer and supplication with thanksgiving let your requests be made known unto God."

2. Does God know the hearts of men?

Yes
Acts 1:24 "Thou, Lord, which knowest the hearts of all men, shew whether of these two thou hast chosen"
Psalm 44:21 "He knoweth the secrets of the heart"

Psalm 139:2-3 "Thou knowest my downsitting and mine uprising, thou understandest my thought afar off. Thou compassest my path and my lying down, and art acquainted with all my ways."

No, God did not know what was in Abraham's heart
Genesis 22:12 "He said, Lay not thine hand upon the lad, neither do thou any thing unto him: for now I know that thou fearest God, seeing thou hast not withheld thy son, thine only son from me."

No, God did not know what was in the hearts of the Israelites
Deuteronomy 8:2 "Thou shalt remember all the way which the Lord thy God led thee these forty years in the wilderness ... to know what was in thine heart, whether thou wouldest keep his commandments, or no."

No, God did not know what was in Hezekiah's heart II
Chronicles 32:31 "God left him [Hezekiah], to try him, that he might know all that was in his heart."

3. Does God know what we need?

Yes
Matthew 6:8 "Be not ye therefore like unto them: for your Father knoweth what things ye have need of, before ye ask him."

No
Philippians 4:6 "Be careful for nothing; but in every thing by prayer and supplication with thanksgiving let your requests be made known unto God."

E. How good is God?

1. Is God good?

Yes, God is good
Psalm 25:8 "Good and upright is the Lord."
Psalm 92:15 "The Lord is upright ... there is no unrighteousness in him."

No, God is not good to all, God is the source of evil
Genesis 22:1-2 "God did tempt Abraham ... he said, Take now thy son ... and offer him there for a burnt offering ..."
Judges 9:23 "God sent an evil spirit ..."

2. Is God the only one holy?

Yes, only God is holy
Revelation 15:4 "For thou alone are holy."

Not only God is holy

Exodus 22:31 "Ye shall be holy men unto me."
Leviticus 11:44-45 "Ye shall be holy; for I am holy."
Leviticus 19:2 "Ye shall be holy: for I the Lord your God am holy."

3. Is the word of God pure?

Yes
Psalm 12:6 "The words of the Lord are pure words: as silver tried in a furnace of earth, purified seven times."

No
II Kings 18:27 "Hath he not sent me to the mean which sit on the wall, that they may eat their own dung, and drink their own piss with you?"
Ezekiel 23:20 "For she doted upon their paramours, whose flesh is as the flesh of asses, and whose issue is like the issue of horses."
Jeremiah 8:8 "How do ye say, We are wise, and the law of the Lord is with us? Lo, certainly in vain made he it; the pen of the scribes is in vain."
Habakkuk 2:16 "Drink thou also, and let thy foreskin be uncovered."
Malachi 2:3 "Behold, I will corrupt your seed, and spread dung upon your faces."

4. Is the law of God perfect?

Yes
Psalm 18:30 "As for God, his way is perfect: the word of the Lord is tried: he is a buckler to all those that trust in him."
Psalm 19:7 "The law of the Lord is perfect, converting the soul: the testimony of the Lord is sure, making wise the simple."

No
Hebrews 8:6-7 "But now hath he obtained a *more excellent* ministry, by how much also he is the mediator of a *better covenant*, which was established upon *better promises*. For if that first covenant had been faultless, then should no place have been sought for the second."

5. Did God forbid the killing of the innocent?

Yes
Exodus 23:7 "Keep thee far from a false matter; and the innocent and righteous slay thou not: for I will not justify the wicked."

No, God did not forbid the killing of the innocent
Numbers 31:17-18 "Kill every male among the little ones, and kill every woman ..."

Deuteronomy 7:2 "When the Lord thy God shall deliver them before thee; thou shalt smite them, and utterly destroy them; thou shalt make no covenant with them, nor shew mercy unto them:"

Judges 11:30-39 "Jephthah vowed … unto the Lord … If thou shalt … deliver the children of Ammon into mine hands … whatsoever cometh forth of the doors of my house to meet me I will offer it up for a burnt offering … and, behold, his daughter came out to meet him … her father, who did with her according to his vow … And it was a custom in Israel,"

Note: In Judges 11:30-39, Jephthah won the war with the children of Ammon and vowed to offer to the Lord as burnt offering whoever greets him at his doorstep. His only child and daughter Adah greeted him and thus he was forced to kill his daughter to keep his promise.

No, God required the killing of the innocent
Hebrews 9:13-14, 22 "For if the blood of bulls and of goats … sanctifieth to the purifying of the flesh: How much more shall the blood of Christ, who through the eternal Spirit offered himself without spot to God …"

6. Does God keep his promise?

Yes, God keeps his promise
Exodus 34:6 "The Lord, The Lord God, merciful and gracious, longsuffering, and abundant in goodness and truth,"
Deuteronomy 7:9 "The Lord … which keepeth covenant and mercy with them that love him and keep his commandments to a thousand generations."
Titus 1:2 "In hope of eternal life, which God, that cannot lie, promised before the world began;"

No, God breaks his promise
Numbers 14:30 "Doubtless ye shall not come into the land, concerning which *I sware* to make you dwell therein …"

7. What is the fruit of God's spirit?

Love, joy, peace, longsuffering, gentleness, goodness, faith
Galatians 5:22 "But the fruit of the Spirit is love, joy, peace, longsuffering, gentleness, goodness, faith."

Anger and vengeance
Judges 15:14 "The Spirit of the Lord came mightily upon him [Samson], and the cords that were upon his arms became as flax that was burnt with fire, and his bands loosed from off his hands."
I Samuel 18:10-11 "*The evil spirit from God* came upon Saul … and Saul cast the javelin …"

8. Is God peaceable?

Yes, God is peacable
Isaiah 2:4 "They shall beat their swords into plowshares, and their spears into pruning hooks: nation shall not lift up sword against nation, neither shall they learn war any more."
Romans 15:33 "The God of peace."
Acts 10:36 "The word which God sent unto the children of Israel, preaching peace by Jesus Christ: (he is Lord of all:)."

No, God creates discord among men but hates those who do
Genesis 11:7-9 "Let us ... confound their language, that they may not understand one another's speech ... the Lord scatter them abroad upon the face of all the earth."
Proverbs 6:16-19 "These six things doth the Lord hate: yea, seven are an abomination unto him: A proud look, a lying tongue, and hands that shed innocent blood, An heart that deviseth wicked imaginations, feet that be swift in running to mischief, A false witness that speaketh lies, and he that soweth discord among brethren."

No, God is warlike
Exodus 15:3 "The Lord is a man of war."
Exodus 17:16 "Because the Lord hath sworn that the Lord will have war with Amalek from generation to generation."

9. Does God help those who are in need?

Yes
Psalm 22:24 "For he hath not despised nor abhorred the affliction of the afflicted; neither hath he hid his face from him; but when he cried unto him, he heard."
Psalm 46:1 "God is our refuge and our strength, a very present help in trouble."
Psalm 145:18 "The Lord is near to all who call upon him."
Nahum 1:7 "The Lord is good, a strong hold in the day of trouble."

No
I Samuel 8:18 "Ye shall cry out in that day because of your king which ye shall have chosen you; and the Lord will not hear you in that day."

10. Does God give to those who ask?

Yes
Luke 11:10 "For every one that asketh receiveth ... to him that knocketh it shall be opened."

James 1:5 "If any of you lack wisdom, let him ask of God … and it shall be given him."

No
Joshua 11:20 "For it was of the Lord to harden their hearts, that they should come against Israel in battle, that he might destroy them utterly, and that they might have no favour, but that he might destroy them, as the Lord commanded Moses."
Isaiah 63:17 "O Lord, why hast thou made us to err from thy ways, and hardened our heart from thy fear? Return for thy servants' sake, the tribes of thine inheritance."
John 12:40 "He hath blinded their eyes, and hardened their heart; that they should not see with their eyes, nor understand with their heart, and be converted, and I should heal them."

11. Does God forgive sins?

Yes God forgives but the guilty does not go unpunished
Exodus 34:6-7 "The Lord, The Lord God … forgiving iniquity and transgression and sin, and that will by no means clear the guilty ."
I Chronicles 16:34 "O give thanks unto the Lord; for he is good; for his mercy endureth for ever."

No
Joshua 24:19 "Joshua said unto the people, Ye cannot serve the Lord: for he is an holy God; he is a jealous God; he *will not forgive your transgressions nor your sins.*"

12. Does God remember sin, even when it has been forgiven?

Yes
Exodus 34:7 "Keeping mercy for thousands, forgiving iniquity and transgression and sin, and that will by no means clear the guilty; visiting the iniquity of the fathers upon the children, and upon the children's children, unto the third and to the fourth generation."
Hebrews 9:27 "As it is appointed unto men once to die, but after this the judgment"

No
Jeremiah 31:34 "Saith the Lord: for I will forgive their iniquity, and *I will remember their sin no more.*"

13. Will God destroy both the wicked and the righteous?

God destroys both the wicked and the righteous
Job 9:22 "He destroyeth the perfect and the wicked."

Ecclesiastes 7:15 "All things have I seen in the days of my vanity: there is a just man that perisheth in his righteousness, and there is a wicked man that prolongeth his life in his wickedness."
Ezekiel 21:3 "Thus saith the Lord; Behold, I am againsth thee, and will draw forth my sword out of his sheath, and will cut off from thee the righteous and the wicked."

God destroys only the wicked
Ezekiel 18:8-9 "He that hath not given forth upon usury, neither hath taken any increase, that hath withdrawn his hand from iniquity, hath executed true judgment between man and man, Hath walked in my statutes, and hath kept my judgments, to deal truly; he is just, he shall surely live, saith the Lord GOD."

14. Is God just and impartial?

Yes, God is just and impartial
Genesis 18:25 "That be far from thee to do after this manner, to slay the righteous with the wicked: and that the righteous should be as the wicked, that be far from thee: Shall not the Judge of all the earth do right?"
Deuteronomy 10:17 "For the Lord your God ... regardeth not persons."

No, God favored Abel
Genesis 4:4-5 "The Lord had respect unto Abel and to his offering: But unto Cain and to his offering he [Lord] had not respect ..."

No, God favored Jacob who cheated his brother Esau
Genesis 27:18-24 "He came unto his father, and said, My father: and he said, Here am I; who art thou, my son? And Jacob [said] I am Esau thy first born."

No, God punished Miriam but not Aaron
Numbers 12:1-15 "Miriam and Aaron spake against Moses ... And Miriam was shut out from the camp seven days ..."

Note: Aaron and Miriam spoke against Moses for marrying a Cushite woman but God punished only Miriam with leprosy and was shut outside the camp for seven days. God did not punish Aaron only Miriam was punished.

No, God favored the Israelites
Exodus 2:25 "God looked upon the children of Israel, and God had respect unto them."
Exodus 11:7 "But against any of the children of Israel shall not a dog move his tongue, against man or beast: that ye may know how that the Lord doth put a difference between the Egyptians and Israel."

No, God is not impartial
Psalm 138:6 "Though the Lord be high, yet hath he respect for the lowly."
Matthew 13:12 "For whosoever hath, to him shall be given, and he shall have more abundance: but whosoever hath not, from him shall be taken away even that he hath."

15. Should we tempt God?

Yes, we can
Judges 6:36-40 "Gideon said unto God, If thou wilt save Israel by mine hand, as thou hast said, Behold, I will put a fleece of wool in the floor ..."

Note: Gideon asked God for proof by making the fleece wet with dew and the earth beside the fleece dry the following day, and God did as he was told. Then, Gideon again asked God for proof by doing vice versa for the following day and God did so as he was told.

I Kings 18:36-38 "Elijah the prophet came near, and said, Lord God of Abraham ... hear me, that this people may know that thou art the Lord God ... Then the fire of the Lord fell, and consumed the burnt sacrifice, and the wood, and the stones, and the dust, and licked up the water that was in the trench."

Note: Elijah asked God to let the people know about him by giving a sign.

II Kings 20:8-11 "Hezekiah said unto Isaiah, What shall be the sign that the Lord will heal me ... And Isaiah the prophet cried unto the Lord: and he brought the shadow ten degrees backward ... in the dial of Ahaz."

Note: Hezekiah asked Isaiah to tell the Lord to bring the shadow ten degrees backward in the sundial of Ahaz as a sign that the Lord will heal him.

God can be tempted, but God should not be tempted
Exodus 17:2 "Wherefore the people did chide with Moses, and said, Give us water that we may drink. And Moses said unto them, Why chide ye with me? wherefore do ye tempt the Lord?"
Deuteronomy 6:16 "Ye shall not tempt the Lord your God."

No, God cannot be tempted
James 1:13 "Let no man say when he is tempted, I am tempted of God: for God cannot be tempted with evil, neither tempteth he any man."

16. Does God conceal some things from some people?

Yes
Matthew 11:25 "At that time Jesus answered and said, I thank thee, O Father,

Lord of heaven and earth, because thou hast hid these things from the wise
 and prudent, and hast revealed them unto babes."
Mark 4:11-12 "He said unto them, Unto you it is given to know the mystery
of the kingdom of God: but unto them that are without, all these things are
done in parables: That seeing they may see, and not perceive; and hearing
they may hear, and not understand; lest at any time they should be
converted, and their sins should be forgiven them."

No
Mark 4:22 "For there is nothing hid, which shall not be manifested; neither
was any thing kept secret, but that it should come abroad."

17. Is God a deceiver?

Yes
I Kings 22:23 "The Lord hath put a lying spirit in the mouth of all these thy
prophets, and the Lord hath spoken evil concerning thee."
Jeremiah 20:7 "O Lord, thou hast deceived me ..."

No
Exodus 34:6 "The Lord passed by before him, and proclaimed, The Lord, The
Lord God, merciful and gracious, longsuffering, and abundant in goodness
and truth."
Numbers 23:19 "God is not a man, that he should lie ..."

18. Is God the author of confusion?

Yes
Genesis 11:7-9 "Go to, let us go down, and there confound their language,
that they may not understand one another's speech ... and from thence did
the Lord scatter them abroad upon the face of all the earth."
Lamentations 3:38 "Out of the mouth of the most High proceedeth not evil
and good?"
I Corinthians 1:20 "Where is the wise? where is the scribe? where is the
disputer of this world? hath not God made foolish the wisdom of this
world?"
I Corinthians 1:27 "But God hath chosen the foolish things of the world to
confound the wise; and God hath chosen the weak things of the world to
confound the things which are mighty"

No
I Corinthians 14:33 "For God is not the author of confusion, but of peace, as
in all churches of the saints."

19. Does God prohibit stealing, defrauding and robbing?

No, God gave instructions to the Israelites to rob the Egyptians
Exodus 3:20-22 "Every woman shall borrow of her neighbour, and of her that sojourneth in her house, jewels of silver ... ye shall spoil the Egyptians."

No, God told the Israelites to plunder their enemies
Deuteronomy 20:14 "But the women, and the little ones, and the cattle, and all that is in the city, even all the spoil thereof, shalt thou take unto thyself; and thou shalt eat the spoil of thine enemies ..."

Yes
Exodus 20:15, 17 "Thou shalt not steal. Thou shalt not covet thy neighbour's house, thou shalt not covet thy neighbour's wife, nor his manservant, nor his maidservant, nor his ox, nor his ass, nor any thing that is thy neighbour's."
Leviticus 19:13 "Thou shalt not defraud thy neighbour, neither rob him: the wages of him that is hired shall not abide with thee all night until the morning."

20. Does God ever get furious?

No
Isaiah 27:4 "Fury is not in me."

Yes
Isaiah 34:2 "For the indignation of the Lord is upon all nations, and his fury upon all their armies."
Jeremiah 21:5 "I myself will fight against you with an outstretched hand and with a strong arm, even in anger, and in fury, and in great wrath."

21. Is God gentle, loving, kind and merciful?

Yes
Exodus 34:6 "The Lord God, merciful and gracious, longsuffering, and abundant in goodness and truth."
Deuteronomy 4:31 "For the Lord thy God is a merciful God."
Luke 6:36 "Be ye therefore merciful, as your Father also is merciful."

No
Numbers 25:4 "The Lord said to Moses, Take all the heads of the people, and hang them up before the Lord against the sun, that the fierce anger of the Lord may be turned away from Israel."
Deuteronomy 7:16 "Thou shalt consume all the people which the Lord thy God shall deliver thee; thine eye shall have no pity upon them: neither shalt thou serve their gods; for that will be a snare unto thee."

22. Is God's anger fierce and lasting?

Yes, God's anger lasts forever
Jeremiah 17:4 "Ye have kindled a fire in mine anger, which shall burn for ever."
Malachi 1:4 "The people against whom the Lord hath indignation for ever."
Matthew 25:46 "These shall go away into everlasting punishment."

No, God's anger does not last forever
Psalm 30:5 "For his anger endureth but a moment; in his favour is life: weeping may endure for a night, but joy cometh in the morning."
Jeremiah 3:12 "Return, thou backsliding Israel … I will not keep anger for ever."

F. How changeable is God?

1. Does God change his mind?

Yes, Abraham was able to change the mind of the Lord
Genesis 6:6 "It repented the Lord that he had made man … it grieved him"
Genesis 18:23-32 "Abraham … said, Wilt thou also destroy the righteous with the wicked? Peradventure there be fifty righteous within the city … [God] said, I will not destroy it for ten's sake."

Note: Abraham was able to convince the Lord to reduce the required minimum number of righteous people in Sodom to avoid destruction, from fifty to ten people.

Yes, Moses was able to convince the Lord not to destroy his people
Exodus 32:14 "The Lord repented of the evil which he thought to do unto his people."
Exodus 33:1, 3 "The Lord said … Depart … Unto a land flowing with milk and honey: for I will not go up in the midst of thee; for thou art a stiff necked people: lest I consume thee in the way."
Exodus 33:14 "[God] said, My presence shall go with thee … I will give thee rest."

Note: In Exodus 33:3, the Lord said I will not go with you [the Israelites] and I might even destroy you. But through the convincing words of Moses, the Lord changed his mind and in Exodus 33:14, the Lord said, 'My presence shall go with thee and I will give thee rest'.

Numbers 14:11-16 "The Lord said unto Moses, How long will this people provoke me? … I will smite them with the pestilence, and disinherit them ..."
Numbers 14:20-21 "The Lord said, I have pardoned according to thy word: But as truly as I live, all the earth shall be filled with the glory of the Lord."

Note: In Numbers 14:12, the Lord said, 'I will smite them with the pestilence and disinherit them.' But after the convincing words of Moses, the Lord changed his mind and said, 'I have pardoned according to thy word'.

Yes, God said he will not give the land of the Ammonites to the Israelites, but God changed His mind
Deuteronomy 2:19, 37 "When you come to the Ammonites, do not harass them or provoke them to war, for *I will not give you possession of any land belonging to the Ammonites* ... in accordance with the command of the Lord our God, you did not encroach on any of the land of the Ammonites ..."
Zephaniah 2:9 "As surely as I live," declares the Lord Almighty ... "surely Moab will become like Sodom, the Ammonites like Gomorrah — a place of weeds and salt pits, a wasteland forever. The remnant of my people will plunder them; *the survivors of my nation will inherit their land."*

Note: In Deuteronomy 2, God wanted the Ammonites to keep their land. But in Zephaniah 2:9, God decided to let the Israelites plunder the land of the Ammonites.

Yes, God repented making Saul a king
I Samuel 15:11 "It repenteth me [God] that I have set up Saul to be king."
I Samuel 15:35 "The Lord repented that he had made Saul king over Israel."

Yes, God repented destroying the people
II Samuel 24:16 "The Lord repented of the evil, and said to the angel that destroyed the people, it is enough: stay now thine hand."
I Chronicles 21:15 "The Lord beheld, and he repented him of the evil, and said to the angel that destroyed, It is enough, stay now thine hand."

Note: God sent an angel to destroy Jerusalem. But the Lord saw the calamity and destruction and changed his mind and told the angel stop.

Yes, God said Hezekiah will not recover, but God changed his mind when Hezekiah prayed
Isaiah 38:1-5 "In those days was Hezekiah sick unto death. And Isaiah ... said unto him, Thus saith the Lord, Set thine house in order: for thou shalt die, and not live ... .Thus saith the Lord ... I have heard thy prayer, I have seen thy tears: behold, I will add unto thy days fifteen years."

Note: In II Kings 20:1-7 and Isaiah 38:1-5, God told Isaiah that Hezekiah is sick and will not recover. Hezekiah prayed for his life and God changed his mind and gave Hezekiah fifteen years more to live.

Yes, God repented many times
Jeremiah 15:6 "I [God] am weary of repenting."

Jeremiah 18:8 "I [God] will repent of the evil that I thought to do unto them."

No, God does not repent
Numbers 23:19 "God is not a man, that he should lie; *neither the son of man, that he should repent*"
Malachi 3:6 "For I am the Lord; I change not."

2. Was God pleased with His creation?

Yes
Genesis 1:31 "God saw every thing that he had made, and, behold, it was very good. And the evening and the morning were the sixth day."

No
Genesis 6:6 "It repented the Lord that he had made man on the earth, and it grieved him at his heart."

Note: This is inconsistent with the concept that God is omniscient.

G. Can God be seen and heard?

1. Has anyone seen God?

Yes, God appeared to Abraham
Genesis 12:7 "The Lord appeared unto Abram ..."

Yes, God appeared to Isaac
Genesis 26:2, 24 "The Lord appeared unto him [Isaac] ... the Lord appeared unto him [Isaac] ..."

Yes, God appeared to Jacob
Genesis 32:30; 35:9 "For I [Jacob] have seen God face to face ..."
Genesis 48:3 "Jacob said ... God Almighty appeared unto me at Luz ..."

Yes, God appeared to Moses
Exodus 3:16 "The Lord God of your fathers ... appeared unto me [Moses] ..."

Yes, God appeared to Isaiah
Isaiah 6:1, 5 "I [Isaiah] saw also the Lord sitting upon a throne ... For mine [Isaiah] eyes have seen the King, the Lord of hosts."

Yes, God appeared to Ezekiel
Ezekiel 1:27 "I [Ezekiel] saw ... the appearance of his loins ..."
Ezekiel 20:35 "There will I [Lord GOD] plead with you face to face."

Yes, God appeared to Amos
Amos 7:7 "Thus he shewed me [Amos]: and, behold, the Lord stood upon a

wall made by a plumbline, with a plumbline in his hand."
Amos 9:1 "I [Amos] saw the Lord standing beside the altar ..."

Yes, other people saw God
Exodus 6:3 "I appeared unto Abraham, unto Isaac, and unto Jacob ..."
I Kings 22:19 "Micaiah said: I saw the Lord sitting on his throne ..."
Job 42:5 "I [Job] have heard of thee ... but now mine eye seeth thee."

No
Exodus 33:20 "Thou canst not see my face: for there shall no man see me, and live."
John 1:18 "No man hath seen God at any time."
I John 4:12 "No man hath seen God at any time."

Note: Several people saw God. However, in Exodus 33:20, it says that no man will see God and live.

2. Will everyone see the majesty of God?

Yes
Isaiah 40:5 "The glory of the Lord shall be revealed, and *all flesh shall see it together."*

No, the wicked will not see the majesty of God
Isaiah 26:10 "The wicked ... will not behold the majesty of the Lord."

3. Has anyone heard God?

Yes
Exodus 20:22 "Then the Lord said to Moses, "Tell the Israelites this: 'You have seen for yourselves that I have spoken to you from heaven"
Deuteronomy 4:12 "Then the Lord spoke to you out of the fire. You heard the sound of words but saw no form; there was only a voice. "

No
John 5:37 "The Father himself, which hath sent me, hath borne witness of me. Ye have neither heard his voice at any time, nor seen his shape."

4. Can God be found through reason alone?

Yes
Romans 1:20 "For the invisible things of him from the creation of the world are clearly seen, being understood by the things that are made, even his eternal power and Godhead; so that they are without excuse."

No
Job 11:7 "Canst thou by searching find out God?"

H. Is God like a man?

1. Is God a man?

God is not a man
Numbers 23:19 "God is not a man, that he should lie; neither the son of man, that he should repent: hath he said, and shall he not do it? or hath he spoken, and shall he not make it good?"

God has mouth and nostrils
Genesis 2:7 "The Lord God formed man … and breathed …"
Deuteronomy 8:3 "Every word … out of the mouth of the Lord …"
[Also in **II Samuel 22:9, Psalm 18:8**]

God has feet
Genesis 3:8 "The Lord God walking in the garden …"
Exodus 24:10 "There was under his [God] feet …"
Nahum 1:3 "The clouds are the dust of his feet."

God has a finger
Exodus 8:19 "Then the magicians said … This is the finger of God …"
Exodus 31:18 "Two tables of testimony … written with the finger of God."

God has a face
Exodus 33:11 "The Lord spake unto Moses face to face …"
Job 13:24 "Wherefore hidest thou thy face, and holdest me for thine enemy?"

God has eyes
Deuteronomy 11:12 "The eyes of the Lord thy God …"

God has eyelids
Psalm 11:4 "The Lord is in his holy temple … his eyelids try …"

God has lips
Psalm 17:4 "By the word of *thy lips* …"

God has wings
Ruth 2:12 "The Lord God of Israel, under whose wings …"
Psalm 17:8 "Hide me under the shadow of thy wings"

Note: The God being described to have wings may be Horus the Greek god.

God has a hand
Exodus 33:22 "Will cover thee with my [God] hand while I pass by:"
Job 19:21 "Have pity upon me … the hand of God hath touched me."
Ezekiel 8:3 "He [God] put forth the form of an hand …"

God has an arm
Job 40:9 "Hast thou an arm like God?"

God has ears
Psalm 130:2 "Lord, hear my voice: let thine ears be attentive …"

God has loins
Ezekiel 8:2 "Then I beheld … from the appearance of his loins …"

2. Does God have a body?

Yes
Genesis 3:8 "They heard the voice of the Lord God walking in the garden …"
Deuteronomy 23:13 "The Lord thy God walketh in the midst of thy camp …"
Habakkuk 3:3-4 "God … had horns coming out of his hand."

No
Luke 24:39 "For a spirit hath not flesh and bones."
John 4:24 "God is a spirit."

3. Does God stand or sit to judge?

God stands to judge
Isaiah 3:13 "The Lord standeth up to plead, and standeth to judge …"

God sits to judge
Joel 3:12 "Let the heathen be wakened, and come up to the valley of Jehoshaphat: for there will I sit to judge all the heathen round about."

4. Does God drink wine?

Judges 9:13 "The vine said … Should I leave my wine, which cheereth God and man …?"

5. Does God get tired and rest?

Yes
Genesis 2:2 "On the seventh day God … rested …"
Jeremiah 15:6 "I am weary with repenting."

No
Isaiah 40:28 "The everlasting God … fainteth not, neither is weary?"

6. Does God fall asleep?

God never sleeps
Psalm 121:3-4 "He who keeps Israel shall neither slumber nor sleep."

God sometimes sleeps
Psalm 44:23 "Awake, why sleepest thou, O Lord?"

I. Is God love?

1. God is love?

God is love
I John 4:8 "He that loveth not knoweth not God; for God is love."

God is a jealous God
Exodus 20:5 "Thou shalt not bow ... to them ... for I ... am a jealous God ..."

But love is not jealous
I Corinthians 13:4 "Charity suffereth long, and is kind; charity envieth not; charity vaunteth not itself, is not puffed up"

Jealousy is sinful, if God is jealous does God sin?
Exodus 20:5 "Thou shalt not bow ... to them ... for I ... am a jealous God ..."
II Corinthians 12:20 "For I fear, lest, when I come, I shall not find you such as I would, and that I shall be found unto you such as ye would not: lest there be debates, envyings, wraths, strifes, backbitings, whisperings, swellings, tumults"

2. Should we love or fear God?

Yes, we should fear God
Leviticus 25:17 "Thou shalt fear thy God: for I am the Lord your God."
Psalm 103:11 "Great is his mercy toward them that fear him."
Psalm 112:1 "Blessed is the man that feareth the Lord."

3. We should fear God but there is no fear in love

II Timothy 1:7 "For God hath not given us the spirit of fear; but of power, and of love, and of a sound mind."
I John 4:18 "There is no fear in love; but perfect love casteth out fear: because fear hath torment. He that feareth is not made perfect in love."

4. We should love God with all our heart

Deuteronomy 6:5 "Thou shalt love the Lord thy God with all thine heart, and with all thy soul, and with all thy might."
Matthew 22:37 "Thou shalt love the Lord thy God with all thy heart, and with all thy soul, and with all thy mind."

5. Does God want the salvation of all?

Yes

I Timothy 2:3-4 "For this is good and acceptable in the sight of God our Saviour; Who will have all men to be saved, and to come unto the knowledge of the truth."

II Peter 3:9 "The Lord is not slack concerning his promise ... not willing that any should perish, but that all should come to repentance."

No

Proverbs 16:4 "The Lord hath made all things ... even the wicked for the day of evil."

John 6:44 "No man can come to me, except the Father which hath sent me draw him: and I will raise him up at the last day."

Romans 9:18 "Therefore hath he mercy on whom he will have mercy, and whom he will he hardeneth."

6. Does God withhold blessings?

Yes

Joshua 11:20 "For it was of the Lord to harden their hearts, that they should come against Israel in battle, that he might destroy them utterly ..."

Isaiah 63:17 "O Lord, why hast thou made us to err from thy ways, and hardened our heart from thy fear? Return for thy servants' sake, the tribes of thine inheritance."

John 12:40 "He hath blinded their eyes, and hardened their heart; that they should not see with their eyes, nor understand with their heart, and be converted, and I should heal them."

No

Luke 11:10 "For every one that asketh receiveth; and he that seeketh findeth; and to him that knocketh it shall be opened."

James 1:5 "If any of you lack wisdom, let him ask of God, that giveth to all men liberally, and upbraideth not; and it shall be given him."

7. Do we get deliverance calling on the Lord?

Yes

Joel 2:32 "Whosoever shall call on the name of the Lord shall be delivered."

Acts 2:21 "Whosoever shall call on the name of the Lord shall be saved."

Romans 10:13 "For whosoever shall call upon the name of the Lord shall be saved."

No

Matthew 7:21 "Not every on that saith unto me Lord, Lord, shall enter the kingdom of heaven."

J. God did ... what!

God wants the smell of burning dead animals
Genesis 8:20-21 "[Noah] offered burnt offerings ... the Lord smelled a sweet savour ..."

God ordered all uncircumcised man child to be abandoned
Genesis 17:14 "The uncircumcised man child ... shall be cut off from his people ..."

God dined with Abraham
Genesis 18:1, 8 "He [Abraham] took butter, and milk, and the calf which he had dressed, and set it before them ... and they did eat."

God wrestled with Jacob and Jacob won
Genesis 32:24, 28 "Jacob ... wrestled a man ... And he said, Thy name shall be ... Israel: for as a prince hast thou power with God ... and hast prevailed."

God said Jacob should be called Israel but still calls Jacob Jacob
Genesis 35:10; 46:2 "God said ... thy name shall not be called any more Jacob, but Israel ... And God ... said, Jacob, Jacob ..."

God hardened the Pharaoh's heart many times so he will not let the Israelites go
Exodus 4:21 "The Lord said, I will harden his [Pharaoh] heart, that he shall not let the people go."

God will send plagues so people will know more about him
Exodus 9:14 "I will [send plagues] thou may know ... there is none like me"

God will send diseases if you do not obey him
Exodus 15:26 "[God] said, If thou wilt diligently hearken to the voice of the Lord thy God ... I will put none of these diseases upon thee ..."

God ordered the total destruction of the Amalekites
Exodus 17:14 "I [Lord] will utterly put out the remembrance of Amalek ..."
Deuteronomy 25:19 "The Lord said ... you shall blot out the memory of Amalek ..."
I Samuel 15:1-3 "God said ... smite Amalek ... destroy all they have ... spare them not."

God ordered the killing of anybody who goes to the mountain or touch its border
Exodus 19:12-13 "[The Lord said] ... ye go not up into the mount, or touch the border of it: whosoever toucheth the mount shall be surely put to death."

God gave instructions to Moses about carpentry, dressmaking, craftmanship, etc
Exodus 25-31 "The Lord spake unto Moses, saying ..."

God tells how to make garments, girdles, and bonnets for glory and beauty
Exodus 28:2, 20, 40 "Thou shalt make holy garments for Aaron ... girdles, and bonnets ... for glory and for beauty."

God has a magical Urim and Thummim
Exodus 28:30 "The Urim and the Thummim ..."
[Also in **Leviticus 8:8**]

God told Aaron to wear a bell when he enters the holy place or he will die
Exodus 28:34-35 "A golden bell and a pomegranate upon the hem of the robe ... and his sound shall be heard when he goeth in unto the holy place ... that he die not."

God gave detailed instructions on how to make and wear underwear
Exodus 28:42 "Thou shalt make them linen breeches to cover their nakedness; from the loins even unto the thighs they shall reach"

God asked for the Israelites to pay a ransom for their soul
Exodus 30:11-16 "The Lord spake ... shall they give every man a ransom for his soul unto the Lord...they shall give ... half a shekel ... the offering of the Lord ..."

God told Aaron and his sons to wash their hands and feet, or they will die
Exodus 30:17-21 "Aaron and his sons shall wash their hands and their feet ... that they die not."

God said anybody who puts holy anointing oil on strangers will be cut off from his people
Exodus 30:33 "Whosoever ... putteth any of it (holy anointing oil) upon a stranger, shall even be cut off from his people."

God forbids anybody to use or smell His special favorite perfume
Exodus 30:37-38 "As for the perfume ... ye shall not make to yourselves according to the composition thereof ... Whosoever shall make like unto that, to smell thereto, shall even be cut off from his people."

God orders the offering of male firstborns
Exodus 34:19-20 "All that openeth the matrix is mine ... All the firstborn of thy sons thou shalt redeem ..."

God orders a step-by-step instruction regarding ritualistic animal killings
Leviticus 1-9 (God gave detailed step-by-step instructions on how to perform

ritualistic animal sacrifices. The animals must be killed, the blood sprinkled around, the animal cut to pieces and then burned.)

God said do not eat animal fat because it is for the Lord
Leviticus 3:16-17 "The priest shall burn them upon the altar: it is the food of the offering made by fire for a sweet savour: all the fat is the Lord's ... ye eat neither fat nor blood."

God will kill the priests and send his wrath to all if the priests misbehave at the tabernacle
Leviticus 10:6-7 "Uncover not your heads, neither rend your clothes; lest ye die, and lest wrath come upon all the people ..."

God gave instructions about killing lambs and pigeons and using their blood for lepers
Leviticus 14:1-25 "The Lord spake [the law of the leper] ... he shall sprinkle (bird blood) upon him ... seven times ... the priest shall take some of the (lamb's) blood ... put it upon the tip of the right ear of him ... upon the thumb of his right hand, and upon the great toe of his right foot ..."

God said do not wear clothes of different materials, cross breed cattle, plow with an ox and an ass and plant different seeds in the same yard
Leviticus 19:19 "Thou shalt not let thy cattle gender with a diverse kind: thou shalt not sow thy field with mingled seed: neither shall a garment mingled of linen and woollen come upon thee."
Deuteronomy 22:9-11 "Thou shalt not sow thy vineyard with divers seeds ... Thou shalt not plow with an ox and an ass together. Thou shalt not wear a garment of divers sorts, as of woollen and linen together."

God will send wild animals that will eat your children
Leviticus 26:18, 22 "I will also send wild beasts among you, which shall rob you of your children ..."

God will make you eat the flesh of your children
Leviticus 26:27-39 "If ye will not for all this hearken unto me, but walk contrary unto me ... ye shall eat the flesh of your sons, and the flesh of your daughters shall ye eat."

God will feed the Israelites with meat until it comes out of their nostrils
Numbers 11:1, 4, 18-20 "When the people complained, it displeased the Lord ... therefore the Lord will give you flesh, and ye shall eat ... until it come out at your nostrils ..."

God gave the Israelites a feast, changed his mind and killed them with a plague

Numbers 11:31-33 "The Lord ... brought quails ... and they [the Israelites] gathered the quails ... the wrath of the Lord was kindled ... and the Lord smote the people with a very great plague."

God ordered the capture of virgins to be kept as sex slaves
Numbers 31:18 "All the women ... that have not known a man ... keep alive for yourselves."

God had humans offered to him
Numbers 31:40 "The persons were sixteen thousand; of which the Lord's tribute was thirty and two persons."

God orders a genocide
Deuteronomy 7:1-4, 16 "The Lord thy God shall bring thee into the land ... and hath cast out many nations before thee, the Hittites ... seven nations ..."

God gave instructions to the Israelites on what to do with their excrement
Deuteronomy 23:13-14 "When thou wilt ease thyself abroad, thou shalt dig therewith, and shalt turn back and cover that which cometh from thee"

God hurled down rocks to kill the enemies of the Israelites
Joshua 10:11 "The Lord cast down great stones from heaven upon them ..."

God sold the Israelites into slavery
Judges 3:5, 8 "He [Lord] sold them [Israelites] into the hand of the king of Mesopotamia [Chushanrishathaim]: Israel served ... eight years."

God sent Ehud to disembowel Eglon
Judges 3:15, 17, 20-22 "The children of Israel cried ... the Lord raised them up a deliverer, Ehud ... [Ehud] took the dagger ... and thrust it into his [Eglon's] belly ..."

God said only those who drink like a dog will join Gideon's army
Judges 7:2-7 "The Lord said ... every one that lappeth ... as a dog (will join Gideon's army.) ..."

Samuel called God and God sent thunder and rain
I Samuel 12:18 "Samuel called unto the Lord; and the Lord sent thunder and rain."

God withers, then restores, the hand of king Jeroboam
I Kings 13:4-6 "He [King Jeroboam] stretched out his hand ... the hand he stretched out ... shriveled up ... the man of God besought the Lord, and the king's hand was restored him again."

God sends two bears to rip up forty two children for calling Elisha bald

II Kings 2:23-24 "[Elisha] went up ... little children ... mocked him [for being bald] ... and he cursed them ... there came ... two she bears ... and tare forty and two children ..."

God will make your ears tingle
II Kings 21:12 "I [God] am bringing such evil upon Jerusalem and Judah, that whosoever heareth of it ... his ears shall tingle."

God will give you nations to dash to pieces like a potter's vessel
Psalm 2:8-9 "Ask of me, and I shall give thee the heathen ... Thou shalt break them with a rod of iron; thou shalt dash them in pieces like a potter's vessel."

God breaks the teeth of the ungodly
Psalm 3:7 "O Lord ... thou hast broken the teeth of the ungodly."

God rode on top of an angel
Psalm 18:10 "He rode upon a cherub, and did fly ..."

God will smote you in the hinder parts
Psalm 78:66 "He smote his enemies in the hinder parts"

God will smite your head with a scab and discover your secret parts
Isaiah 3:17 "Therefore the Lord will smite with a scab the crown of the head of the daughters of Zion, and the Lord will discover their secret parts."

God will make you eat your arm
Isaiah 9:19-20 "Through the wrath of the Lord ... the people shall be as the fuel of the fire... they shall eat every man the flesh of his own arm."

God will let your children be dashed to pieces and your wives ravished
Isaiah 13:16 "Their children also shall be dashed to pieces before their eyes; their houses shall be spoiled, and their wives ravished."

God will make you err as drunkards stagger in their vomit
Isaiah 19:14 "The Lord hath mingled a perverse spirit in the midst thereof: and they have caused Egypt to err in every work thereof, as a drunken man staggereth in his vomit."

God made Isaiah walk naked and barefoot for three years
Isaiah 20:2-4 "Spake the Lord by Isaiah ... saying, Go and loose the sackcloth from off thy loins, and put off thy shoe from thy foot. And he [Isaiah] did so, walking naked and barefoot ... [and] Isaiah hath walked naked and barefoot three years ..."

God told the women to strip naked
Isaiah 32:11 "Tremble, ye women that are at ease; be troubled, ye careless ones: strip you, and make you bare, and gird sackcloth upon your loins."

God will make you eat your own flesh and drink your own blood
Isaiah 49:26 "I will feed them … with their own flesh; and they shall be drunken with their blood"

God ordered Ezekiel to make and eat bread with human dung
Ezekiel 4:9 "Thou shalt eat it as barley cakes, and thou shalt bake it with dung …"

God is against your pillows and your kerchiefs
Ezekiel 13:18-21 "The Lord [said] Woe to the women that sew pillows to all armholes, and make kerchiefs… saith the Lord GOD…I am against your pillows…Your kerchiefs also will I tear …"

God instructs Hosea to take a wife of whoredom
Hosea 1:2 "The Lord said to Hosea, Go, take unto thee a wife of whoredoms and children of whoredoms: for the land hath committed great whoredom, departing from the Lord."

God sent a drought as the Israelites fixed their homes but not His temple that He destroyed
Haggai 1:9-11 "When ye brought it home, I did blow upon it. Why? saith the Lord of hosts. Because of mine house that is waste, and ye run every man unto his own house … I called for a drought upon the land … and upon all the labour of the hands."

God causes us to believe lies
II Thessalonians 2:11-12 "God shall send them strong delusion, that they should believe a lie."

3. The other gods of the Bible

Adrammelech / Adramelech / Adar-malik
II Kings 17:31 "The Sepharvites burnt their children in fire to Adrammelech"

Note: A character in the video game Final Fantasy. In the story Basileus by Robert Silverberg, he is an enemy of God. In Paradise Lost by John Milton, he is a fallen angel.

Anammelech
II Kings 17:31 "The Sepharvites burnt their children ... and Anammelech ..."

Artemis / Diana
Acts 19:24 "Silver shrines for Diana ..."

Ashima
II Kings 17:30 "The men of Hamath made Ashima ..."

Ashtaroth / Ashtoreth / Astarte / Ishtar / Asherah
Judges 2:13, 10:6 "Baal and Ashtaroth ..."

Baal (Baalim)
Judges 6:28 "The altar of Baal was cast down"

Baal-Berith
Judges 8:33, 9:4 "Baalberith their god ..."

Baal-peor
Numbers 25:3 "Israel joined himself unto Baalpeor."

Baal-Zebub
II Kings 1:2-3 "Ahaziah ... enquire of Baalzebub the god of Ekron?"

Bel
Isaiah 46:1 "Bel boweth down ... their idols were upon the beasts ..."

Castor and Pollux
Acts 28:11 "We departed in a ship ... whose sign was Castor and Pollux."

Chemosh
Numbers 21:19 "O people of Chemosh ..."

Chiun / Kaiwan
Amos 5:26 "The tabernacle of your Moloch and Chiun ..."

Dagon
I Samuel 5:7 "Dagon our god."

Note: Dagon is a dream god in the movie Conan the Destroyer.

Marduk / Merodach
Jeremiah 50:2 "Merodach is broken in pieces."

Mercury / Hermes
Acts 14:12 "They called … Paul, Mercurius …"

Molech / Moloch / Malcom / Malcham / Milcom
Leviticus 18:21 "Thou shalt not let any … pass through the fire to Molech …"

Molten calf
Exodus 32:4 "He … made it a molten calf."

Nebo
Isaiah 46:1 "Nebo stoopeth, their idols were upon the beasts …"

Nergal / Nirgal / Nirgali
II Kings 17:30 "The men of Cuth made Nergal …"

Nibhaz
II Kings 17:31 "The Avites made Nibhaz …"

Nisroch
II Kings 19:37 "He was worshipping in the house of Nisroch his god …"

Note: Nisroch is a devil in the game Dungeons and Dragons.

Remphan / Raphan
Acts 7:43 "The star of your god Remphan …"

Rimmon
II Kings 5:18 "My master goeth into the house of Rimmon to worship there"

Succoth Benoth
II Kings 17:30 "The men of Babylon made Succothbenoth …"

Tammuz / Dumuzi / Duzu / Dumuzid
Ezekiel 8:14 "There sat women weeping for Tammuz."

Tartak
II Kings 17:31 "The Avites made Nibhaz and Tartak …"

Zeus/Jupiter
Acts 14:12-13 "They called Barnabas, Jupiter … the priest of Jupiter …"

VI. Books and writings mentioned in the Bible

1. Writings that may have been lost or may have never existed

Book of the Covenant (Covenant Code)
Exodus 24:7 "He took the book of the covenant, and read in the audience ..."

Note: It is commonly believed that The Covenant Code is a set of laws mentioned in Exodus 20:2 – 23:19.

Book of the Wars of the Lord
Numbers 21:14 "Wherefore it is said in the book of the wars of the Lord ..."

Book of Jasher
Joshua 10:13 "The sun stood still ... Is not this written in the book of Jasher?"
II Samuel 1:18 "Behold, it is written in the book of Jasher."

Note: A copy of this book may still exist today or such copy may be a pseudepigrapha.

Manner of the Kingdom/Book of Statutes
I Samuel 10:25 "Samuel told the manner of the kingdom [wrote] it in a book"

Letter of David to Joab
II Samuel 11:14 "David wrote a letter to Joab ..."

Acts of Solomon
I Kings 11:41 "The acts of Solomon ... the book of the acts of Solomon?"

Chronicles of the Kings of Israel
I Kings 14:19 "The book of the Chronicles of the Kings of Israel?"

Chronicles of the Kings of Judah
I Kings 14:29 "The book of the Chronicles of the Kings of Judah?"

Book of the Law
II Kings 22:8 "I have found the Book of the Law ..."

Book of the Kings of Israel and Judah
I Chronicles 9:1 "The Book of the Kings of Israel and Judah."

Last Words of David
I Chronicles 23:27 "By the last words of David the Levites were numbered"

Book of Shemaiah the Prophet
I Chronicles 24:6 "Shemaiah ... wrote them before the king ..."

Chronicles of King David / Annals of King David
I Chronicles 27:24 "Joab the son of Zeruiah began to number ... neither was the number put in the account of the chronicles of king David."

Book of Samuel the Seer
I Chronicles 29:29 "The acts of David ... book of Samuel the seer ..."

Book of Gad the Seer
II Chronicles 9:29 "The acts of David ... book of Gad the seer"

Book of Nathan the Prophet / History of Nathan the Prophet
I Chronicles 29:29 "In the book of Nathan the prophet ..."
II Chronicles 9:29 ""The acts of David ... book of Nathan the prophet"

Visions of Iddo the Seer
II Chronicles 9:29 "Are they not written in the ... visions of Iddo the seer ..."

Prophecy of Ahijah
II Chronicles 9:29 "Written in the book of ... the prophecy of Ahijah ..."

Iddo Genealogies
II Chronicles 12:15 "The acts of Rehoboam ... are they not written in the book ... of Iddo the seer concerning genealogies?"

Book of Shemaiah the Prophet - The Acts of Rehoboam
II Chronicles 12:15 "Now the acts of Rehoboam ... are they not written in the book of Shemaiah the prophet ..."

Story of Prophet Iddo
II Chronicles 13:22 "Written in the story of the prophet Iddo."

Book of Jehu
II Chronicles 20:34 "They are written in the book of Jehu ..."

Book of the Kings of Israel
II Chronicles 20:34 "The book of the kings of Israel."

Story of the Book of Kings / Annotations of the Book of Kings
II Chronicles 24:27 "Now concerning his sons ... written in the story of the book of the kings."

Acts of Uzziah
II Chronicles 26:22 "The rest of the acts of Uzziah ..."

Commandments of David and Gad and Nathan
II Chronicles 29:25 "He set the Levites in the house of the Lord ... according to the commandment of David, and of Gad the king's seer, and Nathan the prophet."

Vision of Isaiah
II Chronicles 32:32 "Now the rest of the acts of Hezekiah ... are written in the vision of Isaiah the prophet ..."

Sayings of the Seers
II Chronicles 33:19 "His prayer ... written among the sayings of the seers."

Decree of David the King of Israel (Liturgical Writings of David and Solomon)
II Chronicles 35:4 "The writing of David ... and according to the writing of Solomon his son."

Commandment of David and Asaph and Heman and Jeduthun
II Chronicles 35:15 "The singers the sons of Asaph were in their place, according to the commandment of David, and Asaph, and Heman, and Jeduthun the king's seer"

Lamentations (for Josiah)
II Chronicles 35:25-26 "Jeremiah lamented for Josiah ... they are written in the lamentations."

Decree of Cyrus / Letter of Cyrus
II Chronicles 36:22-23 "Now in the first year of Cyrus king of Persia ... that he made a proclamation ... and put it also in writing, saying ..."

Letter of Rehum and Shimshai
Ezra 4:8-16 "Rehum the chancellor and Shimshai the scribe wrote a letter ..."

Letter of Artaxerxes
Ezra 4:17-22 "Then sent the king an answer unto Rehum ... and to Shimshai the scribe ..."

Letter of Tattenai
Ezra 5:6-17 "The copy of the letter that Tattenai ... sent a letter unto him ..."

Memorandum from Babylonian Archives
Ezra 6:1-5 "Then Darius the king made a decree, and search was made in the house of the rolls ... And there was found ... a roll, and therein was a record thus written ..."

Letter of Darius
Ezra 6:1-12 "Then Darius the king made a decree ..."

Letter of Artaxerxes
Ezra 7:11-26 "Now this is the copy of the letter that the king Artaxerxes gave"

Letter of Sanballat
Nehemiah 6:5-7 "Then sent Sanballat his servant ... an open letter in his hand ..."

Chronicles of King Ahasuerus
Esther 2:23 "It was written in the book of the chronicles before the king [Ahasuerus]."
Ester 6:1 "He [King Ahasuerus] commanded to bring the book of records of the chronicles."

Chronicles of the Kings of Media and Persia / The Record Book of Ahasuerus
Ester 10:2 "Are they not written in the book of the chronicles of the kings of Media and Persia?"

Edict of King Xerxes
Ester 8:8-11 "Write ye ... he wrote in the king Ahasuerus' name ..."

Epistle to Corinth
I Corinthians 5:9 "I wrote unto you in an epistle ..."

Epistle to the Ephesians
Ephesians 3:3 "By revelation he made known unto me the mystery; as I wrote afore in few words"

Epistle from Laodicea
Colossians 4:16 "And that ye likewise read the epistle from Laodicea."

Epistle to the Thessalonians (spurious)
II Thessalonians 2:2 "That ye be not soon shaken in mind ... neither by spirit, nor by word, nor by letter as from us, as that the day of Christ is at hand."

Jude, the missing Epistle
Jude 1:3 "Beloved, when I gave all diligence to write unto you of the common salvation ..."

Prophecies of Enoch
Jude 1:14 "Enoch ... prophesied of these ..."

2. Books and writings mentioned in the apocrypha

Memoirs of Nehemiah
II Maccabees 2:13 "The memoirs ... of Nehemias..."

Epistles of the Kings
II Maccabees 2:13 "The epistles of the kings"

The King's Letter
II Maccabees 11:22 "But the king's letter contained these words ..."

3. Books that concern the fate of mankind

The Book of Remembrance
Malachi 3:16 "A book of remembrance was written before him ..."

The Book of Life
Daniel 12:1 "Every one ... found written in the book."
Revelation 3:5 "I will not blot out his name out of the book of life."

Note: The Book of Life may be what is considered as the Akashic record. Tto the mystics it is the Mind of God, the memory of all events past, present and future.

The Book of Judgment
Daniel 7:10 "The judgment was set, and the books were opened."
Revelation 20:12 "The dead were judged out of those things which were written in the books ..."

The seven-sealed book
Revelation 5:1-5 "I saw [a book] ... sealed with seven seals ..."

An angel's book
Revelation 10:2, 9 "I saw [a] mighty angel ... he had a little book open ..."

VII. Salvation

1. What does the Bible say about salvation?

A. Are we saved through works?

Yes, through works
Psalm 62:12 "Thou renderest to every man according to his work."
Jeremiah 17:10 "I the Lord search the heart, I try the reins, even to give every man according to his ways, and according to the fruit of his doings."

No, by faith alone
Mark 16:16 "He that believeth and is baptized shall be saved; but he that believeth not shall be damned."
John 3:16 "For God so loved the world, that he gave his only begotten Son, that whosoever believeth in him should not perish, but have everlasting life."

Neither, but by divine predestination
Romans 9:11-16 "For the children being not yet born … the purpose of God according to election might stand … it is not of him that willeth … but of God that sheweth mercy."

B. Are we saved by grace?

Yes
Ephesians 2:8-9 "For by grace are ye saved through faith; and that not of yourselves: it is the gift of God: Not of works, lest any man should boast."

No
James 2:14 "What doth it profit, my brethren, though a may say he hath faith, and have not works? Can faith save him?"
James 2:17 "Even so faith, if it hath not works, is dead, being alone."

C. Who will be saved?

Those who endures till the end will be saved
Matthew 10:22; 24:13 "He that endureth to the end shall be saved."
Mark 13:13 "But he that shall endure unto the end, the same shall be saved."

Those who say the right things will be saved
Matthew 12:37 "For by thy words thou shalt be justified …"

Those who believe the right things will be saved
Romans 3:28 "Therefore we conclude that a man is justified by faith …"

Those who do the right things will be saved
Matthew 16:27 "He shall reward every man according to his works."

Those who believe and do the right things will be saved
James 2:17 "In the same way, faith by itself, if it is not accompanied by action, is dead."

Those who call the name of the Lord will be saved
Acts 2:21 "Whosoever shall call on the name of the Lord shall be saved."

Not everyone who calls the name of the Lord will be saved
Matthew 7:21 "Not every one that saith … Lord, Lord, shall enter into the kingdom of heaven."

Those who are washed by the Holy Ghost will be saved
Titus 3:5 "He saved us … through the washing of rebirth and renewal by the Holy Spirit"

Those who ask will be saved
Matthew 7:7-8 "Ask, and it shall be given you; seek, and ye shall find; knock, and it shall be opened unto you: For every one that asketh receiveth … to him that knocketh it shall be opened."

Those who love will be saved
I John 4:7 "Let us love one another … every one that loveth is born of God, and knoweth God."
Luke 10:25, 27 "Master, what shall I do to inherit eternal life? And he answering said, Thou shalt love the Lord thy God with all thy heart, and with all thy soul, and with all thy strength, and with all thy mind; and thy neighbour as thyself."

Those who are more righteous than the scribes and Pharisees will be saved
Matthew 5:20 "For I say unto you, That except your righteousness shall exceed the righteousness of the scribes and Pharisees, ye shall in no case enter into the kingdom of heaven."

Those who keep the commandments will be saved
Matthew 19:17 "Jesus replied … If you want to enter life, obey the commandments.'"
Revelation 22:14 "Blessed are they that do his commandments, that they may have right to the tree of life, and may enter in through the gates into the city."

Those who keep the commandments, give all their wealth to the poor, and follow Jesus Christ will be saved
Luke 18:18-22 "A certain ruler asked him [Jesus], "Good teacher, what must I do to inherit eternal life?" [know] the commandments … sell everything

you have and give to the poor, and you will have treasure in heaven. Then come, follow me."

Those who believe in Jesus Christ will be saved
Acts 16:31 "Believe on the Lord Jesus Christ, and thou shalt be saved ..."

Those who hear the words of Jesus and believe in whoever sent him will be saved
John 5:24 "He that heareth my word, and believeth on him that sent me, hath everlasting life..."

Those who keep the commandments and believe in Jesus Christ will be saved
Revelation 14:12 "This calls for patient endurance on the part of the saints who obey God's commandments and remain faithful to Jesus."

Those who believe that God raised Jesus from the dead and confesses with their mouths 'Jesus is Lord' will be saved
Romans 10:9 "That if thou shalt confess with thy mouth the Lord Jesus, and shalt believe in thine heart that God hath raised him from the dead, thou shalt be saved."

Those who have babies (for women) will be saved
I Timothy 2:14-15 "The woman being deceived was in the transgression. Notwithstanding she shall be saved in childbearing ..."

Only virgin men will be saved
Revelation 14:3-4 "They sung as it were a new song before the throne, and before the four beasts, and the elders: and no man could learn that song but the hundred and forty and four thousand, which were redeemed from the earth. These are they which were not defiled with women; for they are virgins."

Note: How can the women have babies in order to be saved if the men should be virgins in order to be saved?

Only those who are converted and become like a little child will be saved
Matthew 18:3 "He said ... unless you change and become like little children, you will never enter the kingdom of heaven."

Only those who believed and is baptized will be saved
Mark 16:16 "He that believeth and is baptized shall be saved; but he that believeth not shall be damned."

Only those who are born of water and spirit will be saved
John 3:3, 5 "Jesus answered ... Except a man be born of water and of the Spirit, he cannot enter into the kingdom of God."

Only those who are chosen, predestined, those God will call to himself will be saved
Matthew 22:14 "For many are called, but few are chosen."

Only those who are not rich or wealthy will be saved
Matthew 19:23-24 "Then said Jesus … That a rich man shall hardly enter into the kingdom of heaven … It is easier for a camel to go through the eye of a needle, than for a rich man to enter into the kingdom of God."

Only those who eat the body and blood of Jesus will be saved
John 6:53-54 "Then Jesus said … Whoso eateth my flesh, and drinketh my blood, hath eternal life; and I will raise him up at the last day."

Only those who are circumcised will be saved
Acts 15:1 "Except ye be circumcised after the manner of Moses, ye cannot be saved."

Jesus implied that all will be saved
John 12:32 "I, if I be lifted up from the earth, will draw all men unto me."

Yet, some will not be saved
Romans 9:27 "Esaias also crieth concerning Israel, Though the number of the children of Israel be as the sand of the sea, a remnant shall be saved"
I Timothy 4:1 "Now the Spirit speaketh expressly, that in the latter times some shall depart from the faith, giving heed to seducing spirits, and doctrines of devils"

2. Arguments against Jesus Christ as the Messiah

The Bible contains verses that contradict themselves, leading to the possible conclusion that Jesus Christ is not the Messiah. The following are the contradictory verses regarding the messianic role of Jesus Christ:

A. Jesus Christ denied he is God
The books in the Bible that say Jesus Christ is God were mainly written by Paul who never met Jesus in person. Jesus Christ himself admitted that he is just a man.

The following passages in the Gospels of Matthew, Mark, and Luke indicate that Jesus was a man and not a God:

Matthew 19:17 "He [Jesus] said ... *Why callest thou me good? There is none good but one, that is, God*: but if thou wilt enter into life, keep the commandments."
Mark 10:18 "Jesus said ... *Why callest thou me good? there is none good but one, that is, God.*"
Luke 18:18-19 "A certain ruler asked him, 'Good teacher, what must I do to inherit eternal life?' 'Why do you call me good?' *Jesus answered. 'No one is good - except God alone.'*"

Only the Gospel of John implies that Jesus is God in the following verse:

John 10:30 "I and my Father are one."

Of the four Gospels, only the Gospel of John implies that Jesus Christ is God. However, the Gospel of John was written last, and is far different from the three other Gospels. The Gospel of John was said to be written about ninety years after the crucifixion of Jesus, and therefore cannot be considered a historically accurate book about the life of Jesus Christ.

The people who knew and saw Jesus through the years were those from his own country, who said, "Is not this the carpenter's son?"

Matthew 13:54-55 "When he [Jesus] was come into his own country ... they were astonished, and said ... Is not this the carpenter's son? is not his mother called Mary? and his brethren, James, and Joses, and Simon, and Judas?"

Jesus claimed that he is not God. If Jesus is God, yet denied this, his denial would then contradict the Bible, which states that God cannot lie.

Hebrews 6:18 "It was impossible for God to lie."

B. God cannot be tempted, but Jesus Christ was tempted

The Bible states the God cannot be tempted, but Jesus Christ was tempted.

If Jesus is God, he cannot and should not be tempted by the devil. In Mark 1:12-13, Jesus was tempted by the devil in the wilderness. But James 1:13 states that God cannot be tempted by the devil. Therefore, Jesus Christ is not God.

Mark 1:12-13 "And immediately the spirit driveth him into the wilderness. And he was there in the wilderness forty days, tempted of Satan; and was with the wild beasts; and the angels ministered unto him."
James 1:13 "Let no man say when he is tempted, I am tempted of God: for God cannot be tempted with evil, neither tempteth he any man."

Whether Jesus Christ is God or man, was discussed, argued, voted, fought, and died for by various sects, cults and councils for centuries, several hundred years after his lifetime.

Arguments regarding the nature and mission of Jesus Christ brought about the following widely varied doctrines:

DOCTRINE	BELIEF
Adoptionism	Jesus was born fully human, and adopted by God as God's son
Albigensis	Jesus was sent by God but was fully human
Anomoeanism	Jesus had a different nature, but was not God
Apollinarism	Jesus had a divine mind, but also had a human body and emotions
Arianism	Jesus was not eternal and not fully God
Arminianism	Jesus died for everyone
Armstrongism	God consists of two individuals, the Father and Jesus Christ who was born a man
Bogomilism	Jesus was the son of God through grace
Calvinism	Jesus saved only the elect, not the whole world
Carpocratianism	Jesus was just a man, the son of Joseph and Mary
Catharism	Jesus Christ cannot be the son of God and an incarnate
Catholicism	Jesus is the Son of God, both God and human, born of Mary
Cerinthianism	Jesus was not of virgin birth, was a man of virtue, knowledge and

	wisdom
Christadelphianism	Jesus Christ is the promised Jewish Messiah and is a separate being from God his father
Christianism	Jesus is the Son of God, both God and human, born of Mary
Docetism	Jesus was a completely divine being, that only seemed human
Ebionitism	Jesus was not divine, nor was he the savior of all mankind
Eutychianism	Jesus was part God and part human
Gnosticism	Jesus was not a real person but a phantom who appeared human sent by God to reveal to mankind about the true God
Henopysitism (Miaphysitism)	Jesus is a united combination of humanity and divinity
Judaism	Jesus was neither God nor Messiah
Mandeism (Sabeanism)	Jesus was a false prophet and somewhat evil
Manicheanism	Jesus was not a real man
Marcionism	Jesus was sent by the good God but not the god of the Jews
Monophysitism	Jesus has only one nature, the divine nature
Monothelitism	Jesus Christ has two natures but only one will
Nestorianism	Jesus Christ exists as two persons, the man and the divine son of God
Notzrimism	Jesus was just a literary invention and is not the Messiah
Patripassianism (Sabellianism)	It was God the Father who was crucified and not Jesus because there is only one God
Pelagianism	Jesus was only a good example
Psilanthropism	Jesus was only human
Socianism	Jesus did not pre-exist before birth
Unitarianism	Jesus was a great man, but not God himself

C. Jesus Christ was baptized for repentance

Jesus Christ was baptized by John the Baptist for repentance. If Jesus Christ is God, why does he need to be baptized for repentance?

Matthew 3:11 "I indeed baptize you with water unto repentance."

D. The savior must be a biological descendant of King David

The Bible says the savior must be a biological descendant of King David. The following verses require the messiah to be a biological descendant of David:

Romans 1:3-4 "Concerning his Son Jesus Christ our Lord which is made of the seed of David according to the flesh; and declared to be the Son of God with power according to the spirit of holiness, by the resurrection from the dead."

Acts 2:30 "Therefore being a prophet, and knowing that God had sworn with an oath to him, that of the fruit of his [David] loins, according to the flesh, he would raise up Christ to sit on his throne."

Acts 13:23 "Of this man's [David] seed hath God according to his promise raised unto Israel a Saviour, Jesus:"

But, according to **Matthew 1:18**, Joseph, a biological descendant of David is not the biological father of Jesus.

Matthew 1:18 "Now the birth of Jesus Christ was on this wise; When as his mother Mary was espoused to Joseph, before they came together, she was found with child of the Holy Ghost."

The Bible does not show that Jesus is a biological descendant of David through Mary's bloodline. Some theologians argue that the genealogy written in Luke 3:23-38, being completely different from the genealogy in the book of Matthew, is actually the genealogy of Mary. But the Bible explicitly mentions that the genealogy in Luke is the genealogy of Joseph, and not Mary's.

Luke 3:23 "Jesus (was supposed) the son of Joseph ... son of Heli."

E. The curse of Jeconiah and Jehoiakim

The curse of Jeconiah and Jehoiakim indicates that Jesus, being a descendant of Jeconiah and Jehoiakim, cannot and should not be considered a messiah.

The curse of Jeconiah:
Jeremiah 22:30 "This is what the Lord says: "Record this man as if childless, a man who will not prosper in his lifetime, for none of his offspring will prosper, none will sit on the throne of David or rule anymore in Judah.""

The curse of Jehoiakim:
Jeremiah 36:30 "Therefore thus saith the Lord of Jehoiakim king of Judah; He shall have none to sit upon the throne of David: and his dead body shall be cast out in the day to the heat, and in the night to the frost."

Jehoiakim is the father of Jeconiah an ancestor of Jesus
I Chronicles 3:10-19 "The sons of Jehoiakim: Jeconiah his son, Zedekiah his son."

The book of Matthew (**Matthew 1:1-16**) lists Jeconiah as an ancestor of

Jesus which, according to this prophecy, disqualifies Jesus as the Messiah.

Matthew 1:1, 12, 16 "The book of the generation of Jesus Christ ... Jechonias begat Salathiel ... And Jacob begat Joseph the husband of Mary, of whom was born Jesus, who is called Christ."

F. The Messiah will be a military king

The Messiah will be a military king who will rule from sea to sea. The Gospels of Matthew and John claim that Jesus Christ fulfilled the prophecy of Zechariah as the Messiah:

Matthew 21:4-5 "All this was done, that it might be fulfilled which was spoken by the prophet, saying, Tell ye the daughter of Sion, Behold, thy King cometh unto thee, meek, and sitting upon an ass, and a colt the foal of an ass."
John 12:14-15 "Jesus, when he had found a young ass, sat thereon; as it is written, Fear not, daughter of Sion: behold, thy King cometh, sitting on an ass's colt."
Zechariah 9:9 "Rejoice greatly, O daughter of Zion; shout, O daughter of Jerusalem: behold, thy King cometh unto thee: he is just, and having salvation; lowly, and riding upon an ass, and upon a colt the foal of an ass."

But Jesus does not fit the description of the said 'King' described in the subsequent verse:

Zechariah 9:10 "He shall speak peace unto the heathen: and his dominion shall be from sea even to sea, and from the river even to the ends of the earth."

Jesus was never a king with a kingdom and an army that had dominion from sea to sea and to the ends of the earth. Therefore, Jesus could not have fulfilled the prophecy of Zechariah.

G. The Messiah must come from the family of Bethlehem Ephratah

The ruler of Israel was prophesied to come from the family of Bethlehem Ephratah.

Jesus was born in Bethlehem (although this is widely disputed by historians and achaeologists) but he did not come from the clan of Bethlehem Ephratah.

Matthew 2:5-6 "They said unto him, In Bethlehem of Judaea ... for out of thee shall come a Governor, that shall rule my people Israel."
Micah 5:2, 6 "Bethlehem Ephratah ... out of thee shall he come forth unto me that is to be ruler in Israel ... they shall waste the land of Assyria with the sword, and the land of Nimrod in the entrances thereof: thus shall he deliver us from the Assyrian ..."
I Chronicles 2:50-54 "These were the sons of Caleb the son of Hur, the firstborn of Ephratah; Shobal the father of Kirjathjearim. Salma the father of Bethlehem ... The sons of Salma; Bethlehem, and the Netophathites ..."

The Bethlehem mentioned in Micah refers to a clan mentioned in **I Chronicles 2:50-54**. But in Matthew, the Bethlehem mentioned is a place. Micah also predicted that the future ruler would lead the Israelites against Assyria. However, Jesus never led the Israelites against Assyria.

H. Jesus does not fit the messiah described in the Book of Isaiah

Jesus does not fit the description of the messiah mentioned in the Book of Isaiah. Jesus was not named Immanuel, and had nothing to do with Rezin and Pekah.

Isaiah 7:14 "Therefore the Lord himself shall give you a sign; Behold, a virgin shall conceive, and bear a son, and shall call his name Immanuel. Butter and honey shall he eat, that he may know to refuse the evil, and choose the good. For before the child shall know to refuse the evil, and choose the good, the land that thou abhorrest shall be forsaken of both her kings."
Matthew 1:22-23 "Now all this was done, that it might be fulfilled which was spoken of the Lord by the prophet, saying, Behold, a virgin shall be with child, and shall bring forth a son, and they shall call his name Emmanuel, which being interpreted is, God with us."

Isaiah was referring to a child who would be born during his lifetime. The original text also refers to a young woman (but not a virgin) living at the time of the prophecy. In effect, this is a prophecy that Judah will be saved from the threat of Rezin and Pekah, as detailed in the following verses:

Isaiah 7:14, 16 "Therefore the Lord himself shall give you a sign; Behold, a virgin shall conceive, and bear a son, and shall call his name Immanuel. For before the child shall know to refuse the evil, and choose the good, the land that thou abhorrest shall be forsaken of both her kings (Rezin and Pekah)."

Jesus was not named Immanuel, and had nothing to do with Rezin and Pekah.

I. Jesus Christ had some unpure blood lines

1. Jesus had Ammonite blood

I Kings 14:21 "His [Rehoboam] mother's name was Naamah an Ammonitess."
I Kings 14:31 "His mother's name was Naamah an Ammonitess."
II Chronicles 12:13 "His [Rehoboam] mother's name was Naamah an Ammonitess."

2. Jesus had Moabite blood

Ruth 4:9-10, 13, 16 "Then Boaz announced to the elders and all the people … I have also acquired Ruth the Moabitess. So Boaz took Ruth and she became his wife … and she gave birth to a son … And they named him Obed. He was the father of Jesse, the father of David."

God declared that an Ammonite or a Moabite shall not enter into the congregation of the Lord. This was primarily because the Ammonites and the Moabites prohibited the Israelites from passing through their lands during the Exodus.

Aside from the unfavorable Exodus event, the Ammonites and the Moabites came from the incestuous union of Lot and his daughters and hired Balaam to curse the Israelites.

Genesis 19:30, 36-38 "He [Lot] dwelt in a cave, he and his two daughters. Thus were both the daughters of Lot with child by their father. The first born bare a son … Moab: the same is the father of the Moabites unto this day. And the younger, she also bare a son … Benammi: the same is the father of the children of Ammon unto this day."
Deuteronomy 23:2 "A bastard shall not enter into the congregation of the Lord; even to his tenth generation shall he not enter into the congregation of the Lord."
Deuteronomy 23:3-4 "No Ammonite or Moabite or any of his descendants may enter the assembly of the Lord, even down to the tenth generation. Because they met you not with bread and with water in the way, when ye came forth out of Egypt; and because they hired against thee Balaam … to curse thee."
Nehemiah 13:1-3 "The Book of Moses was read … and there it was found written that no Ammonite or Moabite should ever be admitted into the assembly of God, because they had not met the Israelites with food and water but had hired Balaam to call a curse down on them. (Our God,

however, turned the curse into a blessing.) When the people heard this law, they excluded from Israel all who were of foreign descent."

3. Jesus descended from Pharez, the fruit of the union of Tamar and her father-in-law while Tamar acted as a prostitute and seduced her father-in-law.

J. Jesus Christ, being a descendant of Judah was not a Levite

The following statements indicate that only the descendants of Aaron are allowed to perform priestly duties to God. But Jesus Christ descended from Judah, not from Aaron.

Exodus 29:9 "The priest's office shall be theirs [Levites] for a perpetual statute: and thou shalt consecrate Aaron and his sons."
Exodus 40:13, 15 "Thou shalt put upon Aaron the holy garments, and anoint him … that he may minister unto me in the priest's office. And thou shalt anoint them [Aaron's sons] … *for their anointing shall surely be an everlasting priesthood throughout their generations.*"

K. Jesus Christ was conceived out of wedlock

In Deuteronomy, God declared that a bastard shall not enter the congregation of the Lord.

Deuteronomy 23:2 "A bastard shall not enter into the congregation of the Lord; even to his tenth generation shall he not enter into the congregation of the Lord."

King David is a tenth-generation descendant (Luke 3:23-38) of Perez, a bastard son of Judah and Tamar. Tamar was Judah's daughter-in-law who pretended to be a prostitute in order to seduce Judah, and in so doing bore a son named Perez, an ancestor of King David and Jesus. Like King David, Jesus Christ himself was conceived out of wedlock.

L. Jesus Christ was substitute for the Goat of Azazel

The idea that Jesus Christ died for the atonement of our sins was most likely a belief derived from a Jewish ritual that uses the Goat of Azazel.

The Christian doctrine that Jesus Christ died for the sins of the world evolved from a Jewish rite held during Yom Kippur, as shown in the following biblical passages:

Leviticus 16:10 "But the goat, on which the lot fell to be the scapegoat, shall be presented alive before the Lord, to make an atonement with him, and to let him go for a scapegoat into the wilderness."

Hebrews 9:7, 11-14, 22 "The high priest [went to the second tabernacle] alone once every year, not without blood, which he offered for himself, and for the errors of the people: But Christ being come an high priest of good things to come ... *Neither by the blood of goats and calves, but by his own blood* he entered in once into the holy place, having obtained eternal redemption for us. For *if the blood of bulls and of goats, and the ashes of an heifer sprinkling the unclean, sanctifieth to the purifying of the flesh: How much more shall the blood of Christ,* who through the eternal Spirit offered himself without spot to God, purge your conscience from dead works to serve the living God? And almost all things are by the law purged with blood; and without shedding of blood is no remission."

During the Jewish holiday of Yom Kippur, one ancient ritual involved placing one's sins on a goat, then sending the goat to the wilderness or pushing it to a cliff. The idea behind this ritual was that if a person confessed their sins to a goat called the Goat of Azazel their sins would transfer to the goat and perish with the animal.

This Jewish ritual bears a close resemblance to the Christian doctrine that states that we are cleansed of our sins due to the death of Jesus Christ. As stated in **Hebrews 9**, instead of having the blood of goats and calves for forgiveness, we now have the blood of Christ.

M. Jesus Christ did not die on a cross

It is unlikely that Jesus died on the cross. Jesus was hanged on the cross for about six hours, but this kind of torture is usually survived for about three to six days.

N. Most writings about Jesus were made by Paul

The writings which state that Jesus Christ was crucified for our sins were written after the fact by Paul, who never met Jesus.

The statement that Jesus Christ died for our sins can be attributed to Paul, who was Jewish. Paul's writings are based on a hodgepodge of Jewish traditions, superstitions and the writings of others. An analysis of Paul's writings reveals that many of his ideas were borrowed from *The Testaments of the Twelve Patriarchs* and other ancient writings.

The Gospel of John also states that Jesus Christ is God; he is said to be the Lamb of God, who removes the sins of the world:

John 1:29 "The next day John seeth Jesus coming unto him, and saith, 'Behold the Lamb of God, which taketh away the sin of the world'."

Casting Jesus in the role of the 'Lamb of God' may have its origins in the book of Leviticus which describes how animal sacrifice, along with offerings, should be practiced for the forgiveness of one's sins.

O. Why was Jesus crucified?

Several verses in the Bible explain why Jesus Christ was crucified. The following reasons are the most explicit explanation for his crucifixion:

Charge One: Public Disorder
Jesus chased the moneychangers from the temple, and went to the house of Lazarus. After three or six days, (depending on which gospel), he came back, riding on a donkey, and was arrested. The chief priests even contemplated putting Lazarus to death, as stated in the following verses:

John 12:10-11 "But the chief priests consulted that they might put Lazarus also to death; Because that by reason of him many of the Jews went away, and believed on Jesus."

Charge Two: Blasphemy
Jesus claimed to be the Messiah, the Son of God. The high priests decided to sentence Jesus to death for claiming that he is the Messiah, the Son of God. The following conversations eventually led to his execution:

Matthew 26:63-66 "The high priest [said] … thou tell us whether thou be the Christ, the Son of God. Jesus saith unto him, Thou hast said: nevertheless I say unto you, Hereafter shall ye see the Son of man sitting on the right hand of power, and coming in the clouds of heaven. Then the high priest … saying, He hath spoken blasphemy … What think ye? They answered and said, *He is guilty of death.*" [Also in **Mark 14:61-64**]
Luke 22:70-71 "Then said they all, Art thou then the Son of God? And he said unto them, Ye say that I am. And they said, What need we any further witness? for we ourselves have heard of his own mouth."

Charge Three: Sedition

Jesus is accused of telling the people not to pay tribute to Caesar and for claiming he is king:

Luke 23:2 "They began to accuse him, saying, We found this fellow perverting the nation, and forbidding to give tribute to Caesar, saying that he himself is Christ a King."

Charge Four: Violation of the Sabbath law
Violating the Sabbath law during Jesus' time is punishable by death:

Mark 2:27-28 "He [Jesus] said unto them, The sabbath was made for man, and not man for the sabbath: Therefore the Son of man is Lord also of the sabbath."
John 5:18 "Therefore the Jews sought the more to kill him [Jesus], because he not only had broken the sabbath, but said also that God was his Father, making himself equal with God."

P. The original sin was conceived in the Council of Trent

The original sin was conceived in the Council of Trent on June 7, 1546.

The original sin did not come from the book of Genesis, but was a declaration made by the Council of Trent on June 7, 1546. This doctrine was voted upon, based on a passage from **Romans 5:12**, written by Paul around 58 AD:

Romans 5:12 "Wherefore, as by one man sin entered into the world, and death by sin; and so death passed upon all men, for that all have sinned."

Did the sin of Adam and Eve cause the fall of all mankind? The story of Adam and Eve is most likely a derivative of the Hindu folk tale about Adimo and Heva. This folk tale was written by Ramutsariar, in the book The Prophecies, at least fifteen centuries prior to the birth of Jesus Christ. It was copied and retold in the Bible as a true story. The biblical characters Adam, Eve, Shem, Ham, and Japeth are nearly identical to the earlier heroic Hindu characters Adimo, Heva, Sherma, Hama and Jiapheta.

Jesus was proclaimed as the Messiah by those who had never met him, those who had never known him, as well as those who had their own personal agendas, invested in the belief of Jesus as God.

VIII. Paul and the New Testament

Paul, the self-proclaimed Apostle of Jesus Christ, has the most writings in the Bible about Jesus, yet Paul and Jesus Christ never actually met. Paul's only claim for such knowledge and authority are his so called visions. After Paul converted to Christianity on his way to Damascus, Paul claimed that he consistently received instructions from Jesus through his visions.

Paul wrote most of the books in the New Testament, however, claiming to have utmost knowledge and authority about Jesus Christ. These books include: Romans, First Corinthians, Second Corinthians, Galatians, Philippians, First Thessalonians, Second Thessalonians, First Timothy, Second Timothy, Titus, and Philemon. It is also believed that Paul also wrote the Ephesians, Colossians, and Hebrews. If Paul did indeed receive divine visions from Jesus Christ, why would Jesus choose Paul - who never met him in person, instead of any of the apostles, who were closest to Jesus during his lifetime? The Jesus Christ depicted in Paul's writings is based only on Paul's perceptions, without firsthand knowledge of the real, historic Jesus Christ.

The following is a brief timeline and discussion about the man who, through his visions, claimed to know the most about Jesus Christ:

1. Paul asks for letters from the priest in Jerusalem to be sent to Damascus

This request is odd, since the high priest in Jerusalem had no jurisdiction in Damascus.

Acts 9:1-2 "Saul ... went unto the high priest, And desired of him letters to Damascus to the synagogues, that if he found any ... whether men or women, he might bring them bound unto Jerusalem."

2. Paul takes pleasure in watching people die

Acts 22:4 "I persecuted this way unto the death, binding and delivering into prisons both men and women."
Acts 22:20 "When the blood of thy martyr Stephen was shed, I also was standing by, and consenting unto his death, and kept the raiment of them that slew him."

3. Paul claims to have met Jesus on his way to Damascus

Paul's first version of his encounter with Jesus on his way to Damascus:

Acts 9:3-7 "As he journeyed, he came near Damascus: and suddenly there shined round about him a light from heaven ..."

Note:
1) **Only Paul** fell on the ground
2) Paul heard a voice but **saw no one**
3) Jesus said, "Saul, Saul, why persecutest thou me? ... **I am Jesus** whom thou persecutest: it is hard for thee to kick against the pricks."
4) Paul's companions **heard** a voice
5) Jesus gave **no details** about tasks to be done in Damascus

Paul's second version of his encounter with Jesus on his way to Damascus:

Acts 22:6-11 "It came to pass, that, as I made my journey, and was come nigh unto Damascus about noon, suddenly there shone from heaven ..."

Note:
1) **Only Paul** fell on the ground
2) Paul heard a voice but **saw no one**
3) Jesus said 'Saul, Saul, why persecutest thou me? **I am Jesus of Nazareth**, whom thou persecutest.''
4) Paul's companions **did not** hear a voice
5) Jesus gave **no details** about tasks to be done in Damascus

Paul's third version of his encounter with Jesus on his way to Damascus:

Acts 26:13-18 "At midday, O king, I saw in the way a light from heaven ..."

Note:
1) **Paul and his companions** fell on the ground
2) Paul heard a voice but **saw no one**
3) Jesus said 'Saul, Saul, why persecutest thou me? it is hard for thee to kick against the pricks. **I am Jesus** whom thou persecutest ...'
4) Paul's companions **did not** hear a voice
5) Jesus **gave detailed** instructions about the tasks to be done in Damascus

The different versions given by Paul about his encounter with Jesus on his way to Damascus raise doubts about the veracity of his claims. In **I Corinthians 15:5-8**, Paul claims to have *seen* Jesus. But in three separate versions in the Book of Acts, Paul *only heard a voice* without seeing Jesus on his way to Damascus, and in most likelihood Paul *never saw Jesus* at all.

I Corinthians 15:5-8 "That he [Jesus] was seen of Cephas, then of the twelve … And last of all he was seen of me also …"

Paul's account of his encounter with Jesus on the road to Damascus may be a case of severe heatstroke, having traveled on foot for several hours during midday, in a place where temperatures can rise above forty degrees Celsius.

A person suffering from heatstroke is characterized by the following symptoms: high body temperature, rapid pulse, difficulty sweating, strange behavior, mental confusion, hallucination, agitation, disorientation, temporary blindness, seizure, and coma.

Paul's main foundation and basis for preaching Christianity was his single strange encounter on the road to Damascus.

4. Ananias meets Paul in Damascus

Ananias said Paul *saw* Jesus. But in all three separate accounts Paul said he heard a voice but *saw no one:*

Acts 9:11-17 "The Lord said unto him [Ananias], Arise, and go into … the house of Judas for one called Saul … Ananias … entered into the house; [and] said, Brother Saul, the Lord, even Jesus, that appeared unto thee in the way as thou camest, hath sent me, that thou mightest receive thy sight, and be filled with the Holy Ghost."

5. The apostles help Paul escape certain death

The apostles save Paul from certain death:

Acts 9:23-25 "The Jews took counsel to kill him: But their laying await was known of Saul. And they watched the gates day and night to kill him. Then the disciples took him by night, and let him down by the wall in a basket."

6. The apostles doubt Paul's sincerity, rejecting him

Paul was rejected by the apostles who doubt his sincerity (although Barnabas vouched for Paul's character); thus to support his case and say that he is indeed a disciple of Jesus Christ, he claims that Jesus Christ keeps giving him messages thru visions:

Acts 9:26-27 "When Saul was come to Jerusalem, he assayed to join himself to the disciples: but they were all afraid of him, and believed not that he was a disciple. But Barnabas took him ... and declared unto them how he had seen the Lord in the way ..."
Galatians 1:12 "For I neither received it of man, neither was I taught it, but by the revelation of Jesus Christ."

7. Paul claims he receives messages from Jesus through his visions

However, Paul admits he is not sure of his visions about Jesus Christ. Why should Paul be trusted if he himself is not sure of what he saw? In Paul's statement about his divine encounter in Damascus, he says he saw no one, but heard a voice:

II Corinthians 12:1-4 "I will come to visions and revelations of the Lord. I knew a man in Christ above fourteen years ago, (*whether in the body, I cannot tell; or whether out of the body, I cannot tell: God knoweth;*) such an one caught up to the third heaven. And I knew such a man, (*whether in the body, or out of the body, I cannot tell: God knoweth;*) How that he was caught up into paradise, and heard unspeakable words, which it is not lawful for a man to utter."

8. Paul has a falling-out with Barnabas and the apostles

After getting favors from Barnabas, Paul and Barnabas had a falling-out:

Acts 15:39 "The contention was so sharp between them, that they departed asunder one from the other ..."

9. Paul appoints himself an apostle of Jesus

Paul calls himself the Apostle of Jesus Christ, even though Paul never met Jesus. Paul is not the thirteenth Apostle and is not the replacement of Judas, since Mathias had already replaced Judas (Acts 1:26):

Romans 1:1 "Paul, a servant of Jesus Christ, called to be an apostle ..."
I Corinthians 1:1 "Paul called to be an apostle of Jesus Christ through the will of God ..."

10. Paul claims he has worked more than any other apostle for the church

According to Paul he did the most work for the church of Jesus Christ:

I Corinthians 15:10 "But by the grace of God I am what I am ... I laboured more abundantly than they all ..."

Paul disagrees with the apostles:

Galatians 2:11-13 "But when Peter was come to Antioch, I withstood him to the face, because he was to be blamed. For before that certain came from James, he did eat with the Gentiles: but when they were come, he withdrew and separated himself, fearing them which were of the circumcision. And the other Jews dissembled likewise with him; insomuch that Barnabas also was carried away with their dissimulation."

11. Paul contradicts himself, saying he never met the apostles in Jerusalem

Paul contradicts himself, saying he did not go to Jerusalem and has never met the apostles.

Yes, Paul went to Jerusalem:

Acts 9:26 "When Saul was come to Jerusalem, he assayed to join himself to the disciples: but they were all afraid of him, and believed not that he was a disciple."

No, Paul went to Jerusalem three years after:

Galatians 1:15-20 "But when it pleased God, who separated me from my mother's womb, and called me by his grace, To reveal his Son in me, that I might preach him among the heathen; immediately I conferred not with flesh and blood: *Neither went I up to Jerusalem to them which were apostles before me; but I went into Arabia,* and returned again unto Damascus. Then after three years I went up to Jerusalem to see Peter, and abode with him fifteen days. *But other of the apostles saw I none,* save James the Lord's brother. Now the things which I write unto you, behold, *before God, I lie not.*"

Paul claims to be specially chosen by God. He also claims he never met the apostles and was not in Jerusalem for the three years after his conversion. Paul swears he was not lying. Why does Paul contradict himself? What was the purpose of Paul's contradiction; was it to hide the fact that he had a close call with death, escaping by hiding in a basket? Why does Paul volunteer that he never went to Jerusalem when no one had questioned him? Is it because he had a falling-out with Barnabas and the rest of the apostles?

Paul tried to be part of the Twelve Apostles of Jesus. Paul had disagreements with the apostles, which could explain why he denied even meeting them in person.

12. Paul's definition of the fulfillment of the law is different from what Jesus said

Paul said, *"Love your neighbor as yourself."* is the fulfillment of the law:

Romans 13:9-10 "Thou shalt love thy neighbour as thyself. Love worketh no ill to his neighbour: therefore love is the fulfilling of the law."

Jesus said, *"Love God with all your heart and love your neighbor as yourself."* is the fulfillment of the law:

Matthew 22:37-40 "Jesus said … Thou shalt love the Lord thy God with all thy heart, and with all thy soul, and with all thy mind. This is the first and great commandment. And the second is … Thou shalt love thy neighbour as thyself. On these two commandments hang all the law and the prophets."

If Paul, received instructions from Jesus thru his visions, why is his definition of the fulfillment of the law different from what Jesus said?

13. Paul claims that Jesus said, "It is more blessed to give than to receive."

Acts 20:35 "The words of [Jesus] 'It is more blessed to give than to receive."

There is no biblical evidence that Jesus ever made this statement.

What was the motive behind Paul's conversion to Christianity?

To become the head of a religion he created.

Paul sees the opportunity for a new religion; a new following he can create, manipulate, and claim as his own:

I Corinthians 4:16 "Wherefore I beseech you, be ye followers of me."
I Corinthians 11:1 "Be ye followers of me, even as I also am of Christ."

Paul tries to be part of the apostles' group by claiming himself an apostle. After some time, Paul claims he is "superior" to all Twelve Apostles because he allegedly keeps receiving instruction from Jesus Christ through his visions:

II Corinthians 11:5 "For I suppose I was not a whit behind the very chiefest apostles. But though I be rude in speech, yet not in knowledge; but we have been throughly made manifest among you in all things."
Galatians 1:11-12 "But I certify you, brethren, that the gospel which was preached of me is not after man. For I neither received it of man, neither was I taught [it], but by the revelation of Jesus Christ."

Paul claims he will do anything for people to follow him:

I Corinthians 9:20-22 "To the Jews I became like a Jew, to win the Jews. To those under the law I became like one under the law (though I myself am not under the law), so as to win those under the law. To those not having the law I became like one not having the law (though I am not free from God's law but am under Christ's law), so as to win those not having the law."

Paul claims that the *suffering of Christ is still not sufficient for the salvation of mankind,* and that *he himself is suffering to make up* for what is lacking in the suffering of Jesus Christ.

At this point, Paul is likening himself to Jesus Christ:

Colossians 1:24 "Now I rejoice in what I am suffering for you, and *I fill up* in my flesh what is *still lacking in regard to Christ's afflictions*, for the sake of his body, which is the church."

Paul claims the old law is dead and that he is the new law. Paul states, All things are lawful unto me.:

Romans 7:6 "But now we are delivered from the law, that being dead wherein we were held; that we should serve in newness of spirit, and not in the oldness of the letter."
I Corinthians 6:12 "All things are lawful unto me, but all things are not expedient: all things are lawful for me, but I will not be brought under the power of any."
Galatians 3:10-13 "For as many as are of the works of the law are under the curse: for it is written, Cursed is every one that continueth not in all things which are written in the book of the law to do them. But that no man is justified by the law in the sight of God, it is evident: for, The just shall live by faith. And the law is not of faith: but, The man that doeth them shall live in them. Christ hath redeemed us from the curse of the law, being made a curse

for us: for it is written, Cursed is every one that hangeth on a tree"
Hebrews 8:13 "In that he saith, A new covenant, he hath made the first old. Now that which decayeth and waxeth old is ready to vanish away."

Paul warns that people might be led astray if they believe *other than what he* teaches:

II Corinthians 11:3-6 "But I fear, lest by any means, as the serpent beguiled Eve through his subtilty, so your minds should be corrupted from the simplicity that is in Christ. For if he that cometh preacheth another Jesus, whom we have not preached, or if ye receive another spirit, which ye have not received, or another gospel, which ye have not accepted, ye might well bear with him."

Paul further says that anybody who contradicts him will be accursed:

Galatians 1:8-9 "But though we, or an angel from heaven, preach any other gospel unto you than that which we have preached unto you, let him be accursed. As we said before, so say I now again, if any man preach any other gospel unto you than that ye have received, let him be accursed."

According to Paul, if you do everything he says, you will be at peace with God:

Philippians 4:9 "Those things, which ye have both learned, and received, and heard, and seen in me, do: and the God of peace shall be with you."

Paul invented the whole concept of original sin. The "fall of mankind" attributed to the sin of Adam and Eve is stated nowhere in the Bible (not even in the book of Genesis), but in the book of Romans. The doctrine of original sin was defined in the Fourth Council of Trent based on Romans 5:12:

Romans 5:12 "Wherefore, as by one man sin entered into the world, and death by sin; and so death passed upon all men, for that all have sinned"

Paul claims that our salvation is based on our belief in the death of Jesus Christ. Only those who believe in the death of Jesus Christ will be saved and accepted by God:

Romans 10:9 "If thou shalt confess with thy mouth the Lord Jesus, and shalt believe in thine heart that God hath raised him from the dead, thou shalt be saved."

Paul expects the end of the world to come soon; there is no time for marriage:

I Corinthians 7:29 "But this I say, brethren, the time is short: it remaineth, that both they that have wives be as though they had none"

Paul states that Jesus will be descending from heaven immediately. When, after some time, Jesus still does not return, Paul changes his mind and says Jesus will not return immediately:

II Thessalonians 2:2-6 "That ye be not soon shaken in mind, or be troubled, neither by spirit, nor by word, nor by letter as from us, as that the day of Christ is at hand. Let no man deceive you by any means: for that day shall not come, except there come a falling away first, and that man of sin be revealed, the son of perdition ... And now ye know what withholdeth that he might be revealed in his time."

Paul claims he is deceitful:

II Corinthians 12:16 "But be it so ... being crafty, I caught you with guile."

Paul claims he is the most sinful of men:

I Timothy 1:15 "This is a faithful saying, and worthy of all acceptation, that Christ Jesus came into the world to save sinners; of whom I am chief."

Paul says to drink not water, but wine:

I Timothy 5:23 *"Drink no longer water,* but use a little wine for thy stomach's sake and thine often infirmities."

It is written in Hebrews that God failed to fulfill his promises to Abraham and all others who believe God talked to them and made promises:

Hebrews 11:13 "These all died in faith, *not having received the promises*, but having seen them afar off, and were persuaded of them, and embraced them"

What makes Paul think that God is indeed talking to him?

It makes one wonder how Jesus and Paul would have carried their conversation if they ever met in person based on Paul's background and character. Perhaps the following verses can give us some answers:

Acts 23:6 "[Paul] cried out in the council … 'I am a Pharisee, the son of a Pharisee.'"

Matthew 23:15 "[Jesus said] Woe unto you, scribes and Pharisees, hypocrites! for ye compass sea and land to make one proselyte, and when he is made, ye make him twofold more the child of hell than yourselves."

Some of Paul's writings may have been alluded to or copied from other writings, such as the works of Cleanthes, Euripides, Menander, and Epimenides, as well as other ancient writings, such as the Testaments of the Twelve Patriarchs. If Paul received his messages from his visions, why are his writings similar to other writers in more ways than one? It is widely believed that the doctrines introduced by Paul and other church leaders were mostly derived from the Mithra religion. The celebration of Jesus' birthday on December 25th coincides with the birthday of Mithra. Like Jesus, Mithra died and was resurrected on Easter after three days.

The Christian concept of being a 'born-again' is a Mithraic doctrine that can be found in a prayer addressed to Mithra:

"Spirit of Spirit, if it be your will, give me over to immortal birth so that I
may be born again - and the sacred spirit may breathe in me."
Prayer to Mithras

The McGuffin of the whole Christian religion is not the crucifixion of Jesus Christ, but Paul's hallucination on his way to Damascus, and his writings based on his claims of receiving instructions from Jesus through visions.

IX. What does the Bible say about?

1. Abortion

Exodus 21:22-23 "If men strive, and hurt a woman with child, so that her fruit depart from her, and yet no mischief follow: he shall be surely punished, according as the woman's husband will lay upon him; and he shall pay as the judges determine. And if any mischief follow, then thou shalt give life for life."

Note: Anyone who caused a woman to lose her child by miscarriage or abortion should be punished by the woman's husband.

2. Adultery

Adulterous women are tested and punished, but nothing is mentioned about adulterous men
Numbers 5:12-31 "Speak unto the children of Israel, and say unto them, If any man's wife go aside, and commit a trespass against him..."

Summary: The woman suspected of adultery must drink a concoction prepared by the priest. The priest will utter curses meant to harm the woman (if she is guilty), and the woman must respond 'Amen, amen'. If the woman is guilty of adultery, the drink is expected to cause her great pain, but if she is innocent, the said drink will not affect her.

Note: The infidelity test only applies for women. Since women were deemed as properties of men, only the women were tried for infidelity.

A man who copulates with a married woman is committing adultery
Deuteronomy 22:22 "If a man be found lying with a woman married to an husband, then they shall both of them die, [both] the man that lay with the woman, and the woman: so shalt thou put away evil from Israel."

Note: However, the rule does not apply for a woman fornicating with a married man.

Looking at a woman with lust is already an act of adultery
Matthew 5:28 - But I say unto you, That whosoever looketh on a woman to lust after her hath committed adultery with her already in his heart.

Note: Pope John Paul II went further by saying, that if you look at your wife with lust, you are already committing adultery. Pope John Paul II delivered a sermon saying, "The husband must not use his wife, her femininity, to fulfill his instinctive desire."

A man who marries a divorced woman has committed adultery
Matthew 5:32; 19:9 "Whosoever shall put away his wife, except [it be] for fornication, and shall marry another, committeth adultery: and who so marrieth her which is put away doth commit adultery.
Luke 16:18 "Whosoever marrieth her that is put away from [her] husband committeth adultery."

A divorced man who marries another woman has committed adultery
Luke 16:18 "Whosoever putteth away his wife, and marrieth another, committeth adultery"

3. Amputation and castration

About castration
A castrate cannot enter the Lord's congregation
Deuteronomy 23:1 "He that is wounded in the stones, or hath his privy member cut off, shall not enter into the congregation of the LORD."
[Also in **Leviticus 21:17-23**]

A castrate will be favored
Isaiah 56:4-5 "For thus saith the Lord unto the eunuchs that keep my Sabbaths ... I will give them an everlasting name, that shall not be cut off."
Matthew 19:12 "For there are some eunuchs, which were so born from their mother's womb: ... some were made eunuchs of men: and there be eunuchs, which have made themselves eunuchs for the kingdom of heaven's sake. He that is able to receive it, let him receive it."

4. Astrology

Astrology is condemned
Deuteronomy 18:10-12 "There shall not be found among you any ... that useth divination, or an observer of times.... For all that do these things are an abomination unto the LORD."
Leviticus 19:26 "Neither shall ye use enchantment, nor observe times."

Astrology is practiced
Daniel 2:1-5 "Nebuchadnezzar dreamed dreams ... [and] commanded to call the magicians, and the astrologers ... to shew the king his dreams.
[Also in **Job 38:32**]

Jesus was visited by wise men guided by a star
Matthew 2:1-2 "When Jesus was born ... there came wise men [Saying] Where is [the] King of the Jews? for we have seen his star in the east ..."

5. Capital punishment

Capital punishment must be imposed for the following:

For murder
Genesis 9:6 "Whoso sheddeth man's blood, by man shall his blood be shed."

For going to Mount Sinai during the giving of the commandments by God
Exodus 19:13 "Whosoever toucheth the mount shall be surely put to death."

For stealing slaves
Exodus 21:16 "He that stealeth a man, and selleth him [will be] put to death."

The owner of an animal that killed a person
Exodus 21:29 "If the ox …hath killed a man or a woman; the ox shall be stoned, and his owner also shall be put to death."

For giving your children to Molech
Leviticus 20:2 "Whosoever … giveth any of his seed unto Molech; he shall surely be put to death."

For witches and wizards
Exodus 22:18 "Thou shalt not suffer a witch to live."
Leviticus 20:27 "A man also or woman that hath a familiar spirit, or that is a wizard, shall surely be put to death"

Children who are disobedient to their parents
Exodus 21:15, 17 "He that smiteth his father, or his mother … he that curseth his father, or his mother, shall surely be put to death."

For a woman who is not a virgin on her wedding night
Deuteronomy 22:13-21 "If any man take a wife, [and] found her not a maid … the men of her city shall stone her with stones that she die."

6. Disability

People with disabilities are not allowed to approach the altar of God
Leviticus 21:17-23 "Whosoever … hath any blemish, let him not approach to offer the bread of his God … a blind man, or a lame, or he that hath a flat nose, or any thing superfluous, Or a man that is brokenfooted, or brokenhanded, Or crookbackt, or a dwarf, or that hath a blemish in his eye, or be scurvy, or scabbed, or hath his stones broken."

7. Divorce

Only the man can divorce his wife
Deuteronomy 24:1-22 "When a man hath taken a wife … and it come to pass that she find no favour in his eyes, because he hath found some uncleanness in her: then let him write her a bill of divorcement …"

Note: The law states that a man can divorce his wife. However, it does not state that a woman can divorce her husband.

Matthew 5:32; 19:9 "Whosoever shall put away his wife, saving for the cause of fornication, causeth her to commit adultery: and whosoever shall marry her that is divorced committeth adultery."
[Also in **Mark 10:11-12; Luke 16:18**]

Note: Only the man can divorce his wife. A man should divorce his wife only for sexual immorality, otherwise he is committing adultery. And a man who marries a divorced woman commits adultery.

The woman is bound by the law to her husband as long as he lives
Romans 7:2-3 "For the woman which hath an husband is bound by the law to her husband so long as he liveth ... So then if, while her husband liveth, she be married to another man, she shall be called an adulteress"
[Also in **I Corinthians 7:39**]

Note: The woman is only freed from her husband if the husband dies.

I Corinthians 7:10-11 "Let not the wife depart from her husband: But and if she depart, let her remain unmarried, or be reconciled to [her] husband: and let not the husband put away [his] wife."

Note: A man who marries a divorced woman commits adultery.

8. Food

We must all be vegetarians
Genesis 1:29-30 "God said, Behold, I have given you every herb bearing seed ... and every tree ... to you it shall be for meat. And to every ... thing that creepeth upon the earth ... I have given every green herb for meat."

Note: If God created all the plants and trees for human consumption, why are some plants and trees inedible and poisonous?

We can eat any living thing except blood
Genesis 9:3-4 "Every moving thing that liveth shall be meat for you ... But flesh with the life thereof, which is the blood thereof, shall ye not eat."

We should not eat fat or blood
Leviticus 3:17 "It shall be a perpetual statute for your generations ... that ye eat neither fat nor blood."

Animals that we can eat

Leviticus 11:2-3 "These are the beasts which ye shall eat … Whatsoever parteth the hoof, is clovenfooted, and cheweth the cud … that shall ye eat."

Note: These rules exclude the camel, the rabbit, the hare, and the swine.

We must not eat sea creatures with no fins and scales
Leviticus 11:9-12 "These shall ye eat of all … whatsoever hath fins and scales … all that have not fins and scales … they shall be an abomination unto you"
Deuteronomy 14:9-10 "All that have fins and scales shall ye eat: whatsoever hath not fins and scales ye may not eat; it is unclean unto you."

Note: The rules stated above exclude shrimps, lobsters, clams, oysters, crabs and other sea creatures without fins and scales.

9. Homosexuality

Homosexuality rule in the Bible
Leviticus 18:22 "You shall not lie with man as one lies with a women; this is an abomination."
Leviticus 20:13 "If a man also lie with mankind as he lieth with a woman … they should surely be put to death."

Note: However, the rule in Leviticus seems to apply only for homosexual males but not for homosexual females.

Romans 1:26-28 "God gave them up unto vile affections: for even their women did change the natural use into that which is against nature: And likewise also the men, leaving the natural use of the woman …"
I Corinthians 6:9 "The unrighteous shall not inherit the kingdom of God? Neither fornicators … nor effeminate …"

Was David gay?
I Samuel 20:16-17, 30-31, 41-42 "Jonathan caused David to swear again, because he loved him: for he loved him as he loved his own soul … Then Saul's anger was kindled against Jonathan, and he said unto him, Thou son of the perverse rebellious woman, do not I know that thou hast chosen the son of Jesse (David) to thine own confusion, and unto the confusion of thy mother's nakedness? ... and they (David and Jonathan) kissed one another"
II Samuel 1:26 "Thy love to me was wonderful, passing the love of women."

Ruth and Naomi
Ruth 1:14 "They … wept again: and Orpah kissed her mother in law; but Ruth clave unto her."
Ruth 1:16-17 "Ruth said, Intreat me not to leave thee, or to return from following after thee: for whither thou goest, I will go …"

Note: Ruth and Naomi are known to be the lesbian couple in the Bible.

Daniel and Ashpenaz
Daniel 1:9 "Now God had brought Daniel into favour and tender love with the prince of the eunuchs."

The centurion and his servant
Matthew 8:5-13 "When Jesus was entered into Capernaum, there came unto him a centurion ... saying, Lord, my servant lieth at home sick of the palsy ... and Jesus saith ... I will come and heal him ..."

Note: In some writings the centurion and his servant were described as same-gender partners.

Was Jesus Gay?
John 13:23-25 "Now there was leaning on Jesus' bosom one of his disciples, whom Jesus loved. Simon Peter therefore beckoned to him, that he should ask who it should be of whom he spake. *He then lying on Jesus' breast* saith unto him, Lord, who is it?"
John 19:26 "When Jesus ... saw his mother, and the disciple [whom he loved], he saith ... Woman, behold thy son!
John 21:20 "Then Peter, turning about, seeth the disciple whom Jesus loved following; which also leaned on his breast at supper ..."

Salvation of virgin men?
Revelation 14:1-4 "A Lamb stood on the mount Sion, and with him an hundred forty and four thousand ... which were redeemed from the earth ... they which were not defiled with women; for they are virgins."

Note: Are these virgin men homosexuals?

10. Incest

Leviticus 18:6-18; 20:11-21 "None of you shall approach to any that is near of kin to him, to uncover their nakedness ..."

Note: The rules of incest mentioned apply to the following: father, mother, brother, sister, nephews, nieces, uncles, aunts and in-laws.

11. Necromancy

It is not condoned
Deuteronomy 18:10-11 "There shall not be found among you any one that maketh his son or his daughter to pass through the fire ... or a consulter with familiar spirits, or a wizard, or a necromancer."

It is practiced

I Samuel 28:8-12 "Saul disguised himself … [and] came to the woman by night: and he said, I pray thee, divine unto me by the familiar spirit, and bring me him up, whom I shall name unto thee."

12. Polygamy

Polygamy is condoned
I Samuel 1:1-2 "Elkanah ... had two wives; the name of the one was Hannah, and … the other Peninnah."
II Samuel 12:7-8 "Thus saith the LORD God of Israel ... I gave thee ... thy master's wives …"
I Kings 11:2-3 "[Solomon] had seven hundred wives ... three hundred concubines."
[Also in **Genesis 4:19; 16:1-4; 26:34; Judges 8:30; II Chronicles 11:21; 13:21**]

13. Racism

God set a mark upon Cain
Genesis 4:15 "The Lord set a mark upon Cain, lest any finding him should kill him."

Note: The mark of Cain, also called the curse of Cain was believed to be the reason and justification of racism and slavery. Because Cain married a foreign woman it is believed that the colored peoples of the world came from Cain.

14. Rape

About rape and women
God instructed Moses to keep the virgins for themselves
Numbers 31:1-2, 15-18 "The LORD spake unto Moses, saying … kill every woman …But all the women children, that have not known a man by lying with him, keep alive for yourselves."
Judges 21:12 "And they found among the inhabitants of Jabeshgilead four hundred young virgins … and they brought them unto the camp to Shiloh"

An engaged rape victim must be executed if she was raped in the city and did not scream
Deuteronomy 22:23-24 "If a damsel that is a virgin be betrothed unto an husband, … and a man find her in the city, and lie with her; Then ye shall … stone them with stones that they die; the damsel, because she cried not …"

The rapist must be executed if he raped an engaged woman in the country
Deuteronomy 22:25-27 "If a man find a betrothed damsel in the field, and … lie with her: then the man … shall die. … For he found her in the field, and the betrothed damsel cried, and there was none to save her."

Women should marry the men who raped them
Deuteronomy 22:28-29 "If a man ... lay hold on her, and lie with her ... the man that lay with her shall give unto the damsel's father fifty shekels of silver, and she shall be his wife; because he hath humbled her, he may not put her away all his days."

Note: If the rape victim is not engaged, the rapist must pay fifty shekels to the woman's father and the woman must marry her rapist.

15. Reincarnation

Did we exist before we were born?
Jeremiah 1:45 "*Before* I formed you in the womb, I knew you; and *before* you were born I consecrated you ..."

Note: This passage explains that we existed before we were born.

Elias and John the Baptist
Matthew 11:10-15 "Verily I say unto you, Among them that are born of women there hath not risen a greater than John the Baptist ... this is Elias, which was for to come."
Matthew 17:10-13 "Jesus answered ... Elias is come already, and they knew him not ... the disciples understood that he spoke unto them of John the Baptist."

Jesus and Abraham
John 8:56-58 "Jesus answered, "Your father Abraham rejoiced that he was to see the time of my coming. They said unto him, "You are not even fifty years old – and you have seen Abraham?" "I am telling you the truth," Jesus replied. Before Abraham was born, I am."

The Blind man
John 9:1-3 "As Jesus was walking along, he saw a man who had been born blind. His disciples asked him, Teacher, who did sin? His parents or he that he was born blind?"

Note: The disciples were thinking that the blind man sinned in his previous life and thus was born blind.

Esau, a case of reincarnation or predestination?
Romans 9:13 "As it is written, Jacob have I loved, but Esau have I hated".

Note: God hated Esau even before he was born. Was this a case of reincarnation or predestination? Was Esau hated because of what he did in a previous lifetime?

16. Slavery

Genesis 9:22-25 "Ham, the father of Canaan, saw the nakedness of his father [Noah] … and he [Noah] said, Cursed be Canaan; a servant of servants shall he be unto his brethren."

Note: Noah cursed Canaan because Ham saw him naked. Noah disrobed himself when he was drunk thus none of his sons were at fault for seeing him naked. Because of a belief that the people of Black African ancestry descended from Ham, the curse of Canaan (also called the curse of Ham) uttered by Noah became a justification for racism and Negro enslavement. Members of the Mormon religion of Black African ancestry were banned from priesthood until 1978 because of this belief.

A father can sell his daughter into slavery
Exodus 21:7-11 "If a man sell his daughter to be a maidservant …"

Note: However, the bible does not say the father can sell his son.

17. Tattoos and body piercings

Tattoos and body piercings are not allowed
Leviticus 19:28 "Ye shall not make any cuttings in your flesh for the dead, nor print any marks upon you: I am the Lord."

Note: Leviticus forbids the cutting of any flesh. However, this seems to contradict the covenant God made with Abraham (See Genesis 17:10-14) that requires the circumcision of every male?

Ear piercing is allowed among servants
Exodus 21:6 "His master shall bore his ear through with an aul; and he shall serve him forever."
Deuteronomy 15:17 "Then thou shalt take an aul, and thrust it through his ear … and he shall be thy servant …"

Note: A pierced ear of a bought servant means that the servant had chosen to serve his master until death.

God promised to clothed his people and put earrings on their ears
Ezekiel 16:12 "I put a jewel on thy forehead, and earrings in thine ears …"

X. Other Facts about the Bible

1. Jacob's ladder

Genesis 28:11-19 "And he lighted upon a certain place ... and lay down in that place to sleep. And he dreamed, and behold a ladder set up on the earth, and the top of it reached to heaven ..."

Note: Jacob's dream of a ladder that reached up to heaven was the basis for the song Nearer My God To Thee. It is alleged that this was the song played by the band during the sinking of the RMS Titanic.

2. A Stranger in a Strange Land

Exodus 2:22 "And she [Zipporah] bare him a son, and he [Moses] called his name Gershom: for he said, I have been *a stranger in a strange land.*"

Note: The novel A Stranger in a Strange Land was written by Robert Heinlein in reference to the statement made by Moses in Exodus 2:22. It is about a person named Michael Valentine Smith, who came back to earth after growing up in Mars.

3. King Henry VIII and the Book of Leviticus

Leviticus 20:21 "If a man shall take his brother's wife, it is an unclean thing: he hath uncovered his brother's nakedness; they shall be childless."

Note: Because of Leviticus 20:21, King Henry VIII asked the dispensation of Pope Julius II before marrying Catherine of Aragon in 1509, a Spanish princess and his brother's widow.

4. The Liberty Bell and the Book of Leviticus

Leviticus 25:10 "Ye shall hallow the fiftieth year, and *proclaim liberty throughout all the land unto all the inhabitants thereof:* it shall be a jubile unto you; and ye shall return every man unto his possession, and ye shall return every man unto his family."

Note: The Liberty Bell that tolled during the reading of the Declaration of Independence on July 8, 1776 is inscribed with the words from Leviticus 25:10, "Proclaim liberty throughout all the land unto all the inhabitants thereof."

5. Joan of Arc and the Biblical Clothing Law

Deuteronomy 22:5 "The woman shall not wear that which pertaineth unto a man, neither shall a man put on a woman's garment: for all that do so are abomination unto the Lord thy God."

Note: Deuteronomy 22:5 was the technical reason for the conviction of Joan of Arc.

6. Shibboleth

Judges 12:5-6 "Art thou an Ephraimite? If he said, Nay; Then said they unto him, Say now Shibboleth: and he said Sibboleth: for he could not frame to pronounce it right. Then they took him, and slew him at the passages of Jordan."

Note: Originally the term shibboleth refers to a flowing stream or part of a plant that contains grains (i.e. ear of a corn). However, the biblical passage in Judges 12:5-6 gave rise to a new meaning of shibboleth. It refers to any distinguishing practice that reveals the social, ethnic or cultural origin of the subject involved such as peculiarity of pronunciation, behavior or mode of dress.

7. My father, my father the chariot of Israel and the horsemen thereof

As Elisha watched Elijah being taken into the clouds he uttered a phrase
II Kings 2:12 "Elisha cried, My father, my father, the chariot of Israel, and the horseman thereof."

As Joash watched Elisha on his deathbed, he uttered the same phrase
II Kings 13:14 "Elisha was fallen sick ... Joash ... wept over his face, and said, O my father, my father, the chariot of Israel, and the horsemen thereof."

8. The Longest word in the Bible – Maher-shalal-hash-baz

Isaiah 8:1 "Moreover the Lord said unto me, Take thee a great roll, and write in it with a man's pen concerning Mahershalalhashbaz."

9. The Legend of the Wandering Jew

Matthew 16:28 "Verily I say unto you, There be some standing here, which shall not taste of death, till they see the Son of man coming in his kingdom."
John 21:22-23 "Jesus saith ... If I will that he tarry till I come, what is that to thee? follow thou me. Then went this saying abroad among the brethren, that that disciple should not die: yet Jesus said not unto him, He shall not die; but, If I will that he tarry till I come, what is that to thee?"

Note: The verses Matthew 16:28 and John 21:22-23 brought about a legend alleging that the Wandering Jew will continue to wander all over the world until Judgment Day or the second coming of Jesus. Music, novels and poetry were written in different cultures about the legend of the Wandering Jew. One famous work is The Wandering Jew by Eugene Sue. An enigmatic figure in the movie The Seventh Sign, the Wandering Jew is sometimes called Ahasuerus, Cartaphilus or Malchus.

10. The Blood Libel

Matthew 27:25 "Then answered all the people, and said, His blood be on us, and on our children."

Note: When Pilate asked the crowd to make a choice between Jesus and Barabbas, they chose to release Barabbas instead of Jesus. Thus, the Jewish people take the blame for the death of Jesus in perpetuity.
Several superstitous beliefs have evolved concerning the Jews such as the kidnapping and murder of Christian children to use their blood for Jewish rituals and the making of the unleavened bread.

11. The Spear of Destiny

John 19:34 "But one of the soldiers with a spear pierced his side ..."

Note: The verse John 19:34 is the basis for the legend about the Spear of Destiny also called the Spear of Longinus. It was the spear used by Gaius Cassius Longinus to pierce the side of Jesus Christ during crucifixion. The said spear changed hands from one political leader to another and was acquired by Hitler during World War II.

12. Psalm 46 and Shakespeare

Psalm 46 "God is our refuge and strength, a very present help in trouble. Therefore will not we fear, though the earth be removed, and though the mountains be carried into the midst of the sea; Though the waters thereof roar and be troubled, though the mountains shake ... spear in sunder; he burneth the chariot in the fire. Be still, and know that I am God: I will be exalted among the heathen, I will be exalted in the earth. The Lord of hosts is with us; the God of Jacob is our refuge. Selah."

Note: The name of Shakespeare is said to be in Psalm 46. Count 46 letters from the beginning and from the end of Psalm 46 and you get the words shake and spear.

XI. Conclusion

The concept of having a messiah is a psychological characteristic of a beleaguered nation suffering from Lemming syndrome such as the Israelites during the time of Moses. The belief in a messiah is also created in the minds of peoples and cultures that are 'lost', as in the case of an out-of-luck, downtrodden person wishing for someone to give a helping hand. This type of mindset is both good and bad. It can be positive, since this way of thinking gives some form of hope to those in a seemingly hopeless, inescapable situation. But reaching for a savior can also be dangerous, giving false hope and encouraging complacency instead of self-reliance, inhibiting a person from embracing reality and becoming self-directed.

History is full of kings and other rulers with hidden agendas who used religion as a control mechanism. Religion has been used to rule not just the body, but also the mind and soul. More wars have been fought in the name of religion. The world does not need religion, but a universal code of ethics that would settle differences in belief systems. The Lemming syndrome and the Myrmidon complex are major characteristics of primitive societies who do not have a defined sense of direction as a group, government, or institution. We can still observe these behavioral patterns in economically distressed groups and societies that believe in an outside religious force that will rescue them from their predicament.

What we need is a universal code of ethics that could serve as a road map, settling differences and serving as a guide for all humanity. While some societies have already developed a sophisticated mode of governance, many are still in the dark, mired in ignorance, bigotry, and superstition. Why reinvent the wheel when we can share, compare, and grow from other people's ideas and follies? More often than not, a law or code is passed because of an unprecedented event, misfortune, or tragedy of catastrophic proportions. How many tragedies does the world need before putting the proper order in place? We all belong to one body; the pain of one is the pain of all. The suffering of one nation reverberates throughout all mankind. Because we are all interconnected, all creation belongs to the oneness of life, the oneness of existence.

Bibliography

Acharya S, The Christ Conspiracy, Adventures Unlimited Press, 1999

Asimov, Isaac, Asimov's Guide to the Bible, Random House, 1981

Bardon, Franz, The Key to the True Quabbalah, Dieter Ruggeberg Wuppertal, 1956

Callahan, Tim, Secret Origins of the Bible, Millenium Press, 2002

Callaway, Joseph, The New Encyclopedia of Archaeological Excavations in the Holy Land, Simon and Schuster, 1993

Ehrman, Bart, Lost Scriptures, Oxford University Press, 2003

Handbook of Indulgencies, Catholic Book Publishing, Co, 1992

Litt, Charles, Testaments of the Twelve Patriarchs, 1925

Mysteries of the Bible, The Reader's Digest Association, Inc., 1997

Peters, Edward, Heresy and Authority in Medieval Europe, 1980

Rev. H. J. Schroeder O.P., The Cannons and Decrees of The Council of Trent, Tan Books, 1978

Schaff, Phillip, Schaff-Herzog Encyclopedia of Religious Knowledge, 1914